Toward Excellence

A READER

Toward Excellence

A READER

Vincent Milosevich

CHICO STATE COLLEGE

Harcourt Brace Jovanovich, Inc.

NEW YORK / CHICAGO / SAN FRANCISCO / ATLANTA

G

ISBN: 0-15-592194-0

Library of Congress Catalog Card Number: 72-92270

Printed in the United States of America

Copyrights and Acknowledgments

THE ABBEY OF THELEME by François Rabelais is reprinted from *Gargantua,* translated by Sir Thomas Urquhart and Peter Motteux.

THE AIMS OF EDUCATION by Alfred North Whitehead is reprinted from *The Aims of Education,* copyright 1929 by The Macmillan Company and renewed 1957 by Evelyn Whitehead. Reprinted by permission of The Macmillan Company.

ALIENATED LABOUR by Karl Marx is reprinted from *Karl Marx: Early Writings* Edited and Translated by T. B. Bottomore. © T. B. Bottomore, 1963. Used with permission of McGraw-Hill Book Company and C. A. Watts, London.

APOLOGY by Plato is reprinted from *The Dialogues of Plato,* translated by Benjamin E. Jowett.

THE BIRTH OF TRAGEDY by Friedrich Nietzsche translated by Clifton P. Fadiman is reprinted from *The Philosophy of Nietzsche,* copyright 1927 and renewed 1955 by The Modern Library Inc. Reprinted by permission of Random House, Inc.

THE GRAND INQUISITOR by Fyodor Dostoevsky is reprinted from *The Brothers Karamazov* translated by Constance Garnett. Reprinted by Permission of Random House, Inc.

ICAROMENIPPUS, AN AERIAL EXPEDITION by Lucian is reprinted from *The Works of Lucian of Samosata,* translated by W. H. and G. F. Fowler.

ORATION ON THE DIGNITY OF MAN by Pico della Mirandola is reprinted from *On the Dignity of Man* translated by Charles Glenn Wallis, The Library of the Liberal Arts, copyright 1965 by Bobbs-Merrill Book Company. Reprinted by permission of Eleanor Van T. Glenn, Trustee under the Will of Eleanor S. Wallis.

THE SOCIAL CONTRACT by Jean-Jacques Rousseau is reprinted from *The Social Contract* translated anonymously in 1791 and revised by Charles Frankel, copyright 1947, 1957 by Hafner Publishing Company, Inc. Reprinted by permission of Hafner Publishing Company, Inc.

THIRD PROLUSION by John Milton is reprinted from *John Milton: Complete Poems and Major Prose* edited by Merritt Y. Hughes, copyright © 1957, by The Odyssey Press, Inc. Reprinted by permission of The Bobbs-Merrill Book Company.

TONIO KRÖGER by Thomas Mann, copyright 1936 and renewed 1964 by Alfred A. Knopf, Inc. Reprinted from *Stories of Three Decades* by Thomas Mann, by permission of Alfred A. Knopf, Inc. [translated by H. T. Lowe-Porter].

Preface

My purpose in this anthology is primarily to bring together, in one volume, writings that have indisputably earned the label "excellent," both for their quality of thought and felicity of expression. The reader will quickly note that writers of the modern period are conspicuously absent. Their absence does not arise from a simplistic idea that there is nothing new under the sun. Rather, this circumstance comes about because I have found in my own reading and teaching that true relevance is not measured by topical considerations nearly so much as by the writer's ability to recognize the full import of his subject and by what may be called his rhetorical control of that subject. For it is far more the rule than the exception that the most perceptive thinkers unite the power of their insights with an ability to communicate their thought clearly.

At the same time, the writings I have chosen do not, of course, exhaust the store of great human utterances. This collection is but a sampling of the best that men have thought and written over the centuries and each reader can undoubtedly nominate additional worthy selections. I have chosen these particular writings because they show a continuity and commonality of social concerns and because I am convinced that acquaintance with the thought contained here will give the reader a perspective from which to view current ideas and events.

I must make an observation about the general tone of the selections, which the reader will discover for himself as he gets into the book. In his *Journals,* André Gide remarks, "What an amazing anthology one could make . . . grouping and bringing out of all the great writings of the past [that which is] the revolutionary element. It seems that school work consists in taming the classics; they appear tempered, sobered, softened, inoffensive;

familiarity has dulled their sharpest weapons. They cannot be *properly* read without giving them back some of their edge." There is, in much great writing, an attitude of disaffection from the here-and-now; not mere nay-saying, but dissatisfaction with man's failure to achieve—or even to attempt—perfection, be it in the area of education, politics, or social organization. The writers represented in *Toward Excellence* are frequently critical of man and the institutions he has created, but their criticism grows out of their deep commitment to an ethical idea that they believe can be realized. In this sense, then, they can truly be called "revolutionary."

Finally, *Toward Excellence* is not an "easy" book, one to breeze through casually while waiting for important events to occur, like the laundry to be completed or the dentist to call the reader into his office. The close study this book requires, however, will be amply repaid. As Spinoza has said, "All things excellent are difficult as they are rare."

I would like to thank W. B. Carnochan of Stanford University and M. M. Riordan of City College, San Francisco for their interest and valuable suggestions.

VINCENT MILOSEVICH

Contents

Society and Social Institutions

Literature and Art

Education

The Aims of Education

Alfred North Whitehead

(1861-1948)

"What is Education?" "What purpose does it serve?" As you will discover from reading the following selections, the answers to these questions are many and complex. Traditionally, education is defined as the transmission of past knowledge. As simple as this answer may seem, it raises any number of other questions, some of which we are already familiar with. For example, the past is vast and could not possibly be taught in toto; *therefore we must select the past we decide to teach. Hence, "What portions of the past should we choose and what principles of selection should we adopt?" Moreover, "How should we teach the material we do select?" The answers vary enormously and are usually determined by the way you conceive the purpose of education. Our goals must thus be decided on before we can fully answer the question of what we mean by "education."*

In his essay, "The Aims of Education," Alfred North Whitehead sets out what he believes our educational goals should be. Central to his thesis is an attack on the unthinking reproduction of what he pointedly calls "inert ideas" received from the past. Whitehead was well placed to criticize our inherited notions. Together with Bertrand Russell he undertook, in the Principia Mathematica, *a major critique of logic that eventually revolutionized the field. Whitehead's other writings in esthetics, epistemology, and metaphysics have made him an important contributor to twentieth-century philosophy. In all these areas he submitted received notions to the finely honed critical intelligence displayed on the following pages. All his works might be thought of as "a protest against dead knowledge," to borrow his own phrase.*

The following essay was adapted by Whitehead from a talk he gave before a conference of teachers, and it forms part of a series of essays on education that have been very influential in England. Some of his other major writings are Science and the Modern World, Process and Reality, *and* The Function of Reason.

CULTURE is activity of thought, and receptiveness to beauty and humane feeling. Scraps of information have nothing to do with it. A merely well-informed man is the most useless bore on God's earth. What we should aim at producing is men who possess both culture and expert knowledge in some special direction. Their expert knowledge will give them the ground to start from, and their culture will lead them as deep as philosophy and as high as art. We have to remember that the valuable intellectual development is self-development, and that it mostly takes place between the ages of sixteen and thirty. As to training, the most important part is given by mothers before the age of twelve. A saying due to Archbishop Temple illustrates my meaning. Surprise was expressed at the success in after-life of a man, who as a boy at Rugby had been somewhat undistinguished. He answered,

"It is not what they are at eighteen, it is what they become afterwards that matters."

In training a child to activity of thought, above all things we must beware of what I will call "inert ideas"—that is to say, ideas that are merely received into the mind without being utilised, or tested, or thrown into fresh combinations.

In the history of education, the most striking phenomenon is that schools of learning, which at one epoch are alive with a ferment of genius, in a succeeding generation exhibit merely pedantry and routine. The reason is, that they are overladen with inert ideas. Education with inert ideas is not only useless: it is, above all things, harmful—*Corruptio optimi, pessima.* Except at rare intervals of intellectual ferment, education in the past has been radically infected with inert ideas. That is the reason why uneducated clever women, who have seen much of the world, are in middle life so much the most cultured part of the community. They have been saved from this horrible burden of inert ideas. Every intellectual revolution which has ever stirred humanity into greatness has been a passionate protest against inert ideas. Then, alas, with pathetic ignorance of human psychology, it has proceeded by some educational scheme to bind humanity afresh with inert ideas of its own fashioning.

Let us now ask how in our system of education we are to guard against this mental dryrot. We enunciate two educational commandments, "Do not teach too many subjects," and again, "What you teach, teach thoroughly."

The result of teaching small parts of a large number of subjects is the passive reception of disconnected ideas, not illumined with any spark of vitality. Let the main ideas which are introduced into a child's education be few and important, and let them be thrown into every combination possible. The child should make them his own, and should understand their application here and now in the circumstances of his actual life. From the very beginning of his education, the child should experience the joy of discovery. The discovery which he has to make, is that general ideas give an understanding of that stream of events which pours through his life, which is his life. By understanding I mean more than a mere logical analysis, though that is included. I mean "understanding" in the sense in which it is used in the French proverb, "To understand all, is to forgive all." Pedants sneer at an education which is useful. But if education is not useful, what is it? It is a talent, to be hidden away in a napkin? Of course, education should be useful, whatever your aim in life. It was useful to Saint Augustine and it was useful to Napoleon. It is useful, because understanding is useful.

I pass lightly over that understanding which should be given by the literary side of education. Nor do I wish to be supposed to pronounce on the relative merits of a classical or a modern curriculum. I would only remark that the understanding which we want is an understanding of an insistent present. The only use of a knowledge of the past is to equip us for the present. No more deadly harm can be done to young minds than by depreciation of the present. The present contains all that there is. It is holy ground; for it is the past, and it is the future. At the same time it must be observed that an age is no less past if it existed two hundred years ago than if it existed two thousand years ago. Do not be deceived by the pedantry of dates. The ages of Shakespeare and of Molière are no less past than are the ages of Sophocles and of Virgil. The communion of saints is a great and inspiring assemblage, but it has only one possible hall of meeting, and that is, the present; and the mere lapse of time through which any particular group of saints must travel to reach that meeting-place, makes very little difference.

Passing now to the scientific and logical side of education, we remember that here also ideas which are not utilised are positively harmful. By utilising an idea, I mean relating it to that stream, compounded of sense perceptions, feelings, hopes, desires, and of mental activities adjusting thought to thought, which forms our life. I can imagine a set of beings which might fortify their souls by passively reviewing disconnected ideas. Humanity is not built that way—except perhaps some editors of newspapers.

In scientific training, the first thing to do with an idea is to prove it. But allow me for one moment to extend the meaning of "prove"; I mean—to prove its worth. Now an idea is not worth much unless the propositions in which it is embodied are true. Accordingly an essential part of the proof of an idea is the proof, either by experiment or by logic, of the truth of the propositions. But it is not essential that this proof of the truth should constitute the first introduction to the idea. After all, its assertion by the authority of respectable teachers is sufficient evidence to begin with. In our first contact with a set of propositions, we commence by appreciating their importance. That is what we all do in after-life. We do not attempt, in the strict sense, to prove or to disprove anything, unless its importance makes it worthy of that honour. These two processes of proof, in the narrow sense, and of appreciation, do not require a rigid separation in time. Both can be proceeded with nearly concurrently. But in so far as either process must have the priority, it should be that of appreciation by use.

Furthermore, we should not endeavour to use propositions in isolation. Emphatically I do not mean, a neat little set of experiments to illustrate Proposition I and then the proof of Proposition I, a neat little set of experiments to illustrate Proposition II and then the proof of Proposition II, and so on to the end of the book. Nothing could be more boring. Interrelated truths are utilised *en bloc,* and the various propositions are employed in any order, and with any reiteration. Choose some important applications of your theoretical subject; and study them concurrently with the systematic theoretical exposition. Keep the theoretical exposition short and simple, but let it be strict and rigid so far as it goes. It should not be too long for it to be easily known with thoroughness and accuracy. The consequences of a plethora of half-digested theoretical knowledge are deplorable. Also the theory should not be muddled up with the practice. The child should have no doubt when it is proving and when it is utilising. My point is that what is proved should be utilised, and that what is utilised should—so far as is practicable—be proved. I am far from asserting that proof and utilisation are the same thing.

At this point of my discourse, I can most directly carry forward my argument in the outward form of a digression. We are only just realising that the art and science of education require a genius and a study of their own; and that this genius and this science are more than a bare knowledge of some branch of science or of literature. This truth was partially perceived in the past generation; and headmasters, somewhat crudely, were apt to supersede learning in their colleagues by requiring left-hand bowling and a taste for football. But culture is more than cricket, and more than football, and more than extent of knowledge.

Education is the acquisition of the art of the utilisation of knowledge. This is an art very difficult to impart. Whenever a textbook is written of real educational worth, you may be quite certain that some reviewer will say that it will be difficult to teach from it. Of course it will be difficult to teach from it. If it were easy, the book ought to be burned; for it cannot be educational. In education, as elsewhere, the broad primrose path leads to a nasty place. This evil path is represented by a book or a set of lectures which will practically enable the student to learn by heart all the questions likely to be asked at the next external examination. And I may say in passing that no educational system is possible unless every question directly asked of a pupil at any examination is either framed or modified by the actual teacher of that pupil in that subject. The external assessor may report on the curriculum or on the performance of the pupils, but never should be allowed to ask the pupil a question which has not been strictly supervised by the actual teacher, or at least inspired by a long conference with him. There are a few exceptions to this rule, but they are exceptions, and could easily be allowed for under the general rule.

We now return to my previous point, that theoretical ideas should always find important applications within the pupil's curriculum. This is not an easy doctrine to apply, but a very hard one. It contains within itself the problem of keeping knowledge alive, of preventing it from becoming inert, which is the central problem of all education.

The best procedure will depend on several factors, none of which can be neglected, namely, the genius of the teacher, the intellectual type of the pupils, their prospects in life, the opportunities offered by the immediate surroundings of the school, and allied factors of this sort. It is for this reason that the uniform external examination is so deadly. We do not denounce it because we are cranks, and like denouncing established things. We are not so childish. Also, of course, such examinations have their use in testing slackness. Our reason of dislike is very definite and very practical. It kills the best part of culture. When you analyse in the light of experience the central task of education, you find that its successful accomplishment depends on a delicate adjustment of many variable factors. The reason is that we are dealing with human minds, and not with dead matter. The evocation of curiosity, of judgment, of the power of mastering a complicated tangle of circumstances, the use of theory in giving foresight in special cases—all these powers are not to be imparted by a set rule embodied in one schedule of examination subjects.

I appeal to you, as practical teachers. With good discipline, it is always possible to pump into the minds of a class a certain quantity of inert knowledge. You take a text-book and make them learn it. So far, so good. The child then knows how to solve a quadratic equation. But what is the point of teaching a child to solve a quadratic equation? There is a traditional answer to this question. It runs thus: The mind is an instrument, you first sharpen it, and then use it; the acquisition of the power of solving a quadratic equation is part of the process of sharpening the mind. Now there is just enough truth in this answer to have made it live through the ages. But for all its half-truth, it embodies a radical error which bids fair to stifle the genius of the modern world. I do not know who was first responsible for this analogy of the mind to a dead instrument. For aught I know, it may have been one of the seven wise men of Greece, or a committee of the whole lot of them. Whoever was the originator, there can be no doubt of the authority which it has acquired by the continuous approval bestowed upon it by eminent persons. But whatever its weight of authority, whatever the high approval which it can quote, I have no hesitation in denouncing it as one of the most fatal, erroneous, and dangerous conceptions ever introduced into the theory of education. The mind is never passive; it is a perpetual activity, delicate, receptive, responsive to stimulus. You cannot postpone its life until you have sharpened it. Whatever interest attaches to your subject-matter must be evoked here and now; whatever powers you are strengthening in the pupil, must be exercised here and now; whatever possibilities of mental life your teaching should impart, must be exhibited here and now. That is the golden rule of education, and a very difficult rule to follow.

The difficulty is just this: the apprehension of general ideas, intellectual habits of mind, and pleasurable interest in mental achievement can be evoked by no form of words, however accurately adjusted. All practical teachers know that education is a patient process of the mastery of details, minute by minute, hour by hour, day by day. There is no royal road to learning through an airy path of brilliant generalisations. There is a proverb about the difficulty of seeing the wood because of the trees. That difficulty is exactly the point which I am enforcing. The problem of education is to make the pupil see the wood by means of the trees.

The solution which I am urging, is to eradicate the fatal disconnection of subjects which kills the vitality of our modern curriculum. There is only one subject-matter for education, and that is Life in all its manifestations. Instead of this single unity, we offer children—Algebra, from which nothing follows; Geometry, from which nothing follows; Science, from which nothing follows; History, from which nothing follows; a Couple of Languages, never mastered; and lastly, most dreary of all, Literature, represented by plays of Shakespeare, with philological notes and short analyses of plot and character to be in substance committed to memory. Can such a list be said to represent Life, as it is known in the midst of the living of it? The best that can be said of it is, that it is a rapid table of contents which a deity might run over in his mind while he was thinking of creating a world, and has not yet determined how to put it together.

Let us now return to quadratic equations. We still have on hand the unanswered question. Why should children be taught their solution? Unless quadratic equations fit into a connected curriculum, of course there is no reason to teach anything about them. Furthermore, extensive as should be the place of mathematics in a complete culture, I am a little doubtful whether for many types of boys algebraic solutions of quadratic equations do not lie on the specialist side of mathematics. I may here remind you that as yet I have not said anything of the psychology or the content of the specialism, which is so necessary a part of an ideal education. But all that is an evasion of our real question, and I merely state it in order to avoid being misunderstood in my answer.

Quadratic equations are part of algebra, and algebra is the intellectual instrument which has been created for rendering clear the quantitative aspects of the world. There is no getting out of it. Through and through the world is infected with quantity. To talk sense, is to talk in quantities. It is no use saying that the nation is large,—How large? It is no use saying that radium is scarce,—How scarce? You cannot evade quantity. You may fly to poetry and to music, and quantity and number will face you in your rhythms and your octaves. Elegant intellects which despise the theory of quantity, are but half developed. They are more to be pitied than blamed. The scraps of gibberish, which in their school-days were taught to them in the name of algebra, deserve some contempt.

This question of the degeneration of algebra into gibberish, both in word and in fact, affords a pathetic instance of the uselessness of reforming educational schedules without a clear conception of the attributes which you wish to evoke in the living minds of the children. A few years ago there was an outcry that school algebra was in need of reform, but there was a general agreement that graphs would put everything right. So all sorts of things were extruded, and graphs were introduced. So far as I can see, with no sort of idea behind them, but just graphs. Now every examination paper has one or two questions on graphs. Personally I am an enthusiastic adherent of graphs. But I wonder whether as yet we have gained very much. You cannot put life into any schedule of general education unless you succeed in exhibiting its relation to some essential characteristic of all intelligent or emotional perception. It is a hard saying, but it is true; and I do not see how to make it any easier. In making these little formal alterations you are beaten by the very nature of things. You are pitted against too skilful an adversary, who will see to it that the pea is always under the other thimble.

Reformation must begin at the other end. First, you must make up your mind as to those quantitative aspects of the world which are simple enough to be introduced into general education; then a schedule of algebra should be framed which will about find its exemplification in these applications. We need not fear for our pet graphs, they will be there in plenty when we once begin to treat algebra as a serious means of studying the world. Some of the simplest applications will be found in the quantities which occur in the simplest study of society. The curves of history are more vivid and more informing than the dry catalogues of names and dates which comprise the greater part of that arid school study. What purpose is effected by a catalogue of undistinguished kings and queens? Tom, Dick, or Harry, they are all dead. General resurrections are failures, and are better postponed. The quantitative flux of the forces of modern society is capable of very simple exhibition. Meanwhile, the idea of the variable, of the function, of rate of change, of equations and their solution, of elimination, are being studied as an abstract science for their own sake. Not, of course, in the pompous phrases with which I am alluding to them here, but with that iteration of simple special cases proper to teaching.

If this course be followed, the route from Chaucer to the Black Death, from the Black Death to modern Labour troubles, will connect the tales of the mediaeval pilgrims with the abstract science of algebra, both yielding diverse aspects of that single theme, Life. I know what most of you are thinking at this point. It is that the exact course which I have sketched out is not the particular one which you would have chosen, or even see how to work. I quite agree. I am not claiming that I could do it myself. But your objection is the precise reason why a common external examination system is fatal to education. The process of exhibiting the applications of knowledge must, for its success, essentially depend on the character of the pupils and the genius of the teacher. Of course I have left out the easiest applications with which most of us are more at home. I mean the quantitative sides of sciences, such as mechanics and physics.

Again, in the same connection we plot the statistics of social phenomena against the time. We then eliminate the time between suitable pairs. We can speculate how far we have exhibited a real causal connection, or how far a mere temporal coincidence. We notice that we might have plotted against the time one set of statistics for one country and another set for another country, and thus, with suitable choice of subjects, have obtained graphs which certainly exhibited mere coincidence. Also other graphs exhibit obvious causal connections. We wonder how to discriminate. And so are drawn on as far as we will.

But in considering this description, I must beg you to remember what I have been insisting on above. In the first place, one train of thought will not suit all groups of children. For example, I should expect that artisan children will want something more concrete and, in a sense, swifter than I have set down here. Perhaps I am wrong, but that is what I should guess. In the second place, I am not contemplating one beautiful lecture stimulating, once and for all, an admiring class. That is not the way in which education proceeds. No; all the time the pupils are hard at work solving examples, drawing graphs, and making experiments, until they have a thorough hold on the whole subject. I am describing the interspersed explanations, the directions which should be given to their thoughts. The pupils have got to be made to feel that they are studying something, and are not merely executing intellectual minuets.

Finally, if you are teaching pupils for some general examination, the problem of sound teaching is greatly complicated. Have you ever noticed the zig-zag moulding round a Norman arch? The ancient work is beautiful, the modern work is hideous. The reason is, that the modern work is done to exact measure, the ancient work is varied according to the idiosyncrasy of the workman. Here it is crowded, and there it is expanded. Now the essence of getting pupils through examinations is to give equal weight to all parts of the schedule. But mankind is naturally specialist. One man sees a whole subject, where another can find only a few detached examples. I know that it seems contradictory to allow for specialism in a curriculum especially designed for a broad culture. Without contradictions the world would be simpler, and perhaps duller. But I am certain that in education wherever you exclude specialism you destroy life.

We now come to the other great branch of a general mathematical education, namely Goemetry. The same principles apply. The theoretical part should be clear-cut, rigid, short, and important. Every proposition not absolutely necessary to exhibit the main connection of ideas should be cut out, but the great fundamental ideas should be all there. No omission of concepts, such as those of Similarity and Proportion. We must remember that, owing to the aid rendered by the visual presence of a figure, Geometry is a field of unequalled excellence for the exercise of the deductive faculties of reasoning. Then, of course, there follows Geometrical Drawing, with its training for the hand and eye.

But, like Algebra, Geometry and Geometrical Drawing must be extended beyond the mere circle of geometrical ideas. In an industrial neighbourhood, machinery and workshop practice form the appropriate extension. For example, in the London Polytechnics this has been achieved with conspicuous success. For many secondary schools I suggest that surveying and maps are the natural applications. In particular, plane-table surveying should lead pupils to a vivid apprehension of the immediate application of geometric truths. Simple drawing apparatus, a surveyor's chain, and a surveyor's compass, should enable the pupils to rise from the survey and mensuration of a field to the construction of the map of a small district. The best education is to be found in gaining the utmost information from the simplest apparatus. The provision of elaborate instruments is greatly to be deprecated. To have constructed the map of a small district, to have considered its roads, its contours, its geology, its climate, its relation to other districts, the effects on the status of its inhabitants, will teach more history and geography than any knowledge of Perkin Warbeck or of Behren's Straits. I mean not a nebulous lecture on the subject, but a serious investigation in which the real facts are definitely ascertained by the aid of accurate theoretical knowledge. A typical mathematical problem should be: Survey such and such a field, draw a plan of it to such and such a scale, and find the area. It would be quite a good procedure to impart the necessary geometrical propositions without their proofs. Then, concurrently in the same term, the proofs of the propositions would be learnt while the survey was being made.

Fortunately, the specialist side of education presents an easier problem than does the provision of a general culture. For this there are many reasons. One is that many of the principles of procedure to be observed are the same in both cases, and it is unnecessary to recapitulate. Another reason it that specialist training takes place—or should take place—at a more advanced stage of the pupil's course, and thus there is easier material to work upon. But undoubtedly the chief reason is that the specialist study is normally a study of peculiar interest to the student. He is studying it because, for some reason, he wants to know it. This makes all the difference. The general culture is designed to foster an activity of mind; the specialist course utilises this activity. But it does not do to lay too much stress on these neat antitheses. As we have already seen, in the general course foci of special interest will arise; and similarly in the special study, the external connections of the subject drag thought outwards.

Again, there is not one course of study which merely gives general culture, and another which gives special knowledge. The subjects pursued for the sake of a general education are special subjects specially studied; and, on the other hand, one of the ways of encouraging general mental activity is to foster a special devotion. You may not divide the seamless coat of learning. What education has to impart is an intimate sense for the power of ideas, for the beauty of ideas, and for the structure of ideas, together with a particular body of knowledge which has peculiar reference to the life of the being possessing it.

The appreciation of the structure of ideas is that side of a cultured mind which can only grow under the influence of a special study. I mean that eye for the whole chess-board, for the bearing of one set of ideas on another. Nothing but a special study can give any appreciation for the exact formulation of general ideas, for their relations when formulated, for their service in the comprehension of life. A mind so disciplined should be both more abstract and more concrete. It has been trained in the comprehension of abstract thought and in the analysis of facts.

Finally, there should grow the most austere of all mental qualities; I mean the sense for style. It is an aesthetic sense, based on admiration for the direct attainment of a foreseen end, simply and without waste. Style in art, style in literature, style in science, style in logic, style in practical execution have fundamentally the same aesthetic qualities, namely, attainment and restraint. The love of a subject in itself and for itself, where it is not the sleepy pleasure of pacing a mental quarter-deck, is the love of style as manifested in that study.

Here we are brought back to the position from which we started, the utility of education. Style, in its finest sense, is the last acquirement of the educated mind; it is also the most useful. It pervades the whole being. The administrator with a sense for style hates waste; the engineer with a sense for style economises his material; the artisan with a sense for style prefers good work. Style is the ultimate morality of mind.

But above style, and above knowledge, there is something, a vague shape like fate above the Greek gods. That something is Power. Style is the fashioning of power, the restraining of power. But, after all, the power of attainment of the desired end is fundamental. The first thing is to get there. Do not bother about your style, but solve your problem, justify the ways of God to man, administer your province, or do whatever else is set before you.

Where, then, does style help? In this, with style the end is attained without side issues, without raising undesirable inflammations. With style you attain your end and nothing but your end. With style the effect of your activity is calculable, and foresight is the last gift of gods to men. With style your power is increased, for your mind is not distracted with irrelevancies, and you are more likely to attain your object. Now style is the exclusive privilege of the expert. Whoever heard of the style of an amateur painter, of the style of an amateur poet? Style is always the product of specialist study, the peculiar contribution of specialism to culture.

English education in its present phase suffers from a lack of definite aim, and from an external machinery which kills its vitality. Hitherto in this address I have been considering the aims which should govern education. In this respect England halts between two opinions. It has not decided whether to produce amateurs or experts. The profound change in the world which the nineteenth century has produced is that the growth of knowledge has given foresight. The amateur is essentially a man with appreciation and with immense versatility in mastering a given routine. But he lacks the foresight which comes from special knowledge. The object of this address is to suggest how to produce the expert without loss of the essential virtues of the amateur. The machinery of our secondary education is rigid where it should be yielding, and lax where it should be rigid. Every school is bound on pain of extinction to train its boys for a small set of definite examinations. No headmaster has a free hand to develop his general education or his specialist studies in accordance with the opportunities of his school, which are created by its staff, its environment, its class of boys, and its endowments. I suggest that no system of external tests which aims primarily at examining individual scholars can result in anything but educational waste.

Primarily it is the schools and not the scholars which should be inspected. Each school should grant its own leaving certificates, based on its own curriculum. The standards of these schools should be sampled and corrected. But the first requisite for educational reform is the school as a unit, with its approved curriculum based on its own needs, and evolved by its own staff. If we fail to secure that, we simply fall from one formalism into another, from one dung-hill of inert ideas into another.

In stating that the school is the true educational unit in any national system for the safeguarding of efficiency, I have conceived the alternative system as being the external examination of the individual scholar. But every Scylla is faced by its Charybdis—or, in more homely language, there is a ditch on both sides of the road. It will be equally fatal to education if we fall into the hands of a supervising department which is under the impression that it can divide all schools into two or three categories, each type being forced to adopt a rigid curriculum. When I say that the school is the education unit, I mean exactly what I say, no larger unit, no smaller unit. Each school must have the claim to be considered in relation to its special circumstances. The classifying of schools for some purposes is necessary. But no absolutely rigid curriculum, not modified by its own staff, should be permissible. Exactly the same principles apply, with the proper modifications, to universities and to technical colleges.

When one considers in its length and in its breadth the importance of this question of the education of a nation's young, the broken lives, the defeated hopes, the national failures, which result from the frivolous inertia with which it is treated, it is difficult to restrain within oneself a savage rage. In the conditions of modern life the rule is absolute, the race which does not value trained intelligence is doomed. Not all your heroism, not all your social charm, not all your wit, not all your victories on land or at sea, can move back the finger of fate. To-day we maintain ourselves. To-morrow science will have moved forward yet one more step, and there will be no appeal from the judgment which will then be pronounced on the uneducated.

We can be content with no less than the old summary of educational ideal which has been current at any time from the dawn of our civilisation. The essence of education is that it be religious.

Pray, what is religious education?

A religious education is an education which inculcates duty and reverence. Duty arises from our potential control over the course of events. Where attainable knowledge could have changed the issue, ignorance has the guilt of vice. And the foundation of reverence is this perception, that the present holds within itself the complete sum of existence, backwards and forwards, that whole amplitude of time, which is eternity.

Icaromenippus, An Aerial Expedition

Lucian

(A.D. 125-c. 200)

Whitehead protested against the "mental dryrot" fostered by the educational system of his day. His principal charge was that educators were bent on purveying disconnected ideas that bore little or no relation to life experiences. About 1700 years earlier the Greek satirist, Lucian of Samosata, leveled a similar charge against the schools of philosophy current at his time. It seemed to Lucian that his contemporaries in philosophy were out of touch with reality—and moreover were not even interested in knowing reality. Instead they held rigidly to obscure or absurd notions and were primarily interested only in the image they projected.

Using as his central character the Greek satirist Menippus, who was himself no slouch in ridiculing the foibles of mankind, Lucian mocked the philosopher's claim to teach us anything, much less the truth. In reading the following work it is important to remember that in Lucian's day educators called themselves philosophers, generally taught privately, and were usually in competition with one another for pupils. In other works Lucian attacked the notion of paying teachers on the grounds that this practice militated against the disinterested search for truth.

The Icaromenippus *is one of Lucian's most notable "Satirical Dialogues." Some of his others are* Dialogues of the Gods *and* Dialogues of the Dead, *both of which contributed to his subsequent reputation as the "blasphemer." Lucian also wrote literary criticism and novels, one of which,* The True History, *is perhaps the earliest example of the genre later developed by Jonathan Swift in* Gulliver's Travels *and by Voltaire in* Candide.

MENIPPUS AND A FRIEND

ME. Let me see, now. First stage, Earth to Moon, 350 miles. Second stage, up to the Sun, 500 leagues. Then the third, to the actual Heaven and Zeus' citadel, might be put at a day's journey for an eagle in light marching order.

FR. In the name of goodness, Menippus, what are these astronomical sums you are doing under your breath? I have been dogging you for some time, listening to your suns and moons, queerly mixed up with common earthly stages and leagues.

ME. Ah, you must not be surprised if my talk is rather exalted and ethereal; I was making out the mileage of my journey.

FR. Oh, I see; using stars to steer by, like the Phoenicians?

ME. Oh no, traveling among them.

FR. Well, to be sure, it must have been a longish dream, if you lost yourself in it for whole leagues.

ME. Dream, my good man? I am just come straight from Zeus. Dream, indeed!

FR. How? What? Our Menippus a literal godsend from Heaven?

ME. 'Tis even so; from very Zeus I come this day, eyes and ears yet full of wonders. Oh, doubt, if you will. That my fortune should pass belief makes it only the more gratifying.

FR. Nay, my worshipful Olympian, how should I, "a man begotten, treading this poor earth," doubt him who transcends the clouds, a "denizen of Heaven," as Homer says? But vouchsafe to tell me how you were uplifted, and where you got your mighty tall ladder. There is hardly enough of Ganymede in your looks to suggest that you were carried off by the eagle for a cupbearer.

ME. I see you are bent on making a jest of it. Well, it *is* extraordinary; you could not be expected to see that it is not a romance. The fact is, I needed neither ladder nor amorous eagle; I had wings of my own.

FR. Stranger and stranger! This beats Daedalus. What, you turned into a hawk or a crow on the sly?

ME. Now that is not a bad shot; it was Daedalus' wing trick that I tried.

FR. Well, talk of foolhardiness! Did you like the idea of falling into the sea, and giving us a *Mare Menippeum* after the precedent of the *Icarium?*

ME. No fear. Icarus' feathers were fastened with wax, and of course, directly the sun warmed this, he molted and fell. No wax for me, thank you.

FR. How did you manage, then? I declare I shall be believing you soon, if you go on like this.

ME. Well, I caught a fine eagle, and also a particularly powerful vulture, and cut off their wings above the shoulder-joint. . . . But no; if you are not in a hurry, I may as well give you the enterprise from the beginning.

FR. Do, do; I am rapt aloft by your words already, my mouth open for your *bonne bouche;* as you love me, leave me not in those upper regions hung up by the ears!

ME. Listen, then; it would be a sorry sight, a friend deserted, with his mouth open, and *sus. per aures.*—Well, a very short survey of life had convinced me of the absurdity and meanness and insecurity that pervade all human objects, such as wealth, office, power. I was filled with contempt for them, realized that to care for them was to lose all chance of what deserved care, and determined to grovel no more, but fix my gaze upon the great All. Here I found my first problem in what wise men call the universal order; I could not tell how it came into being, who made it, what was its beginning, or what its end. But my next step, which was the examination of details, landed me in yet worse perplexity. I found the stars dotted quite casually about the sky, and I wanted to know what the sun was. Especially the phenomena of the moon struck me as extraordinary, and quite passed my comprehension; there must be some mystery to account for those many phases, I conjectured. Nor could I feel any greater certainty about such things as the passage of lightning, the roll of thunder, the descent of rain and snow and hail.

In this state of mind, the best I could think of was to get at the truth of it all from the people called philosophers; they of course would be able to give it me. So I selected the best of them, if solemnity of visage, pallor of complexion and length of beard are any criterion—for there could not be a moment's doubt of their soaring words and heaven-high thoughts—and in their hands I placed myself. For a considerable sum down, and more to be paid when they should have perfected me in wisdom, I was to be made an airy metaphysician and instructed in the order of the universe. Unfortunately, so far from dispelling my previous ignorance, they perplexed me more and more, with their daily drenches of beginnings and ends, atoms and voids, matters and forms. My greatest difficulty was that, though they differed among themselves, and all they said was full of inconsistency and contradiction, they expected me to believe them, each pulling me in his own direction.

FR. How absurd that wise men should quarrel about facts, and hold different opinions on the same things!

ME. Ah, but keep your laughter till you have heard something of their pretentious mystifications. To begin with, their feet are on the ground; they are no taller than the rest of us "men that walk the earth"; they are no sharper-sighted than their neighbors, some of them purblind, indeed, with age or indolence; and yet they say they can distinguish the limits of the sky, they measure the sun's circumference, take their walks in the supralunar regions, and specify the sizes and shapes of the stars as though they had fallen from them; often one of them could not tell you correctly the number of miles from Megara to Athens, but has no hesitation about the distance in feet from the sun to the moon. How high the atmosphere is, how deep the sea, how far it is round the earth—they have the figures for all that; and moreover, they have only to draw some circles, arrange a few triangles and squares, and certain complicated spheres, and lo, they have the cubic contents of Heaven.

Then, how reasonable and modest of them, dealing with subjects so debatable, to issue their views without a hint of uncertainty; thus it must be and it shall be; *contra gentes* they will have it so; they will tell you on oath the sun is a molten mass, the moon inhabited, and the stars water-drinkers, moisture being drawn up by the sun's rope and bucket and equitably distributed among them.

How their theories conflict is soon apparent; next-door neighbors? No, they are miles apart. In the first place, their views of the world differ. Some say it had no beginning, and cannot end; others boldly talk of its creator and his procedure; what particularly entertained me was that these latter set up a contriver of the universe, but fail to mention where he came from, or what he stood on while about his elaborate task, though it is by no means obvious how there could be place or time before the universe came into being.

FR. You really do make them out very audacious conjurers.

ME. My dear fellow, I wish I could give you their lucubrations on ideas and incorporeals, on finite and infinite. Over that point, now, there is fierce battle; some circumscribe the All, others will have it unlimited. At the same time they declare for a plurality of worlds, and speak scornfully of others who make only one. And there is a bellicose person who maintains that war is the father of the universe.

As to Gods, I need hardly deal with that question. For some of them God is a number; some swear by dogs and geese and plane trees. Some again banish all other Gods, and attribute the control of the universe to a single one; I got rather depressed on learning how small the supply of divinity was. But I was comforted by the lavish souls who not only make many, but classify; there was a First God, and second and third classes of divinity. Yet again, some regard the divine nature as unsubstantial and without form, while others conceive it as a substance. Then they were not all disposed to recognize a Providence; some relieve the Gods of all care, as we relieve the superannuated of their civic duties; in fact, they treat them exactly like supernumeraries on the stage. The last step is also taken, of saying that Gods do not exist at all, and leaving the world to drift along without a master or a guiding hand.

Well, when I heard all this, I dared not disbelieve people whose voices and beards were equally suggestive of Zeus. But I knew not where to turn for a theory that was not open to exception, nor combated by one as soon as propounded by another. I found myself in the state Homer has described; many a time I would vigorously start believing one of these gentlemen;

But then came second thoughts.

So in my distress I began to despair of ever getting any knowledge about these things on earth; the only possible escape from perplexity would be to take to myself wings and go up to Heaven. Partly the wish was father to the thought; but it was confirmed by Aesop's Fables, from which it appears that Heaven is accessible to eagles, beetles, and sometimes camels. It was pretty clear that I could not possibly develop feathers of my own. But if I were to wear vulture's or eagle's wings—the only kinds equal to a man's weight—I might perhaps succeed. I caught the birds, and effectually amputated the eagle's right, and the vulture's left wing. These I fastened together, attached them to my shoulders with broad thick straps, and provided grips for my hands near the end of the quill-feathers. Then I made experiments, first jumping up and helping the jump by flapping my hands, or imitating the way a goose raises itself without leaving the ground and combines running with flight. Finding the machine obedient, I next made a bolder venture, went up the Acropolis, and launched myself from the cliff right over the theater.

Getting safely to the bottom that time, my aspirations shot up aloft. I took to starting from Parnes or Hymettus, flying to Geranea, thence to the top of the Acrocorinthus, and over Pholoë and Erymanthus to Taÿgetus. The training for my venture was now complete; my powers were devoloped, and equal to a lofty flight; no more fledgling essays for me. I went up Olympus, provisioning myself as lightly as possible. The moment was come; I soared skywards, giddy at first with that great void below, but soon conquering this difficulty. When I approached the Moon, long after parting from the clouds, I was conscious of fatigue, especially in the left or vulture's wing. So I alighted and sat down to rest, having a bird's-eye view of the Earth, like the Homeric Zeus,

Surveying now the Thracian horsemen's land,
Now Mysia,

and again, as the fancy took me, Greece or Persia or India. From all which I drew a manifold delight.

FR. Oh well, Menippus, tell me all about it. I do not want to miss a single one of your travel experiences; if you picked up any stray information, let me have that too. I promise myself a great many facts about the shape of the Earth, and how everything on it looked to you from your point of vantage.

ME. And you will not be disappointed there, friend. So do your best to get up to the Moon, with my story for traveling companion and showman of the terrestrial scene.

Imagine yourself first descrying a tiny Earth, far smaller than the Moon looks; on turning my eyes down, I could not think for some time what had become of our mighty mountains and vast sea. If I had not caught sight of the Colossus of Rhodes and the Pharus tower, I assure you I should never have made out the Earth at all. But their height and projection, with the faint shimmer of Ocean in the sun, showed me it must be the Earth I was looking at. Then, when once I had got my sight properly focused, the whole human race was clear to me, not merely in the shape of nations and cities, but the individuals, sailing, fighting, plowing, going to law; the women, the beasts, and in short every breed "that feedeth on earth's foison."

FR. Most unconvincing and contradictory. Just now you were searching for the Earth, it was so diminished by distance, and if the Colossus had not betrayed it, you would have taken it for something else; and now you develop suddenly into a Lynceus, and distinguish everything upon it, the men, the beasts, one might almost say the gnat-swarms. Explain, please.

ME. Why, to be sure! how did I come to leave out so essential a particular? I had made out the Earth, you see, but could not distinguish any details; the distance was so great, quite beyond the scope of my vision; so I was much chagrined and baffled. At this moment of depression—I was very near tears—who should come up behind me but Empedocles the physicist? His complexion was like charcoal variegated with ashes, as if he had been baked. I will not deny that I felt some tremors at the sight of him, taking him for some lunar spirit. But he said: "Do not be afraid, Menippus;

A mortal I, no God; how vain thy dreams.

I am Empedocles the physicist. When I threw myself into the crater in such a hurry, the smoke of Etna whirled me off up here; and now I live in the Moon, doing a good deal of high thinking on a diet of dew. So I have come to help you out of your difficulty; you are distressed, I take it, at not being able to see everything on the Earth." "Thank you so much, you good Empedocles," I said; "as soon as my wings have brought me back to Greece, I will remember to pour libations to you up the chimney, and salute you on the first of every month with three moonward yawns." "Endymion be my witness," he replied, "I had no thought of such a bargain; I was touched by the sight of your distress. Now, what do you think is the way to sharpen your sight?"

"I have no idea, unless you were to remove the mist from my eyes for me; the sight seems quite bleared." "Oh, you can do without me; the thing that gives sharp sight you have brought with you from Earth." "Unconsciously, then; what is it?" "Why, you know that you have on an eagle's right wing?" "Of course I do; but what have wings and eyes to do with one another?" "Only this," he said; "the eagle is far the strongest-eyed of all living things, the only one that can look straight at the sun; the test of the true royal eagle is, his meeting its rays without blinking." "So I have heard; I wish I had taken out my own eyes when I was starting, and substituted the eagle's. I am an imperfect specimen now I am here, not up to the royal standard at all, but like the rejected bastards." "Well, you can very soon acquire one royal eye. If you will stand up for a minute, keep the vulture wing still, and work the other, your right eye, corresponding to that wing, will gain strength. As for the other, its dimness cannot possibly be obviated, as it belongs to the inferior member." "Oh, I shall be quite content with aquiline vision for the right eye only," I said; "I have often observed that carpenters in ruling their wood find one better than two." So saying, I proceeded to carry out my instructions at once. Empedocles began gradually to disappear, and at last vanished in smoke.

I had no sooner flapped the wing than a flood of light enveloped me, and things that before I had not even been aware of became perfectly clear. I turned my eyes down earthwards, and with ease discerned cities, men, and all that was going on, not merely in the open, but in the fancied security of houses. There was Ptolemy in his sister's arms, the son of Lysimachus plotting against his father, Seleucus' son Antiochus making signs to his step-mother Stratonice, Alexander of Pherae being murdered by his wife, Antigonus corrupting his daughter-in-law, the son of Attalus putting the poison in his cup; Arsaces was in the act of slaying his mistress, while the eunuch Arbaces drew his sword upon him; the guards were dragging Spatinus the Mede out from the banquet by foot, with the lump on his brow from the golden cup. Similar sights were to be seen in the palaces of Libya and Scythia and Thrace—adulteries, murders, treasons, robberies, perjuries, suspicions, and monstrous betrayals.

Such was the entertainment afforded me by royalty; private life was much more amusing; for I could make that out too. I saw Hermodorus the Epicurean perjuring himself for £40, Agathocles the Stoic suing a pupil for his fees, lawyer Clinias stealing a bowl from the temple of Aesculapius, and Herophilus the Cynic sleeping in a brothel. Not to mention the multitude of burglars, litigants, usurers, duns; oh, it was a fine representative show!

FR. I must say, Menippus, I should have liked the details here too; it all seems to have been very much to your taste.

ME. I could not go through the whole of it, even to please you; to take it in with the eyes kept one busy. But the main divisions were very much what Homer gives from the shield of Achilles: here junketings and marriages, there courts and councils, in another compartment a sacrifice, and hard by a mourning. If I glanced at Getica, I would see the Getae at war; at Scythia, there were the Scythians wandering about on their wagons; half a turn in another direction gave me Egyptians at the plow, or Phoenicians chaffering, Cilician pirates, Spartan flagellants, Athenians at law.

All this was simultaneous, you understand; and you must try to conceive what a queer jumble it all made. It was as if a man were to collect a number of choristers, or rather of choruses, and then tell each individual to disregard the others and start a strain of his own; if each did his best, went his own way, and tried to drown his neighbor, can you imagine what the musical effect would be?

FR. A very ridiculous confusion.

ME. Well, friend, such are the earthly dancers; the life of man is just such a discordant performance; not only are the voices jangled, but the steps are not uniform, the motions not concerted, the objects not agreed upon—until the impresario dismisses them one by one from the stage, with a "not wanted." Then they are all alike, and quiet enough, confounding no longer their undisciplined rival strains. But as long as the show lasts in its marvelous diversity, there is plenty of food for laughter in its vagaries.

The people who most amused me, however, were those who dispute about boundaries, or pride themselves on cultivating the plain of Sicyon, or holding the Oenoë side of Marathon, or a thousand acres at Acharnae. The whole of Greece, as I then saw it, might measure some four inches; how much smaller Athens on the same scale. So I realized what sort of sized basis for their pride remains to our rich men. The widest-acred of them all, methought, was the proud cultivator of an Epicurean atom. Then I looked at the Peloponnese, my eyes fell on the Cynurian district, and the thought occurred that it was for this little plot, no broader than an Egyptian lentil, that all those Argives and Spartans fell in a single day. Or if I saw a man puffed up by the possession of seven or eight gold rings and half as many gold cups, again my lungs would begin to crow; why, Pangaeus with all its mines was about the size of a grain of millet.

FR. You lucky man! what a rare sight you had! And how big, now, did the towns and the people look from there?

ME. You must often have seen a community of ants, some of them a seething mass, some going abroad, others coming back to town. One is a scavenger, another is a bustling porter loaded with a bit of bean-pod or half a wheat grain. They no doubt have, on their modest myrmecic scale, their architects and politicians, their magistrates and composers and philosophers. At any rate, what men and cities suggested to me was just so many ant-hills. If you think the similitude too disparaging, look into the Thessalian legends, and you will find that the most warlike tribe there was the Myrmidons, or ants turned men. Well, when I had had enough of contemplation and laughter, I roused myself and soared

To join the Gods, where dwells the Lord of storms.

I had only flown a couple of hundred yards, when Selene's feminine voice reached me: "Menippus, do me an errand to Zeus, and I will wish you a pleasant journey." "You have only to name it," I said, "provided it is not something to carry." "It is a simple message of entreaty to Zeus. I am tired to death, you must know, of being slandered by these philosophers; they have no better occupation than impertinent curiosity about me—What am I? how big am I? why am I halved? why am I gibbous? I am inhabited; I am just a mirror hung over the sea; I am—whatever their latest fancy suggests. It is the last straw when they say my light is stolen, sham, imported from the sun, and keep on doing their best to get up jealousy and ill feeling between brother and sister. They might have been contented with making *him* out a stone or a red-hot lump.

"These gentry who in the day look so stern and manly, dress so gravely, and are so revered by common men, would be surprised to learn how much I know of their vile nightly abominations. I see them all, though I never tell; it would be too indecent to make revelations, and show up the contrast between their nightly doings and their public performances; so, if I catch one of them in adultery or theft or other nocturnal adventure, I pull my cloud veil over me; I do not want the vulgar to see old men disgracing their long beards and their virtuous calling. But they go on giving tongue and worrying me all the same, and, so help me Night, I have thought many a time of going a long, long way off, out of reach of their impertinent tongues. Will you remember to tell Zeus all this? and you may add that I cannot remain at my post unless he will pulverize the physicists, muzzle the logicians, raze the Porch, burn the Academy, and put an end to strolling in the Lyceum. That might secure me a little peace from these daily mensurations."

"I will remember," said I, and resumed my upward flight to Heaven, through

A region where nor ox nor man had wrought.

For the Moon was soon but a small object, with the Earth entirely hidden behind it. Three days' flight through the stars, with the Sun on my right hand, brought me close to Heaven; and my first idea was to go straight in as I was; I should easily pass unobserved in virtue of my half-eagleship; for of course the eagle was Zeus' familiar; on second thoughts, though, my vulture wing would very soon betray me. So, thinking it better not to run any risks, I went up to the door and knocked. Hermes opened, took my name, and hurried off to inform Zeus. After a brief wait I was asked to step in; I was now trembling with apprehension, and I found that the Gods, who were all seated together, were not quite easy themselves. The unexpected nature of the visit was slightly disturbing to them, and they had visions of all mankind arriving at my heels by the same conveyance.

But Zeus bent upon me a Titanic glance, awful, penetrating, and spoke:

Who art thou? where thy city? who thy kin?

At the sound, I nearly died of fear, but remained upright, though mute and paralyzed by that thunderous voice. I gradually recovered, began at the beginning, and gave a clear account of myself—how I had been possessed with curiosity about the heavens, had gone to the philosophers, found their accounts conflicting, and grown tired of being logically rent in twain; so I came to my great idea, my wings, and ultimately to Heaven; I added Selene's message. Zeus smiled and slightly unbent his brow. "What of Otus and Ephialtes now?" he said; "here is Menippus scaling Heaven! Well, well, for today consider yourself our guest. Tomorrow we will treat with you of your business, and send you on your way." And therewith he rose and walked to the acoustic center of Heaven, it being prayer time.

As he went, he put questions to me about earthly affairs, beginning with, What was wheat a quarter in Greece? had we suffered much from cold last winter, and did the vegetables want more rain? Then he wished to know whether any of Phidias' kin were alive, why there had been no Diasia at Athens all these years, whether his Olympeum was ever going to be completed, and had the robbers of his temple at Dodona been caught? I answered all these questions, and he proceeded: "Tell me, Menippus, what are men's feelings towards me?" "What should they be, Lord, but those of absolute reverence, as to the King of all Gods?" "Now, now, chaffing as usual," he said; "I know their fickleness very well, for all your dissimulation. There was a time when I was their prophet, their healer, and their all,

And Zeus filled every street and gathering-place.

In those days Dodona and Pisa were glorious and farfamed, and I could not get a view for the clouds of sacrificial steam. But now Apollo has set up his oracle at Delphi, Aesculapius his temple of health at Pergamum, Bendis and Anubis and Artemis their shrines in Thrace, Egypt, Ephesus; and to these all run; theirs the festal gatherings and the hecatombs. As for me, I am superannuated; they think themselves very generous if they offer me a victim at Olympia at four-year intervals. My altars are cold as Plato's *Laws* or Chrysippus' *Syllogisms*."

So talking, we reached the spot where he was to sit and listen to the prayers. There was a row of openings with lids like well-covers, and a chair of gold by each. Zeus took his seat at the first, lifted off the lid and inclined his ear. From every quarter of Earth were coming the most various and contradictory petitions; for I too bent down my head and listened. Here are specimens. "O Zeus, that I might be king!" "O Zeus, that my onions and garlic might thrive!" "Ye Gods, a speedy death for my father!" Or again, "Would that I might succeed to my wife's property!" "Grant that my plot against my brother be not detected." "Let me win my suit." "Give me an Olympic garland." Of those at sea, one prayed for a north, another for a south wind; the farmer asked for rain, the fuller for sun. Zeus listened, and gave each prayer careful consideration, but without promising to grant them all;

Our Father this bestowed, and that withheld.

Righteous prayers he allowed to come up through the hole, received and laid them down at his right, while he sent the unholy ones packing with a downward puff of breath, that Heaven might not be defiled by their entrance. In one case I saw him puzzled; two men praying for opposite things and promising the same sacrifices, he could not tell which of them to favor, and experienced a truly Academic suspense of judgment, showing a reserve and equilibrium worthy of Pyrrho himself.

The prayers disposed of, he went on to the next chair and opening, and attended to oaths and their takers. These done with, and Hermodorus the Epicurean annihilated, he proceeded to the next chair to deal with omens, prophetic voices, and auguries. Then came the turn of the sacrifice aperture, through which the smoke came up and communicated to Zeus the name of the devotee it represented. After that, he was free to give his wind and weather orders: Rain for Scythia today, a thunderstorm for Libya, snow for Greece. The north wind he instructed to blow in Lydia, the west to raise a storm in the Adriatic, the south to take a rest; a thousand bushels of hail to be distributed over Cappadocia.

His work was now pretty well completed, and as it was just dinner time, we went to the banquet hall. Hermes received me, and gave me my place next to a group of Gods whose alien origin left them in a rather doubtful position—Pan, the Corybants, Attis, and Sabazius. I was supplied with bread by Demeter, wine by Dionysus, meat by Heracles, myrtle-blossoms by Aphrodite, and sprats by Poseidon. But I also got a sly taste of ambrosia and nectar; good-natured Ganymede, as often as he saw that Zeus' attention was engaged elsewhere, brought round the nectar and indulged me with a half-pint or so. The Gods, as Homer (who I think must have had the same opportunities of observation as myself) somewhere says, neither eat bread nor drink the ruddy wine; they heap their plates with ambrosia, and are nectar-bibbers; but their choicest dainties are the smoke of sacrifice ascending with rich fumes, and the blood of victims poured by their worshipers round the altars. During dinner, Apollo harped, Silenus danced his wild measures, the Muses uprose and sang to us from Hesiod's *Birth of Gods,* and the first of Pindar's odes. When we had our fill and had well drunken, we slumbered, each where he was.

Slept all the Gods, and men with plumed helms,
That livelong night; but me kind sleep forsook;

for I had much upon my mind; most of all, how came it that Apollo, in all that time, had never grown a beard? And how was night possible in Heaven, with the sun always there taking his share of the good cheer? So I had but a short nap of it. And in the morning Zeus arose, and bade summon an assembly.

When all were gathered, he thus commenced: "The immediate occasion of my summoning you is the arrival of this stranger yesterday. But I have long intended to take counsel with you regarding the philosophers, and now, urged by Selene and her complaints, I have determined to defer the consideration of the question no longer. There is a class which has recently become conspicuous among men; they are idle, quarrelsome, vain, irritable, lickerish, silly, puffed up, arrogant, and, in Homeric phrase, vain cumberers of the earth. These men have divided themselves into bands, each dwelling in a separate word-maze of its own construction, and call themselves Stoics, Epicureans, Peripatetics, and more farcical names yet. Then they take to themselves the holy name of Virtue, and with uplifted brows and flowing beards exhibit the deceitful semblance that hides immoral lives; their model is the tragic actor, from whom if you strip off the mask and the gold-spangled robe, there is nothing left but a paltry fellow hired for a few shillings to play a part.

"Nevertheless, quite undeterred by their own characters, they scorn the human and travesty the divine; they gather a company of guileless youth, and feed them with solemn chatter upon Virtue and quibbling verbal puzzles; in their pupils' presence they are all for fortitude and temperance, and have no words bad enough for wealth and pleasure: when they are by themselves, there is no limit to their gluttony, their lechery, their licking of dirty pence. But the head and front of their offending is this: they neither work themselves nor help others' work; they are useless drones,

Of no avail in council nor in war;

which notwithstanding, they censure others; they store up poisoned words, they con invectives, they heap their neighbors with reproaches; their highest honors are for him who shall be loudest and most overbearing and boldest in abuse.

"Ask one of these brawling bawling censors, And what do *you* do? in God's name, what shall we call *your* contribution to progress? and he would reply, if conscience and truth were anything to him: I consider it superfluous to sail the sea or till the earth or fight for my country or follow a trade; but I have a loud voice and a dirty body; I eschew warm water and go barefoot through the winter; I am a Momus who can always pick holes in other people's coats; if a rich man keeps a costly table or a mistress, I make it my business to be properly horrified; but if my familiar friend is lying sick, in need of help and care, I am not aware of it. Such, your Godheads, is the nature of this vermin.

"There is a special insolence in those who call themselves Epicureans; these go so far as to lay their hands on our character; we take no interest in human affairs, they say, and in fact have nothing to do with the course of events. And this is a serious question for you; if once they infect their generation with this view, you will learn what hunger means. Who will sacrifice to you, if he does not expect to profit by it? As to Selene's complaints, you all heard them yesterday from this stranger's lips. And now decide upon such measures as shall advantage mankind and secure your own safety."

Zeus had no sooner closed his speech than clamor prevailed, all crying at once: "Blast! burn! annihilate! to the pit with them! to Tartarus! to the Giants!" Zeus ordered silence again, and then, "Your wishes," he said, "shall be executed; they shall all be annihilated, and their logic with them. But just at present chastisement is not lawful; you are aware that we are now in the four months of the long vacation; the formal notice has lately been issued. In the spring of next year, the baleful levinbolt shall give them the fate they deserve."

He spake, and sealed his word with lowering brows.

"As to Menippus," he added, "my pleasure is this. He shall be deprived of his wings, and so incapacitated for repeating his visit, but shall today be conveyed back to Earth by Hermes."

So saying, he dismissed the assembly. The Cyllenian accordingly lifted me up by the right ear, and yesterday evening deposited me in the Ceramicus. And now, friend, you have all the latest from Heaven. I must be off to the Poecile, to let the philosophers loitering there know the luck they are in.

Oration on the Dignity of Man

Pico della Mirandola

(1463-1494)

The assumption underlying the arguments of both Whitehead and Lucian is that knowledge has a positive value. Lucian would qualify this statement by insisting that it be "true knowledge" rather than the spurious doctrines peddled by the sages of his day. Whitehead asserted that knowledge is valuable only when it forms a nexus of general and specialized ideas that contribute to "an understanding of an insistent present." However differently they may have defined knowledge, both thinkers probably would agree that its main function is to enlarge the capacities of humankind.

But what are the capacities of humankind? Toward the end of the fifteenth century an answer was proposed by one of the leading figures of the Italian Renaissance, Count Giovanni Pico della Mirandola. Pico was part of a circle of writers and artists that formed around the Medici and were known as the

Florentine Academy. It was within the Academy that the principal ideas of Renaissance Platonism were formulated and afterward influenced the Tudor and Elizabethan writers of the sixteenth century as well as the artists and poets of the Italian late Renaissance.

In his oration Pico suggests that man is a "chameleon" capable of descending to the lowest form of life or of standing "ahead of all things," depending on the qualities in himself that he chooses to cultivate. Central to the development of man's highest qualities, in Pico's view, was the cultivation of a thoroughgoing familiarity with the past—Christian, Judaic, Classical, and occult. This typically Renaissance syncretism led Pico, as it did many others of the period, to an attempted synthesis of ideas derived from ancient Greek, Biblical, Gnostic, Neoplatonic, Patristic, Arabic, Scholastic, and Cabalistic sources.

"On the Dignity of Man" was first planned by Pico as a preface to 900 theses, which he published in 1486 and intended to debate with the Church fathers in Rome. Some of his theses, however, were declared heretical and the debate was prohibited. As a consequence Pico fled to France until the Medici were able to arrange for his safe return to Florence. He later wrote biblical exegesis, and attempt to harmonize the teachings of Plato and Aristotle, and an attack on astrology.

Most venerable fathers, I have read in the records of the Arabians that Abdul the Saracen, on being asked what thing on, so to speak, the world's stage, he viewed as most greatly worthy of wonder, answered that he viewed nothing more wonderful than man. And Mercury's, "a great wonder, Asclepius, is man!" agrees with that opinion. On thinking over the reason for these sayings, I was not satisfied by the many assertions made by many men concerning the outstandingness of human nature: that man is the messenger between creatures, familiar with the upper and king of the lower; by the sharpsightedness of the senses, by the hunting-power of reason, and by the light of intelligence, the interpreter of nature; the part in between the standstill of eternity and the flow of time; and, as the Persians say, the bond tying the world together, nay, the nuptial bond; and, according to David, "a little lower than the angels." These reasons are great but not the chief ones, that is, they are not reasons for a lawful claim to the highest wonder as to a prerogative. Why should we not wonder more at the angels themselves and at the very blessed heavenly choirs?

Finally, it seemed to me that I understood why man is the animal that is most happy, and is therefore worthy of all wonder; and lastly, what the state is that is allotted to man in the succession of things, and that is capable of arousing envy not only in the brutes but also in the stars and even in minds beyond the world. It is wonderful and beyond belief. For this is the reason why man is rightly said and thought to be a great marvel and the animal really worthy of wonder. Now hear what it is, fathers; and with kindly ears and for the sake of your humanity, give me your close attention:

Now the highest Father, God the master-builder, had, by the laws of his secret wisdom, fabricated this house, this world which we see, a very superb temple of divinity. He had adorned the super-celestial region with minds. He had animated the celestial globes with eternal souls; he had filled with a diverse throng of animals the cast-off and residual parts of the lower world. But, with the work finished, the Artisan desired that there be someone to reckon up the reason of such a big work, to love its beauty, and to wonder at its greatness. Accordingly, now that all things had been completed, as Moses and Timaeus testify, He lastly considered creating man. But there was nothing in the archetypes from which He could mold a new sprout, nor anything in His storehouses which He could bestow as a heritage upon a new son, nor was there an empty judiciary seat where this contemplator of the universe could sit. Everything was filled up; all things had been laid out in the highest, the lowest, and the middle orders. But it did not belong to the paternal power to have failed in the final parturition, as though exhausted by childbearing; it did not belong to wisdom, in a case of necessity, to have been tossed back and forth through want of a plan; it did not belong to the loving-kindness which was going to praise divine liberality in others to be forced to condemn itself. Finally, the best of workmen decided that that to which nothing of its very own could be given should be, in composite fashion, whatsoever had belonged individually to each and every thing. Therefore He took up man, a work of indeterminate form; and, placing him at the midpoint of the world, He spoke to him as follows:

"We have given to thee, Adam, no fixed seat, no form of thy very own, no gift peculiarly thine, that thou mayest feel as thine own, have as thine own, possess as thine own the seat, the form, the gifts which thou thyself shalt desire. A limited nature in other creatures is confined within the laws written down by Us. In conformity with thy free judgment, in whose hands I have placed thee, thou are confined by no bounds; and thou wilt fix limits of nature for thyself. I have placed thee at the center of the world, that from there thou mayest more conveniently look around and see whatsoever is in the world. Neither heavenly nor earthly, neither mortal nor immortal have We made thee. Thou, like a judge appointed for being honorable, art the molder and maker of thyself; thou mayest sculpt thyself into whatever shape thou dost prefer. Thou canst grow downward into the lower natures which are brutes. Thou canst again grow upward from thy soul's reason into the higher natures which are divine."

O great liberality of God the Father! O great and wonderful happiness of man! It is given him to have that which he chooses and to be that which he wills. As soon as brutes are born, they bring with them, "from their dam's bag," as Lucilius says, what they are going to possess. Highest spirits have been, either from the beginning or soon after, that which they are going to be throughout everlasting eternity. At man's birth the Father placed in him every sort of seed and sprouts of every kind of life. The seeds that each man cultivates will grow and bear their fruit in him. If he cultivates vegetable seeds, he will become a plant. If the seeds of sensation, he will grow into brute. If rational, he will come out a heavenly animal. If intellectual, he will be an angel, and a son of God. And if he is not contented with the lot of any creature but takes himself up into the center of his own unity, then, made one spirit with God and settled in the solitary darkness of the Father, who is above all things, he will stand ahead of all things. Who does not wonder at this chameleon which we are? Or who at all feels more wonder at anything else whatsoever? It was not unfittingly that Asclepius the Athenian said that man was symbolized by Prometheus in the secret rites, by reason of our nature sloughing its skin and transforming itself; hence metamorphoses were popular among the Jews and the Pythagoreans. For the more secret Hebrew theology at one time reshapes holy Enoch into an angel of divinity, whom they call *malach hashechina,* and at other times reshapes other men into other divinities. According to the Pythagoreans, wicked men are deformed into brutes and, if you believe Empedocles, into plants too. And copying them, Mohammed often had it on his lips that he who draws back from divine law becomes a brute. And his saying so was reasonable: for it is not the rind which makes the plant, but a dull and non-sentient nature; not the hide which makes a beast of burden, but a brutal and sensual soul; not the spherical body which makes the heavens, but right reason; and not a separateness from the body but a spiritual intelligence which makes an angel. For example, if you see a man given over to his belly and crawling upon the ground, it is a bush not a man that you see. If you see anyone blinded by the illusions of his empty and Calypso-like imagination, seized by the desire of scratching, and delivered over to the senses, it is a brute not a man that you see. If you come upon a philosopher winnowing out all things by right reason, he is a heavenly not an earthly animal. If you come upon a pure contemplator, ignorant of the body, banished to the innermost places of the mind, he is not an earthly, not a heavenly animal; he more superbly is a divinity clothed with human flesh.

Who is there that does not wonder at man? And it is not unreasonable that in the Mosaic and Christian holy writ man is sometimes denoted by the name "all flesh" and at other times by that of "every creature"; and man fashions, fabricates, transforms himself into the shape of all flesh, into the character of every creature. Accordingly, where Evantes the Persian tells of the Chaldaean theology, he writes that man is not any inborn image of himself, but many images coming in from the outside: hence that saying of the Chaldaeans: *enosh hu shinuy vekamah tevaoth baal chayim,* that is, man is an animal of diverse, multiform, and destructible nature.

But why all this? In order for us to understand that, after having been born in this state so that we may be what we will to be, then, since we are held in honor, we ought to take particular care that no one may say against us that we do not know that we are made similar to brutes and mindless beasts of burden. But rather, as Asaph the prophet says: "Ye are all gods, and sons of the most high," unless by abusing the very indulgent liberality of the Father, we make the free choice, which he gave to us, harmful to ourselves instead of helpful toward salvation.

Let a certain holy ambition invade the mind, so that we may not be content with mean things but may aspire to the highest things and strive with all our forces to attain them: for if we will to, we can. Let us spurn earthly things; let us struggle toward the heavenly. Let us put in last place whatever is of the world; and let us fly beyond the chambers of the world to the chamber nearest the most lofty divinity. There, as the sacred mysteries reveal, the seraphim, cherubim, and thrones occupy the first places. Ignorant of how to yield to them and unable to endure the second places, let us compete with the angels in dignity and glory. When we have willed it, we shall be not at all below them.

But by what method? or by doing what? Let us see what they are doing, what life they are living. If we too live that life—for we can—we shall equal their lot. The seraph burns with the fire of charity; the cherub shines with the radiance of intelligence; the throne stands in steadfastness of judgment. Hence, if, dedicated to an active life, we undertake the care of lower things with a right weighing of them, we shall be made steadfast in the fixed firmness of the thrones. If, being tired of actions and meditating on the workman in the work, on the work in the workman, we are busy with the leisure of contemplation, we shall flash on every side with cherubic light. If by charity we, with his devouring fire, burn for the Workman alone, we shall suddenly burst into flame in the likeness of a seraph. Upon the throne, that is, upon the just judge, sits God, the judge of the ages. He flies above the cherub, that is, the contemplator, and warms him, as if by brooding over him. The Spirit of the Lord is borne above the waters—I mean those waters which are above the heavens, the waters which in Job praise the Lord with hymns before daybreak. He who is a seraph, that is, a lover, is in God; and more, God is in him, and God and he are one.

But in what way can anyone either judge or love things which are unknown? Moses loved God whom he saw, and as judge, he administered to the people what he formerly saw as contemplator on the mountain. Therefore with his own light the cherub in the middle makes us ready for the seraphic fire, and at the same time illuminates us for the judgment of the thrones. He is the bond of the first minds, the order of Pallas, the ruler over contemplative philosophy. We must first rival him and embrace him and lay hold of him. Let us make ourselves one with him and be caught up to the heights of love. And let us descend to the duties of action, well instructed and prepared.

But if our life is to be shaped after the model of a cherub's life, it is well worth while to have in readiness and before our eyes what that life is and what sort it is, what actions and what works are theirs. Since we may not attain to this through ourselves, because we are flesh and our wisdom is of the earth, let us go to the ancient fathers who can give us a very substantial and sure faith in these things as things familiar and akin to them. Let us consult the Apostle Paul, the vessel of election, because, when he was lifted up to the third heaven, he saw the armies of the cherubim in action. According to Dionysius' interpretation, he will answer that the cherubim are being purged, then are being illuminated, and lastly are being prefected. Therefore, by rivaling the life of a cherub upon the earth, by confining the onslaughts of the affections by means of moral science, and by shaking off the mist of reason by means of dialectic, as if washing off the filth of ignorance and vice, let us purge the soul, that the affections may not audaciously run riot, nor an imprudent reason sometime rave. Then, over a soul which has been set in order and purified, let us pour the light of natural philosophy, that lastly we may perfect it with the knowledge of divine things.

And lest our Christians be insufficient for us, let us consult the patriarch Jacob, whose image flashes forth, carven in the seat of glory. That very wise father will give us advice by showing himself asleep in the lower world and awake in the upper. But his advice will be given figuratively; that is the way all things happen there. A ladder stretching from the lowness of earth to the heights of heaven and divided by the succession of many steps, with the Lord sitting at the top: the angels, contemplating, climb, by turns, up and down the steps. But if we who are in pursuit of an angelic life must try to do this same thing, I ask, who can touch the ladder of the Lord with dirty feet or unwashed hands? As the mysteries put it, it is sacrilegious for the impure to touch that which is pure. But what are these feet, and what are these hands? Naturally, the feet of the soul are that most despicable portion which alone rests upon matter as upon the earth, I mean the nutritive and the food-taking power, kindling-wood of lust and teacher of voluptuous softness. As for the hands of the soul, we might as well have spoken of anger, which struggles as a defender for appetite and, like a robber under the dust and sunshine, carries off the things which will be squandered by the appetite, which is dozing away in the shade. But, so as not to be hurled back from the ladder as profane and unclean, let us wash these hands and these feet in moral philosophy as in living water—that is, the whole sensual part wherein the allurement of the body resides, the allurement from which, they say, the soul gets a twisted neck, while being held back. But, if we want to be the companions of the angels moving up and down Jacob's ladder, this will not be enough, unless we have first been well trained and well taught to move forward duly from rung to rung, never to turn aside from the main direction of the ladder, and to make sallies up and down. When we have attained that by means of the speaking or reasoning art, then, besouled by a cherub's spirit, philosophizing along the rungs of the ladder of nature, and penetrating through everything from center to center, we shall at one time be descending, tearing apart, like Osiris, the one into many by a titanic force; and we shall at another time be ascending and gathering into one the many, like the members of Osiris, by an Apollonian force; until finally we come to rest in the bosom of the Father, who is at the top of the ladder, and are consumed by a theological happiness.

Let us inquire too of Job the just, what covenant he entered into with the God of life before he was begotten into life, the covenant which, among those million who stand before him, the highest God most strongly desired. He will doubtlessly answer, Peace. Accordingly, since we read in Job that God makes peace in the highest, and that the middle order interprets the prophecies of the highest order to the lower orders—let Empedocles the philosopher interpret for us the words of Job the theologian: he signifies to us that two natures are planted in our souls; by the one nature we are lifted upward to the heavens, and by the other, shoved downward to the lower world; and this by strife and friendship or by war and peace, according to his songs, in which he complains that, driven by strife and discord like a madman and banished from the gods, he is tossed upon the deep. Indeed, fathers, there is multiple discord in us, and we have severe, intestine, and more than civil wars at home: if we are unwilling to have these wars, if we will strive for that peace which so lifts us up to the heights that we are made to stand among the exalted of the Lord, moral philosophy alone will still those wars in us, will bring calm successfully. First, if our man will seek a truce with the enemy, he will subdue the uncurbed forays of the multiple brute, the quarrelings of the lion, and the feelings of wrath. Then if we take the right counsel, and desire for ourselves the security of everlasting peace, it will come and will fulfill our prayers liberally. The slaying of both beasts, like stuck sows, will establish most solemnly a most holy treaty between the flesh and the spirit. Dialectic will calm the turmoils of a reason shoved about between the fistfights of oratory and the deceits of the syllogism. Natural philosophy will calm the strifes and discords of opinion, which shake the unquiet soul up and down, pull her apart, and mangle her. But natural philosophy will bring calm in such a way as to command us to remember that, according to Heraclitus, our nature is born of war, and therefore is called a struggle by Homer; and hence, that in natural philosophy true quiet and lasting peace cannot offer themselves to us, and that this is the office and prerogative of their mistress, most holy theology. Theology herself will show the way to that peace and be our companion and guide; and, as from afar she sees us hurrying, she will cry out, "Come unto me, ye that labor, and I will refresh you. Come unto me, and I will give unto you peace which the world and nature cannot give unto you!" As we are called so sweetly and are invited with such kindness, let us fly on winged feet like earthly Mercuries into the embrace of our most blessed mother and enjoy the longed-for peace: the most holy peace, the indivisible bond, the friendship which is one soul, the friendship whereby all minds do not merely accord in one intellect that is above every intellect but in some inexpressible fashion become absolutely one. This is that friendship which the Pythagoreans say is the end of all philosophy. This is that peace which God makes on his heights and which the angels descending to earth announced to men of good will, that by this peace the men themselves ascending into heaven might become angels. Let us desire this peace for our friends, for our age. Let us desire this peace for every house into which we enter. Let us desire it for our soul, that through this peace she may become the house of God; that after she has, through morals and dialectics, cast off her meanness and has adorned herself with manifold philosophy as with a princely garment, and has crowned with garlands of theology the summits of the gates, the King of Glory may descend, and, coming with the Father, may make his residence in her. If she shows herself worthy of such a great guest, as his mercy is great, then, in a golden gown as in a wedding dress, wrapped in a multiple variety of teachings, she will welcome her beautiful guest not as a guest but as a bridegroom. That she may never be divorced from him, she will long to be divorced from her own people and, forgetful of the house of her father, nay, forgetful of herself, she will long to die in herself that she may live in her bridegroom, in whose sight the death of his saints is surely precious —I mean death, if that should be called death which is the fullness of life, the meditation upon which the wise have said is the study of philosophy.

Let us also cite Moses himself, scarcely inferior to the fountain fullness of holy and inexpressible intelligence, whence the angels are drunken on their own nectar. We shall hear the venerable judge promulgating laws to us who dwell in the desert solitude of this body: "Let those who are still unclean and in need of moral knowledge dwell with the people outside of the tabernacle in the open sky, and let them meanwhile purify themselves like Thessalian priests. Let those who have by now set their lives (*mores*) in order be received into the sanctuary. But let them not yet handle the sacred things; but first, as deacons assiduous in the service that is dialectic, let them minister to the sacred things of philosophy. Then, after they have been admitted to the sacred things, let them in the priesthood of philosophy contemplate sometimes the many-colored, that is, the star-constellated royal decoration of the higher palace of God, at other times the celestial candelabra divided by seven lights, and at other times the skin-covered elements, that finally they may be received through the merits of sublime theology into the sanctuary of the temple and may enjoy the glory of divinity without the veil of any image coming in between." Moses gives us these direct commands, and in giving them he advises us, arouses us, urges us to make ready our way through philosophy to future celestial glory, while we can.

But in truth, not only the Mosaic or Christian mysteries but also the theology of the ancients show the advantages for us and the dignity of these liberal arts about which I have come here to dispute. For what else is meant by the degrees of initiation that are customary in the secret rites of the Greeks? First, to those who had been purified by moral and dialectic arts, which we have called, as it were, purgative, befell the reception of the mysteries. And what else can this reception be but the interpretation of more hidden nature by means of philosophy? Then lastly, to those who had been thus prepared, came that ἐποπτεία, that is, a vision of divine things by means of the light of theology. Who does not seek to be initiated into such rites? Who does not set all human things at a lower value and, contemning the goods of fortune and neglecting the body, does not desire, while still continuing on earth, to become the drinking-companion of the gods; and, drunken with the nectar of eternity, to bestow the gift of immortality upon the mortal animal? Who does not wish to have breathed into him the Socratic frenzies sung by Plato in the *Phaedrus,* that by the oarlike movement of wings and feet he may quickly escape from here, that is, from this world where he is laid down as in an evil place, and be carried in speediest flight to the heavenly Jerusalem. We shall be possessed, fathers, we shall be possessed by these Socratic frenzies, which will so place us outside of our minds that they will place our mind and ourselves in God. We shall be possessed by them if we have first done what is in us to do. For if through morality the forces of the passions will have been so stretched to the [proper] measure, through due proportions, that they sound together in fixed concord, and if through dialectic, reason will have moved, keeping time in her forward march, then, aroused by the frenzy of the muses, we shall drink in the heavenly harmony of our ears. Then Bacchus the leader of the muses, in his own mysteries, that is, in the visible signs of nature, will show the invisible things of God to us as we philosophize, and will make us drunk with the abundance of the house of God. In this house, if we are faithful like Moses, holiest theology will approach, and will inspire us with a twofold frenzy. We, raised up into the loftiest watchtower of theology, from which, measuring with indivisible eternity the things that are, will be, and shall have been, and looking at their primeval beauty, shall be prophets of Phoebus, his winged lovers, and finally, aroused with ineffable charity as with fire, placed outside of ourselves like burning Seraphim, filled with divinity, we shall now not be ourselves, but He himself who made us.

The sacred names of Apollo, if anyone examines their meanings and hidden mysteries, will sufficiently show that that god is no less philosopher than prophet. Since Ammonius has followed this up sufficiently, there is no reason why I should handle it in another way. But there come to mind, fathers, three Delphic precepts, very necessary for those who are to enter into the sacrosanct and very august temple of the true, not the invented Apollo, who illuminates every soul coming into this world. You will see that they give us no other advice than to embrace with all our strength this three-fold philosophy which the present disputation is about. For that *μηδὲν ἄγαν*, that is, nothing too much, rightly prescribes the measure and rule of all virtues through the principle of moderation, with which morals is concerned. Then that *γνῶθι σεαυτόν*, that is, know thyself, arouses us and urges us towards the knowledge of all nature, of which man's nature is the medium and, as it were, the union. For he who knows himself, knows all things in himself, as first Zoroaster, and then Plato wrote in the *Alcibiades*. At last, illuminated by this knowledge through natural philosophy, now near to God, saying *εἶ*, that is, Thou art, we shall address the true Apollo with a theological greeting, familiarly and so happily.

Let us also consult the very wise Pythagoras, who was wise especially in that he never thought himself worthy of the name of wise. First, he will warn us not to sit too much, that is, not to let go the rational part, by which the soul measures, judges, and examines everything, and relax in idle inactivity. But let us direct it diligently and arouse it by dialectical exercise and rule. Then he will signify that we are to pay special attention to two things, not to make water against the sun nor trim our nails during the sacrifices. But after we have, through morals, relieved ourselves of the appetite for overflowing sensual pleasures and, as it were, trimmed the tips of our nails, the sharp pricks of anger and the stings of animosity, only then may we begin to take part in the aforementioned sacred mysteries of Bacchus, and to be at leisure for our contemplation, whose father and leader is rightly said to be the Sun. At last, he will advise us to feed the cock, that is, to nourish the divine part of our soul with knowledge of divine things as with solid food and heavenly ambrosia. This is the cock at the sight of which the lion, that is, every earthly power, feels fear and awe. This is that cock to which intelligence was given, as we read in Job. At the crowing of this cock, erring man returns to his senses. In the morning dawn this cock daily crows in harmony with the morning stars praising God. Socrates at the point of death, when he hoped to unite the divinity of his soul to the divinity of a greater world, said that he owed this cock to Asclepius, that is, to the physician of souls, now that he was placed beyond all danger of sickness.

Let us also examine the records of the Chaldaeans. We shall

see, if we can believe them, that through these same arts, the way to happiness is opened to men. The Chaldaean interpreters write that it was a saying of Zoroaster that the soul has wings; when the feathers fall off, she is borne headlong into the body, when they sprout again, she flies up to the heights. When his students asked him how they might obtain souls flying with well feathered wings, he said "You moisten the wings with the waters of life." When they again questioned him where they might seek these waters, he answered them figuratively (as was the custom of the man), "The paradise of God is washed and watered by four rivers. From the same place you may draw healthful waters for yourselves. The name of the river from the north is Pischon, which means straight, that from the west is Dichon, which signifies atonement, that from the east is Chiddekel, which means light, that from the south is Perath, which we can translate as piety." Give close attention, fathers, and consider carefully that these doctrines of Zoroaster really mean nothing else than that by moral science, as by western waters, we may wash dirt from our eyes; by dialectic, as by a ruler pointing north, we may direct our eyesight along a straight line. Then, let us accustom our eyes in natural contemplation to bear the still weak light of truth, the beginning of the rising sun, as it were, so that finally by theological piety and the most sacred worship of God, we may, like the eagles of heaven, endure bravely the very radiant brightness of the midday sun. These are perhaps those morning, noon, and evening knowledges sung first by David and explained more fully by Augustine. This is that midday light, which, perpendicular, inflames the Seraphim, and at the same time illuminates the Cherubim. This is that land toward which old father Abraham was always setting out. This is that place where there is no room for unclean spirits, as the doctrines of the Cabalists and Moors teach. And if it is right to make public, even enigmatically, something from more hidden mysteries, after the sudden fall of man from heaven has condemned our heads to dizziness, and, according to Jeremiah, death has entered through the windows and stricken liver and breast, let us call Raphael the heavenly physician to free us by morals and dialectic as by saving medicines. When we are restored to good health, Gabriel, the strength of God, will now dwell in us. Leading us through the wonders of nature, and pointing out the virtue and power of God everywhere, he will finally hand us over to the high priest

Michael, who will distinguish the veterans in the service of philosophy with the priesthood of theology, as with a crown of precious stones.

These are the reasons, most reverend fathers, that have not merely inspired me but compelled me to the study of philosophy. I was certainly not going to state them, except as a reply to those accustomed to condemning the study of philosophy in princes especially, or more generally, in men of ordinary fortune. Already (and this is the misfortune of our age) all this philosophizing makes for contempt and contumely rather than for honor and glory. This destructive and monstrous opinion that no one, or few, should philosophize, has much invaded the minds of almost everybody. As if it were absolutely nothing to have the causes of things, the ways of nature, the reason of the universe, the counsels of God, the mysteries of heaven and earth very certain before our eyes and hands, unless someone could derive some benefit from it or acquire profit for himself. It has already reached the point that now (what sorrow!) those only are considered wise who pursue the study of wisdom for the sake of money; so that one may see chaste Pallas, who stays among men by a gift of the gods, chased out, hooted, hissed; who loves and befriends her does not have her unless she, as it were prostituting herself and receiving a pittance for her deflowered virginity, bring back the ill-bought money to her lover's money-box. I say all these things not without great grief and indignation, not against the princes, but against the philosophers of this age, who believe and preach that there should be no philosophizing because there is no money for philosophers, no prizes awarded them; as if they did not show by this one word that they are not philosophers. Since their whole life is set on money-making or ambition, they do not embrace the knowledge of truth for itself. I shall give myself this credit and shall not blush to praise myself in this respect, that I have never philosophized for any reason other than for the sake of philosophizing, that I have neither hoped nor sought from my studies, from my lucubrations, any other gain or profit than cultivation of soul and knowledge of truth, always so greatly desired by me. I have always been so desirous of this truth and so much in love with it that, abandoning all care of public and private affairs, I gave my whole self over to the leisure of contemplating, from which no disparaging of the envious, no curses from the enemies of wisdom, have been able so far or will be able later to frighten me away. Philosophy herself has taught me to weigh things rather by my own conscience than by the judgments of others, and to consider not so much whether I should be badly spoken of as whether I myself should say or do anything bad. In fact, I was not ignorant, most reverend fathers, that this disputation of mine will be as pleasant and enjoyable to all you who delight in good arts and have wished to honor it with your most august presence, as it will be heavy and burdensome to many others; and I know that there are some who have condemned my undertaking before this, and who condemn it now under many names. Thus there are usually no fewer, not to say more, growlers who carry on well and in a holy way against virtue, than there are who do so wickedly and wrongly against vice.

There are some who do not approve of this whole class of disputes and this practice of debating in public about letters, asserting that it makes rather for the display of talent and learning than for acquiring knowledge. There are some who do not disapprove of this type of exercise, but who do not approve of it at all in my case, because I at my age, in only my twenty-fourth year, have dared, in the most famous city, in the largest assembly of the most learned men, in the apostolic senate, to propose a disputation on the sublime mysteries of Christian theology, on the loftiest questions of philosophy, on unknown teachings. Others who give me leave to dispute are unwilling to give me leave to dispute about nine hundred questions, saying in slander that the proposal was made as needlessly and ambitiously as it was beyond my powers. I should have immediately surrendered to their objections if the philosophy which I profess had so taught me; and now, at her teaching me, I would not answer if I believed this disputation among us were set up for brawling and quarreling. Consequently, let every intent of detraction and irritation depart, and let malice, which, Plato writes, is always absent from the divine chorus, also depart from our minds. And let us learn in friendly fashion whether I ought to dispute, and on so many questions.

First, to those who slander this practice of disputing publicly, I am not going to say much, except that this crime, if they judge it a crime, is the joint work not only of all you very excellent doctors—who have often discharged this office not without very great praise and glory—but also of Plato and Aristotle and the most upright philosophers of every age, together with me. To them it was most certain that they had nothing better for reaching the knowledge of the truth which they sought than that they be very often in the exercise of disputing. As through gymnastics the forces of the body are strengthened, so doubtless in this, as it were, literary gymnasium, the forces of the soul become much stronger and more vigorous. I would not believe that the poets signified anything else to us by the celebrated arms of Pallas, or the Hebrews when they say *barzel,* iron, is the symbol of wise men, than that this sort of contest is very honorable, exceedingly necessary for gaining wisdom. Perhaps that is why the Chaldaeans, too, desire that at the birth of him who is to become a philosopher, Mars should behold Mercury with triangular aspect, as if to say that if you take away these encounters, these wars, then all philosophy will become drowsy and sleepy.

But to those who say that I am not equal to this business, the reason in my defense is more difficult. For if I say that I am equal to it, perhaps I shall seem liable to the charge of boastfulness and self-conceit; if I confess myself unequal, of audacity and imprudence. You see what difficulties I have fallen into, in what a position I am, where I cannot without blame make a promise about myself which I cannot then without blame fail to fulfill. Perhaps I could bring forward that saying of Job, that the spirit is in all, and hear with Timothy, "Let no one scorn your young manhood." But from my conscience I shall say this truly, that there is nothing great or singular in us. Though I do not deny that I am very studious and desirous of the good arts, nevertheless I do not take to myself or lay claim to the name of learned man. Wherefore I laid such a great burden on my shoulders not because I was unconscious of our infirmity, but because I knew that this sort of struggle, that is, literary, was peculiar in that here it is a gain to lose. Consequently, anyone very weak can and should not only not disparage them, but also seek them voluntarily, since the loser truly receives benefit and not injury from the winner, for through him the loser returns home richer, that is, more learned and readier for future fights. Inspired by this hope, I, weak soldier though I be, have not been afraid to challenge the bravest and strongest of all to such a heavy battle. Whether it was an act of boldness or not can in any case be judged more rightly from the outcome of the fight than from my age.

It remains in the third place for me to answer those who are offended by the numerous multitude of things proposed, as if this burden sat upon their shoulders, and as if it were not I alone who have to endure this toil, howsoever great. It is certainly unbecoming and peevish to wish to set limits to another's industry, and, as Cicero says, to desire mediocrity in a case where the greater is the better. All in all, it was necessary for me either to fail or to succeed in such great undertakings. If I should succeed, I do not see why it is praiseworthy for me to distinguish myself on ten questions, while it is thought blameworthy for me to have distinguished myself on nine hundred. If I should fail, they will have grounds for accusing me, if they hate me; for excusing me, if they love me. This is so because a young man of modest talents and scanty learning who has failed in such a serious and great matter will merit pardon rather than accusation. Indeed, according to the poet, "If strength fails, boldness will surely be glory: in great things it is enough to have willed." But if in our age many men, imitating Gorgias the Leontine, have been accustomed not without praise to propose a disputation not merely on nine hundred questions but on all questions about all arts, why am I not allowed to dispute without blame on many questions indeed, but still on a fixed and determinate number? But, they say, this is needless and ambitious. Yet I contend that I did this not needlessly, but of necessity. But if they should consider with me my reasons for philosophizing, let them reluctantly confess that it is clearly of necessity.

Those who have devoted themselves to any one of the schools of philosophy, inclining for example to Thomas or Scotus, who now are much followed, can bring their doctrine into danger in the discussion of a few questions. But I have resolved not to swear by anyone's word, that I may base myself on all teachers of philosophy, examine all writings, recognize every school. Wherefore, since I had to speak on all questions (lest, if as defender of a personal doctrine, neglecting others, I should seem to be hampered by it), even if few questions might be raised about individual doctrines, there could not fail to be very many that were brought forward simultaneously concerning all. Nor should anyone condemn in me that wherever the tempest bears me, I am brought as a guest. For it was a practice of the ancients to study every school of writers, and if possible, to pass over no treatises unread; and especially those of Aristotle, who because of this was called by Plato ἀναγνώστης, that is, reader. And it indeed belongs to a narrow mind to have kept oneself within one Porch or Academy. Nor can anyone have selected rightly his own doctrine from all, unless he has first made himself familiar with all.

Further, in each school there is something notable that it does not have in common with the others. But let me now begin with ourselves, whom philosophy has at last reached. In John Scotus there is certain vigor and breadth. In Thomas, a solidity and equilibrium. In Aegidius, a terseness and precision. In Francis, a sharpness and pointedness. In old Albert, spaciousness and grandeur. In Henry, so it seems to me, there is always something sublime and venerable. Among the Arabs, there is in Averroes a firmness and steadiness. In Avempace and in Alfarabi, something grave and well meditated. In Avicenna, something divine and Platonic. Among the Greeks universally there is, especially, a certain brilliance and chasteness of philosophy. In Simplicius, richness and abundance. In Themistius, elegance and concision. In Alexander, steadfastness and learning. In Theophrastus, a serious working out of things. In Ammonius, a smoothness and pleasingness. And if you turn to the Platonists, to go over a few of them: in Prophyry you will be pleased by an abundance of materials and a complex religion. In Jamblichus you will feel awe at a more hidden philosophy and at the mysteries of the barbarians. In Plotinus there is no one thing in particular for you to wonder at, for he offers himself to our wonder in every part; and while he speaks in a divine manner about divine things, and of human things in a manner far above man, with a learned indirectness of discourse, the sweating Platonists scarcely understand. I pass over the more recent: Proclus, abounding in Asiatic fertility, and those who have flowed from him, Hermias, Damascius, Olympiodorus and many others, in all of whom there always shines that τὸ θεῖον, that is, divine something, the peculiar emblem of the Platonists. Further, if there is a school which attacks truer doctrines and ridicules with calumny the good causes of thought, it strengthens rather than weakens truth, and as by motion it excites the flame rather than extinguishing it. Moved by this reasoning, I have wished to bring into view the things taught not merely according to one doctrine (as some would desire), but things taught according to every sort of doctrine, that by this comparison of very many sects and by the discussion of manifold philosophy, that radiance of truth which Plato mentions in his *Letters* might shine more clearly upon our minds, like the sun rising from the deep. What good was it if only the philosophy of the Latins would be treated, namely, Thomas,

Scotus, Aegidius, Francis, and Henry, without the Greek and Arab philosophers? All wisdom flowed from the barbarians to the Greeks, and from the Greeks to us. So our people, in their way of philosophizing, always thought it enough for them if they remained with foreign discoveries and cultivated foreign things. What good was it to treat of natural things with the Peripatetics, unless the academy of the Platonists was also summoned, whose doctrine on divine things has always been held very sacred among all philosophies (witness Augustine), and also has by me now, for the first time after many centuries (as I know, and may there be no envy at the word), been brought forward publicly to undergo the test of disputation.

What good was it to have dealt with the opinions of others in any number, if, as though coming to a banquet of the wise without contributing anything, we brought nothing which would be our own, given birth and perfected by our mind. Indeed it is ignoble, as Seneca says, to know only by way of commentary, and, as if the discoveries of the ancients had closed the road for our industry, as if the force of nature in us were exhausted, to give birth to nothing from ourselves, which, if it does not demonstrate truth, at least points to it as from a distance. But if a farmer hates sterility in a field, and a husband in a wife, certainly a barren soul is hated by the divine mind woven into it and allied with it, the more a far nobler offspring is desired from it.

Consequently I was not content to have added, beside the common teachings, much on the ancient theology of Hermes Trismegistus, much on the doctrines of the Chaldaeans and of Pythagoras, and much on the more secret mysteries of the Jews, and I also proposed for disputation very many things discovered and thought out by us on natural and divine matters.

First, I have proposed the concord of Plato and Aristotle, believed by many before now, but adequately proved by no one. Among the Latins, Boethius, who promised to prove it, is not found ever to have done what he always wished to do. Among the Greeks, Simplicius made the same declaration: would that he had fulfilled his promise. Augustine too wrote in his *Academica* that there have been many who have attempted to prove the same thing in their very subtle disputations, namely, that the philosophy of Plato and of Aristotle is the same. Again, John the Grammarian, although he says that Plato seems to differ from Aristotle only to those who do not understand what Plato says, nevertheless left no proof of this to posterity. Further, we have added several points where the thoughts of Scotus and Thomas, of Averroes and Avicenna, which are considered to be discordant, we have maintained to be in concord.

Second, we have put down the seventy-two new physical and metaphysical doctrines which we have thought out in Aristotelian and Platonic philosophy. If one holds to them he will be able, unless I am wrong, as will soon be clear to me, to solve any question proposed about the things of nature or of God, in a fashion far other than we are taught by that philosophy which is read in the schools and cultivated by the doctors of these times. And, fathers, no one should wonder that in my early years, at a tender age at which it has been hardly permitted me (as some maintain) to read the meditations of others, I should wish to bring forward a new philosophy. They should either praise this philosophy if it is defended, or condemn it if it is refuted; and finally, since they are to judge of these our discoveries and our learning, they should reckon up not the years of the author, but rather the merits or demerits of these things.

Besides this we have brought forward something else new, the ancient system of philosophizing through numbers. It was held to by the early theologians, by Pythagoras in particular, by Aglaophamus, by Philolaus, by Plato and the early Platonists. But in this age, this doctrine, like other famous ones, has so passed out of use by the negligence of posterity, that scarcely any traces of it are to be found. Plato writes in the *Epinomis* that among all liberal arts and theoretical sciences the science of numbering is chief and most divine. Again, asking why man is the wisest animal, he answers that it is because he knows how to number. Aristotle also records this opinion in his *Problemata.* Abumasar writes that there was a saying of Avenzoar the Babylonian that he who knows how to number knows all things. These things could not in any way be true if they had understood by the art of numbering that art at which now the merchants are expert above all. Plato also witnesses this, warning us in a loud voice not to confuse this divine arithmetic with mercantile arithmetic. Therefore, when, after many lucubrations, it seemed to me that I had explored that arithmetic which is so praised, I went to put this thing to a test, and I promised I would answer publicly, in order, to the seventy-four questions that are thought to be among the principal questions on nature and God.

I have proposed theorems about magic, too, wherein I have signified that magic is twofold. The first sort is put together by the work and authorship of demons, and is a thing, as God is true, execrable and monstrous. The other sort is, when well explored, nothing but the absolute consummation of the philosophy of nature. When the Greeks mention these, they call the first sort *γοητείαν*, not dignifying it in any way by the name magic. They call the second sort by its proper and peculiar name, *μαγείαν*, the perfect and highest wisdom, as it were. Porphyry says that in the language of the Persians, magician means the same thing as interpreter and lover of divine things means in our language. Now there is a great, or rather, fathers, there is the greatest disparity and unlikeness between these arts. Not only the Christian religion, but all laws, every well ordered state, condemns and curses the first. All wise men, all nations studious of things heavenly and divine, approve and embrace the second. The first is the most fraudulent of arts, the second is firm, faithful, and solid. Whoever cultivated the first always dissimulated it, because it would be in ignominy and disgrace of the author. From the second comes the highest splendor and glory of letters, desired in ancient times and almost always since then. No man who was a philosopher and desirous of learning good arts has ever been studious of the first. Pythagoras, Empedocles, Democritus, Plato, traveled across seas to learn the second. When they came back, they preached it and held it chief among their esoteric doctrines. The first can be proved by no arguments nor certain founders; the second, honored as it were by most illustrious parents, has two principal founders: Xalmosis, whom Abbaris the Hyperborean imitated, and Zoroaster, not the one whom you perhaps think, but the son of Oromasus. If we question Plato as to what is the magic of each of them, he will answer in the *Alcibiades* that Zoroaster's magic is nothing but that knowledge of divine things wherein the kings of Persia educated their sons, that after the pattern of the republic of the world they might themselves be taught to rule their own republic. He will reply in the *Charmides* that the magic of Xalmosis is medicine of the soul, by which temperance is obtained for the soul, as health is obtained for the body by medicine. Afterwards Carondas, Damigeron, Apollonius, Hostanes, and Dardanus continued in their foosteps. So did Homer, whom we shall prove sometime in our *Poetic Theology* to have disguised this magic too, just as he did all other wisdoms, under the wanderings of

Ulysses. Eudoxus and Hermippus continued in their footsteps. Nearly all who have examined closely the Pythagorean and Platonic mysteries have continued also. I find three among the moderns who have caught the scent of it, Alchindus the Arab, Roger Bacon, and William of Paris. Plotinus too mentions it, where he shows that the magician is the minister and not the maker of nature. That most wise man proves and asserts this second magic, so abhorring the other that, invited to the rites of evil demons, he replied that it was more fitting for them to come to him than for him to go to them, and rightly so. For as the first magic makes man subject to and delivered over to the powers of wickedness, so the second makes him their prince and lord. Finally, the first cannot claim for itself the name of either art or science. The second is full of the deepest mysteries and includes the most profound and hidden contemplation of things, and finally, the knowledge of all nature. The second, among the virtues sown by the kindness of God and planted in the world, as if calling them out from darkness into light, does not so much make wonders as carefully serve nature which makes them. Having carefully investigated the harmony of the universe, which the Greeks very expressively call *συμπάθειαν*, and having looked closely into the knowledge that natures have of each other, this second magic, applying to each thing its innate charms, which are called by magicians *ἰύγγες*, as if it were itself the maker, discloses in public the wonders lying hidden in the recesses of the world, in the bosom of nature, in the storerooms and secrets of God. And as the farmer marries elm to vine, so the magician marries earth to heaven, that is, lower things to the qualities and virtues of higher things. Hence the first magic appears as monstrous and harmful as the second, divine and salutary. And especially because the first magic delivers man over to the enemies of God, calls him away from God, this second magic arouses that admiration at the works of God which so prepares that charity, faith, and hope most surely follow. For nothing impels more toward religion and the worship of God than assiduous contemplation of the wonders of God. When we shall have well explored these wonders by means of this natural magic we are speaking of, we shall be inspired more ardently to the worship and love of the maker, and shall be driven to sing: "The heavens are full, all the earth is full of the majesty of Thy glory."

And this is enough about magic, about which I have said these things because I know there are many people who, as dogs always bark at strangers, so also often condemn and hate what they do not understand.

I come now to those things that I have dug up from the ancient mysteries of the Hebrews and have brought forward in order to confirm the holy and Catholic faith. And lest by chance they be thought by those to whom they are unknown to be fictitious nonsense or tales about rumors, I wish everyone to understand what and of what sort they are, whence sought, by which and how famous authors they are guaranteed, and how they were stored away, how divinely inspired they are, and how necessary to us for defending religion against the rude slanders of the Hebrews. Not only do celebrated doctors of the Hebrews, but also among us Esdras, Hilary, and Origen write that Moses on the mountain received from God not only the law, which, as written down in five books, he left to posterity, but also a more secret and true interpretation of the law. But God commanded him to publish the law indeed to the people, yet not to pass on in writing the interpretation of the law, or to make it generally known, but to reveal it himself under a great holy seal of silence to Jesus Nave alone, and afterwards he to the other high priests succeeding him. It was enough to recognize by means of the plain story, now the power of God, now his anger against the wicked, his mercy toward the good, and his justice toward all; and by means of the divine and saving precepts to be taught to live well and blessedly, and the worship of the true religion. But to disclose to the people the more secret mysteries, things hidden under the bark of the law and the rough covering of words, the secrets of the highest divinity, what was that other than to give what is holy to dogs and to cast pearls among swine? Consequently it was not human prudence but divine command to keep these things secret from the people, and to communicate them to the perfect, among whom alone Paul says that he spoke wisdom. The ancient philosophers observed this custom very faithfully. Pythagoras wrote nothing but a few little things which, on dying, he entrusted to his daughter Dama. The sphinxes carved on the temples of the Egyptians warned them to guard mystical doctrines inviolate from the profane multitude, in the entanglements of enigmas. Plato, writing to Dionysius some things about the highest substances, says, "I must speak in enigmas, so that if the letter by chance comes into the hands of others, what I have written you may not be understood by them." Aristotle said that his books of *Metaphysics,* which treat of divine things, are published and not published. What more? Origen asserts that Jesus Christ the master of life revealed many things to his disciples which they did not want to write down, lest they become common to the vulgar. Dionysius the Areopagite especially confirms this, who says that the more secret mysteries were handed down by the founders of our religion ἐκ νοῦ εἰς νοῦν διὰ μέσον λόγον, from soul to soul, without writing, by means of words passing down. Because that divinely given, true interpretation of the law of Moses was revealed by command of God in just this same way, it is called Cabala, which means the same thing among the Hebrews as *reception* does among us. This is so because one man would receive this doctrine from another not through written records, but by regular succession of disclosure, by law of inheritance, as it were. But after the Hebrews had been liberated by Cyrus from captivity in Babylon, and the temple had been restored under Zorobabel, they turned their minds to repairing the law. Esdras, then governor of the church, after he corrected the book of Moses, clearly knew that the custom instituted by the forefathers of passing the doctrine on by hand could not be preserved through the exiles, slaughters, flights, and captivity of the people of Israel, and that the secrets of heavenly doctrine, granted to him by God, would henceforth perish, as they could not remain long in memory without the mediation of writings. Consequently, he decreed that all the wise men who were then left should be called together, and each of them should bring together what he remembered about the mysteries of the law. After scribes were summoned, it should then be written down in seventy volumes, for there were about that many wise men in the Sanhedrin. Do not take my word only for this, fathers, but listen to Esdras himself speaking, thus: "When forty days had passed, the most high spoke, saying: 'Place in the open what you formerly wrote, so that the worthy and unworthy may read. But you will save the last seventy books so that you may pass them on to the wise among your people. For in them is the heart of understanding and the fountain of wisdom and the river of knowledge.' And so I have done." These are the words of Esdras. These are the books of the knowledge of Cabala. Esdras proclaimed at the beginning in a clear voice that in these books was rightly the heart of understanding, that is, an ineffable theology of supersubstantial deity, the fountain of wisdom, that is, an exact metaphysics of intelligible angels and forms, and the river of knowledge, that is, a most sure philosophy of natural things.

Pope Sixtus IV, who preceded Innocent VIII under whom we happily live, provided with the greatest care and zeal that these books should be translated into Latin for the public advantage of our faith. And so, when he died, three of them came through to the Latins. In this age these books are cherished among the Hebrews with such religious awe that no one is allowed to touch them unless he is forty years old.

When I had procured myself these books at no small expense and had read them through with the greatest diligence and unwearied labor, I saw in them (God is my witness) a religion not so much Mosaic as Christian. There is the mystery of the Trinity, there the incarnation of the Word, there the divinity of the Messiah; there I read the same things on original sin, on Christ's atonement for it, on the heavenly Jerusalem, on the fall of demons, on the orders of angels, on purgatory, on the punishments of hell, which we daily read in Paul and Dionysius, in Jerome and Augustine. In those matters that regard philosophy, you may really hear Pythagoras and Plato, whose doctrines are so akin to Christian faith that our Augustine gives great thanks to God that the books of the Platonists came into his hands. In short, there is hardly any dispute between us and the Hebrews on this wherein they cannot be so disproved and refuted from the books of the Cabalists that there is no corner left in which they may hide. I have Antonius Cronicus, a most learned man, as a very trustworthy witness to this. When I was at his house at a banquet he heard with his own ears Dactylus the Hebrew, who was learned in this science, come down on his feet and hands to the exact belief of Christians on the Trinity.

But to return to the review of the topics of my disputation, we have advanced our opinion on the interpretation of the poems of Orpheus and Zoroaster. Orpheus is read almost wholly in Greek, Zoroaster partly in Greek, but more completely in Chaldaean. Both are believed to be the fathers and founders of ancient wisdom. I am silent about Zoroaster, who is frequently mentioned by the Platonists, always with the greatest veneration. Jamblichus the Chalcidean writes that Pythagoras had the Orphic theology as the model after which he molded and informed his own philosophy. In fact, they say that the words of Pythagoras are called holy only because they flowed from the teachings of Orpheus: thence as from their primal source flowed the secret doctrine of numbers, and whatever Greek philosophy had that was great and sublime. But, as was the practice of ancient theologians, Orpheus covered the mysteries of his doctrines with the wrappings of fables, and disguised them with a poetic garment, so that whoever reads his hymns may believe there is nothing underneath but tales and the purest nonsense. I wished to say this so that it may be known with what labor, with what difficulty I dug out the hidden meanings of a secret philosophy from the calculated meshes of riddles and from hiding-places in fables, especially with no help from the work and industry of other interpreters in such a weighty, abstruse, and unexplored field.

And still these dogs of mine bark that I have heaped up minutiae and trifles for a display of many questions, as if the questions were not all those which are doubtful and most controversial, with which the principal schools struggle; as if I did not advance many utterly unknown and untried questions to those very people who criticize mine and believe themselves the most eminent of philosophers.

I am so free from that guilt that I have taken care to reduce my disputation to as few headings as I could. If, as others usually do, I had wished to divide the disputation into its parts and cut it up fine, it would have expanded into a truly innumerable number. And, not to speak of the others, who is there who does not know that I could have spun out one of the nine hundred theses, that is, that the philosophies of Plato and Aristotle are to be reconciled, into six hundred headings, not to say more, beyond all suspicion of artificial multiplicity, enumerating one by one all the places wherein others think they disagree and I think they agree? But certainly (though I shall say something neither modest nor in accord with my character), I shall say, because the envious force me to speak, detractors force me, that I wished by this assembly of mine to show not that I know many things, but that I know things which many people do not know.

So that the fact itself may now be made evident to you, most venerable fathers, so that my discourse may no longer delay your desire, most excellent doctors, whom not without great delight I see ready and equipped, awaiting battle (may it be happy and fortunate), let us now, as by a trumpet summons, engage hands in combat.

Of Studies, Learning, and Idols

Francis Bacon

(1561-1626)

If Pico della Mirandola can be taken as the culmination of Renaissance thought, then Sir Francis Bacon can be, and often is, considered the beginning of modern thought. It was Bacon who said, "knowledge is power," an aphorism taken as an axiom by contemporary apologists of education. But Bacon would never have accepted the notion that knowledge per se *has much value. Instead, he would have agreed with Whitehead that "a merely well-informed man is the most useless bore on God's earth." To Bacon, knowledge was valuable only insofar as it was useful.*

In order to correct what he considered to be the errors that passed for knowledge in his day, he planned a vast critique or, in his words, "a total reconstruction of . . . all human knowledge." Our selections from the Advancement of Learning *and the* Novum Organum *are parts of this undertaking, which*

Bacon unfortunately never finished. One can say in explanation only that the real world was too much with him.

It might be interesting for the reader to reflect on Bacon's argument in the Advancement *for adequate support of teachers in contrast to the notions expressed on the same subject by Lucian and Pico della Mirandola. One should also note that the same down-to-earth realism is present in Bacon's critique of "false notions," the famous four idols. Here, incidentally, we have an early statement of the inductive method that was to become a governing principle of experimental science. A number of other notions in our selection can be seen as harbingers of the future. Bacon's attack on the subjectivity of rationalism and his critique of language as a faulty tool for precise description can serve as two examples. These have now become our current shibboleths.*

Of Studies

STUDIES serve for delight, for ornament, and for ability. Their chief use for delight is in privateness and retiring; for ornament, is in discourse; and for ability, is in the judgment and disposition of business. For expert men can execute, and perhaps judge of particulars, one by one; but the general counsels, and the plots and marshalling of affairs come best from those that are learned. To spend too much time in studies is sloth; to use them too much for ornament is affectation; to make judgment wholly by their rules is the humor of a scholar. They perfect nature, and are perfected by experience: for natural abilities are like natural plants, that need pruning by study; and studies themselves do give forth directions too much at large, except they be bounded in by experience. Crafty men contemn studies, simple men admire them, and wise men use them; for they teach not their own use; but that is a wisdom without them and above them, won by observation. Read not to contradict and confute, nor to believe and take for granted, nor to find talk and discourse, but to weigh and consider. Some books are to be tasted, others to be swallowed, and some few to be chewed and digested; that is, some books are to be read only in parts; others to be read, but not curiously; and some few to be read wholly, and with diligence and attention. Some books also may be read by deputy, and extracts made of them by others; but that would be only in the less important arguments and the meaner sort of books; else distilled books are, like common distilled waters, flashy things. Reading maketh a full man; conference a ready man; and writing an exact man. And, therefore, if a man write little, he had need have a great memory; if he confer little, he had need have a present wit; and if he read little, he had need have much cunning, to seem to know that he doth not. Histories make men wise; poets, witty; the mathematics, subtile; natural philosophy, deep; moral, grave; logic and rhetoric, able to contend. *Abeunt studia in mores.* Nay, there is no stond or impediment in the wit but may be wrought out by fit studies, like as diseases of the body may have appropriate exercises. Bowling is good for the stone and reins, shooting for the lungs and breast, gentle walking for the stomach, riding for the head, and the like. So if a man's wit be wandering, let him study the mathematics; for in demonstrations, if his wit be called away never so little, he must begin again. If his wit be not apt to distinguish or find differences, let him study the schoolmen; for they are *Cymini sectores.* If he be not apt to beat over matters, and to call up one thing to prove and illustrate another, let him study the lawyers' cases. So every defect of the mind may have a special receipt.

from Advancement of Learning

BOOK II

DEFECTS OF COLLEGES AND UNIVERSITIES

8. First therefore, amongst so many great foundations of colleges in Europe, I find strange that they are all dedicated to professions, and none left free to arts and sciences at large. For if men judge that learning should be referred to action, they judge well; but in this they fall into the error described in the ancient fable, in which the other parts of the body did suppose

the stomach had been idle, because it neither performed the office of motion, as the limbs do, nor of sense, as the head doth: but yet notwithstanding it is the stomach that digesteth and distributeth to all the rest. So if any man think philosophy and universality to be idle studies, he doth not consider that all professions are from thence served and supplied. And this I take to be a great cause that hath hindered the progression of learning, because these fundamental knowledges have been studied but in passage. For if you will have a tree bear more fruit than it hath used to do, it is not anything you can do to the boughs, but it is the stirring of the earth and putting new mould about the roots that must work it. Neither is it to be forgotten, that this dedicating of foundations and dotations to professory learning hath not only had a malign aspect and influence upon the growth of sciences, but hath also been prejudicial to states and governments. For hence it proceedeth that princes find a solitude in regard of able men to serve them in causes of estate, because there is no education collegiate which is free; where such as were so disposed might give themselves to histories, modern languages, books of policy and civil discourse, and other the like enablements unto service of estate.

9. And because founders of colleges do plant, and founders of lectures do water, it followeth well in order to speak of the defect which is in public lectures; namely, in the smallness and meanness of the salary or reward which in most places is assigned unto them; whether they be lectures of arts, or of professions. For it is necessary to the progression of sciences that readers be of the most able and sufficient men; as those which are ordained for generating and propagating of sciences, and not for transitory use. This cannot be, except their condition and endowment be such as may content the ablest man to appropriate his whole labor and continue his whole age in that function and attendance; and therefore must have a proportion answerable to that mediocrity or competency of advancement, which may be expected from a profession or the practice of a profession. So as, if you will have sciences flourish, you must observe David's military law, which was, "That those which staid with the carriage should have equal part with those which were in the action"; else will the carriages be ill attended. So readers in sciences are indeed the guardians of the stores and provisions of sciences, whence men in active courses are furnished, and therefore ought

to have equal entertainment with them; otherwise if the fathers in sciences be of the weakest sort or be ill maintained,

Et patrum invalidi referent jejunia nati.

10. Another defect I note, wherein I shall need some alchemist to help me, who call upon men to sell their books, and to build furnaces; quitting and forsaking Minerva and the Muses as barren virgins, and relying upon Vulcan. But certain it is, that unto the deep, fruitful, and operative study of many sciences, specially natural philosophy and physic, books be not only the instrumentals; wherein also the beneficence of men hath not been altogether wanting. For we see spheres, globes, astrolabes, maps, and the like, have been provided as appurtenances to astronomy and cosmography, as well as books. We see likewise that some places instituted for physic have annexed the commodity of gardens for simples of all sorts, and do likewise command the use of dead bodies for anatomies. But these do respect but a few things. In general, there will hardly be any main proficience in the disclosing of nature, except there be some allowance for expenses about experiments; whether they be experiments appertaining to Vulcanus or Daedalus, furnace or engine, or any other kind. And therefore as secretaries and spials of princes and states bring in bills for intelligence, so you must allow the spials and intelligencers of nature to bring in their bills; or else you shall be ill advertised.

11. And if Alexander made such a liberal assignation to Aristotle of treasure for the allowance of hunters, fowlers, fishers, and the like, that he might compile an history of nature, much better do they deserve it that travail in arts of nature.

12. Another defect which I note, is an intermission or neglect, in those which are governors in universities, of consultation, and in princes or superior persons, of visitation: to enter into account and consideration, whether the readings, exercises, and other customs appertaining unto learning, anciently began and since continued, be well instituted or no; and thereupon to ground an amendment or reformation in that which shall be found inconvenient. For it is one of your Majesty's own most wise and princely maxims, "That in all usages and precedents, the times be considered wherein they first began; which if they were weak or ignorant, it derogateth from the authority of the usage, and leaveth it for suspect." And therefore inasmuch as most of the

usages and orders of the universities were derived from more obscure times, it is the more requisite they be re-examined. In this kind I will give an instance or two, for example sake, of things that are the most obvious and familiar. The one is a matter, which though it be ancient and general, yet I hold to be an error; which is, that scholars in universities come too soon and too unripe to logic and rhetoric, arts fitter for graduates than children and novices. For these two, rightly taken, are the gravest of sciences, being the arts of arts; the one for judgment, the other for ornament. And they be the rules and directions how to set forth and dispose matter: and therefore for minds empty and unfraught with matter, and which have not gathered that which Cicero called *sylva* and *supellex,* stuff and variety, to begin with those arts (as if one should learn to weigh or to measure or to paint the wind) doth work but this effect, that the wisdom of those arts, which is great and universal, is almost made contemptible, and is degenerate into childish sophistry and ridiculous affectation. And further, the untimely learning of them hath drawn on by consequence the superficial and unprofitable teaching and writing of them, as fitteth indeed to the capacity of children. Another is a lack I find in the exercises used in the universities, which do make too great a divorce between invention and memory. For their speeches are either premeditate, in *verbis conceptis,* where nothing is left to invention; or merely extemporal, where little is left to memory. Whereas in life and action there is least use of either of these, but rather of intermixtures and premeditation and invention, notes and memory. So as the exercise fitteth not the practice, nor the image the life; and it is ever a true rule in exercises, that they be framed as near as may be to the life of practice; for otherwise they do pervert the motions and faculties of the mind, and not prepare them. The truth whereof is not obscure, when scholars come to the practices of professions, or other actions of civil life; which when they set into, this want is soon found by themselves, and sooner by others. But this part, touching the amendment of the institutions and orders of universities, I will conclude with the clause of Caesar's letter to Oppius and Balbus, *Hoc quemadmodum fieri possit, nonnulla mihi in mentem veniunt, et multa reperiri possunt: de iis rebus rogo vos ut cogitationem suscipiatis.*[1]

[1] As to how this may be done, a few things occur to me, and many more may be thought of; I ask you to give thought to these matters.

13. Another defect which I note ascendeth a little higher than the precedent. For as the proficience of learning consisteth much in the orders and institutions of universities in the same states and kingdoms, so it would be yet more advanced, if there were more intelligence mutual between the universities of Europe than now there is. We see there be many orders and foundations, which though they be divided under several sovereignties and territories, yet they take themselves to have a kind of contract, fraternity, and correspondence one with the other, insomuch as they have provincials and generals. And surely as nature createth brotherhood in families, and arts mechanical contract brotherhoods in communalties, and the anointment of God superinduceth a brotherhood in kings and bishops, so in like manner there cannot but be a fraternity in learning and illumination, relating to that paternity which is attributed to God, who is called the Father of illuminations or lights.

14. The last defect which I will note is, that there hath not been, or very rarely been, any public designation of writers or inquirers, concerning such parts of knowledge as may appear not to have been already sufficiently labored or undertaken; unto which point it is an inducement to enter into a view and examination what parts of learning have been prosecuted and what omitted. For the opinion of plenty is amongst the causes of want, and the great quantity of books maketh a show rather of superfluity than lack; which surcharge nevertheless is not to be remedied by making no more books, but by making more good books, which, as the serpent of Moses, might devour the serpents of the enchanters.

from Novum Organum

IDOLS AND FALSE NOTIONS

19. There are and can be only two ways of searching into and discovering truth. The one flies from the senses and particulars to the most general axioms, and from these principles, the truth of which it takes for settled and immovable, proceeds to judgment and to the discovery of middle axioms. And this way is now in fashion. The other derives axioms from the senses and particulars, rising by a gradual and unbroken ascent, so that it

arrives at the most general axioms last of all. This is the true way, but as yet untried.

. . . . .

38. The Idols and false notions which are now in possession of the human understanding, and have taken deep root therein, not only so beset men's minds that truth can hardly find entrance, but even after entrance obtained, they will again in the very instauration of the sciences meet and trouble us, unless men being forewarned of the danger fortify themselves as far as may be against their assaults.

39. There are four classes of Idols which beset men's minds. To these for distinction's sake I have assigned names—calling the first class *Idols of the Tribe;* the second, *Idols of the Cave;* the third, *Idols of the Market-place;* the fourth, *Idols of the Theater.*

40. The formation of ideas and axioms by true induction is no doubt the proper remedy to be applied for the keeping off, and clearing away of Idols. To point them out, however, is of great use; for the doctrine of Idols is to the interpretation of Nature what the doctrine of the refutation of Sophisms is to common Logic.

41. The *Idols of the Tribe* have their foundation in human nature itself, and in the tribe or race of men. For it is a false assertion that the sense of man is the measure of things. On the contrary, all perceptions as well of the sense as of the mind are according to the measure of the individual and not according to the measure of the universe. And the human understanding is like a false mirror, which, receiving rays irregularly, distorts and discolors the nature of things by mingling its own nature with it.

42. The *Idols of the Care* are the idols of the individual man. For every one (besides the errors common to human nature in general) has a cave or den of his own, which refracts and discolors the light of nature; owing either to his own proper and peculiar nature; or to his education and conversation with others; or to the reading of books, and the authority of those whom he esteems and admires; or to the differences of impressions, accordingly as they take place in a mind preoccupied and predisposed or in a mind indifferent and settled; or the like. So that the spirit of man (according as it is meted out to different individuals) is in fact a thing variable and full of perturbation, and governed as it were by chance. Whence it was well observed

by Heraclitus that men look for sciences in their own lesser worlds, and not in the greater or common world.

43. There are also Idols formed by the intercourse and association of men with each other, which I call *Idols of the Market-place,* on account of the commerce and consort of men there. For it is by discourse that men associate; and words are imposed according to the apprehension of the vulgar. And therefore the ill and unfit choice of words wonderfully obstructs the understanding. Nor do the definitions or explanations wherewith in some things learned men are wont to guard and defend themselves, by any means set the matter right. But words plainly force and overrule the understanding, and throw all into confusion, and lead men away into numberless empty controversies and idle fancies.

44. Lastly, there are Idols which have immigrated into men's minds from the various dogmas of philosophies, and also from wrong laws of demonstration. These I call *Idols of the Theater;* because in my judgment all the received systems are but so many stage-plays, representing worlds of their own creation after an unreal and scenic fashion. Nor is it only of the systems now in vogue, or only of the ancient sects and philosophies, that I speak; for many more plays of the same kind may yet be composed and in like artificial manner set forth; seeing that errors the most widely different have nevertheless causes for the most part alike. Neither again do I mean this only of entire systems, but also of many principles and axioms in science, which by tradition, credulity, and negligence have come to be received.

But of these several kinds of Idols I must speak more largely and exactly, that the understanding may be duly cautioned.

. . . . .

53. The *Idols of the Cave* take their rise in the peculiar constitution, mental or bodily, of each individual; and also in education, habit, and accident. Of this kind there is a great number and variety. But I will instance those the pointing out of which contains the most important caution, and which have most effect in disturbing the clearness of the understanding.

54. Men become attached to certain particular sciences and speculations, either because they fancy themselves the authors and inventors thereof, or because they have bestowed the greatest pains upon them and become most habituated to them. But men

of this kind, if they betake themselves to philosophy and contemplations of a general character, distort and color them in obedience to their former fancies; a thing especially to be noticed in Aristotle, who made his natural philosophy a mere bond-servant to his logic, thereby rendering it contentious and well-nigh useless.

. . . . .

56. There are found some minds given to an extreme admiration of antiquity, others to an extreme love and appetite for novelty; but few so duly tempered that they can hold the mean, neither carping at what has been well laid down by the ancients, nor despising what is well introduced by the moderns. This, however, turns to the great injury of the sciences and philosophy; since these affectations of antiquity and novelty are the humors of partisans rather than judgments; and truth is to be sought for not in the felicity of any age, which is an unstable thing, but in the light of nature and experience, which is eternal.

. . . . .

58. Let such then be our provision and contemplative prudence for keeping off and dislodging the *Idols of the Cave,* which grow for the most part either out of the predominance of a favorite subject, or out of an excessive tendency to compare or to distinguish, or out of partiality for particular ages, or out of the largeness or minuteness of the objects contemplated. And generally let every student of nature take this as a rule—that whatever his mind seizes and dwells upon with peculiar satisfaction is to be held in suspicion, and that so much the more care is to be taken in dealing with such questions to keep the understanding even and clear.

59. But the *Idols of the Market-place* are the most troublesome of all: idols which have crept into the understanding through the alliance of words and names. For men believe that their reason governs words; but it is also true that words react on the understanding; and this it is that has rendered philosophy and the sciences sophistical and inactive. Now words, being commonly framed and applied according to the capacity of the vulgar, follow those lines of division which are most obvious to the vulgar understanding. And whenever an understanding of

greater acuteness or a more diligent observation would alter those lines to suit the true divisions of nature, words stand in the way and resist the change. Whence it comes to pass that the high and formal discussions of learned men end oftentimes in disputes about words and names; with which (according to the use and wisdom of the mathematicians) it would be more prudent to begin, and so by means of definitions reduce them to order. Yet even definitions cannot cure this evil in dealing with natural and material things; since the definitions themselves consist of words, and those words beget others: so that it is necessary to recur to individual instances, and those in due series and order; as I shall say presently when I come to the method and scheme for the formation of notions and axioms.

60. The Idols imposed by words on the understanding are of two kinds. They are either names of things which do not exist (for as there are things left unnamed through lack of observation, so likewise are there names which result from fantastic suppositions and to which nothing in reality corresponds), or they are names of things which exist, but yet confused and ill-defined, and hastily and irregularly derived from realities. Of the former kind are Fortune, the Prime Mover, Planetary Orbits, Element of Fire, and like fictions which owe their origin to false and idle theories. And this class of idols is more easily expelled, because to get rid of them it is only necessary that all theories should be steadily rejected and dismissed as obsolete.

But the other class, which springs out of a faulty and unskilful abstraction, is intricate and deeply rooted. Let us take for example such a word as *humid;* and see how far the several things which the word is used to signify agree with each other; and we shall find the word *humid* to be nothing else than a mark loosely and confusedly applied to denote a variety of actions which will not bear to be reduced to any constant meaning. For it both signifies that which easily spreads itself round any other body; and that which in itself is indeterminate and cannot solidize; and that which readily yields in every direction; and that which easily divides and scatters itself; and that which easily unites and collects itself; and that which readily flows and is put in motion; and that which readily clings to another body and wets it; and that which is easily reduced to a liquid, or being solid easily melts. Accordingly when you come to apply the word—if you take it in one sense, flame is humid; if in another, air is not humid; if in another, fine dust is humid; if in another, glass is humid. So that it is easy to see that the notion is taken by abstraction only from water and common and ordinary liquids, without any due verification.

There are, however, in words certain degrees of distortion and error. One of the least faulty kinds is that of names of substances, especially of lowest species and well-deduced (for the notion of *chalk* and of *mud* is good, of *earth* bad); a more faulty kind is that of actions, as *to generate, to corrupt, to alter;* the most faulty is of qualities (except such as are the immediate objects of the sense), as *heavy, light, rare, dense,* and the like. Yet in all these cases some notions are of necessity a little better than others, in proportion to the greater variety of subjects that fall within the range of the human sense.

61. But the *Idols of the Theater* are not innate, nor do they steal into the understanding secretly, but are plainly impressed and received into the mind from the play-books of philosophical systems and the perverted rules of demonstration. To attempt refutations in this case would be merely inconsistent with what I have already said: for since we agree neither upon principles nor upon demonstrations there is no place for argument. And this is so far well, inasmuch as it leaves the honor of the ancients untouched. For they are no wise disparaged—the question between them and me being only as to the way. For as the saying is, the lame man who keeps the right road outstrips the runner who takes a wrong one. Nay, it is obvious that when a man runs the wrong way, the more active and swift he is the further he will go astray.

But the course I propose for the discovery of sciences is such as leaves but little to the acuteness and strength of wits, but places all wits and understandings nearly on a level. For as in the drawing of a straight line or perfect circle, much depends on the steadiness and practice of the hand, if it be done by aim of hand only, but if with the aid of rule or compass, little or nothing; so is it exactly with my plan. But though particular confutations would be of no avail, yet touching the sects and general divisions of such systems I must say something; something also touching the external signs which show that they are unsound; and finally something touching the causes of such great infelicity and of such lasting and general agreement in error; that so the access to truth may be made less difficult, and the human understanding may the more willingly submit to its purgation and dismiss its idols.

62. *Idols of the Theater,* or of Systems, are many, and there can be and perhaps will be yet many more. For were it not that now for many ages men's minds have been busied with religion and theology; and were it not that civil governments, especially monarchies, have been averse to such novelties, even in matters speculative; so that men labor therein to the peril and harming of their fortunes—not only unrewarded, but exposed also to contempt and envy; doubtless there would have arisen many other philosophical sects like to those which in great variety flourished once among the Greeks. For as on the phenomena of the heavens many hypotheses may be constructed, so likewise (and more also) many various dogmas may be set up and established on the phenomena of philosophy. And in the plays of this philosophical theater you may observe the same thing which is found in the theater of the poets, that stories invented for the stage are more compact and elegant, and more as one would wish them to be, than true stories out of history.

In general, however, there is taken for the material of philosophy either a great deal out of a few things, or a very little out of many things; so that on both sides philosophy is based on too narrow a foundation of experiment and natural history, and decides on the authority of too few cases. For the rational school of philosophers snatches from experience a variety of common instances, neither duly ascertained nor diligently examined and weighed, and leaves all the rest to meditation and agitation of wit.

. . . . .

Third Prolusion

John Milton

(1608-1674)

If one were to sum up the general position of the authors we just read one would have to say that they felt the schoolroom needed a breath of fresh air. This view Milton wholeheartedly endorses in his "Third Prolusion." In this early exercise in oratory, composed while still a student and delivered to his fellows while still in school, Milton advises them to abandon the "gamesome quarrels of gloomy oldsters" and to "rove . . . over all the lands drawn on the map." Written in a direct and spirited style, very different from Milton's later and mature prose, the "Third Prolusion" unhesitatingly compares the material the speaker had to study with the stuff Hercules had to shovel out of the Augean stables. It is a familiar comparison.

Against Scholastic Philosophy

A STRENUOUS search for a rhetorical display that would fascinate you, my collegiate audience, was by no means the least of my recent worries until suddenly I bethought myself of what was so often laid down in the writings of Cicero (whose name I not inauspiciously set on my masthead): that the business of a speaker is to inform, to regale, and to convince his hearers. And so the task which I have set myself in this affair is—to the best of my ability—not to fall short of this triple function of the orator.

But since there is no subject about which I should presume to inform scholars so universally erudite as you are, nor about which you would submit to my instruction, I can only hope for your permission to come close to it by saying something which perhaps will not be entirely off our subject. As for regaling you—as I fear I am far from talented enough to do—it is my dearest hope, and if I attain it, the result will certainly be much the same as convincing you. And now I shall abundantly convince you out of my own heart's judgment, if I shall succeed in persuading you, O my auditors, to relax your study of those enormous and near monstrous volumes of the so-called subtle doctors and to be less strenuous in your enjoyment of the warty disputes of the sophists. Yes truly, so as to make the soundness and rightness of my thesis plain to everyone, I shall briefly prove in my little half hour that the mind is neither entertained nor educated by these studies, nor any good done by them for society.

And at the outset, O Collegians, I put it to you (if I can guess your feelings by my own), and I ask what possible pleasure can lurk in these gamesome quarrels of gloomy oldsters. If they were not born in the cave of Trophonius, their stench betrays their birth in the caves of the monks, they reek with the grim harshness of their authors and are as wrinkled as their fathers. Their style is terse but in spite of it they are so prolix that they bore us and nauseate us. When they are read at any length, they generate an almost instinctive aversion and an even stronger natural hatred in their readers. Too often, my hearers, when it has been my bad luck to be saddled with assignments of research in their contemptible sophistries, when both my eyes and my mind were dull with long reading—too often, I say, I have stopped for breath, and sought some miserable relief in measuring the task before me. But when—as always—I found more ahead of me than I had yet got through, how often have I wished that I had been set to shovel out the Augean ox-stalls rather than struggle with such absurd assignments. And I have called Hercules happy because Juno was so easy-going as never to give him a job like mine to struggle through.

No flowers of rhetoric relieve this lifeless, flaccid, crawling stuff, but the jejune, juiceless style matches its thin substance, so that I might easily believe that it was written under melancholy Saturn were it not that the innocent simplicity of his times knew nothing of the tricks and impertinences which swarm in these books. Believe me, O most erudite young gentlemen, while I peruse these inane arguments I seem to myself to be ploughing my way through deserts and impassable places, through enormous wastes and narrow mountain gorges. It is incredible that the lovely and fastidious Muses preside over these wretched, squalid studies or could patronize their crazy fans. I am sure that there was never a place for them on Parnassus except perhaps some abandoned spot at the bottom of the mountain, some ugly place, thick and bristling with thornbushes and brambles, and covered with thistles and stinging nettles, where the chorus of the goddesses never comes, where no laurels or flowers are found, and where the sound of Apollo's lyre never reaches.

For surely divine poetry has the heaven-given power to lift the soul with its crust of earthly filth aloft and enshrine it in the skies, to breathe the perfume of nectar upon it, to bathe it with ambrosia, to fill it with heavenly bliss and whisper to it of immortal joy. Rhetoric so ensnares men's minds and so sweetly lures them with her chains that at one moment she can move them to pity, at another she can drive them to hatred, at another she can fire them with warlike passion, and at another lift them up to contempt of death itself. History, when it is handsomely related, can allay and compose the anxious troubles of the mind or anoint it with joy or, again, evoke tears, but gentle and calm tears, tears that bring a strange pleasure with their flow.

But these futile and barren controversies and wordy disputes are impotent to move the affections of the heart; they simply stupefy and benumb the mind. And so they please no one except a boor or a hairy ape with a secret craving for disputes and quarrels, a chatterer whose back is forever turned on true and sound wisdom. Chase him off with his sophisms either to Mount Caucasus or to any region where blind savagery prevails, and let him set up shop with his subtleties and quibbles and twist and torture himself as much as he likes until too much worry eats out his vitals, as the vulture ate out the heart of Prometheus.

But these studies which teach us nothing about things can give us no profit and no pleasure. Let us conjure up a vision of those crowds of old fellows in cowls, the prime contrivers of these sophisms: how many of them have ever enriched literature with anything good? No doubt, their crude violence has almost deformed Philosophy, who once was splendid, cultured, and gentler than she is now. Like an evil spirit, they have filled men's breasts with thorns and briars and have brought endless discord into the schools, which has marvellously impeded the scholars' happy progress.

What's the matter? Do these agile philosophasters box the compass with their arguments? One establishes a solid position and another struggles mightily to knock it down; and what you think has been fortified with impregnable logic is swiftly and handily knocked over by his opponent. Meanwhile the unhappy reader is in a quandary, as if at a crossroads, uncertain which way to turn and which road to take, while all around him the missiles fly so thick that they shut out the light and involve things in deep darkness. So, at last the reader is obliged to imitate the long suffering of Ceres and go searching with a lighted torch for truth through the whole wide world, and find it nowhere; until he is brought so close to insanity as to think that he is miserably blind because there is nothing that he can see.

And further, when those who yield and dedicate themselves entirely to the darkness of these disputations happen to stumble upon something foreign to their silliness, they usually betray their ignorance and laughable childishness. And finally, the great reward of all your hard work is that you emerge a more polished fool and contriver of nonsense. And it is no wonder that you grow more expertly ignorant, when all these things on which so much toil has been desperately and painfully spent have no existence in reality anywhere. Yet empty fancies and airy phantoms mislead puzzled and empty heads that lack sounder wisdom. As for the rest and as for the main matter, which is the nothing that these fooleries contribute to integrity of life and moral education, though I may say nothing, the facts are perfectly plain to you.

And so now the last point which I proposed to discuss becomes clear: namely, that this impudent battle of words does nothing for the good of society or for the honor or profit of our fatherland, the first priority, by common consent, in the sciences.

Now I have observed that our country is pre-eminently strengthened and honored by two things: by clear speaking and by brave deeds. And surely this contentious duel of clashing opinions seems impotent either to teach eloquence or to develop wisdom or to stir men to brave actions. So away with these clever disputants and their formalities; whose lot after death should be to twist ropes in Hades with that notorious Oenus.

But how much more satisfaction there would be, gentlemen, and how much worthier it would be of your name to rove with your eyes over all the lands which are drawn on the map, to look at the places where the heroes walked of old, to explore the regions made glorious by wars, triumphs, and the tales of famous poets; to cross the surging Adriatic unhurt; to ascend Mount Aetna in eruption; then to scrutinize the manners of men and the well-ordered governments of nations; then to search out and examine the natures of all living creatures; and from them to turn to the study of the hidden virtues of stones and herbs. Nor should you hesitate, gentlemen, to fly into the heavens and contemplate the manifold shapes of the clouds, the compacted power of the snow, and the source of the morning dews; then examine the chambers of the hail and the armories of the thunderbolts. Let there be nothing secret from you about the purpose of either Jove or Nature when a dire, tremendous comet threatens to set the skies on fire. Not even the tiniest stars should be hidden from you—however numerous they are, scattered and dispersed between the two poles. You must follow the sun on his journey—be his companions and call time itself to a reckoning, and demand an account of its eternal flight.

But your mind should not consent to be limited and circumscribed by the earth's boundaries, but should range beyond the confines of the world. Let it reach the summit of knowledge and learn to know itself and at the same time to know those blessed minds and intelligences with whom hereafter it will enter into eternal fellowship.

What can I say more? Let your teacher in all these studies be the famous man who is already your favorite, Aristotle, who has written learnedly and diligently about almost all the things that should be studied. At his name I see that you start up, gentlemen, and you are gradually being brought to this way of thinking and inclining to it as if he were inviting you to come on. If this is so, you should praise and thank him for anything that you have got out of this affair. As far as I am concerned, I am content if I can persuade you in your kindness of heart to forgive me for speaking at such length. And now my last word has been said.

Politics and Government

Apology

Plato

(c. 427-347 B.C.)

In the preceding unit we encountered thinkers who on one level or another, for one reason or another, were critical of the educational concepts of their day. As we saw with Pico della Mirandola, criticism of established ideas was a sometimes risky undertaking. Perhaps no one ran a greater risk or suffered a sterner penalty for his critical independence than Socrates, the ancient Greek teacher of us all and the central character in most of Plato's dialogues.

Whitehead once noted that "All of western philosophy is a footnote to Plato." Without much strain we can include political philosophy in this assessment. Plato's Republic, Laws, *and* Apology *still contain some of the most suggestive thinking on the political questions troubling our culture. The* Apology *addresses itself to the problem of a citizen's obligations to the state and the need for the freedom to dissent and think inde-*

pendently as the best means of fulfilling that obligation. In his defense Socrates says that he is a "gadfly" much needed by the state if it is to pursue the course of justice, and underlying his entire argument is the assumption that the just society cannot survive without severe criticism.

A stonemason by trade, Socrates was born in Athens about 469 B.C. *and died by drinking hemlock in 399* B.C., *an event described in Plato's dialogue, the* Phaedo. *Since Socrates himself did not write down his thoughts, our knowledge of him comes principally from his students, Plato and Xenephon, and from the comic playwright Aristophanes, who mocked Socrates in his comedy* The Clouds. *Socrates pursued what he conceived to be the truth by engaging opposing views in a dialogue, a technique that has since come to be known as the Socratic method and has had a permanent effect on our thinking processes.*

How you, O Athenians, have been affected by my accusers, I cannot tell; but I know that they almost made me forget who I was—so persuasively did they speak; and yet they have hardly uttered a word of truth. But of the many falsehoods told by them, there was one which quite amazed me;—I mean when they said that you should be upon your guard and not allow yourselves to be deceived by the force of my eloquence. To say this, when they were certain to be detected as soon as I opened my lips and proved myself to be anything but a great speaker, did indeed appear to me most shameless—unless by the force of eloquence they mean the force of truth; for if such is their meaning, I admit that I am eloquent. But in how different a way from theirs! Well, as I was saying, they have scarcely spoken the truth at all; but from me you shall hear the whole truth: not, however, delivered after their manner in a set oration duly ornamented with words and phrases. No, by heaven! but I shall use the words and arguments which occur to me at the moment; for I am confident in the justice of my cause: at my time of life I ought not to be appearing before you, O men of Athens, in the character of a juvenile orator—let no one expect it of me. And I must beg of you to grant me a favour:—If I defend myself in my accustomed manner, and you hear me using the words which I have been in the habit of using in the agora, at the tables of the moneychangers, or anywhere else, I would ask you not to be surprised, and not to interrupt me on this account. For I am more than seventy years of age, and appearing now for the first time in a court of law, I am quite a stranger to the language of the place; and therefore I would have you regard me as if I were really a stranger, whom you would excuse if he spoke in his native tongue, and after the fashion of his country:—Am I making an unfair request of you? Never mind the manner, which may or may not be good; but think only of the truth of my words, and give heed to that: let the speaker speak truly and the judge decide justly.

And first, I have to reply to the older charges and to my first accusers, and then I will go on to the later ones. For of old I have had many accusers, who have accused me falsely to you during many years; and I am more afraid of them than of Anytus and his associates, who are dangerous, too, in their own way. But far more dangerous are the others, who began when you were children, and took possession of your minds with their falsehoods, telling of one Socrates, a wise man, who speculated about the heaven above, and searched into the earth beneath, and made the worse appear the better cause. The disseminators of this tale are the accusers whom I dread; for their hearers are apt to fancy that such enquirers do not believe in the existence of the gods. And they are many, and their charges against me are of ancient date, and they were made by them in the days when you were more impressible than you are now—in childhood, or it may have been in youth—and the cause when heard went by default, for there was none to answer. And hardest of all, I do not know and cannot tell the names of my accusers; unless in the chance case of a comic poet. All who from envy and malice have persuaded you—some of them having first convinced themselves—all this class of men are most difficult to deal with; for I cannot have them up here, and cross-examine them, and therefore I must simply fight with shadows in my own defence, and argue when there is no one who answers. I will ask you then to assume with me, as I was saying, that my opponents are of two kinds; one recent, the other ancient: and I hope that you will see the propriety of my answering the latter first, for these accusations you heard long before the others, and much oftener.

Well, then, I must make my defence, and endeavour to clear away in a short time a slander which has lasted a long time. May I succeed, if to succeed be for my good and yours, or likely to avail me in my cause! The task is not an easy one; I quite understand the nature of it. And so leaving the event with God, in obedience to the law I will now make my defence.

I will begin at the beginning, and ask what is the accusation which has given rise to the slander of me, and in fact has encouraged Meletus to prefer this charge against me. Well, what do the slanderers say? They shall be my prosecutors, and I will sum up their words in an affidavit: "Socrates is an evildoer, and a curious person, who searches into things under the earth and in heaven, and he makes the worse appear the better cause; and he teaches the aforesaid doctrines to others." Such is the nature of the accusation: it is just what you have yourselves seen in the comedy of Aristophanes,[1] who has introduced a man whom he calls Socrates, going about and saying that he walks in air, and talking a deal of nonsense concerning matters of which I do not pretend to know either much or little—not that I mean to speak disparagingly of any one who is a student of natural philosophy. I should be very sorry if Meletus could bring so grave a charge against me. But the simple truth is, O Athenians, that I have nothing to do with physical speculations. Very many of those here present are witnesses to the truth of this, and to them I appeal. Speak then, you who have heard me, and tell your neighbours whether any of you have ever known me hold forth in few words or in many upon such matters. . . . You hear their answer. And from what they say of this part of the charge you will be able to judge of the truth of the rest.

As little foundation is there for the report that I am a teacher, and take money; this accusation has no more truth in it than the other. Although, if a man were really able to instruct mankind, to receive money for giving instruction would, in my opinion, be an honour to him. There is Gorgias of Leontium, and Prodicus of Ceos, and Hippas of Elis, who go the round of the cities, and are able to persuade the young men to leave their own citizens by whom they might be taught for nothing, and come to them whom they not only pay, but are thankful if

[1] Aristoph., Clouds, 225 ff.

they may be allowed to pay them. There is at this time a Parian philosopher residing in Athens, of whom I have heard; and I came to hear of him in this way:—I came across a man who has spent a world of money on the Sophists, Callias, the son of Hipponicus, and knowing that he had sons, I asked him: "Callias," I said, "if your two sons were foals or calves, there would be no difficulty in finding some one to put over them; we should hire a trainer of horses, or a farmer, probably, who would improve and perfect them in their own proper virtue and excellence; but as they are human beings, whom are you thinking of placing over them? Is there any one who understands human and political virtue? You must have thought about the matter, for you have sons; is there any one?" "There is," he said. "Who is he?" said I; "and of what country? and what does he charge?" "Evenus the Parian," he replied; "he is the man, and his charge is five minae." Happy is Evenus, I said to myself, if he really has this wisdom, and teaches at such a moderate charge. Had I the same, I should have been very proud and conceited; but the truth is that I have no knowledge of the kind.

I dare say, Athenians, that some one among you will reply, "Yes, Socrates, but what is the origin of these accusations which are brought against you; there must have been something strange which you have been doing? All these rumours and this talk about you would never have arisen if you had been like other men: tell us, then, what is the cause of them, for we should be sorry to judge hastily of you." Now, I regard this as a fair challenge, and I will endeavour to explain to you the reason why I am called wise and have such an evil fame. Please to attend then. And although some of you may think that I am joking, I declare that I will tell you the entire truth. Men of Athens, this reputation of mine has come of a certain sort of wisdom which I possess. If you ask me what kind of wisdom, I reply, wisdom such as may perhaps be attained by man, for to that extent I am inclined to believe that I am wise; whereas the persons of whom I was speaking have a superhuman wisdom, which I may fail to describe, because I have it not myself; and he who says that I have, speaks falsely, and is taking away my character. And here, O men of Athens, I must beg you not to interrupt me, even if I seem to say something extravagant. For the word which I will speak is not mine. I will refer you to a witness who is worthy of credit; that witness shall be the God of Delphi—he will tell you about my wisdom, if I have any, and of what sort it is. You must have known Chaerephon; he was early a friend of mine, and also a friend of yours, for he shared in the recent exile of the people, and returned with you. Well, Chaerephon, as you know, was very impetuous in all his doings, and he went to Delphi and boldly asked the oracle to tell him whether—as I was saying, I must beg you not to interrupt—he asked the oracle to tell him whether any one was wiser than I was, and the Pythian prophetess answered, that there was no man wiser. Chaerephon is dead himself; but his brother, who is in court, will confirm the truth of what I am saying.

Why do I mention this? Because I am going to explain to you why I have such an evil name. When I heard the answer, I said to myself, What can the God mean? and what is the interpretation of his riddle? for I know that I have no wisdom, small or great. What then can he mean when he says that I am the wisest of men? And yet he is a god, and cannot lie; that would be against his nature. After long consideration, I thought of a method of trying the question. I reflected that if I could only find a man wiser than myself, then I might go to the god with a refutation in my hand. I should say to him, "Here is a man who is wiser than I am; but you said that I was the wisest." Accordingly I went to one who had the reputation of wisdom, and observed him—his name I need not mention; he was a politician whom I selected for examination—and the result was as follows: When I began to talk with him, I could not help thinking that he was not really wise, although he was thought wise by many, and still wiser by himself; and thereupon I tried to explain to him that he thought himself wise, but was not really wise; and the consequence was that he hated me, and his enmity was shared by several who were present and heard me. So I left him, saying to myself, as I went away: Well, although I do not suppose that either of us knows anything really beautiful and good, I am better off than he is,—for he knows nothing, and thinks that he knows; I neither know nor think that I know. In this latter particular, then, I seem to have slightly the advantage of him. Then I went to another who had still higher pretensions to wisdom, and my conclusion was exactly the same. Whereupon I made another enemy of him, and of many others besides him.

Then I went to one man after another, being not unconscious of the enmity which I provoked, and I lamented and feared this: but necessity was laid upon me,—the word of God, I thought, ought to be considered first. And I said to myself, Go

I must to all who appear to know, and find out the meaning of the oracle. And I swear to you, Athenians, by the dog I swear!—for I must tell you the truth—the result of my mission was just this: I found that the men most in repute were all but the most foolish; and that others less esteemed were really wiser and better. I will tell you the tale of my wanderings and of the "Herculean" labours, as I may call them, which I endured only to find at last the oracle irrefutable. After the politicians, I went to the poets; tragic, dithyrambic, and all sorts. And there, I said to myself, you will be instantly detected; now you will find out that you are more ignorant than they are. Accordingly I took them some of the most elaborate passages in their own writings, and asked what was the meaning of them—thinking that they would teach me something. Will you believe me? I am almost ashamed to confess the truth, but I must say that there is hardly a person present who would not have talked better about their poetry than they did themselves. Then I knew that not by wisdom do poets write poetry, but by a sort of genius and inspiration; they are like diviners or soothsayers who also say many fine things, but do not understand the meaning of them. The poets appeared to me to be much in the same case; and I further observed that upon the strength of their poetry they believed themselves to be the wisest of men in other things in which they were not wise. So I departed, conceiving myself to be superior to them for the same reason that I was superior to the politicians.

At last I went to the artisans, I was conscious that I knew nothing at all, as I may say, and I was sure that they knew many fine things; and here I was not mistaken, for they did know many things of which I was ignorant, and in this they certainly were wiser than I was. But I observed that even the good artisans fell into the same error as the poets;—because they were good workmen they thought that they also knew all sorts of high matters, and this defect in them overshadowed their wisdom; and therefore I asked myself on behalf of the oracle, whether I would like to be as I was, neither having their knowledge nor their ignorance, or like them in both; and I made answer to myself and to the oracle that I was better off as I was.

This inquisition has led to my having many enemies of the worst and most dangerous kind, and has given occasion also to many calumnies. And I am called wise, for my hearers always imagine that I myself possess the wisdom which I find wanting in others: but the truth is, O men of Athens, that God only is wise; and by his answer he intends to show that the wisdom of men is worth little or nothing; he is not speaking of Socrates, he is only using my name by way of illustration, as if he said, He, O men, is the wisest, who, like Socrates, knows that his wisdom is in truth worth nothing. And so I go about the world obedient to the god, and search and make enquiry into the wisdom of any one, whether citizen or stranger, who appears to be wise; and if he is not wise, then in vindication of the oracle I show him that he is not wise; and my occupation quite absorbs me, and I have no time to give either to any public matter of interest or to any concern of my own, but I am in utter poverty by reason of my devotion to the god.

There is another thing:—young men of the richer classes, who have not much to do, come about me of their own accord; they like to hear the pretenders examined, and they often imitate me, and proceed to examine others; there are plenty of persons, as they quickly discover, who think that they know something, but really know little or nothing; and then those who are examined by them instead of being angry with themselves are angry with me: This confounded Socrates, they say; this villainous misleader of youth!—and then if somebody asks them, Why, what evil does he practise or teach? they do not know, and cannot tell; but in order that they may not appear to be at a loss, they repeat the ready-made charges which are used against all philosophers about teaching things up in the clouds and under the earth, and having no gods, and making the worse appear the better cause; for they do not like to confess that their pretence of knowledge has been detected—which is the truth; and as they are numerous and ambitious and energetic, and are drawn up in battle array and have persuasive tongues, they have filled your ears with their loud and inveterate calumnies. And this is the reason why my three accusers, Meletus and Anytus and Lycon, have set upon me; Meletus, who has a quarrel with me on behalf of the poets; Anytus, on behalf of the craftsmen and politicians; Lycon, on behalf of the rhetoricians: and, as I said at the beginning, I cannot expect to get rid of such a mass of calumny all in a moment. And this, O men of Athens, is the truth and the whole truth; I have concealed nothing, I have dissembled nothing. And yet, I know that my plainness of speech makes them hate me, and what is their hatred but a proof that I am speaking the truth? Hence has arisen the prejudice against me; and this is the reason of it, as you will find out either in this or in any future enquiry.

I have said enough in my defence against the first class of my accusers; I turn to the second class. They are headed by Meletus, that good man and true lover of his country, as he calls himself. Against these, too, I must try to make a defence:—Let their affidavit be read; it contains something of this kind: It says that Socrates is a doer of evil, who corrupts the youth; and who does not believe in the gods of the State, but has other new divinities of his own. Such is the charge; and now let us examine the particular counts. He says that I am a doer of evil, and corrupt the youth; but I say, O men of Athens, that Meletus is a doer of evil, in that he pretends to be in earnest when he is only in jest, and is so eager to bring men to trial from a pretended zeal and interest about matters in which he really never had the smallest interest. And the truth of this I will endeavour to prove to you.

Come hither, Meletus, and let me ask a question of you. You think a great deal about the improvement of youth?

Yes, I do.

Tell the judges, then, who is their improver; for you must know, as you have taken the pains to discover their corrupter, and are citing and accusing me before them. Speak, then, and tell the judges who their improver is.—Observe, Meletus, that you are silent, and have nothing to say. But is not this rather disgraceful, and a very considerable proof of what I was saying, that you have no interest in the matter? Speak up, friend, and tell us who their improver is.

The laws.

But that, my good sir, is not my meaning. I want to know who the person is, who, in the first place, knows the laws.

The judges, Socrates, who are present in court.

What, do you mean to say, Meletus, that they are able to instruct and improve youth?

Certainly they are.

What, all of them, or some only and not others?

All of them.

By the goddess Here, that is good news! There are plenty of improvers, then. And what do you say of the audience,—do they improve them?

Yes, they do.

And the senators?

Yes, the senators improve them.

But perhaps the members of the assembly corrupt them?—or do they improve them?

They improve them.

Then every Athenian improves and elevates them; all with the exception of myself; and I alone am their corrupter? Is that what you affirm?

That is what I stoutly affirm.

I am very unfortunate if you are right. But suppose I ask you a question: How about horses? Does one man do them harm and all the world good? Is not the exact opposite the truth? One man is able to do them good, or at least not many;—the trainer of horses, that is to say, does them good, and others who have to do with them rather injure them? Is not that true, Meletus, of horses, or of any other animals? Most assuredly it is; whether you and Anytus say yes or no. Happy indeed would be the condition of youth if they had one corrupter only, and all the rest of the world were their improvers. But you, Meletus, have sufficiently shown that you never had a thought about the young: your carelessness is seen in your not caring about the very things which you bring against me.

And now, Meletus, I will ask you another question—by Zeus I will: Which is better, to live among bad citizens, or among good ones? Answer, friend, I say; the question is one which may be easily answered. Do not the good do their neighbours good, and the bad do them evil?

Certainly.

And is there any one who would rather be injured than benefited by those who live with him? Answer, my good friend, the law requires you to answer—does any one like to be injured?

Certainly not.

And when you accuse me of corrupting and deteriorating the youth, do you allege that I corrupt them intentionally or unintentionally?

Intentionally, I say.

But you have just admitted that the good do their neighbours good, and the evil do them evil. Now, is that a truth which your superior wisdom has recognized thus early in life, and am I, at my age, in such darkness and ignorance as not to know that if a man with whom I have to live is corrupted by me, I am very likely to be harmed by him; and yet I corrupt him, and intentionally, too—so you say, although neither I nor any other human being is ever likely to be convinced by you. But either I do not corrupt them, or I corrupt them unintentionally; and on either view of the case you lie. If my offence is unintentional, the law has no cognizance of unintentional offences: you ought to have taken me privately, and warned and admonished me; for if I had been better advised, I should have left off doing what I only did unintentionally—no doubt I should; but you would have nothing to say to me and refused to teach me. And now you bring me up in this court, which is a place not of instruction, but of punishment.

It will be very clear to you, Athenians, as I was saying, that Meletus has no care at all, great or small, about the matter. But still I should like to know, Meletus, in what I am affirmed to corrupt the young. I suppose you mean, as I infer from your indictment, that I teach them not to acknowledge the gods which the State acknowledges, but some other new divinities or spiritual agencies in their stead. These are the lessons by which I corrupt the youth, as you say.

Yes, that I say emphatically.

Then, by the gods, Meletus, of whom we are speaking, tell me and the court, in somewhat plainer terms, what you mean! For I do not as yet understand whether you affirm that I teach other men to acknowledge some gods, and therefore that I do believe in gods, and am not an entire atheist—this you do not lay to my charge,—but only you say that they are not the same gods which the city recognizes—the charge is that they are different gods. Or, do you mean that I am an atheist simply, and a teacher of atheism?

I mean the latter—that you are a complete atheist.

What an extraordinary statement! Why do you think so, Meletus? Do you mean that I do not believe in the godhead of the sun or moon, like other men?

I assure you, judges, that he does not: for he says that the sun is stone, and the moon earth.

Friend Meletus, you think that you are accusing Anaxagoras: and you have but a bad opinion of the judges, if you fancy them illiterate to such a degree as not to know that these doctrines are found in the books of Anaxagoras the Clazomenian, which are full of them. And so, forsooth, the youth are said to be taught them by Socrates, when there are not infrequently exhibitions of them at the theatre (price of admission one drachma at the most); and they might pay their money, and laugh at Socrates if he pretends to father these extraordinary views. And so, Meletus, you really think that I do not believe in any god?

I swear by Zeus that you believe absolutely in none at all.

Nobody will believe you, Meletus, and I am pretty sure that you do not believe yourself. I cannot help thinking, men of Athens, that Meletus is reckless and impudent, and that he has written this indictment in a spirit of mere wantonness and youthful bravado. Has he not compounded a riddle, thinking to try me? He said to himself:—I shall see whether the wise Socrates will discover my facetious contradiction, or whether I shall be able to deceive him and the rest of them. For he certainly does appear to me to contradict himself in the indictment as much as if he said that Socrates is guilty of not believing in the gods, and yet of believing in them—but this is not like a person who is in earnest.

I should like you, O men of Athens, to join me in examining what I conceive to be his inconsistency; and do you, Meletus, answer. And I must remind the audience of my request that they would not make a disturbance if I speak in my accustomed manner:

Did ever man, Meletus, believe in the existence of human things, and not of human beings? . . . I wish, men of Athens, that he would answer, and not be always trying to get up an interruption. Did ever any man believe in horsemanship, and not in horses? or in flute-playing, and not in flute-players? No, my friend; I will answer to you and to the court, as you refuse to answer for yourself. There is no man who ever did. But now please to answer the next question: Can a man believe in spiritual and divine agencies, and not in spirits or demigods?

He cannot.

How lucky I am to have extracted that answer, by the assistance of the court! But then you swear in the indictment that I teach and believe in divine or spiritual agencies (new or old, no matter for that); at any rate, I believe in spiritual agencies,—so you say and swear in the affidavit; and yet if I believe in divine beings, how can I help believing in spirits or demigods;—must I not? To be sure I must; and therefore I may assume that your silence gives consent. Now what are spirits or demigods? are they not either gods or the sons of gods?

Certainly they are.

But this is what I call the facetious riddle invented by you:

the demigods or spirits are gods, and you say first that I do not believe in gods, and then again that I do believe in gods; that is, if I believe in demigods. For if the demigods are the illegitimate sons of gods, whether by the nymphs or by any other mothers, of whom they are said to be the sons—what human being will ever believe that there are no gods if they are the sons of gods? You might as well affirm the existence of mules, and deny that of horses and asses. Such nonsense, Meletus, could only have been intended by you to make trial of me. You have put this into the indictment because you had nothing real of which to accuse me. But no one who has a particle of understanding will ever be convinced by you that the same men can believe in divine and superhuman things, and yet not believe that there are gods and demigods and heroes.

I have said enough in answer to the charge of Meletus: any elaborate defence is unnecessary; but I know only too well how many are the enmities which I have incurred, and this is what will be my destruction if I am destroyed;—not Meletus, nor yet Anytus, but the envy and detraction of the world, which has been the death of many good men, and will probably be the death of many more; there is no danger of my being the last of them.

Some one will say: And are you not ashamed, Socrates, of a course of life which is likely to bring you to an untimely end? To him I may fairly answer: There you are mistaken: a man who is good for anything ought not to calculate the chance of living or dying; he ought only to consider whether in doing anything he is doing right or wrong—acting the part of a good man or of a bad. Whereas, upon your view, the heroes who fell at Troy were not good for much, and the son of Thetis above all, who altogether despised danger in comparison with disgrace; and when he was so eager to slay Hector, his goddess mother said to him, that if he avenged his companion Patroclus, and slew Hector, he would die himself—"Fate," she said, in these or the like words, "waits for you next after Hector"; he, receiving this warning, utterly despised danger and death, and instead of fearing them, feared rather to live in dishonour, and not to avenge his friend. "Let me die forthwith," he replies, "and be avenged of my enemy, rather than abide here by the beaked ships, a laughing-stock and a burden of the earth." Had Achilles any thought of death and danger? For wherever a man's place is, whether the place which he has chosen or that in which he has been placed by a commander, there he ought to remain in the hour of danger; he should not think of death or of anything but of disgrace. And this, O men of Athens, is a true saying.

Strange, indeed, would be my conduct, O men of Athens, if I, who, when I was ordered by the generals whom you chose to command me at Potidaea and Amphipolis and Delium, remained where they placed me, like any other man, facing death —if now, when, as I conceive and imagine, God orders me to fulfil the philosopher's mission of searching into myself and other men, I were to desert my post through fear of death, or any other fear; that would indeed be strange, and I might justly be arraigned in court for denying the existence of the gods, if I disobeyed the oracle because I was afraid of death, fancying that I was wise when I was not wise. For the fear of death is indeed the pretence of wisdom, and not real wisdom, being a pretence of knowing the unknown; and no one knows whether death, which men in their fear apprehend to be the greatest evil, may not be the greatest good. Is not this ignorance of a disgraceful sort, the ignorance which is the conceit that a man knows what he does not know? And in this respect only I believe myself to differ from men in general, and may perhaps claim to be wiser than they are:—that whereas I know but little of the world below, I do not suppose that I know: but I do know that injustice and disobedience to a better, whether God or man, is evil and dishonourable, and I will never fear or avoid a possible good rather than a certain evil. And therefore if you let me go now, and are not convinced by Anytus, who said that since I had been prosecuted I must be put to death; (or if not that I ought never to have been prosecuted at all); and that if I escape now, your sons will all be utterly ruined by listening to my words—if you say to me, Socrates, this time we will not mind Anytus, and you shall be let off, but upon one condition, that you are not to enquire and speculate in this way any more, and that if you are caught doing so again you sall die;—if this was the condition on which you let me go, I should reply: Men of Athens, I honour and love you; but I shall obey God rather than you, and while I have life and strength I shall never cease from the practice and teaching of philosophy, exhorting any one whom I meet and saying to him after my manner: You, my friend,—a citizen of the great and mighty and wise city of Athens,—are you not ashamed of heaping up the greatest amount of money and honour and reputation, and caring so little about wisdom and truth and the greatest improvement of the soul, which you never regard or heed at all? And if the person with whom I am arguing, says: Yes, but I do care; then I do not leave him or let him go at once; but I proceed to interrogate and examine and cross-examine him, and if I think that he has no virtue in him, but only says that he has, I reproach him with undervaluing the greater, and overvaluing the less. And I shall repeat the same words to every one whom I meet, young and old, citizen and alien, but especially to the citizens, inasmuch as they are my brethren. For know that this is the command of God; and I believe that no greater good has ever happened in the State than my service to the God. For I do nothing but go about persuading you all, old and young alike, not to take thought for your persons or your properties, but first and chiefly to care about the greatest improvement of the soul. I tell you that virtue is not given by money, but that from virtue comes money and every other good of man, public as well as private. This is my teaching, and if this is the doctrine which corrupts the youth, I am a mischievous person. But if any one says that this is not my teaching, he is speaking an untruth. Wherefore, O men of Athens, I say to you, do as Anytus bids or not as Anytus bids, and either acquit me or not; but whichever you do, understand that I shall never alter my ways, not even if I have to die many times.

Men of Athens, do not interrupt, but hear me; there was an understanding between us that you should hear me to the end: I have something more to say, at which you may be inclined to cry out; but I believe that to hear me will be good for you, and therefore I beg that you will not cry out. I would have you know, that if you kill such an one as I am, you will injure yourselves more than you will injure me. Nothing will injure me, not Meletus nor yet Anytus—they cannot, for a bad man is not permitted to injure a better than himself. I do not deny that Anytus may, perhaps, kill him, or drive him into exile, or deprive him of civil rights; and he may imagine, and others may imagine, that he is inflicting a great injury upon him: but there I do not agree. For the evil of doing as he is doing—the evil of unjustly taking away the life of another—is greater far.

And now, Athenians, I am not going to argue for my own sake, as you may think, but for yours, that you may not sin against the God by condemning me, who am his gift to you. For if you kill me you will not easily find a successor to me, who, if I may use such a ludicrous figure of speech, am a sort of gadfly, given to the State by God; and the State is a great and noble steed who is tardy in his motions owing to his very size, and requires to be stirred into life. I am that gadfly which God has attached to the State, and all day long and in all places am always fastening upon you, arousing and persuading and reproaching you. You will not easily find another like me, and therefore I would advise you to spare me. I dare say that you may feel out of temper (like a person who is suddenly awakened from sleep), and you think that you might easily strike me dead as Anytus advises, and then you would sleep on for the remainder of your lives, unless God in his care of you sent you another gadfly. When I say that I am given to you by God, the proof of my mission is this:—if I had been like other men, I should not have neglected all my own concerns or patiently seen the neglect of them during all these years, and have been doing yours, coming to you individually like a father or elder brother, exhorting you to regard virtue; such conduct, I say, would be unlike human nature. If I had gained anything, or if my exhortations had been paid, there would have been some sense in my doing so; but now, as you will perceive, not even the impudence of my accusers dares to say that I have ever exacted or sought pay of any one; of that they have no witness. And I have a sufficient witness to the truth of what I say—my poverty.

Some one may wonder why I go about in private giving advice and busying myself with the concerns of others, but do not venture to come forward in public and advise the State. I will tell you why. You have heard me speak at sundry times and in divers places of an oracle or sign which comes to me, and is the divinity which Meletus ridicules in the indictment. This sign, which is a kind of voice, first began to come to me when I was a child; it always forbids but never commands me to do anything which I am going to do. This is what deters me from being a politician. And rightly, as I think. For I am certain, O men of Athens, that if I had engaged in politics, I should have perished long ago, and done no good either to you or to myself. And do not be offended at my telling you the truth: for the truth is, that no man who goes to war with you or any other multitude, honestly striving against the many lawless and unrighteous deeds which are done in a state, will save his life; he who will fight for the right, if he would live even for a brief space, must have a private station and not a public one.

I can give you convincing evidence of what I say, not words

only, but what you value far more—actions. Let me relate to you a passage of my own life which will prove to you that I should never have yielded to injustice from any fear of death and that "as I should have refused to yield" I must have died at once. I will tell you a tale of the courts, not very interesting perhaps, but nevertheless true. The only office of State which I ever held, O men of Athens, was that of senator: the tribe Antiochis, which is my tribe, had the presidency at the trial of the generals who had not taken up the bodies of the slain after the battle of Arginusae; and you proposed to try them in a body, contrary to law, as you all thought afterwards; but at the time I was the only one of the Prytanes who was opposed to the illegality, and I gave my vote against you; and when the orators threatened to impeach and arrest me, and you called and shouted, I made up my mind that I would run the risk, having law and justice with me, rather than take part in your injustice because I feared imprisonment and death. This happened in the days of the democracy. But when the oligarchy of the Thirty was in power, they sent for me and four others into the rotunda, and bade us bring Leon the Salaminian from Salamis, as they wanted to put him to death. This was a specimen of the sort of commands which they were always giving with the view of implicating as many as possible in their crimes; and then I showed, not in word only but in deed, that, if I may be allowed to use such an expression, I cared not a straw for death, and that my great and only care was lest I should do an unrighteous or unholy thing. For the strong arm of that oppressive power did not frighten me into doing wrong; and when we came out of the rotunda the other four went to Salamis and fetched Leon, but I went quietly home. For which I might have lost my life, had not the power of the Thirty shortly afterwards come to an end. And many will witness to my words.

Now, do you really imagine that I could have survived all these years, if I had led a public life, supposing that like a good man I had always maintained the right and had made justice, as I ought, the first thing? No, indeed, men of Athens, neither I nor any other man. But I have been always the same in all my actions, public as well as private, and never have I yielded any base compliance to those who are slanderously termed my disciples, or to any other. Not that I have any regular disciples. But if any one likes to come and hear me while I am pursuing my mission, whether he be young or old, he is not excluded. Nor do

I converse only with those who pay; but any one, whether he be rich or poor, may ask and answer me and listen to my words; and whether he turns out to be a bad man or a good one, neither result can be justly imputed to me; for I never taught or professed to teach him anything. And if any one says that he has ever learned or heard anything from me in private which all the world has not heard, let me tell you that he is lying.

But I shall be asked, Why do people delight in continually conversing with you? I have told you already, Athenians, the whole truth about this matter: they like to hear the cross-examination of the pretenders to wisdom; there is amusement in it. Now, this duty of cross-examining other men has been imposed upon me by God; and has been signified to me by oracles, visions, and in every way in which the will of divine power was ever intimated to any one. This is true, O Athenians; or, if not true, would be soon refuted. If I am or have been corrupting the youth, those of them who are now grown up and have become sensible that I gave them bad advice in the days of their youth should come forward as accusers, and take their revenge; or if they do not like to come themselves, some of their relatives, fathers, brothers, or other kinsmen, should say what evil their families have suffered at my hands. Now is their time. Many of them I see in the court. There is Crito, who is of the same age and of the same deme with myself, and there is Critobulus his son, whom I also see. Then again there is Lysanias of Sphettus, who is the father of Aeschines—he is present; and also there is Antiphon of Cephisus, who is the father of Epigenes; and there are the brothers of several who have associated with me. There is Nicostratus the son of Theosdotides, and the brother of Theodotus (now Theodotus himself is dead, and therefore he, at any rate, will not seek to stop him); and there is Paralus the son of Demodocus, who had a brother Theages; and Adeimantus the son of Ariston, whose brother Plato is present; and Aeantodorus, who is the brother of Apollodorus, whom I also see. I might mention a great many others, some of whom Meletus should have produced as witnesses in the course of his speech; and let him still produce them, if he has forgotten—I will make way for him. And let him say, if he has any testimony of the sort which he can produce. Nay, Athenians, the very opposite is the truth. For all these are ready to witness on behalf of the corrupter, of the injurer of their kindred, as Meletus and Anytus call me; not the corrupted youth only—there might have been a motive for that—

but their uncorrupted elder relatives. Why should they too support me with their testimony? Why, indeed, except for the sake of truth and justice, and because they know that I am speaking the truth, and that Meletus is a liar.

Well, Athenians, this and the like of this is all the defence which I have to offer. Yet a word more. Perhaps there may be some one who is offended at me, when he calls to mind how he himself on a similar, or even a less serious occasion, prayed and entreated the judges with many tears, and how he produced his children in court, which was a moving spectacle, together with a host of relations and friends; whereas I, who am probably in danger of my life, will do none of these things. The contrast may occur to his mind, and he may be set against me, and vote in anger because he is displeased at me on this account. Now, if there be such a person among you,—mind, I do not say that there is,—to him I may fairly reply: My friend, I am a man, and like other men, a creature of flesh and blood, and not "of wood or stone," as Homer says; and I have a family, yes, and sons, O Athenians, three in number, one almost a man, and two others who are still young; and yet I will not bring any of them hither in order to petition you for an acquittal. And why not? Not from any self-assertion or want of respect for you. Whether I am or am not afraid of death is another question, of which I will not now speak. But, having regard to public opinion, I feel that such conduct would be discreditable to myself, and to you, and to the whole State. One who has reached my years, and who has a name for wisdom, ought not to demean himself. Whether this opinion of me be deserved or not, at any rate the world has decided that Socrates is in some way superior to other men. And if those among you who are said to be superior in wisdom and courage, and any other virtue, demean themselves in this way, how shameful is their conduct! I have seen men of reputation, when they have been condemned, behaving in the strangest manner: they seemed to fancy that they were going to suffer something dreadful if they died, and that they could be immortal if you only allowed them to live; and I think that such are a dishonour to the State, and that any stranger coming in would have said of them that the most eminent men of Athens, to whom the Athenians themselves give honour and command, are no better than women. And I say that these things ought not to be done by those of us who have a reputation; and if they are done, you ought not to permit them; you ought rather to show that you are far more disposed to condemn the man who gets up a doleful scene and makes the city ridiculous, than him who holds his peace.

But, setting aside the question of public opinion, there seems to be something wrong in asking a favour of a judge, and thus procuring an acquittal, instead of informing and convincing him. For his duty is, not to make a present of justice, but to give judgment; and he has sworn that he will judge according to the laws, and not according to his own good pleasure; and we ought not to encourage you, nor should you allow yourselves to be encouraged, in this habit of perjury—there can be no piety in that. Do not then require me to do what I consider dishonourable and impious and wrong, especially now, when I am being tried for impiety on the indictment of Meletus. For if, O men of Athens, by force of persuasion and entreaty I could overpower your oaths, then I should be teaching you to believe that there are no gods, and in defending should simply convict myself of the charge of not believing in them. But that is not so—far otherwise. For I do believe that there are gods, and in a sense higher than that in which any of my accusers believe in them. And to you and to God I commit my cause, to be determined by you as is best for you and me.

There are many reasons why I am not grieved, O men of Athens, at the vote of condemnation. I expected it, and am only surprised that the votes are so nearly equal; for I had thought that the majority against me would have been far larger; but now, had thirty votes gone over to the other side, I should have been acquitted. And I may say, I think, that I have escaped Meletus. I may say more; for without the assistance of Anytus and Lycon, any one may see that he would not have had a fifth part of the votes, as the law requires, in which case he would have incurred a fine of a thousand drachmae.

And so he proposes death as the penalty. And what shall I propose on my part, O men of Athens? Clearly that which is my due. And what is my due? What returns shall be made to the man who has never had the wit to be idle during his whole life; but has been careless of what the many care for—wealth, and family interests, and military offices, and speaking in the assembly, and magistracies, and plots, and parties. Reflecting that I was really too honest a man to be a politician and live, I did not go where I could do no good to you or to myself; but where I could do the greatest good privately to every one of you, thither I went, and sought to persuade every man among you that he must look to himself, and seek virtue and wisdom before he looks to his private interests, and look to the State before he looks to the interests of the State; and that this should be the order which he observes in all his actions. What shall be done to such an one? Doubtless some good thing, O men of Athens, if he has his reward; and the good should be of a kind suitable to him. What would be a reward suitable to a poor man who is your benefactor, and who desires leisure that he may instruct you? There can be no reward so fitting as maintenance in the Prytaneum, O men of Athens, a reward which he deserves far more than the citizen who has won the prize at Olympia in the horse or chariot race, whether the chariots were drawn by two horses or by many. For I am in want, and he has enough; and he only gives you the appearance of happiness, and I give you the reality. And if I am to estimate the penalty fairly, I should say that maintenance in the Prytaneum is the just return.

Perhaps you think that I am braving you in what I am saying now, as in what I said before about the tears and prayers. But this is not so. I speak rather because I am convinced that I never intentionally wronged any one, although I cannot convince you—the time has been too short; if there were a law at Athens, as there is in other cities, that a capital cause should not be decided in one day, then I believe that I should have convinced you. But I cannot in a moment refute great slanders; and, as I am convinced that I never wronged another, I will assuredly not wrong myself. I will not say to myself that I deserve any evil, or propose any penalty. Why should I? Because I am afraid of the penalty of death which Meletus proposes? When I do not know whether death is a good or an evil, why should I propose a penalty which would certainly be an evil? Shall I say imprisonment? And why should I live in prison, and be the slave of the magistrate of the year—of the Eleven? Or shall the penalty be a fine, and imprisonment until the fine is paid? There is the same objection. I should have to lie in prison, for money I have none, and cannot pay. And if I say exile (and this may possibly be the penalty which you will affix), I must indeed be blinded by the love of life, if I am so irrational as to expect that when you, who are my own citizens, cannot endure my discourses and words, and have found them so grievous and odious that you will have no more of them, others are likely to endure me. No, indeed, men of

Athens, that is not very likely. And what a life should I lead, at my age, wandering from city to city, ever changing my place of exile, and always being driven out! For I am quite sure that wherever I go, there, as here, the young men will flock to me; and if I drive them away, their elders will drive me out at their request; and if I let them come, their fathers and friends will drive me out for their sakes.

Some one will say: Yes, Socrates, but cannot you hold your tongue, and then you may go into a foreign city, and no one will interfere with you? Now, I have great difficulty in making you understand my answer to this. For if I tell you that to do as you say would be a disobedience to the God, and therefore that I cannot hold my tongue, you will not believe that I am serious; and if I say again that daily to discourse about virtue, and of those other things about which you hear me examining myself and others, is the greatest good of man, and that the unexamined life is not worth living, you are still less likely to believe me. Yet I say what is true, although a thing of which it is hard for me to persuade you. Also, I have never been accustomed to think that I deserve to suffer any harm. Had I money I might have estimated the offence at what I was able to pay, and not have been much the worse. But I have none, and therefore I must ask you to proportion the fine to my means. Well, perhaps I could afford a mina, and therefore I propose that penalty: Plato, Crito, Critobulus, and Apollodorus, my friends here, bid me say thirty minae, and they will be the sureties. Let thirty minae be the penalty; for which sum they will be ample security to you.

Not much time will be gained, O Athenians, in return for the evil name which you will get from the detractors of the city, who will say that you killed Socrates, a wise man; for they will call me wise, even although I am not wise, when they want to reproach you. If you had waited a little while, your desire would have been fulfilled in the course of nature. For I am far advanced in years, as you may perceive, and not far from death. I am speaking now not to all of you, but only to those who have condemned me to death. And I have another thing to say to them: You think that I was convicted because I had no words of the sort which would have procured my acquittal—I mean, if I had thought fit to leave nothing undone or unsaid. Not so; the deficiency which led to my conviction was not of words—certainly not. But I had not the boldness or impudence or inclination to address you as you would have liked me to do, weeping and wailing and lamenting, and saying and doing many things which you have been accustomed to hear from others, and which, as I maintain, are unworthy of me. I thought at the time that I ought not to do anything common or mean when in danger: nor do I now repent of the style of my defence; I would rather die having spoken after my manner, than speak in your manner and live. For neither in war nor yet at law ought I or any man use every way of escaping death. Often in battle there can be no doubt that if a man will throw away his arms, and fall on his knees before his pursuers, he may escape death; and in other dangers there are other ways of escaping death, if a man is willing to say and do anything. The difficulty, my friends, is not to avoid death, but to avoid unrighteousness; for that runs faster than death. I am old and move slowly, and the slower runner has overtaken me, and my accusers are keen and quick, and the faster runner, who is unrighteousness, has overtaken them. And now I depart hence condemned by you to suffer the penalty of death,—they too go their ways condemned by the truth to suffer the penalty of villainy and wrong; and I must abide by my award—let them abide by theirs. I suppose that these things may be regarded as fated,—and I think that they are well.

And now, O men who have condemned me, I would fain prophesy to you; for I am about to die, and in the hour of death men are gifted with prophetic power. And I prophesy to you who are my murderers, that immediately after my departure punishment far heavier than you have inflicted on me will surely await you. Me you have killed because you wanted to escape the accuser, and not to give an account of your lives. But that will not be as you suppose: far otherwise. For I say that there will be more accusers of you than there are now; accusers whom hitherto I have restrained: and as they are younger they will be more inconsiderate with you, and you will be more offended at them. If you think that by killing men you can prevent some one from censuring your evil lives, you are mistaken; that is not a way of escape which is either possible or honourable; the easiest and the noblest way is not to be disabling others, but to be improving yourselves. This is the prophecy which I utter before my departure to the judges who have condemned me.

Friends, who would have acquitted me, I would like also to talk with you about the thing which has come to pass, while the magistrates are busy, and before I go to the place at which I must die. Stay then a little, for we may as well talk with one another while there is time. You are my friends, and I should like to show you the meaning of this event which has happened to me. O my judges—for you I may truly call judges—I should like to tell you of a wonderful circumstance. Hitherto the divine faculty of which the internal oracle is the source has constantly been in the habit of opposing me even about trifles, if I was going to make a slip or error in any matter; and now as you see there has come upon me that which may be thought, and is generally believed to be, the last and worst evil. But the oracle made no sign of opposition, either when I was leaving my house in the morning, or when I was on my way to the court, or while I was speaking, at anything which I was going to say; and yet I have often been stopped in the middle of a speech, but now in nothing I either said or did touching the matter in hand has the oracle opposed me. What do I take to be the explanation of this silence? I will tell you. It is an intimation that what has happened to me is a good, and that those of us who think that death is an evil are in error. For the customary sign would surely have opposed me had I been going to evil and not to good.

Let us reflect in another way, and we shall see that there is great reason to hope that death is a good; for one of two things—either death is a state of nothingness and utter unconsciousness, or, as men say, there is a change and migration of the soul from this world to another. Now, if you suppose that there is no consciousness, but a sleep like the sleep of him who is undisturbed even by dreams, death will be an unspeakable gain. For if a person were to select the night in which his sleep was undisturbed even by dreams, and were to compare with this the other days and nights of his life, and then were to tell us how many days and nights he had passed in the course of his life better and more pleasantly than this one, I think that any man, I will not say a private man, but even the great king will not find many such days or nights, when compared with the others. Now, if death be of such a nature, I say that to die is gain; for eternity is then only a single night. But if death is the journey to another place, and there, as men say, all the dead abide, what good, O my friends and judges, can be greater than this? If, indeed, when the pilgrim arrives in the world below, he is delivered from the professors of justice in this world, and finds the true judges who are said to give judgment there, Minos and Rhadamanthus and Aeacus and Triptolemus, and other sons of God who were righteous in their own life, that pilgrimage will be worth making. What would not a man give if he might converse with Orpheus and Musaeus and Hesiod and Homer? Nay, if this be true, let me die again and again. I myself, too, shall have a wonderful interest in their meeting and conversing with Palamedes, and Ajax the son of Telamon, and any other ancient hero who has suffered death through an unjust judgment; and there will be no small pleasure, as I think, in comparing my own sufferings with theirs. Above all, I shall then be able to continue my search into true and false knowledge; as in this world, so also in the next; and I shall find out who is wise, and who pretends to be wise, and is not. What would not a man give, O judges, to be able to examine the leader of the great Trojan expedition; or Odysseus or Sisyphus, or numberless others, men and women too! What infinite delight would there be in conversing with them and asking them questions! In another world they do not put a man to death for asking questions: assuredly not. For besides being happier than we are, they will be immortal, if what is said is true.

Wherefore, O judges, be of good cheer about death, and know of a certainty, that no evil can happen to a good man, either in life or after death. He and his are not neglected by the gods; nor has my own approaching end happened by mere chance. But I see clearly that the time had arrived when it was better for me to die and be released from trouble; wherefore the oracle gave no sign. For which reason, also, I am not angry with my condemners, or with my accusers; they have done me no harm, although they did not mean to do me any good; and for this I may gently blame them.

Still, I have a favour to ask of them. When my sons are grown up, I would ask you, O my friends, to punish them; and I would have you trouble them, as I have troubled you, if they seem to care about riches, or anything, more than about virtue; or if they pretend to be something when they are really nothing,—then reprove them, as I have reproved you, for not caring about that for which they ought to care, and thinking that they are something when they are really nothing. And if you do this, both I and my sons will have received justice at your hands.

The hour of departure has arrived, and we go our ways—I to die, and you to live. Which is better God only knows.

from The Social Contract

Jean-Jacques Rousseau

(1712-1778)

Socrates claimed the state owed him a debt. The state in turn condemned him to death for questioning established values. What then are the proper relations of an individual to the state? During the seventeenth and eighteenth centuries, a period torn by ideological conflict and civil war, this question moved to the center of intellectual concerns. Three major thinkers addressed themselves to the problem: Thomas Hobbes in the Leviathan, *John Locke in* Of Civil Government, *and Jean-Jacques Rousseau in* The Social Contract.

Hobbes, the earliest of the three, had proposed the basic argument favoring repressive government: "The natural condition of man . . . is a condition of war of every one against every one." Man finds this condition intolerable, Hobbes further argued, and hence completely surrenders his "natural rights" to a strong sovereign in return for protection. Hobbes's term for this relationship was "covenant," or in modern parlance, "contract."

Somewhat later, both Locke and Rousseau addressed themselves to the naked brutality of the Hobbesian thesis from a liberal vantage point. In doing so they replaced Hobbes's maleficent vision of man's "natural condition" with a far more benign one in which, to quote John Locke, "all men are naturally in . . . a state of perfect freedom" but nevertheless do not have the liberty to destroy themselves nor the right to "harm another in his life, health, liberty, or possessions." Locke further argued that men entered into a "compact" to form a "politic society" only to secure their common good and surrendered only those rights that are necessary to insure their collective interests. When the rulers of the politic society violate the interests of the people, they, according to Locke, have the right to rebel and overthrow their rulers, in other words, to dissolve the "contract" by which they are ruled. In contrast to Hobbes, who proposed that government was founded on superior force, Locke advanced the notion that government was based on the consent of the governed.

Rousseau, the last of the three, was considerably influenced by Locke's theories in writing The Social Contract. *In our excerpt from this work Rousseau attempts to answer the fundamental question posed by the two preceding writers: Whence came government and why, and by what right does government compel or obligate us to obey it? Rousseau's answers to this question have become the ground for the modern radical tradition. In his own day, Rousseau's statement: "Man is born free, and yet we see him everywhere in chains," became the rallying cry of the French Revolution. Today it informs our efforts to achieve a more just and humane society.*

In his epistolary novel, La Nouvelle Héloïse, *Rousseau depicts ideal social relations in opposition to rigid social conventions. His* Confessions, *which ranks with St. Augustine's in the autobiographical genre, reveal a deeply troubled but exceptionally honest individual. Both works had an enormous impact on the development of Romanticism.*

BOOK I

My design in this treatise is to enquire whether, taking men such as they are, and laws such as they may be made, it is not possible to establish some just and certain rule for the administration of the civil order. In the course of my research I shall endeavour to unite what right permits with what interest prescribes, that justice and utility may not be separated.

I shall enter on my enquiry without saying anything about the importance of my subject. If I am asked whether I am a prince or a lawgiver, that I write on politics, I shall answer that I am neither, and for that reason I am a political writer. If I were a prince or a lawgiver, I should not waste in theory the time which I ought to employ in practice; I would act or I would remain silent.

Born a citizen of a free State, and, as such, a member of its Sovereign, however weak the influence of my voice may prove in the determination of public affairs, the right of voting on such occasions imposes on me the duty of informing myself on the subject: and I am happy, whenever I meditate on governments, to find that my researches always afford me new reason to admire that of my own country.

CHAPTER I

SUBJECT OF THE FIRST BOOK

Man is born free, and yet we see him everywhere in chains. Those who believe themselves the masters of others cease not to be even greater slaves than the people they govern. How this happens I am ignorant; but, if I am asked what renders it justifiable, I believe it may be in my power to resolve the question.

If I were only to consider force, and the effects of it, I should say, "When a people is constrained to obey, and does obey, it does well; but as soon as it can throw off its yoke, and does throw it off, it does better: for a people may certainly use, for the recovery of their liberty, the same right that was employed to deprive them of it: it was either justifiably recovered, or unjustifiably torn from them." But the social order is a sacred right which serves for the basis of all others. Yet this right comes not from nature; it is therefore founded on conventions. The question is, what those conventions are. But, before I come to that point, I must establish the principles which I have just asserted.

CHAPTER II

OF THE FIRST SOCIETIES

The earliest and the only natural societies are families: yet the children remain attached to the father no longer than they have need for his protection. As soon as that need ceases, the bond of nature is dissolved. The child, exempt from the obedience he owed the father, and the father, from the duties he owed the child, return equally to independence. If they continue to remain together, it is not in consequence of a natural, but a voluntary union; and the family itself is maintained only by a convention.

This common liberty is a consequence of the nature of man. His first law is that of self-preservation, his first cares those which he owes to himself; and as soon as he has attained the age of reason, being the only judge of the means proper to preserve himself, he becomes at once his own master.

It appears therefore that families are the first models of political societies: the chief represents the father of the family, the children the people; and being all born equal, and all free, they in either case only alienate their liberty in order to obtain what is more useful. All the difference between the two societies is that, in the family, the gratification which paternal tenderness derives from a consciousness of benefiting those who are the objects of it makes a full amends to the father for the care he bestows on the children; while, in the State, the pleasure of commanding takes the place of that love which the chief does not feel for his people.

Grotius denies that all human power is established for the

benefit of those who are governed; and he instances slavery in proof of his assertion. But his constant manner of reasoning is to establish right by fact.[1] A more satisfactory mode might be employed, but none more favourable to tyrants.

It is therefore doubtful, according to Grotius, whether the whole human race belongs to about one hundred men, or this hundred men to the human race; and he appears throughout his book to incline to the former opinion, which is also the idea of Hobbes: so that, according to them, mankind is divided into herds of cattle, each herd having its master who protects it in order to devour it.

As the herdsman is of a nature superior to that of his cattle, so the herdsmen of men, that is, their chiefs, are of a nature superior to their people. So reasoned, according to Philo's account, the Emperor Caligula, who concluded very justly from analogy that either kings were gods, or men were beasts.

The reasoning of Caligula comes to just the same point as that of Grotius and Hobbes. Aristotle had said, before any of them, that men are not naturally equal, but that some are born for slavery and others for dominion.

Aristotle was right; but he mistook the effect for the cause. Nothing is more certain than that all men who are born in slavery are born for slavery. Slaves become so debased by their chains as to lose even the desire of breaking from them; they love their servitude, even as the companions of Ulysses loved their brutishness.[2] If there are some who are slaves by nature, the reason is that men were made slaves against nature. Force made the first slaves, and slavery, by degrading and corrupting its victims, perpetuated their bondage.

I have not said anything of King Adam, or Emperor Noah, the father of three great monarchs, who parted the universe among them, like the children of Saturn, whom they are by many supposed to be. I expect to be applauded for this moderation; because, as I am descended in a direct line from one of these princes, and perhaps from the eldest branch, who can tell whether, in the verification of titles, I might not find myself the legitimate king of the human race? However it be, we can

[1] "Learned studies of public right are often only the history of past abuses; and it is foolish and stubborn to take the trouble to study them too deeply." (*Essay on the Interests of France in Relation to its Neighbours,* by the Marquis d'Argenson.) This is precisely what Grotius did.

[2] See a short treatise by Plutarch entitled *That Animals Use Reason.*

discover nothing but that Adam was sovereign of the world, as Robinson Crusoe was of his island, because he was its only inhabitant; and the happiest circumstance attending the empire was that the monarch was secure in his throne, having nothing to apprehend from rebellions, wars, or conspiracies.

CHAPTER III

OF THE RIGHT OF THE STRONGEST

The strongest are still never sufficiently strong to ensure them continual mastership, unless they find means of transforming force into right, and obedience into duty. Hence the right of the strongest—a right which seems ironical in appearance, but is really established as a principle. But shall we never have an explanation of this term? Force is a physical power; I do not see what morality can result from its effects. To yield to force is an act of necessity, not of inclination; or it is at best only an act of prudence. In what sense then can it be a duty?

Let us suppose for a moment the existence of this pretended right. I see nothing that can arise from it but inexplicable nonsense. For, if we admit that force constitutes right, the effect changes with the cause: all force which overcomes the first succeeds to its right. As soon as men can disobey with impunity, they can do so justifiably; and because the strongest is always in the right, strength is the only thing men should seek to acquire. But what sort of right is that which perishes with the force that gave it existence? If it is necessary to obey by force, there can be no occasion to obey from duty; and when force is no more, all obligation ceases with it. We see, therefore, that this word "right" adds nothing to force, but is indeed an unmeaning term.

If in saying, "Let us obey the powerful," they mean to say, "Let us yield to force," the precept is good, but it is superfluous, for it never is or can be violated. All power, we are told, comes from God. I grant it does; but all diseases likewise come from the same hand, and yet who ever forbade us to call in a physician? If a robber surprises me in a corner of a wood, is it necessary that I should not only give him my purse when forced to do so, but am I in conscience obliged to give it to him, though I should be in a position to escape? For the fact is, the pistol which he holds is also a power.

We must grant, therefore, that force does not constitute right, and that obedience is only due to legitimate powers. Thus everything goes back to my first question.

CHAPTER IV

OF SLAVERY

Since no man has any natural authority over his fellows, and since force produces no right to any, all justifiable authority among men must be established on the basis of conventions.

If an individual, says Grotius, can alienate his liberty, and become the slave of a master, why may not a whole people alienate theirs, and become the subject of a king? There are some equivocal words in this sentence, which require an explanation; but I will confine myself to the word "alienate." To alienate is to give or sell. But a man who becomes the slave of another, cannot give but must sell himself, at least for a subsistence. But for what do a people sell themselves? A king, so far from furnishing his subjects with subsistence, draws his own from them; and, according to Rabelais, a king does not subsist upon a little. Do subjects therefore give their persons on condition that the prince will condescend to accept their property also? I see nothing, after such a gratuity, that there remains for them to preserve.

We are told that a despot ensures civil tranquillity for his subjects. Be it so; but what do his subjects gain if the wars which his ambition draws them into, if his insatiable avarice, and the vexations of his administration, desolate the country even more than civil dissensions? What do they gain if this very tranquillity is one of their miseries? We find tranquillity also in dungeons; but is that enough to make them enjoyable? The Greeks enjoyed the same kind of tranquillity while they were shut up in the cave of the Cyclops, and were expecting every moment that it would be their turn to be devoured.

To say that a man gives himself gratuitously is absurd and incomprehensible; such an act is unjustifiable and void, because the person who performed it is not in his proper senses. To say the same of a whole people is to suppose the people are all mad; and folly does not make it right.

If each individual could alienate himself, he could not alienate his descendants; for, being born men and free, their liberty is their own, and no person can dispose of it but they themselves. Before they arrive at the age of reason, the father may, in his children's name, stipulate conditions for their preservation and welfare, but not give them up irrevocably, and unconditionally; for such a gift would be contrary to the designs of nature, and exceed the rights of paternal authority. It would therefore be necessary, in order to make an arbitrary government justifiable, that each generation should be at liberty to admit or reject it: but then such a government would not be arbitrary.

To renounce our liberty is to renounce our quality of man, and with it all the rights and duties of humanity. No adequate compensation can possibly be made for a sacrifice so complete. Such a renunciation is incompatible with the nature of man; whose actions, when once he is deprived of his free will, must be destitute of all morality. Finally, a convention which stipulates absolute authority on one side, and unlimited obedience on the other, must be considered as vain and contradictory. Is it not clear that there can be no obligation to a person from whom everything may be justly required? And does not the single circumstance of there being no equivalence and no exchange also annul the act? For what right can my slave have against me, since everything that he has belongs to me, and, his right being mine, this right of mine against myself is absolute nonsense?

Grotius and others derive from war another origin for this pretended right of slavery. The victor having, according to them, a right to kill the vanquished, the latter may purchase his life at the expense of his liberty; a convention which is so much the more justifiable because it tends to benefit both parties.

But it is clear that this pretended right of killing the vanquished results not in any manner from the state of war; because, while men remain in their primitive independence, there is no intercourse between them sufficiently settled to constitute either peace or war; and they are not naturally enemies. It is a concurrence of things, and not of men, that occasions war; and the state of war cannot rise out of simple personal concerns, but only out of real relations; nor can private war between man and man exist either in the state of nature, where there is no settled property, or in a civil state, where everything is under the authority of the laws.

Private combats, duels, and rencontres are acts which do not constitute a state of war; and with regard to the petty wars authorized by the "Establishments" of Louis IX of France, and suspended by the Peace of God, they were abuses of the feudal government, a system so completely absurd that it contradicted the principles of natural right and of every sound polity.

War is therefore not a concern between man and man but between State and State, in which individuals are only enemies accidentally, not as men, or as citizens, but as soldiers; not as members of a country, but as its defenders. In fine, States can only have other States, and not men, for enemies, because there can be no true relation between things of different natures.

This principle is conformable to the established maxims of all times, and the invariable practice of all politically organized peoples. Declarations of war are not so much to inform the powers as their subjects. The stranger, be it a monarch, a private individual, or a whole people, that robs, kills, or detains the subjects of another prince, without previously declaring war against that prince, is not an enemy but a robber. Even in real war, a just prince, while he carries away whatever he can seize upon in an enemy's country that belongs to the public, respects the persons and property of private people, because he respects the right by which he holds his own. The end of war being to subdue the hostile State, the army of one State has a right to kill the defenders of the other while they have arms in their hands; but, as soon as they lay them down and surrender themselves, they cease to be enemies or the instruments of enemies; they become simply men, and the victors have no longer any right over their lives. Sometimes it may be possible for one State to destroy another State without destroying one of its members: and war does not give a right to do anything beyond what is absolutely necessary to its end. These are not the principles of Grotius, neither are they adopted on the authority of the poets; but they are derived from the nature of things, and founded on reason.

With regard to the right of conquest, it has no other foundation than the law of the strongest. If war does not give the conqueror the right to massacre the conquered, then that right does not exist and cannot serve as a basis for the right to enslave the conquered. Men have no right to kill the enemy but at the time when it is impossible to enslave them; the right of enslaving cannot therefore be derived from the right of killing: it is therefore an iniquitous barter to make them purchase, at the price of their liberty, that life over which the conquerors have no right. In establishing the right of life and death on that of slavery, and of slavery on that of life and death, is it not clear that we become involved in a vicious circle?

But supposing that this terrible right of massacring everybody did exist, the slaves made in war, or a conquered people, could be bound by no obligation at all to their master, and would only obey him while they were compelled by force to do so. In taking his service as an equivalent for sparing his life, the victor confers no favour on the man he has vanquished: instead of killing him—from whence he could derive no advantage—he spares him that he may reap the fruits of his labour. So far, therefore, is the conqueror from having acquired, by saving the life of the conquered, any other authority over him to second that of force, that the state of war continues to subsist between them as formerly, and even their union is the effect of it; and, while the rights of war are exercised, no treaty of peace can be supposed to exist. I shall be told perhaps that they have made a convention. Be it so; but this convention is so far from terminating the state of war that it supposes the continuance of it.

Thus, in whatever light we view things, the right of slavery is found to be null, not only because it is unjustifiable but because it is absurd and has no meaning. The terms "slavery" and "right" contradict and exclude each other. Be it from man to man, or from a man to a people, it would be equally nonsensical to say: I make a covenant with you entirely at your expense, and for my benefit; I will observe it as far as my inclination leads me, and you shall observe it as far as I please.

CHAPTER V

THAT WE MUST ALWAYS GO BACK TO A FIRST CONVENTION

Had I granted all which I have refuted, the favourers of despotism would not have found their cause advanced by it. There will always be a great difference between subduing a multitude and governing a society. When unorganized men are successively subjugated by one individual, whatever number there may be of them, they appear to me only as a master and slaves; I cannot regard them as a people and their chief; they are, if you please, an *aggregation,* but they are not as yet an *association;* for there is neither public property, nor a political body, among them. A man may have enslaved half the world, and yet continue only a private individual; his interest is separate from that of others, and confined to himself alone. When such a man falls, his empire remains unconnected and without any bond of union, as an oak dissolves and becomes a mass of ashes when consumed by fire.

"A people," says Grotius, "can give themselves to a king." According to Grotius, then, they are a people before they give themselves to a king. The donation itself is a civil act, and supposes a public consultation. It would therefore be better before we examine the act by which they elected a king, to enquire into that by which they became a people; for that act, being necessarily anterior to the other, is the true foundation of society.

In fact, if there was no prior convention, where would be—unless the election was unanimous—the obligation which should bind the minority to submit to the choice of the majority? And whence would a hundred men, who wish to submit to a master, derive the right of binding by their votes ten other men who were not disposed to acknowledge any chief? The law which gives the majority of votes the power of deciding for the whole body can only be established by a convention, and proves that there must have been unanimity at one time at least.

CHAPTER VI

OF THE SOCIAL COMPACT

I will suppose that men in the state of nature are arrived at that crisis when the strength of each individual is insufficient to overcome the resistance of the obstacles to his preservation. This primitive state can therefore subsist no longer; and the human race would perish unless it changed its manner of life.

As men cannot create for themselves new forces, but merely unite and direct those which already exist, the only means they can employ for their preservation is to form by aggregation an assemblage of forces that may be able to overcome the resistance, to be put in motion as one body, and to act in concert.

This assemblage of forces must be produced by the concurrence of many; but as the force and the liberty of each man are the chief instruments of his preservation, how can he engage them elsewhere without danger to himself, and without neglecting the care which is due himself? This difficulty, which leads directly to my subject, may be expressed in these words:

"Where shall we find a form of association which will defend and protect with the whole common force the person and the property of each associate, and by which every person, while uniting himself with all, shall obey only himself and remain as free as before?" Such is the fundamental problem of which the Social Contract gives the solution.

The articles of this contract are so unalterably fixed by the nature of the act that the least modification renders them vain and of no effect; so that they are the same everywhere, and are everywhere tacitly understood and admitted, even though they may never have been formally announced; until, the social compact being violated, each individual is restored to his original rights, and resumes his native liberty, while losing the conventional liberty for which he renounced it.

The articles of the social contract will, when clearly understood, be found reducible to this single point: the total alienation of each associate, and all his rights, to the whole community; for, in the first place, as every individual gives himself up entirely, the condition of every person is alike; and being so, it would not be to the interest of any one to render that condition offensive to others.

Nay, more than this, the alienation being made without any reserve, the union is as complete as it can be, and no associate has any further claim to anything: for if any individual retained rights not enjoyed in general by all, as there would be no common superior to decide between him and the public, each person being in some points his own judge, would soon pretend to be so in everything; and thus would the state of nature be continued and the association necessarily become tyrannical or be annihilated.

Finally, each person gives himself to all, and so not to any one individual; and as there is no one associate over whom the same right is not acquired which is ceded to him by others, each gains an equivalent for what he loses, and finds his force increased for preserving that which he possesses.

If, therefore, we exclude from the social compact all that is not essential, we shall find it reduced to the following terms:

Each of us places in common his person and all his power under the supreme direction of the general will; and as one body we all receive each member as an indivisible part of the whole.

From that moment, instead of as many separate persons as there are contracting parties, this act of association produces a moral and collective body, composed of as many members as there are votes in the assembly, which from this act receives its unity, its common self, its life, and its will. This public person, which is thus formed by the union of all other persons, took formerly the name of "city,"[3] and now takes that of "republic" or "body politic." It is called by its members "State" when it is passive, "Sovereign" when in activity, and, whenever it is compared with other bodies of a similar kind, it is denominated "power." The associates take collectively the name of "people," and separately, that of "citizens," as participating in the sovereign authority, and of "subjects," because they are subjected to the laws of the State. But these terms are frequently confounded and used one for the other; and it is enough that a man understands how to distinguish them when they are employed in all their precision.

CHAPTER VII

OF THE SOVEREIGN

It appears from this formula that the act of association contains a reciprocal engagement between the public and individuals, and that each individual, contracting, as it were, with himself, is engaged under a double character; that is, as a member of

[3] The true sense of this word is almost entirely lost among the moderns: the name of "city" is now generally used to signify a town, and that of "citizen" applied to a burgess. Men do not seem to know that *houses* make a "town," but that *citizens* make a "city." The Carthaginians once paid dearly for a mistake of this kind. I have never seen it mentioned that the title of *cives* was ever given to the subjects of any prince, not even to the Macedonians formerly, or to the English at present, although they are nearer liberty than any other people. The French alone use the name of "citizen" familiarly to all, because they have no true idea of it, as appears from their dictionaries; and without knowing its meaning they are in danger of falling into the crime of lèse majesté, by usurping a title to which they have no just claim. The word "citizen" with them means a virtue, and not a right. Bodin made a very gross mistake, when, in speaking of "citizens" and "burgesses," he mistook the one for the other. M. D'Alembert was better acquainted with the meaning of these terms, and in his article "Genève" he has very properly marked the difference between the four orders of men —indeed I may say five, by including the foreigners—which are found there, and of which two orders only compose the republic. No other French author that I know of has comprehended the true sense of the word "citizen."

the Sovereign engaging with individuals, and as a member of the State engaged with the Sovereign. But we cannot apply here the maxim of civil right, that no person is bound by any engagement which he makes with himself; for there is a material difference between an obligation to oneself individually, and an obligation to a collective body of which oneself constitutes a part.

It is necessary to observe here that public deliberation, which can bind all the subjects to the Sovereign, in consequence of the double character under which the members of that body appear, cannot, for the opposite reason, bind the Sovereign to itself; and consequently that it is against the nature of the body politic for the sovereign power to impose on itself any law which it cannot break. Being able to consider itself as acting under one character only, it is in the situation of an individual forming a contract with himself; and we see therefore that there neither is nor can be any kind of fundamental law obligatory for the body of the people, not even the social contract itself. But this does not mean that this body could not very well engage itself to others in any manner which would not derogate from the contract; for, with respect to what is external to it, it becomes a simple being, an individual. But the body politic, or the Sovereign, which derives its existence from the sacredness of the contract, can never bind itself, even towards outsiders, in anything that would derogate from the original act, such as alienating any portion of itself, or submitting to another Sovereign. To violate the contract by which it exists would be to annihilate itself; and that which is nothing can produce nothing.

As soon as this multitude is united in one body, you cannot offend one of its members without attacking the body; much less can you offend the body without incurring the resentment of all the members. Thus duty and interest equally oblige the two contracting parties to lend aid to each other; and the same men must endeavour to unite under this double character all the advantages which attend it.

Further, the Sovereign, being formed only of the individuals who compose it, neither has, nor can have, any interest contrary to theirs; consequently, the sovereign power need give no guarantee to its subjects, because it is impossible that the body should seek to injure all its members; and we shall see presently that it can do no injury to any individual in particular. The Sovereign, by its nature, is always everything it ought to be.

But this is not so with the relation of subjects towards the Sovereign, which, notwithstanding the common interest, has nothing to make them responsible for the performance of their engagements if some means is not found of ensuring their fidelity.

In fact, each individual may, as a man, have a private will, dissimilar or contrary to the general will which he has as a citizen. His own private interest may dictate to him very differently from the common interest; his absolute and naturally independent existence may make him regard what he owes to the common cause as a gratuitous contribution, the omission of which would be less injurious to others than the payment would be burdensome to himself; and considering the moral person which constitutes the State as a creature of the imagination, because it is not a man, he may wish to enjoy the rights of a citizen without being disposed to fulfil the duties of a subject. Such an injustice would in its progress cause the ruin of the body politic.

In order, therefore, to prevent the social compact from becoming an empty formula, it tacitly comprehends the engagement, which alone can give effect to the others—that whoever refuses to obey the general will shall be compelled to it by the whole body: this in fact only forces him to be free; for this is the condition which, by giving each citizen to his country, guarantees his absolute personal independence, a condition which gives motion and effect to the political machine. This alone renders all civil engagements justifiable, and without it they would be absurd, tyrannical, and subject to the most enormous abuses.

CHAPTER VIII

OF THE CIVIL STATE

The passing from the state of nature to the civil state produces in man a very remarkable change, by substituting justice for instinct in his conduct, and giving to his actions a moral character which they lacked before. It is then only that the voice of duty succeeds to physical impulse, and a sense of what is right, to the incitements of appetite. Man, who had till then regarded none but himself, perceives that he must act on other principles, and learns to consult his reason before he listens to his inclinations. Although he is deprived in this new state of many advantages which he enjoyed from nature, he gains in return others so great, his faculties so unfold themselves by being exercised, his ideas are so extended, his sentiments so exalted, and his whole mind so enlarged and refined, that if, by abusing his new condition, he did not sometimes degrade it even below that from which he emerged, he ought to bless continually the happy moment that snatched him forever from it, and transformed him from a circumscribed and stupid animal to an intelligent being and a man.

In order to draw a balance between the advantages and disadvantages attending his new situation, let us state them in such a manner that they may be easily compared. Man loses by the social contract his *natural* liberty, and an unlimited right to all which tempts him, and which he can obtain; in return he acquires *civil* liberty, and proprietorship of all he possesses. That we may not be deceived in the value of these compensations, we must distinguish natural liberty, which knows no bounds but the power of the individual, from civil liberty, which is limited by the general will; and between possession, which is only the effect of force or of the right of the first occupant, from property, which must be founded on a positive title. In addition we might add to the other acquisitions of the civil state that of moral liberty, which alone renders a man master of himself; for it is *slavery* to be under the impulse of mere appetite, and *freedom* to obey a law which we prescribe for ourselves. But I have already said too much on this head, and the philosophical sense of the word "liberty" is not at present my subject.

CHAPTER IX

OF REAL PROPERTY

Each member of the community, at the moment of its formation, gives himself up to it just as he is: himself and all his forces, of which his wealth forms a part. By this act, however, possession does not change in nature when it changes its master, and become property when it falls into the hands of the Sovereign; but as the forces of the city are infinitely greater than those of an individual, it is better secured when it becomes a public possession, without being more justifiable, at least with respect to foreigners. As to its members, the State is made master of all their wealth by the social contract, which within the State serves as the basis of all rights; but with regard to other powers, it claims only under the title of first occupancy, which it derives from individuals.

The right of the first occupant, though more substantial than that of the strongest, does not become a real right, until after the right of property is established. All men have naturally a right to whatever is necessary for them; but the act which renders a man the positive proprietor of any property excludes him from everything else. This being accomplished, the possessor must confine himself to what is thus made his own, and he can claim no right beyond it against the community. It is by this means that the right of the first occupant, so weak in the state of nature, is respected by every man in civil society. In this right we respect less what is another's than what is not our own.

The following conditions are in general necessary to give validity to the right founded on first occupancy in any domain whatever. In the first place, the land must not yet be inhabited by any person; secondly, the party must not occupy more land than is sufficient to supply him with subsistence; thirdly, he must take possession, not by a vain ceremony, but by labour and cultivation, as they are the only proofs of a man's being a proprietor, which, in default of a legal title, deserve to be respected by others.

Is not the thus granting the right of first occupancy to *want* and to *labour* extending it as far as it can go? Cannot the right have some bounds assigned to it? Is it sufficient to set our foot on a common domain, and pretend from thence a right to possess it? Is there nothing necessary but sufficient force to drive others out for a moment in order to deprive them of their right of ever returning thither? And how can a man, or a people, overrun an immense territory, and prevent all other human beings from participating in it without being guilty of a criminal usurpation, since they deprive by that means the rest of mankind of a place of residence and of the means of subsistence which nature gave in common to all? When Nuñez Balboa took possession, on the shores of the South Sea, of that ocean and of all South America in the name of the crown of Castille, was that act sufficient to dispossess the inhabitants of the country, and exclude all the princes of the world from settling there? At this rate these ceremonies would have been multiplied extravagantly, and the

Catholic king might at one stroke have taken possession of the whole universe without going out of his closet, except indeed to have cut off from his empire what had been previously occupied by other princes.

We see how the lands of private persons, contiguous and united, become the public territory, and how the right of sovereignty, extending from the subjects over the lands they occupy, becomes at once real and personal; by which the occupants are rendered more dependent, and their own force made the guarantee of their fidelity; an advantage which does not seem to have been perceived by ancient monarchs, who, styling themselves Kings of the Persians, the Scythians, or the Macedonians, appear to have regarded themselves as the chiefs of men rather than as masters of the country. Those of the present day call themselves more cleverly Kings of France, Spain, England, etc.; and in thus holding the domain, they are sure to hold its inhabitants.

The singular circumstance attending this alienation is that, in accepting the property of individuals, the community is far from despoiling them, and only ensures them justifiable possession, changes usurpation into a true right, and enjoyment into property. By this means, the possessors being considered as depositaries of the public good, their rights are respected by all the members of the State, and protected with all their force against foreigners. So that by a resignation, advantageous to the public, and still more so to the resigners, they may be justly said to have acquired all that they gave up: a paradox which will be easily explained by distinguishing, as I shall do hereafter, between the rights which the Sovereign and the proprietors have in the same property.

It may also happen that men begin to associate before they have any possessions, and that, spreading afterwards over a country sufficient for them all, they may either enjoy it in common, or part it between them equally, or in such proportions as the Sovereign shall direct. In whatever manner the acquisition is made, the right which each individual has over his own property is always subordinate to the right which the community has over all; without which there would be no solidity in the social bond, nor any real force in the exercise of sovereignty.

I shall conclude this chapter and book with a remark which must serve for the basis of the whole social system: it is that, instead of destroying the natural equality of mankind, the fundamental compact substitutes, on the contrary, a moral and legal equality for that physical inequality which nature placed among men, and that, let men be ever so unequal in strength or in genius, they are all equalized by convention and legal right.[4]

[4] Under bad governments this equality is but an illusive appearance, which only serves to keep the poor in misery, and support the rich in their usurpations. In fact, laws are always useful to those who have abundance, and injurious to those who have nothing: from whence it follows that the social state is only advantageous to men when every individual has some property, and no one has too much.

Of Property

John Locke

(1632-1704)

As we have just seen, Locke had, through Rousseau, an enormous effect on the radical tradition stemming from the French Revolution. Locke's influence did not just extend across the channel and throughout Europe. He was at least equally influential at home and is now considered the central thinker of the liberal tradition of America and England. His notion of the consensual society is the core belief of the American and British systems of parliamentary government.

But what was at the center of Locke's political theory? As much as anything, it was his notion of property. And what was Locke's notion of property? The following portion of his Treatise of Civil Government *is his answer to that question. When reading "Of Property" it would be well to keep in mind that Locke himself was part of the landed gentry, a sort of rural middle class. In Locke's day modern manufacturing methods and capitalism were just beginning in England; the country's economy was still mainly agrarian. Hence Locke's contempt for money and his disregard of the exchange value of labor that so plagues modern theorists.*

Of Civil Government *is the second part of* Two Treatises of Government, *an attack on the divine right concept. In addition to this major work on politics Locke wrote several essays advocating religious liberty called "Letters Concerning Toleration" and a major philosophical work on the theory of knowledge titled* Essay Concerning Human Understanding.

25. Whether we consider natural reason, which tells us, that men, being once born, have a right to their preservation, and consequently to meat and drink, and such other things as nature affords for their subsistence; or revelation, which gives us an account of those grants God made of the world to Adam, and to Noah, and his sons; it is very clear, that God, as king David says, Psal. cxv. 16, "has given the earth to the children of men"; given it to mankind in common. But this being supposed, it seems to some a very great difficulty how any one should ever come to have a property in any thing: I will not content myself to answer, that if it be difficult to make out property, upon a supposition that God gave the world to Adam and his posterity in common, it is impossible that any man, but one universal monarch, should have any property, upon a supposition that God gave the world to Adam, and his heirs in succession, exclusive of all the rest of his posterity. But I shall endeavour to show how men might come to have a property in several parts of that which God gave to mankind in common, and that without any express compact of all the commoners.

26. God, who hath given the world to men in common, hath also given them reason to make use of it to the best advantage of life and convenience. The earth, and all that is therein, is given to men for the support and comfort of their being. And though all the fruits it naturally produces, and beasts it feeds, belong to mankind in common, as they are produced by the spontaneous hand of nature; and nobody has originally a private dominion,

exclusive of the rest of mankind, in any of them, as they are thus in their natural state: yet being given for the use of men, there must of necessity be a means to appropriate them some way or other before they can be of any use, or at all beneficial to any particular man. The fruit, or venison, which nourishes the wild Indian, who knows no enclosure, and is still a tenant in common, must be his, and so his, *i.e.* a part of him, that another can no longer have any right to it, before it can do him any good for the support of his life.

27. Though the earth, and all inferior creatures, be common to all men, yet every man has a property in his own person: this nobody has any right to but himself. The labour of his body, and the work of his hands, we may say, are properly his. Whatsoever then he removes out of the state that nature hath provided, and left it in, he hath mixed his labour with, and joined to it something that is his own, and thereby makes it his property. It being by him removed from the common state nature hath placed it in, it hath by this labour something annexed to it that excludes the common right of other men. For this labour being the unquestionable property of the labourer, no man but he can have a right to what that is once joined to, at least where there is enough, and as good, left in common for others.

28. He that is nourished by the acorns he picked up under an oak, or the apples he gathered from the trees in the wood, has certainly appropriated them to himself. Nobody can deny but the nourishment is his. I ask then, when did they begin to be his? when he digested? or when he ate? or when he boiled? or when he brought them home? or when he picked them up? and it is plain, if the first gathering made them not his, nothing else could. That labour put a distinction between them and common: that added something to them more than nature, the common mother of all, had done; and so they became his private right. And will any one say, he had no right to those acorns or apples he thus appropriated, because he had not the consent of all mankind to make them his? was it a robbery thus to assume to himself what belonged to all in common? If such a consent as that was necessary, man had starved, notwithstanding the plenty God had given him. We see in commons, which remain so by compact, that it is the taking any part of what is common, and removing it out of the state nature leaves it in, which begins the property; without which the common is of no use. And the taking of this or that part does not depend on the express consent

of all the commoners. Thus the grass my horse has bit: the turfs my servant has cut; and the ore I have digged in any place, where I have a right to them in common with others; become my property, without the assignation or consent of any body. The labour that was mine, removing them out of that common state they were in, hath fixed my property in them.

29. By making an explicit consent of every commoner necessary to any one's appropriating to himself any part of what is given in common, children or servants could not cut the meat, which their father or master had provided for them in common, without assigning to every one his peculiar part. Though the water running in the fountain be every one's, yet who can doubt but that in the pitcher is his only who drew it out? His labour hath taken it out of the hands of nature, where it was common, and belonged equally to all her children, and hath thereby appropriated it to himself.

30. Thus this law of reason makes the deer that Indian's who hath killed it; it is allowed to be his goods who hath bestowed his labour upon it, though before it was the common right of every one. And amongst those who are counted the civilized part of mankind, who have made and multiplied positive laws to determine property, this original law of nature, for the beginning of property, in what was before common, still takes place; and by virtue thereof, what fish any one catches in the ocean, that great and still remaining common of mankind; or what ambergris any one takes up here, is by the labour that removes it out of that common state nature left it in made his property who takes pains about it. And even amongst us, the hare that any one is hunting is thought his who pursues her during the chase: for being a beast that is still looked upon as common, and no man's private possession; whoever has employed so much labour about any of that kind, as to find and pursue her, has thereby removed her from the state of nature, wherein she was common, and hath begun a property.

31. It will perhaps be objected to this, that "if gathering the acorns, or other fruits of the earth, &c. makes a right to them, then any one may engross as much as he will." To which I answer, Not so. The same law of nature, that does by this means give us property, does also bound that property too. "God has given us all things richly," 1 Tim. vi. 17, is the voice of reason confirmed by inspiration. But how far has he given it us? To enjoy. As much as any one can make use of to any advantage

of life before it spoils, so much he may by his labour fix a property in: whatever is beyond this, is more than his share, and belongs to others. Nothing was made by God for man to spoil or destroy. And thus, considering the plenty of natural provisions there was a long time in the world, and the few spenders; and to how small a part of that provision the industry of one man could extend itself, and engross it to the prejudice of others; especially keeping within the bounds, set by reason, of what might serve for his use; there could be then little room for quarrels or contentions about property so established.

32. But the chief matter of property being now not the fruits of the earth, and the beasts that subsist on it, but the earth itself; as that which takes in, and carries with it all the rest; I think it is plain, that property in that too is acquired as the former. As much land as a man tills, plants, improves, cultivates, and can use the product of, so much is his property. He by his labour does, as it were, enclose it from the common. Nor will it invalidate his right, to say every body else has an equal title to it, and therefore he cannot appropriate, he cannot enclose, without the consent of all his fellow-commoners, all mankind. God, when he gave the world in common to all mankind, commanded man also to labour, and the penury of his condition required it of him. God and his reason commanded him to subdue the earth, *i.e.* improve it for the benefit of life, and therein lay out something upon it that was his own, his labour. He that, in obedience to this command of God, subdued, tilled, and sowed any part of it, thereby annexed to it something that was his property, which another had no title to, nor could without injury take from him.

33. Nor was this appropriation of any parcel of land, by improving it, any prejudice to any other man, since there was still enough, and as good left; and more than the yet unprovided could use. So that, in effect, there was never the less left for others because of his enclosure for himself: for he that leaves as much as another can make use of, does as good as take nothing at all. Nobody could think himself injured by the drinking of another man, though he took a good draught, who had a whole river of the same water left him to quench his thirst; and the case of land and water, where there is enough of both, is perfectly the same.

34. God gave the world to men in common; but since he gave it them for their benefit, and the greatest conveniencies of life they were capable to draw from it, it cannot be supposed he

meant it should always remain common and uncultivated. He gave it to the use of the industrious and rational (and labour was to be his title to it), not to the fancy or covetousness of the quarrelsome and contentious. He that had as good left for his improvement as was already taken up, needed not complain, ought not to meddle with what was already improved by another's labour: if he did, it is plain he desired the benefit of another's pains, which he had no right to, and not the ground which God had given him in common with others to labour on, and whereof there was as good left as that already possessed, and more than he knew what to do with, or his industry could reach to.

35. It is true, in land that is common in England, or any other country, where there is plenty of people under government, who have money and commerce, no one can enclose or appropriate any part without the consent of all his fellow-commoners; because this is left common by compact, *i.e.* by the law of the land, which is not to be violated. And though it be common, in respect of some men, it is not so to all mankind, but is the joint property of this county, or this parish. Besides, the remainder, after such enclosure, would not be as good to the rest of the commoners as the whole was when they could all make use of the whole; whereas in the beginning and first peopling of the great common of the world it was quite otherwise. The law man was under was rather for appropriating. God commanded, and his wants forced him to labour. That was his property which could not be taken from him wherever he had fixed it. And hence subduing or cultivating the earth, and having dominion, we see are joined together. The one gave title to the other. So that God, by commanding to subdue, gave authority so far to appropriate: and the condition of human life, which requires labour and materials to work on, necessarily introduces private possessions.

36. The measure of property nature has well set by the extent of men's labour and the conveniencies of life: no man's labour could subdue, or appropriate all; nor could his enjoyment consume more than a small part; so that it was impossible for any man, this way, to intrench upon the right of another, or acquire to himself a property, to the prejudice of his neighbour, who would still have room for as good and as large a possession (after the other had taken out his) as before it was appropriated. This measure did confine every man's possession to a very moderate proportion, and such as he might appropriate to himself, with-

out injury to any body, in the first ages of the world, when men were more in danger to be lost, by wandering from their company, in the then vast wilderness of the earth, than to be straitened for want of room to plant in. And the same measure may be allowed still without prejudice to any body, as full as the world seems: for supposing a man, or family, in the state they were at first peopling of the world by the children of Adam, or Noah; let him plant in some inland, vacant places of America, we shall find that the possessions he could make himself, upon the measures we have given, would not be very large, nor, even to this day, prejudice the rest of mankind, or give them reason to complain, or think themselves injured by this man's encroachment; though the race of men have now spread themselves to all the corners of the world, and do infinitely exceed the small number was at the beginning. Nay, the extent of ground is of so little value, without labour, that I have heard it affirmed, that in Spain itself a man may be permitted to plough, sow, and reap, without being disturbed, upon land he has no other title to, but only his making use of it. But, on the contrary, the inhabitants think themselves beholden to him, who, by his industry on neglected, and consequently waste land, has increased the stock of corn, which they wanted. But be this as it will, which I lay no stress on; this I dare boldly affirm, that the same rule of propriety, viz. that every man should have as much as he could make use of, would hold still in the world, without straitening any body; since there is land enough in the world to suffice double the inhabitants, had not the invention of money, and the tacit agreement of men to put a value on it, introduced (by consent) larger possessions, and a right to them; which, how it has done, I shall by and by show more at large.

37. This is certain, that in the beginning, before the desire of having more than man needed had altered the intrinsic value of things, which depends only on their usefulness to the life of man; or had agreed, that a little piece of yellow metal, which would keep without wasting or decay, should be worth a great piece of flesh, or a whole heap of corn; though men had a right to appropriate, by their labour, each one to himself, as much of the things of nature as he could use: yet this could not be much, nor to the prejudice of others, where the same plenty was still left to those who would use the same industry. To which let me add, that he who appropriates land to himself by his labour, does not lessen, but increase the common stock of mankind: for

the provisions serving to the support of human life, produced by one acre of enclosed and cultivated land, are (to speak much within compass) ten times more than those which are yielded by an acre of land of an equal richness lying waste in common. And therefore he that encloses land, and has a greater plenty of the conveniencies of life from ten acres, than he could have from an hundred left to nature, may truly be said to give ninety acres to mankind: for his labour now supplies him with provisions out of ten acres, which were by the product of an hundred lying in common. I have here rated the improved land very low, in making its product but at ten to one, when it is much nearer an hundred to one: for I ask, whether in the wild woods and uncultivated waste of America, left to nature, without any improvement, tillage, or husbandry, a thousand acres yield the needy and wretched inhabitants as many conveniencies of life as ten acres equally fertile land do in Devonshire, where they are well cultivated?

Before the appropriation of land, he who gathered as much of the wild fruit, killed, caught, or tamed, as many of the beasts, as he could; he that so employed his pains about any of the spontaneous products of nature, as any way to alter them from the state which nature put them in, by placing any of his labour on them, did thereby acquire a propriety in them: but if they perished, in his possession, without their due use; if the fruits rotted, or the venison putrefied, before he could spend it; he offended against the common law of nature, and was liable to be punished; he invaded his neighbour's share, for he had no right, farther than his use called for any of them, and they might serve to afford him conveniencies of life.

38. The same measures governed the possession of land too: whatsoever he tilled and reaped, laid up and made use of, before it spoiled, that was his peculiar right; whatsoever he enclosed, and could feed, and make use of, the cattle and product was also his. But if either the grass of his enclosure rotted on the ground, or the fruit of his planting perished without gathering and laying up; this part of the earth, notwithstanding his enclosure, was still to be looked on as waste, and might be the possession of any other. Thus, at the beginning, Cain might take as much ground as he could till, and make it his own land, and yet leave enough to Abel's sheep to feed on; a few acres would serve for both their possessions. But as families increased, and industry enlarged their stocks, their possessions enlarged

with the need of them; but yet it was commonly without any fixed property in the ground they made use of, till they incorporated, settled themselves together, and built cities; and then, by consent, they came in time to set out the bounds of their distinct territories, and agree on limits between them and their neighbours; and by laws within themselves settled the properties of those of the same society: for we see that in that part of the world which was first inhabited, and therefore like to be best peopled, even as low down as Abraham's time, they wandered with their flocks, and their herds, which was their substance, freely up and down; and this Abraham did, in a country where he was a stranger. Whence it is plain, that at least a great part of the land lay in common; that the inhabitants valued it not, nor claimed property in any more than they made use of. But when there was not room enough in the same place for their herds to feed together, they by consent, as Abraham and Lot did, Gen. xiii. 5, separated and enlarged their pasture, where it best liked them. And for the same reason Esau went from his father, and his brother, and planted in mount Seir, Gen. xxxvi. 6.

39. And thus, without supposing any private dominion and property in Adam, over all the world, exclusive of all other men, which can no way be proved, nor any one's property be made out from it; but supposing the world given, as it was, to the children of men in common, we see how labour could make men distinct titles to several parcels of it, for their private uses; wherein there could be no doubt of right, no room for quarrel.

40. Nor is it so strange, as perhaps before consideration it may appear, that the property of labour should be able to overbalance the community of land: for it is labour indeed that put the difference of value on every thing; and let any one consider what the difference is between an acre of land planted with tobacco or sugar, sown with wheat or barley, and an acre of the same land lying in common, without any husbandry upon it, and he will find, that the improvement of labour makes the far greater part of the value. I think it will be but a very modest computation to say, that of the products of the earth useful to the life of man, nine-tenths are the effects of labour; nay, if we will rightly estimate things as they come to our use, and cast up the several expenses about them, what in them is purely owing to nature, and what to labour, we shall find, that in most of them ninety-nine hundredths are wholly to be put on the account of labour.

41. There cannot be a clearer demonstration of any thing, than several nations of the Americans are of this, who are rich in land, and poor in all the comforts of life; whom nature having furnished as liberally as any other people with the materials of plenty, *i.e.* a fruitful soil, apt to produce in abundance what might serve for food, raiment, and delight; yet, for want of improving it by labour, have not one-hundredth part of the conveniencies we enjoy: and a king of a large and fruitful territory there feeds, lodges, and is clad worse than a day-labourer in England.

42. To make this a little clear, let us but trace some of the ordinary provisions of life, through their several progresses, before they come to our use, and see how much of their value they receive from human industry. Bread, wine, and cloth, are things of daily use, and great plenty; yet notwithstanding, acorns, water, and leaves, or skins, must be our bread, drink, and clothing, did not labour furnish us with these more useful commodities: for whatever bread is more worth than acorns, wine than water, and cloth or silk than leaves, skins, or moss, that is wholly owing to labour and industry; the one of these being the food and raiment which unassisted nature furnishes us with; the other, provisions which our industry and pains prepare for us; which, how much they exceed the other in value, when any one hath computed, he will then see how much labour makes the far greatest part of the value of things we enjoy in this world: and the ground which produces the materials is scarce to be reckoned in as any, or, at most, but a very small part of it; so little, that even amongst us, land that is left wholly to nature, that hath no improvement of pasturage, tillage, or planting, is called, as indeed it is, waste; and we shall find the benefit of it amount to little more than nothing.

This shows how much numbers of men are to be preferred to largeness of dominions; and that the increase of lands, and the right of employing of them, is the great art of government: and that prince, who shall be so wise and godlike, as by established laws of liberty to secure protection and encouragement to the honest industry of mankind, against the oppression of power and narrowness of party, will quickly be too hard for his neighbours: but this by the by. To return to the argument in hand.

43. An acre of land, that bears here twenty bushels of wheat, and another in America, which, with the same husbandry, would do the like, are, without doubt, of the same natural intrinsic

value: but yet the benefit mankind receives from the one in a year is worth 5*l.* and from the other possibly not worth a penny, if all the profit an Indian received from it were to be valued, and sold here; at least, I may truly say, not one thousandth. It is labour, then, which puts the greatest part of the value upon land, without which it would scarcely be worth any thing: it is to that we owe the greatest part of all its useful products; for all that the straw, bran, bread, of that acre of wheat, is more worth than the product of an acre of as good land, which lies waste, is all the effect of labour: for it is not barely the ploughman's pains, the reaper's and thresher's toil, and the baker's sweat, is to be counted into the bread we eat; the labour of those who broke the oxen, who digged and wrought the iron and stones, who felled and framed the timber employed about the plough, mill, oven, or any other utensils, which are a vast number, requisite to this corn, from its being seed to be sown to its being made bread, must all be charged on the account of labour, and received as an effect of that: nature and the earth furnished only the almost worthless materials, as in themselves. It would be a strange "catalogue of things, that industry provided and made use of, about every loaf of bread," before it came to our use, if we could trace them; iron, wood, leather, bark, timber, stone, bricks, coals, lime, cloth, dyeing, drugs, pitch, tar, masts, ropes, and all the materials made use of in the ship, that brought any of the commodities used by any of the workmen, to any part of the work: all which it would be almost impossible, at least too long, to reckon up.

44. From all which it is evident, that though the things of nature are given in common, yet man, by being master of himself, and "proprietor of his own person, and the actions or labour of it, had still in himself the great foundation of property;" and that which made up the greater part of what he applied to the support or comfort of his being, when invention and arts had improved the conveniencies of life, was perfectly his own, and did not belong in common to others.

45. Thus labour, in the beginning, gave a right of property wherever any one was pleased to employ it upon what was common, which remained a long while the far greater part, and is yet more than mankind makes use of. Men, at first, for the most part, contented themselves with what unassisted nature offered to their necessities: and though afterwards, in some parts of the world, (where the increase of people and stock, with the use of

money, had made land scarce, and so of some value) the several communities settled the bounds of their distinct territories, and by laws within themselves regulated the properties of the private men of their society, and so, by compact and agreement, settled the property which labour and industry began: and the leagues that have been made between several states and kingdoms, either expressly or tacitly disowning all claim and right to the land in the others' possession, have, by common consent, given up their pretences to their natural common right, which originally they had to those countries, and so have, by positive agreement, settled a property amongst themselves, in distinct parts and parcels of the earth; yet there are still great tracts of ground to be found, which (the inhabitants thereof not having joined with the rest of mankind in the consent of the use of their common money) lie waste, and are more than the people who dwell on it do or can make use of, and so still lie in common; though this can scarce happen amongst that part of mankind that have consented to the use of money.

46. The greatest part of things really useful to the life of man, and such as the necessity of subsisting made the first commoners of the world look after, as it doth the Americans now, are generally things of short duration; such as, if they are not consumed by use, will decay and perish of themselves: gold, silver, and diamonds, are things that fancy or agreement hath put the value on, more than real use, and the necessary support of life. Now of those good things which nature hath provided in common, every one had a right (as hath been said) to as much as he could use, and property in all that he could effect with his labour; all that his industry could extend to, to alter from the state nature had put it in, was his. He that gathered a hundred bushels of acorns or apples, had thereby a property in them; they were his goods as soon as gathered. He was only to look that he used them before they spoiled, else he took more than his share, and robbed others. And indeed it was a foolish thing, as well as dishonest, to hoard up more than he could make use of. If he gave away a part to any body else, so that it perished not uselessly in his possession, these he also made use of. And if he also bartered away plums, that would have rotted in a week, for nuts that would last good for his eating a whole year, he did no injury; he wasted not the common stock; destroyed no part of the portion of the goods that belonged to others, so long as nothing perished uselessly in his hands. Again, if he would give

his nuts for a piece of metal, pleased with its colour; or exchange his sheep for shells, or wool for a sparkling pebble or a diamond, and keep those by him all his life, he invaded not the right of others; he might heap as much of these durable things as he pleased; the exceeding of the bounds of his just property not lying in the largeness of his possession, but the perishing of any thing uselessly in it.

47. And thus came in the use of money, some lasting thing that men might keep without spoiling, and that by mutual consent men would take in exchange for the truly useful, but perishable supports of life.

48. And as different degrees of industry were apt to give men possessions in different proportions, so this invention of money gave them the opportunity to continue and enlarge them: for supposing an island, separate from all possible commerce with the rest of the world, wherein there were but an hundred families, but there were sheep, horses, and cows, with other useful animals, wholesome fruits, and land enough for corn for a hundred thousand times as many, but nothing in the island, either because of its commonness, or perishableness, fit to supply the place of money; what reason could any one have there to enlarge his possessions beyond the use of his family and a plentiful supply to its consumption, either in what their own industry produced, or they could barter for like perishable, useful commodities with others? Where there is not something, both lasting and scarce, and so valuable, to be hoarded up, there men will not be apt to enlarge their possessions of land, where it ever so rich, ever so free for them to take: for I ask, what would a man value ten thousand, or an hundred thousand acres of excellent land, ready cultivated, and well stocked too with cattle, in the middle of the inland parts of America, where he had no hopes of commerce with other parts of the world, to draw money to him by the sale of the product? It would not be worth the enclosing, and we should see him give up again to the wild common of nature, whatever was more than would supply the conveniencies of life to be had there for him and his family.

49. Thus in the beginning all the world was America, and more so than that is now; for no such thing as money was any where known. Find out something that hath the use and value of money amongst his neighbours, you shall see the same man will begin presently to enlarge his possessions.

50. But since gold and silver, being little useful to the life

of man in proportion to food, raiment, and carriage, has its value only from the consent of men, whereof labour yet makes, in great part, the measure; it is plain, that men have agreed to a disproportionate and unequal possession of the earth; they having, by a tacit and voluntary consent, found out a way how a man may fairly possess more land than he himself can use the product of, by receiving, in exchange for the overplus, gold and silver, which may be hoarded up without injury to any one; these metals not spoiling or decaying in the hands of the possessor. This partage of things in an inequality of private possessions, men have made practicable out of the bounds of society, and without compact; only by putting a value on gold and silver, and tacitly agreeing in the use of money: for in governments, the laws regulate the right of property, and the possession of land is determined by positive constitutions.

51. And thus, I think, it is very easy to conceive, "how labour could at first begin a title of property" in the common things of nature, and how the spending it upon our uses bounded it. So that there could then be no reason of quarrelling about title, nor any doubt about the largeness of possession it gave. Right and conveniency went together; for as a man had a right to all he could employ his labour upon, so he had no temptation to labour for more than he could make use of. This left no room for controversy about the title, nor for encroachment on the right of others; what portion a man carved to himself was easily seen: and it was useless, as well as dishonest, to carve himself too much, or take more than he needed.

The Doctrine of Continuing Majorities

Thomas Jefferson

(1743-1826)

In his Essay Concerning Human Understading *John Locke proposed that the human mind was like a* tabula rasa, *a blank tablet, on which experiences were etched. Aside from the philosophical importance of this metaphor, the idea had tremendous consequences for political theory. One of the chief implications of this notion was that past political relations had no special virtues and should always be reexamined in the light of current needs. Are we to be bound in our political behavior by the actions of our forefathers? Thomas Jefferson, much influenced by Locke and one of America's greatest forefathers, answered a resounding "No!"*

During the early years of the United States there was considerable argument about the continuity of traditional political and economic arrangements. For example, Jefferson's distant cousin, John Marshall, Chief Justice of the U.S. Supreme

Court, considered the Constitution a contract in perpetuity that was equally binding on future generations as it was on the contracting one. In opposition to this posture Jefferson formulated what political scientists have come to call his "Doctrine of Continuing Majorities." Central to his thesis is the thought that the living should not be bound by the dead, in economics, law, government, science, or the arts. Every generation, he held, has the right to change the laws to suit its current needs, and every new generation constitutes a new majority. Moreover, Jefferson held, men should occupy political office on the basis of merit rather than inherited privilege. At the heart of Jefferson's doctrine was an unquestioning faith in the common people.

TO ROBERT J. GARNETT

Monticello, February 14, 1824

THE real friends of the constitution in its federal form, if they wish it to be immortal, should be attentive by amendments to make it keep pace with the advance of the age in science and experience. Instead of this, the European governments have resisted reformation, until the people, seeing no other resource, undertake it themselves by force, their only weapon, and work it out through blood, desolation, and long-continued anarchy.

TO JOHN CARTWRIGHT

Monticello, June 5, 1824

You will perceive by these details that we have not yet so far perfected our constitutions as to venture to make them unchangeable. But still, in their present state, we consider them not otherwise changeable than by the authority of the people, on a special election of representatives for that purpose expressly; they are until then the *lex legum*.

But can they be made unchangeable? Can one generation bind another, and all others, in succession forever? I think not. The Creator has made the earth for the living, not the dead. (Rights and powers can only belong to persons, not to things, not to mere matter unendowed with will.) The dead are not even things. The particles of matter which composed their bodies make part now of the bodies of other animals, vegetables, or minerals of a thousand forms. To what then are attached the rights and powers they held while in the form of men? A generation may bind itself as long as its majority continues in life; when that has disappeared, another majority is in place, holds all the rights and powers their predecessors once held, and may change their laws and institutions to suit themselves. Nothing then is unchangeable but the inherent and unalienable rights of man.

TO SAMUEL KERCHEVAL

Monticello, July 12, 1816

Where then is our republicanism to be found? Not in our Constitution certainly, but merely in the spirit of our people. That would oblige even a despot to govern us republicanly. Owing to this spirit, and to nothing in the form of our Constitution, all things have gone well. But this fact, triumphantly misquoted by the enemies of reformation, is not the fruit of our Constitution, but has prevailed in spite of it. Our functionaries have done well, because generally honest men. If any were not so, they feared to show it.

But it will be said, it is easier to find faults than to amend them. I do not think their amendments so difficult as is pretended. Only lay down true principles, and adhere to them inflexibly. Do not be frightened into their surrender by the alarms of the timid, or the croakings of wealth against the ascendency of the people. . . . I am not among those who fear the people. They, and not the rich, are our dependence for continued freedom.

Some men look at constitutions with sanctimonious reverence, and deem them like the ark of the covenant, too sacred to be touched. They ascribe to the men of the preceding age a wisdom more than human, and suppose what they did to be beyond amendment. I knew that age well; I belonged to it, and labored with it. It deserved well of its country. It was very like the present, but without the experience of the present; and forty years of experience in government is worth a century of book-reading; and this they would say themselves, were they to rise from the dead. I am certainly not an advocate for frequent and untried changes in laws and constitutions. I think moderate imperfections had better be borne with because, when once known, we accommodate ourselves to them, and find practical means of correcting their ill effects. But I know also, that laws and institutions must go hand in hand with the progress of the human mind. As that becomes more developed, more enlightened, as new discoveries are made, new truths disclosed, and manners and opinions change with the change of circumstances, institutions must advance also, and keep pace with the times. We might as well require a man to wear still the coat which fitted him when a boy, as civilized society to remain ever under the regimen of their barbarous ancestors. It is this preposterous idea which has lately deluged Europe in blood. Their monarchs, instead of wisely yielding to the gradual change of circumstances, of favoring progressive accommodation to progressive improvement, have clung to old abuses, entrenched themselves behind steady habits, and obliged their subjects to seek through blood and violence rash and ruinous innovations, which, had they been referred to the peaceful deliberations and collected wisdom of the nation, would have been put into acceptable and salutary forms. Let us follow no such examples, nor weakly believe that one generation is not as capable as another of taking care of itself, and of ordering its own affairs. Let us, as our sister States have done, avail ourselves of our reason and experience, to correct the crude essays of our first and unexperienced, although wise, virtuous, and well-meaning councils. And lastly, let us provide in our Constitution for its revision at stated periods. What these periods should be, nature herself indicates. By the European tables of mortality, of the adults living at any one moment of time, a majority will be dead in about nineteen years. At the end of that period then, a new majority is come into place; or, in other words, a new generation. Each generation is as independent of the one preceding, as that was of all which had gone before. It has then, like them, a right to choose for itself the form of government it believes most promotive of its own happiness; consequently, to accommodate to the circumstances in which it finds itself, that received from its predecessors; and it is for the peace and good of mankind, that a solemn opportunity of doing this every nineteen or twenty years, should be provided by the Constitution; so that it may be handed on, with periodical repairs, from generation to generation, to the end of time, if anything human can so long endure.

This corporeal globe, and everything upon it, belong to its present corporeal inhabitants, during their generation. They alone have a right to direct what is the concern of themselves alone, and to declare the law of that direction; and this declaration can only be made by their majority. That majority, then, has a right to depute representatives to a convention, and to make the Constitution what they think will be the best for themselves.

TO JAMES MADISON

Paris, September 6, 1789

The question, whether one generation of men has a right to bind another, seems never to have been started either on this or our side of the water. Yet it is a question of such consequences as not only to merit decision, but place also among the fundamental principles of every government. The course of reflection in which we are immersed here, on the elementary principles of society, has presented this question to my mind; and that no such obligation can be transmitted, I think very capable of proof. I set out on this ground, which I suppose to be self-evident, that the *earth belongs in usufruct to the living;* that the dead have neither powers nor rights over it. The portion occupied by any individual ceases to be his when himself ceases to be, and reverts to the society. If the society has formed no rules for the appropriation of its lands in severality, it will be taken by the first occupants, and these will generally be the wife and children of the decedent. If they have formed rules of appropriation, those rules may give it to the wife and children, or to some one of them, or to the legatee of the deceased. So they may give it to its creditor. But the child, the legatee or creditor, takes it, not by natural right, but by a law of the society of which he is a member, and to which he is subject. Then, no man can, by *natural right,* oblige the lands he occupied, or the persons who succeed him in that occupation, to the payment of debts contracted by him. For if he could, he might during his own life, eat up the usufruct of the lands for several generations to come; and then the lands would belong to the dead, and not to the living, which is the reverse of our principle.

What is true of every member of the society, individually, is true of them all collectively; since the rights of the whole can be no more than the sum of the rights of the individuals. To keep our ideas clear when applying them to a multitude, let us suppose a whole generation of men to be born on the same day, to attain mature age on the same day, and to die on the same day, leaving a succeeding generation in the moment of attaining their mature age, all together. Let the ripe age be supposed of twenty-one years, and their period of life thirty-four years more, that being the average term given by the bills of mortality to persons of twenty-one years of age. Each successive generation would, in this way, come and go off the stage at a fixed moment, as individuals do now. Then I say, the earth belongs to each of these generations during its course, fully and in its own right. The second generation receives it clear of the debts and incumbrances of the first, the third of the second, and so on. For if the first could charge it with a debt, then the earth would belong to the dead and not to the living. . . .

To render this conclusion palpable, suppose that Louis the XIV. and XV. had contracted debts in the name of the French nation, to the amount of ten thousand milliards, and that the whole had been contracted in Holland. The interest of this sum would be five hundred milliards, which is the whole rent-roll or net proceeds of the territory of France. Must the present generation of men have retired from the territory in which nature produces them, and ceded it to the Dutch creditors? No; they have the same rights over the soil on which they were produced, as the preceding generations had. They derive these rights not from them, but from nature. They, then, and their soil are, by nature, clear of the debts of their predecessors. To present this in another point of view, suppose Louis XV. and his contemporary generation, had said to the money lenders of Holland, give us money, that we may eat, drink, and be merry in our day; and on condition you will demand no interest till the end of thirty-four years, you shall then, forever after, receive an annual interest of fifteen per cent. The money is lent on these conditions, is divided among the people, eaten, drunk, and squandered. Would the present generation be obliged to apply the produce of the earth and of their labor, to replace their dissipations? Not at all.

I suppose that the received opinion, that the public debts of one generation devolve on the next, has been suggested by our seeing, habitually, in private life, that he who succeeds to lands is required to pay the debts of his predecessor; without considering that this requisition is municipal only, not moral, flowing from the will of the society, which has found it convenient to appropriate the lands of a decedent on the condition of a payment of his debts; but that between society and society, or generation and generation, there is no municipal obligation, no umpire but the law of nature.

On similar ground it may be proved, that no society can make a perpetual constitution, or even a perpetual law. The earth belongs always to the living generation; they may manage it, then, and what proceeds from it, as they please, during their usufruct. They are masters, too, of their own persons, and consequently may govern them as they please. But persons and property make the sum of the objects of government. The constitution and the laws of their predecessors are extinguished then, in their natural course, with those whose will gave them being. This could preserve that being, till it ceased to be itself, and no longer. Every constitution, then, and every law, naturally expires at the end of thirty-four years. If it be enforced longer, it is an act of force, and not of right. It may be said, that the succeeding generation exercising, in fact, the power of repeal, this leaves them as free as if the constitution or law had been expressly limited to thirty-four years only. In the first place, this objection admits the right, in proposing an equivalent. But the power of repeal is not an equivalent. It might be, indeed, if every form of government were so perfectly contrived, that the will of the majority could always be obtained, fairly and without impediment. But this is true of no form. The people cannot assemble themselves; their representation is unequal and vicious. Various checks are opposed to every legislative proposition. Factions get possession of the public councils, bribery corrupts them, personal interests lead them astray from the general interests of their constituents; and other impediments arise, so as to prove to every practical man, that a law of limited duration is much more manageable than one which needs a repeal.

This principle, that the earth belongs to the living and not to the dead, is of very extensive application and consequences in every country, and most especially in France. It enters into the resolution of the questions, whether the nation may change the descent of lands holden in tail; whether they may change the appropriation of lands given anciently to the church, to hospitals, colleges, orders of chivalry, and otherwise in perpetuity; whether they may abolish the charges and privileges attached on lands, including the whole catalogue, ecclesiastical and feudal; it goes to hereditary offices, authorities and jurisdictions, to hereditary orders, distinctions and appellations, to perceptual monopolies in commerce, the arts or sciences, with a long train of *et ceteras*. . . .

TO JOHN W. EPPES

Monticello, June 24, 1813

It is a wise rule, and should be fundamental in a government disposed to cherish its credit, and at the same time to restrain the use of it within the limits of its faculties, "never to borrow a dollar without laying a tax in the same instant for paying the interest annually, and the principal within a given term; and to consider that tax as pledged to the creditors on the public faith." On such a pledge as this, sacredly observed, a government may always command, on a reasonable interest, all the lendable money of their citizens, while the necessity of an equivalent tax is a salutary warning to them and their constituents against oppressions, bankruptcy and its inevitable consequence, revolution. But the terms of redemption must be moderate, and at any rate within the limits of their rightful powers. But what limits, it will be asked, does this prescribe to their powers? What is to hinder them from creating a perpetual debt? The laws of nature, I answer. The earth belongs to the living, not to the dead. . . . We may consider each generation as a distinct nation, with a right, by the will of its majority, to bind themselves, but none to bind the succeeding generation, more than the inhabitants of another country. . . . Suppose the annual births of the State of New York to be twenty-three thousand nine hundred and ninety-four, the whole number of its inhabitants, according to Buffon, will be six hundred and seventeen thousand seven hundred and three, of all ages. Of these there would constantly be two hundred and sixty-nine thousand two hundred and eighty-six minors, and three hundred and forty-eight thousand four hundred and seventeen adults, of which last, one hundred and seventy-four thousand two hundred and nine will be a majority. Suppose that majority, on the first day of the year 1794, had borrowed a sum of money equal to the fee-simple value of the State, and to have consumed it in eating, drinking and making merry in their day; or, if you please, in quarrelling and fighting with their unoffending neighbors. Within eighteen years and eight months, one-half of the adult citizens were dead. Till then, being the majority, they might rightfully levy the interest of their debt annually on themselves and their fellow revelers, or fellow champions. But at that period, say at this moment, a new majority have come into place, in their own right, and not under the rights, the conditions, or laws of their predecessors. Are they bound to acknowledge the debt, to consider the preceding generation as having had a right to eat up the whole soil of their country, in the course of a life, to alienate it from them, (for it would be an alienation to the creditors,) and would they think themselves either legally or morally bound to give up their country and emigrate to another for subsistence? Every one will say no; that the soil is the gift of God to the living, as much as it had been to the deceased generation; and that the laws of nature impose no obligation on them to pay this debt. And although, like some other natural rights, this has not yet entered into any declaration of rights, it is no less a law, and ought to be acted on by honest governments. It is, at the same time, a salutary curb on the spirit of war and indebtment, which, since the modern theory of the perpetuation of debt, has drenched the earth with blood, and crushed its inhabitants under burdens ever accumulating.

TO JOHN ADAMS

Monticello, October 28, 1813

I agree with you that there is a natural aristocracy among men. The grounds of this are virtue and talents. Formerly, bodily powers gave place among the aristoi. But since the invention of gunpowder has armed the weak as well as the strong with missile death, bodily strength, like beauty, good humor, politeness and other accomplishments, has become but an auxiliary ground of distinction. There is also an artificial aristocracy, founded on wealth and birth, without either virtue or talents; for with these it would belong to the first class. The natural aristocracy I consider as the most precious gift of nature, for the instruction, the trusts, and government of society. And indeed, it would have been inconsistent in creation to have formed man for the social state, and not to have provided virtue and wisdom enough to manage the concerns of the society. May we not even say, then that form of government is the best, which provides the most effectually for a pure selection of these natural aristoi into the offices of government.

The artificial aristocracy is a mischievous ingredient in government, and provision should be made to prevent its ascendency. On the question, what is the best provision, you and I differ; but we differ as rational friends, using the free exercise of our own reason, and mutually indulging its errors. You think it best to put the pseudo-aristoi into a separate chamber of legislation where they may be hindered from doing mischief by their co-ordinate branches and where, also, they may be a protection to wealth against the agrarian and plundering enterprises of the majority of the people. I think that to give them power in order to prevent them from doing mischief, is arming them for it, and increasing instead of remedying the evil. For if the co-ordinate branches can arrest their action, so may they that of the co-ordinates. Mischief may be done negatively as well as positively. Of this, a cabal in the Senate of the United States has furnished many proofs. Nor do I believe them necessary to protect the wealthy; because enough of these will find their way into every branch of the legislation, to protect themselves. From fifteen to twenty legislatures of our own, in action for thirty years past, have proved that no fears of an equalization of property are to be apprehended from them. I think the best remedy is exactly that provided by all our constitutions, to leave to the citizens the free election and separation of the aristoi from the pseudo-aristoi, of the wheat from the chaff. In general they will elect the really good and wise. In some instances, wealth may corrupt, and birth blind them; but not in sufficient degree to endanger the society.

It is probable that our difference of opinion may, in some measure, be produced by a difference of character in those among whom we live. From what I have seen of Massachusetts and

Connecticut myself, and still more from what I have heard, and the character given of the former by yourself, who know them so much better, there seems to be in those two States a traditionary reverence for certain families, which has rendered the offices of the government nearly hereditary in those families. I presume that from an early period of your history, members of those families happening to possess virtue and talents, have honestly exercised them for the good of the people, and by their services have endeared their names to them.

In Virginia . . . laws, drawn by myself, laid the axe to the foot of pseudo-aristocracy. And had another which I prepared been adopted by the legislature, our work would have been complete. It was a bill for the more general diffusion of learning. This proposed to divide every county into wards of five or six miles square, like your townships; to establish in each ward a free school for reading, writing and common arithmetic; to provide for the annual selection of the best subjects from these schools, who might receive, at the public expense, a higher degree of education at a district school; and from these district schools to select a certain number of the most promising subjects, to be completed at an university, where all the useful sciences should be taught. Worth and genius would thus have been sought out from every condition of life, and completely prepared by education for defeating the competition of wealth and birth for public trusts.

With respect to aristocracy, we should further consider, that before the establishment of the American States, nothing was known to history but the man of the old world, crowded within limits either small or overcharged, and steeped in the vices which that situation generates. A government adapted to such men would be one thing; but a very different one, that for the man of these States. . . .

But even in Europe a change has sensibly taken place in the mind of man. Science had liberated the ideas of those who read and reflect, and the American example had kindled feelings of right in the people. An insurrection has consequently begun, of science, talents, and courage, against rank and birth, which have fallen into contempt. It has failed in its first effort, because the mobs of the cities, the instrument used for its accomplishment, debased by ignorance, poverty, and vice, could not be restrained to rational action. But the world will recover from the panic of this first catastrophe. Science is progressive, and talents and enterprise on the alert. Resort may be had to the people of the country, a more governable power from their principles and subordination; and rank, and birth, and tinsel-aristocracy will finally shrink into significance, even there. . . .

I have thus stated my opinion on a point on which we differ, not with a view to controversy, for we are both too old to change opinions which are the result of a long life of inquiry and reflection; but on the suggestions of a former letter of yours, that we ought not to die before we have explained ourselves to each other.

TO HENRY LEE

Monticello, August 10, 1824

Men by their constitutions are naturally divided into two parties: 1. Those who fear and distrust the people, and wish to draw all powers from them into the hands of the higher classes. 2. Those who identify themselves with the people, have confidence in them, cherish and consider them as the most honest and safe, although not the most wise depository of the public inetrests. In every country these two parties exist, and in every one where they are free to think, speak, and write, they will declare themselves. Call them, therefore, Liberals and Serviles, Jacobins and Ultras, Whigs and Tories, Republicans and Federalists, Aristocrats and Democrats, or by whatever name you please, they are the same parties still, and pursue the same object. The last appellation of Aristocrats and Democrats is the true one expressing the essence of all.

from

Speech on the Mexican War

Abraham Lincoln

(1809-1865)

Widespread opposition to war is not confined to twentieth-century American history. In the mid-nineteenth century there was considerable opposition to the United States' war with Mexico. In 1847 the state legislature of Massachusetts declared that the war was unconstitutional, leading authors such as Emerson and Thoreau wrote heated tracts against the American attack on Mexico, and in 1848 Congressman Abraham Lincoln of Illinois delivered a stinging rebuke to President James K. Polk for using subterfuge to lure the American people into an aggressive war.

Aside from pointing to the lack of presidential credibility and the absence of rational purpose to the war, Lincoln's speech is interesting for its explicit statement of a people's right to revolution. Lincoln's contention had august precedence, located as it was not only in the Jeffersonian principles of the Declaration of Independence, but also in the political writings of John Locke and earlier in the various defences of regicide by John Milton.

In the Apology *Socrates prophesied that if the state suppressed dissent it would face revolution. Some 2500 years later the political and intellectual leaders of the western world have worked their way to the same conclusion. It yet remains to be seen whether the power structure of government can do so also.*

January 12, 1848

Mr. Chairman: Some if not all the gentlemen on the other side of the House who have addressed the committee within the last two days have spoken rather complainingly, if I have rightly understood them, of the vote given a week or ten days ago declaring that the war with Mexico was unnecessarily and unconstitutionally commenced by the President. I admit that such a vote should not be given in mere party wantonness, and that the one given is justly censurable, if it have no other or better foundation. I am one of those who joined in that vote; and I did so under my best impression of the truth of the case. How I got this impression, and how it may possibly be remedied, I will now try to show. When the war began, it was my opinion that all those who because of knowing too little, or because of knowing too much, could not conscientiously oppose the conduct of the President in the beginning of it should nevertheless, as good citizens and patriots, remain silent on that point, at least till the war should be ended. . . .

The President, in his first war message of May, 1846, declares that the soil was ours on which hostilities were commenced by Mexico, and he repeats that declaration almost in the same language in each successive annual message, thus showing that he deems that point a highly essential one. In the importance of that point I entirely agree with the President.

. . . . .

It is a singular fact that if any one should declare the President sent the army into the midst of a settlement of Mexican people who had never submitted, by consent or by force, to the authority of Texas or of the United States, and that there and thereby the first blood of the war was shed, there is not one word in all the President has said which would either admit or deny the declaration. This strange omission it does seem to me could not have occurred but by design. My way of living leads me to be about the courts of justice; and there I have sometimes seen a good lawyer, struggling for his client's neck in a desperate case, employing every artifice to work round, befog, and cover up with many words some point arising in the case which he dared not admit and yet could not deny. Party bias may help to make it appear so, but with all the allowance I can make for such bias, it still does appear to me that just such, and from just such necessity, is the President's struggle in this case. . . .

I propose to state my understanding of the true rule for ascertaining the boundary between Texas and Mexico. It is that wherever Texas was exercising jurisdiction was hers; and wherever Mexico was exercising jurisdiction was hers; and that whatever separated the actual exercise of jurisdiction of the one from that of the other was the true boundary between them. If, as is probably true, Texas was exercising jurisdiction along the western bank of the Nueces, and Mexico was exercising it along the eastern bank of the Rio Grande, then neither river was the boundary; but the uninhabited country between the two was. The extent of our territory in that region depended not on any treaty-fixed boundary (for no treaty had attempted it), but on revolution. Any people anywhere being inclined and having the power have the right to rise up and shake off the existing government, and form a new one that suits them better. This is a most valuable, a most sacred right—a right which we hope and believe is to liberate the world. Nor is this right confined to cases in which the whole people of an existing government may choose to exercise it. Any portion of such people that can may revolutionize and make their own of so much of the territory as they inhabit. More than this, a majority of any portion of such people may revolutionize, putting down a minority, intermingled with or near about them, who may oppose this movement. Such minority was precisely the case of the Tories of our own revolution. It is a quality of revolutions not to go by old lines or old laws; but to break up both, and make new ones.

As to the country now in question, we bought it of France

in 1803, and sold it to Spain in 1819, according to the President's statements. After this, all Mexico, including Texas, revolutionized against Spain; still later Texas revolutionized against Mexico. In my view, just so far as she carried her resolution by obtaining the actual, willing or unwilling, submission of the people, so far the country was hers, and no farther. Now, sir, for the purpose of obtaining the very best evidence as to whether Texas had actually carried her revolution to the place where the hostilities of the present war commenced, let the President answer the interrogatories I proposed, as before mentioned, or some other similar ones. Let him answer fully, fairly, and candidly. Let him answer with facts and not with arguments. Let him remember he sits where Washington sat, and so remembering, let him answer as Washington would answer. As a nation should not, and the Almighty will not, be evaded, so let him attempt no evasion—no equivocation. And if, so answering, he can show that the soil was ours where the first blood of the war was shed—that it was not within an inhabited country, or, if within such, that the inhabitants had submitted themselves to the civil authority of Texas or of the United States, and that the same is true of the site of Fort Brown—then I am with him for his justification. In that case I shall be most happy to reverse the vote I gave the other day. I have a selfish motive for desiring that the Prseident may do this—I expect to gain some votes, in connection with the war, which, without his so doing, will be of doubtful propriety in my own judgment, but which will be free from the doubt if he does so. But if he can not or will not do this—if on any pretense or no pretense he shall refuse or omit it—then I shall be fully convinced of what I more than suspect already—that he is deeply conscious of being in the wrong; that he feels the blood of this war, like the blood of Abel, is crying to Heaven against him; that originally having some strong motive—what, I will not stop now to give my opinion concerning—to involve the two countries in a war, and trusting to escape scrutiny by fixing the public gaze upon the exceeding brightness of military glory—that attractive rainbow that arises in showers of blood—that serpent's eye that charms to destroy—he plunged into it, and has swept on and on till, disappointed in his calculation of the ease with which Mexico might be subdued, he now finds himself he knows not where. How like the half-insane mumbling of a fever dream is the whole war part of his late message! At one time telling us that

Mexico has nothing whatever that we can get but territory; at another showing us how we can support the war by levying contributions on Mexico. At one time urging the national honor, the security of the future, the prevention of foreign interference, and even the good of Mexico herself as among the objects of the war; at another telling us that "to reject indemnity, by refusing to accept a cession of territory, would be to abandon all our just demands, and to wage the war bearing all its expenses, without a purpose or definite object." So then this national honor, security of the future, and everything but territorial indemnity may be considered the no-purpose and indefinite objects of the war! But, having it now settled that territorial indemnity is the only object, we are urged to seize, by legislation here, all that he was content to take a few months ago, and the whole province of Lower California to boot, and to still carry on the war—to take all we are fighting for, and still fight on. Again, the President is resolved under all circumstances to have full territorial indemnity for the expenses of the war; but he forgets to tell us how we are to get the excess after those expenses shall have surpassed the value of the whole of the Mexican territory. So again, he insists that the separate national existence of Mexico shall be maintained; but he does not tell us how this can be done, after we shall have taken all her territory. Lest the questions I have suggested be considered speculative merely, let me be indulged a moment in trying to show they are not. The war has gone on some twenty months; for the expenses of which, together with an inconsiderable old score, the President now claims about one half of the Mexican territory, and that by far the better half, so far as concerns our ability to make anything out of it. It is comparatively uninhabited; so that we could establish land offices in it, and raise some money in that way. But the other half is already inhabited, as I understand it, tolerably densely for the nature of the country, and all its lands, or all that are valuable, already appropriated as private property. How then are we to make anything out of these lands with this encumbrance upon them? or how remove the encumbrance? I suppose no one would say we should kill the people, or drive them out, or make slaves of them; or confiscate their property. How, then, can we make much out of this part of the territory? If the prosecution of the war has in expenses already equaled the better half of the country, how long its future prosecution will be in equaling the less valuable half is not a speculative, but a practical, question, pressing closely upon us. And yet it is a question which the President seems never to have thought of. As to the mode of terminating the war and securing peace, the President is equally wandering and indefinite. First, it is to be done by a more vigorous prosecution of the war in the vital parts of the enemy's country; and after apparently talking himself tired on this point, the President drops down into a half-despairing tone, and tells us that "with a people distracted and divided by contending factions, and a government subject to constant changes by successive revolutions, the continued success of our arms may fail to secure a satisfactory peace." Then he suggests the propriety of wheedling the Mexican people to desert the counsels of their own leaders, and, trusting in our protestations, to set up a government from which we can secure a satisfactory peace; telling us that "this may become the only mode of obtaining such a peace." But soon he falls into a doubt of this too; and then drops back onto the already half-abandoned ground of "more vigorous prosecution." All this shows that the President is in nowise satisfied with his own positions. First he takes up one, and in attempting to argue us into it he argues himself out of it, then seizes another and goes through the same process, and then, confused at being able to think of nothing new, he snatches up the old one again, which he has some time before cast off. His mind, taxed beyond its power, is running hither and thither, like some tortured creature on a burning surface, finding no position on which it can settle down and be at ease.

Again, it is a singular omission in this message that it nowhere intimates when the President expects the war to terminate. At its beginning, General Scott was by this same President driven into disfavor, if not disgrace, for intimating that peace could not be conquered in less than three or four months. But now, at the end of about twenty months, during which time our arms have given us the most splendid successes, every department and every part, land and water, officers and privates, regulars and volunteers, doing all that men could do, and hundreds of things which it had ever before been thought men could not do—after all this, this same President gives us a long message, without showing us that as to the end he himself has even an imaginary conception. As I have before said, he knows not where he is. He is a bewildered, confounded, and miserably perplexed man. God grant he may be able to show there is not something about his conscience more painful than all his mental perplexity.

Society and Social Institutions

The Abbey of Theleme

Francois Rabelais

(c. 1495-1553)

The ground for Lockean liberalism is the belief that people are essentially good. A corollary of this faith is the belief that social institutions distort human character and are thus the source of much of society's ills. Locke was not the first, just as he was not the last, to hold this belief. Many before him argued somewhat the same and among the most outstanding of these was Rabelais. His Gargantua *and* Pantagruel *are marvelously robust satires on some of the major institutions of the late Middle Ages and early Renaissance. Among his favorite topics were education, marriage, and religion, in particular monastic life.*

In our excerpt from Gargantua *Rabelais provides us with a utopian vision of an ideal society, which he locates in a monastery, the medieval place for ideal societies. Of course Rabelais' ideal of monastic life was somewhat different from that which was current at the time. Spurning the growing puritanism and pious hypocrisy of his own day, Rabelais had his monastery devoted to the complete enjoyment of sensuous pleasure, to the complete freedom of all members of the community, and to the complete thoughtfulness of all social relations. There was but one rule that governed the new Rabelaisian order at the Abbey of Theleme: "Do What Thou Wilt."*

A monk himself, Rabelais' criticism of the monastic life was sharp and more often than not hit close to home. Both Gargantua *and* Pantagruel *were banned twice by the ecclesiastical authorities in France. However, Rabelais enjoyed the protection of some of the most powerful nobles of his day. Some of this aristocratic patronage seems to be reflected in our selection. It is interesting to note that the freedom and pleasures extended to the "well-bred" young people at the Abbey do not seem to apply to the servants who hover in the background and make the beautiful world possible.*

CHAPTER 52

HOW GARGANTUA CAUSED TO BE BUILT FOR THE MONK THE ABBEY OF THELEME

THERE was left only the monk to provide for, whom Gargantua would have made Abbot of Sevillé, but he refused it. He would have given him the Abbey of Bourgueil, or of Sanct Florent, which was better, or both, if it pleased him; but the monk gave him a very peremptory answer, that he would never take upon him the charge nor government of monks. For how shall I be able, said he, to rule over others, that have not full power and command of myself? If you think I have done you, or may hereafter do you any acceptable service, give me leave to found an abbey after my own mind and fancy. The motion pleased Gargantua very well, who thereupon offered him all the country of Theleme by the River of Loire, till within two leagues of the great forest of Port-Huaut. The monk then requested

Gargantua to institute his religious order contrary to all others. First then, said Gargantua, you must not build a wall about your convent, for all other abbeys are strongly walled and mured about. See, said the monk, and not without cause, where there is *mur* before, and *mur* behind, there is store of murmur, envy, and mutual conspiracy. Moreover, seeing there are certain convents in the world, whereof the custom is, if any women come in, I mean chaste and honest women, they immediately sweep the ground which they have trod upon; therefore was it ordained, that if any man or woman, entered into religious orders, should by chance come within this new abbey, all the rooms should be thoroughly washed and cleansed through which they had passed. And because in all other monasteries and nunneries all is compassed, limited, and regulated by hours, it was decreed that in this new structure there should be neither clock nor dial, but that according to the opportunities and incident occasions, all their hours should be disposed of; for, said Gargantua, the greatest loss of time that I know, is to count the hours. What good comes of it? Nor can there be any greater dotage in the world than for one to guide and direct his courses by the sound of a bell, and not by his own judgment and discretion.

Item, Because at that time they put no women into nunneries, but such as were either purblind, blinkards, lame, crooked, ill-favoured, mis-shapen, fools, senseless, spoiled, or corrupt; nor encloistered any men, but those that were either sickly, subject to defluxions, ill-bred louts, simple sots, or peevish trouble-houses. But to the purpose, said the monk. A woman that is neither fair nor good, to what use serves she? To make a nun of, said Gargantua. Yea, said the monk, to make shirts and smocks. Therefore was it ordained, that into this religious order should be admitted no women that were not fair, well-featured, and of a sweet disposition; nor men that were not comely, personable, and well conditioned.

Item, Because in the convents of women, men come not but underhand, privily, and by stealth; it was therefore enacted, that in this house there shall be no women in case there be not men, nor men in case there be not women.

Item, Because both men and women, that are received into religious orders after the expiring of their noviciat or probation year, were constrained and forced perpetually to stay there all the days of their life; it was therefore ordered, that all whatever, men or women, admitted within this abbey, should have full leave to depart with peace and contentment, whensoever it should seem good to them so to do.

Item, for that the religious men and women did ordinarily make three vows, to wit, those of chastity, poverty, and obedience; it was therefore constituted and appointed, that in this convent they might be honourably married, that they might be rich, and live at liberty. In regard of the legitimate time of the persons to be initiated, and years under and above which they were not capable of reception, the women were to be admitted from ten till fifteen, and the men from twelve till eighteen.

CHAPTER 53

HOW THE ABBEY OF THE THELEMITES WAS BUILT AND ENDOWED

For the fabric and furniture of the abbey, Gargantua caused to be delivered out in ready money seven and twenty hundred thousand, eight hundred and one and thirty of those golden rams of Berry, which have a sheet stamped on the one side, and a flowered cross on the other; and for every year until the whole work were completed, he allotted threescore nine thousand crowns of the sun, and as many of the seven stars, to be charged all upon the receipt of the custom. For the foundation and maintenance thereof for ever, he settled a perpetual fee-farm-rent of three and twenty hundred, threescore and nine thousand, five hundred and fourteen rose nobles, exempted from all homage, fealty, service, or burden whatsoever, and payable every year at the gate of the abbey; and of this, by letters patent passed a very good grant. The architecture was in a figure hexagonal, and in such a fashion, that in every one of the six corners there was built a great round tower of threescore feet in diameter, and were all of a like form and bigness. Upon the north-side ran along the river of Loire, on the bank whereof was situated the tower called Arctic. Going towards the east, there was another called Calaer, —the next following Anatole,—the next Mesembrine,—the next Hesperia, and the last Criere. Every tower was distant from the other space of three hundred and twelve paces. The whole edifice was every where six stories high, reckoning the cellars under ground for one. The second was arched after the fashion of a basket-handle, the rest were sealed with pure wainscot, flourished with Flanders fret-work, in the form of the foot of a lamp, and covered above with fine slates, with an indorsement of lead, carrying the antique figures of little puppets, and animals of all sorts, notably well suited to one another, and gilt, together with the gutters, which jetting without the walls from betwixt the cross bars in a diagonal figure, painted with gold and azure, reached to the very ground, where they ended into great conduit-pipes, which carried all away unto the river from under the house.

This same building was a hundred times more sumptuous and magnificent than ever was Bonnivet, Chambourg, or Chantilly; for there were in it nine thousand three hundred and two and thirty chambers, every one whereof had a withdrawing room, a handsome closet, a wardrobe, an oratory, and neat passage, leading into a great and spacious hall. Between every tower, in the midst of the said body of building, there was a pair of winding, such as we now call lanthorn stairs, whereof the steps were part of porphyry, which is a dark red marble, spotted with white, part of Numidian stone, which is a kind of yellowishly-streaked marble upon various colours, and part of serpentine marble, with light spots on a dark green ground, each of those steps being two and twenty feet in length, and three fingers thick, and the just number of twelve betwixt every rest, or, as we now term it, landing place. In every resting place were two fair antique arches where the light came in: and by those they went into a cabinet, made even with, and of the breadth of the said winding, and the re-ascending above the roofs of the house ending conically in a pavilion. By that vize or winding, they entered on every side into a great hall, and from the halls into the chambers. From the Arctic tower unto the Criere, were the fair great libraries in Greek, Latin, Hebrew, French, Italian and Spanish, respectively distributed in their several cantons, according to the diversity of these languages. In the midst there was a wonderful scalier or winding-stair, the entry whereof was without the house, in a vault or arch, six fathoms broad. It was made in such symmetry and largeness, that six men at arms with their lances in their rests might together in a breast ride all up to the very top of all the palace. From the tower Anatole to the Mesembrine were fair spacious galleries, all covered over and painted with the ancient prowesses, histories and descriptions of the world. In the midst thereof there was likewise such another ascent and gate, as we said there was on the river-side. Upon that gate was written in great antique letters that which followeth.

CHAPTER 54

THE INSCRIPTION SET UPON THE GREAT GATE OF THELEME

Here enter not vile bigots, hypocrites,
Externally devoted apes, base snites,
Puft up, wry-necked beasts, worse than the Huns,
Or Ostrogots, forerunners of baboons:
Cursed snakes, dissembling varlets, seeming sancts,
Slipshop caffards, beggars pretending wants,
Fat chuffcats, smell-feast knockers, doltish gulls,
Out-strouting cluster-fists, contentious bulls,
Fomenters of divisions and debates,
Elsewhere, not here, make sale of your deceits.
Your filthy trumperies
Stuffed with pernicious lies,
(Not worth a bubble)
Would only trouble
Our earthly paradise,
Your filthy trumperies.

Here enter not attorneys, barristers,
Nor bridle-champing law-practioners;
Clerks, commissaries, scribes, nor pharisees,
Wilful disturbers of the people's ease:
Judges, destroyers, with an unjust breath,
Of honest men, like dogs, ev'n unto death.
Your salary is at the gibbet-foot:
Go drink there! for we do not here fly out
On those excessive courses, which may draw
A waiting on your courts by suits in law.
Law-suits, debates, and wrangling
Hence are exil'd, and jangling.
Here we are very
Frolic and merry,
And free from all entangling,
Law-suits, debates, and wrangling.

Here enter not base pinching usurers,
Pelf-lickers, everlasting gatherers.
Gold-graspers, coin-grippers, gulpers of mists,

With harpy-griping claws, who, though your chests
Vast sums of money should to you afford,
Would ne'ertheless add more unto that hoard,
And yet not be content,—you clunchfists dastards,
Insatiable fiends, and Pluto's bastards,
Greedy devourers, chichy sneakbill rogues,
Hell-mastiffs gnaw your bones, you rav'nous dogs.
        You beastly-looking fellows,
        Reason doth plainly tell us,
            That we should not
            To you allot
        Room here, but at the gallows,
        You beastly-looking fellows.

Here enter not fond makers of demurs
In love adventures, peevish jealous curs,
Sad pensive dotards, raisers of garboyles,
Hags, goblins, ghosts, firebrands of household broils,
Nor dunkards, liars, cowards, cheaters, clowns,
Thieves, cannibals, faces o'ercast with frowns,
Nor lazy slugs, envious, covetous,
Nor blockish, cruel, nor too credulous,—
Here mangy, pocky folks shall have no place,
No ugly lusks, nor persons of disgrace.
        Grace, honour, praise, delight,
        Here sojourn day and night.
            Sound bodies lin'd
            With a good mind,
        Do here pursue with might
        Grace, honour, praise, delight.

Here enter you, and welcome from our hearts,
All noble sparks, endow'd with gallant parts.
This is the glorious place, which bravely shall
Afford wherewith to entertain you all.
Were you a thousand, here you shall not want
For any thing: for what you'll ask we'll grant.
Stay here you lively, jovial, handsome, brisk.
Gay, witty, frolic, cheerful, merry, frisk,
Spruce, jocund, courteous, furtherers of trades,
And in a word, all worthy, gentle blades.

Blades of heroic breasts
Shall taste here of the feasts,
  Both privily
  And civilly
Of the celestial guests,
Blades of heroic breasts.

Here enter you, pure, honest, faithful, true,
Expounders of the Scriptures old and new.
Whose glosses do not blind our reason, but
Make it to see the clearer, and who shut
Its passages from hatred, avarice.
Pride, factions, covenants, and all sort of vice.
Come, settle here a charitable faith,
Which neighbourly affection nourisheth.
And whose light chaseth all corrupters hence,
Of the blest word, from the aforesaid sense.
The Holy Sacred Word,
May it always afford
  T' us all in common,
  Both man and woman,
A spiritual shield and sword,
The Holy Sacred Word.

Here enter you all ladies of high birth,
Delicious, stately, charming, full of mirth,
Ingenious, lovely, miniard, proper, fair,
Magnetic, graceful, splendid, pleasant, rare,
Obliging, sprightly, virtuous, young, solacious,
Kind, neat, quick, feat, bright, compt, ripe, choice, dear, precious.
Alluring, courtly, comely, fine, complete.
Wise, personable, ravishing, and sweet,
Come joys enjoy. The Lord celestial
Hath given enough, wherewith to please us all.
Gold give us, God forgive us,
And from all woes relieve us;
  That we the treasure
  May reap of pleasure,
And shun whate'er is grievous,
Gold give us, God forgive us.

CHAPTER 55

WHAT MANNER OF DWELLING THE THELEMITES HAD

In the middle of the lower court there was a stately fountain of fair alabaster. Upon the top thereof stood the three Graces, with their cornucopias, or horns of abundance, and did jet out the water at their breasts, mouth, ears, eyes, and other open passages of the body. The inside of the buildings in this lower court stood upon great pillars of Cassydony stone, and Porphyry marble, made archwise after a goodly antique fashion. Within those were spacious galleries, long and large, adorned with curious pictures, the horns of bucks and unicorns; with rhinoceroses, water-horses, called hippopotames; the teeth and tusks of elephants, and other things well worth the beholding. The lodging of the ladies, for so we may call those gallant women, took up all from the tower Arctic unto the gate Mesembrine. The men possessed the rest. Before the said lodging of the ladies, that they might have their recreation, between the two first towers, on the outside, were placed the tiltyard, the barriers or lists for tournaments, the hippodrome or riding court, the theatre or public play-house, and natatory or place to swim in, with most admirable baths in three stages, situated above one another, well furnished with all necessary accommodation, and store of myrtle-water. By the riverside was the fair garden of pleasure, and in the midst of that the glorious labyrinth. Between the two other towers were the courts for the tennis and the baloon. Towards the tower Criere stood the orchard full of all fruit-trees, set and ranged in a quincuncial order. At the end of that was the great park, abounding with all sort of venison. Betwixt the third couple of towers were the butts and marks for shooting with a snap-work gun, an ordinary bow for common archery, or with a cross bow. The office-houses were without the tower Hesperia, of one story high. The stables were beyond the offices, and before them stood the falconry, managed by ostrich-keepers and falconers, very expert in the art, and it was yearly supplied and furnished by the Candians, Venetians, Sarmates, now called Moscoviters, with all sorts of most excellent hawks, eagles, gerfalcons, goshawks, sacres, lanners, falcons, sparhawks, merlins, and other kinds of them, so gentle and perfectly well manned, that, flying of themselves sometimes from the castle for their own disport, they would not fail to catch whatever they encountered. The venery, where the beagles and hounds were kept, was a little farther off, drawing towards the park.

All the halls, chambers, and closets or cabinets were richly hung with tapestry, and hangings of divers sorts, according to the variety of the seasons of the year. All the pavements and floors were covered with green cloth. The beds were all embroidered. In every back-chamber or withdrawing room there was a looking-glass of pure crystal set in a frame of fine gold, garnished all about with pearls, and was of such greatness, that it would represent to the full the whole lineaments and proportion of the person that stood before it. At the going out of the halls, which belong to the ladies' lodgings, were the perfumers and trimmers, through whose hands the gallants past when they were to visit the ladies. Those sweet artificers did every morning furnish the ladies' chambers with the spirit of roses, orange-flower-water, and angelica; and to each of them gave a little precious casket vapouring forth the most odoriferous exhalations of the choicest aromatical scents.

CHAPTER 56

HOW THE MEN AND WOMEN OF THE RELIGIOUS ORDER OF THELEME WERE APPARELLED

The ladies of the foundation of this order were apparelled after their own pleasure and liking. But, since that of their own accord and free will they have reformed themselves, their accoutrement is in manner as followeth. They wore stockings of scarlet crimson, or ingrained purple dye, which reached just three inches above the knee, having a list beautified with exquisite embroideries, and rare incisions of the cutter's art. Their garters were of the colour of their bracelets, and circled the knee a little both over and under. Their shoes, pumps and slippers were either of red, violet, or crimson velvet, pinked and jagged like lobster wadles.

Next to their smock they put on the pretty kirtle or vasquin of pure silk camblet: above that went the taffaty or tabby vardingale, of white, red, tawny grey, or of any other colour. Above this taffaty petticoat they had another of cloth of tissue, or brocade, embroidered with fine gold, and interlaced with needlework, or as they thought good, and according to the temperature and disposition of the weather, had their upper coats of satin, damask, or velvet, and those either orange, tawny, green, ash-coloured, blue, yellow, bright red, crimson, or white, and so forth; or had them of cloth of gold, cloth of silver, or some other choice stuff, enriched with purple, or embroidered according to the dignity of the festival days and times wherein they wore them.

Their gowns being still correspondent to the season, were either of cloth of gold frizzled with a silver-raised work; of red satin, covered with gold purl; of tabby, or taffaty, white, blue, black, tawny, &c., of silk serge, silk camblet, velvet, cloth of silver, silver tissue, cloth of gold, gold wire, figured velvet, or figured satin, tinselled and overcast with golden threads, in divers variously purfled draughts.

In the summer, some days, instead of gowns, they wore light handsome mantles, made either of the stuff of the aforesaid attire, or like Moresco rugs, of violet velvet frizzled, with a raised work of gold upon silver purl, or with a knotted cordwork, of gold embroidery, every where garnished with little Indian pearls. They always carried a fair panache, or plume of feathers, of the colour of their muff, bravely adorned and tricked out with glistering spangles of gold. In the winter time, they had their taffaty gowns of all colours, as above named, and those lined with the rich furrings of hind-wolves, or speckled linxes, black spotted weasels, martlet skins of Calabria, sables, and other costly furs of an inestimable value. Their beads, rings, bracelets, collars, carcanets, and neck-chains were all of precious stones, such as carbuncles, rubies, baleus, diamonds, sapphires, emeralds, turquoises, garnets, agates, beryles, and excellent margarites. Their head-dressing also varied with the season of the year, according to which they decked themselves. In winter it was of the French fashion; in the spring, of the Spanish; in summer, of the fashion of Tuscany, except only upon the holy days and Sundays, at which times they were accoutred in the French mode, because they accounted it more honourable, and better befitting the garb of a matronal pudicity.

The men were apparelled after their fashion. Their stockings were of tamine or of cloth-serge, of white, black, scarlet, or some other ingrained colour. Their breeches were of velvet, of the same colour with their stockings, or very near, embroidered and cut according to their fancy. Their doublet was of cloth of gold, of cloth of silver, of velvet, satin, damask, taffaties, &c., of the same colours, cut, embroidered, and suitably trimmed up in perfection. The points were of silk of the same colours, the tags were of gold well enamelled. Their coats and jerkins were of cloth of gold, cloth of silver, gold, tissue or velvet embroidered, as they thought fit. Their gowns were every whit as costly as those of the ladies. Their girdles were of silk, of the colour of their doublets. Every one had a gallant sword by his side, the hilt and handle whereof were gilt, and the scabbard of velvet, of the colour of his breeches, with a chape of gold, and pure goldsmith's work. The dagger of the same. Their caps or bonnets were of black velvet, adorned with jewels and buttons of gold. Upon that they wore a white plume most prettily and minion-like parted by so many rows of gold spangles, at the end whereof hung dangling in a more sparkling resplendency fair rubies, emeralds, diamonds, &c., but there was such a sympathy betwixt the gallants and the ladies, that every day they were apparelled in the same livery. And that they might not miss, there were certain gentlemen appointed to tell the youths every morning what vestments the ladies would on that day wear; for all was done according to the pleasure of the ladies. In these so handsome clothes, and habiliments so rich, think not that either one or other of either sex did waste any time at all; for the masters of the wardrobes had all their raiments and apparel so ready for every morning, and the chamber-ladies were so well skilled, that in a trice they would be dressed, and completely in their clothes from head to foot. And, to have those accoutrements with the more conveniency, there was about the wood of Theleme a row of houses of the extent of half a league, very neat and cleanly, wherein dwelt the goldsmiths, lapidaries, jewellers, embroiderers, tailors, gold-drawers, velvet-weavers, tapestry-makers, and upholsterers, who wrought there every one in his own trade, and all for the aforesaid jolly friars and nuns of the new stamp. They were furnished with matter and stuff from the hands of the Lord Nausiclete, who every year brought them seven ships from the Perlas and Cannibal Islands, laden with ingots of gold, with raw silk, with pearls and precious stones. And if any margarites, called unions [pearls], began to grow old, and lose somewhat of their natural whiteness and lustre, those by their art they did renew, by tendering them to eat to some pretty cocks, as they use to give casting unto hawks.

CHAPTER 57

HOW THE THELEMITES WERE GOVERNED, AND OF THEIR MANNER OF LIVING

All their life was spent not in laws, statutes, or rules, but according to their own free will and pleasure. They rose out of their beds when they thought good: they did eat, drink, labour, sleep, when they had a mind to it, and were disposed for it. None did awake them, none did offer to constrain them to eat, drink, nor to do any other thing; for so had Gargantua established it. In all their rule, and strictest tie of their order, there was but this one clause to be observed.

Do What Thou Wilt.

Because men that are free, well-born, well-bred, and conversant in honest companies, have naturally an instinct and spur that prompteth them unto virtuous actions, and withdraws them from vice, which is called honour. Those same men, when by base subjection and constraint they are brought under and kept down, turn aside from that noble disposition, by which they formerly were inclined to virtue, to shake off and break that bond of servitude, wherein they are so tyrannously enslaved; for it is agreeable with the nature of man to long after things forbidden, and to desire what is denied us.

By this liberty they entered into a very laudable emulation, to do all of them what they saw did please one. If any of the gallants or ladies should say, Let us drink, they would all drink. If any one of them said, Let us play, they all played. If one said, Let us go a walking into the fields, they went all. If it were to go a hawking or a hunting, the ladies mounted upon dainty well-paced nags, seated in a stately palfrey saddle, carried on their lovely fists, miniardly begloved every one of them, either a sparhawk, or a laneret, or a merlin, and the young gallants carried the other kinds of hawks. So nobly were they taught, that there was neither he nor she amongst them, but could read, write, sing, play upon several musical instruments, speak five or six several languages, and compose in them all very quaintly, both in verse and prose. Never were seen so valiant knights, so noble and worthy, so dexterous and skilful both on foot and a horseback, more brisk and lively, more nimble and quick, or better handling all manner of weapons than were there. Never were seen ladies so proper and handsome, so miniard and dainty, less forward, or more ready with their hand, and with their needle, in every honest and free action belonging to that sex, than were there. For this reason, when the time came, that any man of the said abbey, either at the request of his parents, or for some other cause, had a mind to go out of it, he carried along with him one of the ladies, namely her whom he had before that chosen for his mistress, and they were married together. And if they had formerly in Theleme lived in good devotion and amity, they did continue therein and increase it to a greater height in their state of matrimony: and did entertain that mutual love till the very last day of their life, in no less vigour and fervency, than at the very day of their wedding.

Here must not I forget to set down unto you a riddle, which was found under the ground, as they were laying the foundation of the abbey, engraven in a copper plate, and it was thus as followeth.

CHAPTER 58

A PROPHETICAL RIDDLE

Poor mortals, who wait for a happy day,
Cheer up your hearts, and hear what I shall say;
If it be lawful firmly to believe,
That the celestial bodies can us give
Wisdom to judge of things that are not yet;
Or if from heaven such wisdom we may get,
As may with confidence make us discourse
Of years to come, their destiny and course;
I to my hearers give to understand,
That this next winter, though it be at hand,
Yea and before, there shall appear a race
Of men, who, loth to sit still in one place,
Shall boldly go before all people's eyes,
Suborning men of divers qualities,
To draw them unto covenants and sides,
In such a manner, that whate'er betides,
They'll move you, if you give them ear, no doubt,

With both your friends and kindred to fall out.
They'll make a vassal to gain-stand his lord,
And children their own parents; in a word,
All reverence shall then be banished,
No true respect to other shall be had.
They'll say that every man should have his turn,
Both in his going forth, and his return;
And hereupon there shall arise such woes,
Such jarrings, and confused to's and fro's,
That never was in history such coils
Set down as yet, such tumults and garboyles.
Then shall you many gallant men see by
Valour stirr'd up, and youthful fervency,
Who, trusting too much in their hopeful time,
Live but a while, and perish in their prime.
Neither shall any, who this course shall run,
Leave off the race which he hath once begun,
Till they the heavens with noise by their contention
Have fill'd, and with their steps the earth's dimension.
Then those shall have no less authority,
That have no faith, than those that will not lie;
For all shall be governed by a rude,
Base, ignorant, and foolish multitude;
The veriest lout of all shall be their judge,
A horrible and dangerous deluge!
Deluge I call it, and that for good reason,
For this shall be omitted in no season;
Nor shall the earth of this foul stir be free,
Till suddenly you in great store shall see
The waters issue out, with whose streams the
Most moderate of all shall moisten'd be,
And justly too; because they did not spare
The flocks of beasts that innocentest are,
But did their sinews, and their bowels take,
Not to the gods a sacrifice to make,
But usually to serve themselves for sport:
And now consider, I do you exhort,
In such commotions so continual,
What rest can take the globe terrestrial?
Most happy then are they, that can it hold,
And use it carefully as precious gold,
By keeping it in goal, whence it shall have

No help but him, who being to it gave.
And to increase his mournful accident,
The sun, before it set in th' occident,
Shall cease to dart upon it any light,
More than in an eclipse, or in the night,—
So that at once its favour shall be gone
And liberty with it be left alone.
And yet, before it come to ruin thus,
Its quaking shall be as impetuous
As Etna's was, when Titan's sons lay under,
And yield, when lost, a fearful sound like thunder.
Inarimé did not more quickly move,
When Typheus did the vast huge hills remove,
And for despite into the sea them threw.
  Thus shall it then be lost by ways not few,
And changed suddenly, when those that have it
To other men that after come shall leave it.
Then shall it be high time to cease from this
So long, so great, so tedious exercise;
For the great waters told you now by me,
Will make each think where his retreat shall be;
And yet, before that they be clean dispers't,
You may behold in th' air, where nought was erst.
The burning heat of a great flame to rise,
Lick up the water, and the enterprise.
  It resteth after those things to declare,
That those shall sit content, who chosen are,
With all good things, and with celestial manne,
And richly recompensed every man:
The others at the last all stripp'd shall be,
That after this great work all men may see
How each shall have his due. This is their lot;
O he is worthy praise that shrinketh not.

No sooner was this enigmatical monument read over, but Gargantua, fetching a very deep sigh, said unto those that stood by, It is not now only, I perceive, that people called to the faith of the gospel, and convinced with the certainty of evangelical truths, are persecuted. But happy is that man that shall not be scandalized, but shall always continue to the end, in aiming at that mark, which God by his dear Son hath set before us, without being distracted or diverted, by his carnal affections and depraved nature.

The monk then said, What do you think in your conscience is meant and signified by this riddle? What? said Gargantua,—the progress and carrying on of the divine truth. By St. Goderan, said the monk, that is not my exposition. It is the style of the prophet Merlin. Make upon it as many grave allegories and glosses as you will, and dote upon it you and the rest of the world as long as you please: for my part, I can conceive no other meaning in it, but a description of a set at tennis in dark and obscure terms. The suborners of men are the makers of matches, which are commonly friends. After the two chases are made, he that was in the upper end of the tennis-court goeth out, and the other cometh in. They believe the first, that saith the ball was over or under the line. The waters are the heats that the players take till they sweat again. The cords of the rackets are made of the guts of sheep or goats. The globe terrestrial is the tennis-ball. After playing, when the game is done, they refresh themselves before a clear fire, and change their shirts; and very willingly they make all good cheer, but most merrily those that have gained. And so, farewell.

Alienated Labour

Karl Marx

(1818-1883)

If Rabelais ignored the labor of his servants Karl Marx focused on the labor of his workers. One might easily say that the associated problems of labor, production, and property were at the center of Marx's concerns. His starting point in any consideration of society and social institutions was always the surplus value created by labor and "expropriated by the owners of the means of production." In Marx's view these "owners" would have been in Rabelais' day the great aristocrats, in Locke's day the landed gentry, and in his own day were the capitalists. The value of labor as understood by Marx stands in sharp contrast to the value of labor perceived by Locke. After reading "Alienated Labour" it would be interesting to compare Marx's views with those of Locke expressed in "Of Property" on pages 129–42.

The following selection comes from Marx's earlier writings.

At that point in his career he functioned chiefly as a journalist, serving as editor and writer for a number of newspapers on the Continent that either were suppressed by the government for radicalism or collapsed for lack of funds. The Communist Manifesto *is generally considered the culminating work of this period. Subsequently he was compelled to flee to London where he devoted most of his energies to guiding the First International and writing* Das Kapital, *although during this time he also sporadically produced pieces of journalism, most notably for the New York* Herald Tribune. *Throughout his career Marx held that the intellectual must be directly involved in the political struggles of his time. Hence the polemical tone that runs consistently through his writings.*

WE have begun from the presuppositions of political economy. We have accepted its terminology and its laws. We presupposed private property; the separation of labour, capital and land, as also of wages, profit and rent; the division of labour; competition; the concept of exchange value, etc. From political economy itself, in its own words, we have shown that the worker sinks to the level of a commodity, and to a most miserable commodity; that the misery of the worker increases with the power and volume of his production; that the necessary result of competition is the accumulation of capital in a few hands, and thus a restoration of monopoly in a more terrible form; and finally that the distinction between capitalist and landlord, and between agricultural labourer and industrial worker, must disappear, and the whole of society divide into the two classes of property *owners* and *propertyless* workers.

Political economy begins with the fact of private property; it does not explain it. It conceives the *material* process of private property, as this occurs in reality, in general and abstract formulas which then serve it as laws. It does not *comprehend* these laws; that is, it does not show how they arise out of the nature of private property. Political economy provides no explanation of the basis for the distinction of labour from capital, of capital from land. When, for example, the relation of wages to profits is defined, this is explained in terms of the interests of capitalists; in other words, what should be explained is assumed. Similarly, competition is referred to at every point and is explained in terms of external conditions. Political economy tells us nothing about the extent to which these external and apparently accidental conditions are simply the expression of a necessary development. We have seen how exchange itself seems an accidental fact. The only motive forces which political economy recognizes are *avarice* and the *war between the avaricious, competition.*

Just because political economy fails to understand the interconnexions within this movement it was possible to oppose the doctrine of competition to that of monopoly, the doctrine of freedom of the crafts to that of the guilds, the doctrine of the division of landed property to that of the great estates; for competition, freedom of crafts, and the division of landed property were conceived only as accidental consequences brought about by will and force, rather than as necessary, inevitable and natural consequences of monopoly, the guild system and feudal property.

Thus we have now to grasp the real connexion between this whole system of alienation—private property, acquisitiveness, the separation of labour, capital and land, exchange and competition, value and the devaluation of man, monopoly and competition—and the system of *money.*

Let us not begin our explanation, as does the economist, from a legendary primordial condition. Such a primordial condition does not explain anything; it merely removes the question into a grey and nebulous distance. It asserts as a fact or event what it should deduce, namely, the necessary relation between two things; for example, between the division of labour and exchange. In the same way theology explains the origin of evil by the fall of man; that is, it asserts as a historical fact what it should explain.

We shall begin from a *contemporary* economic fact. The worker becomes poorer the more wealth he produces and the more his production increases in power and extent. The worker becomes an ever cheaper commodity the more goods he creates. The *devaluation* of the human world increases in direct relation with the *increase in value* of the world of things. Labour does not only create goods; it also produces itself and the worker as a *commodity,* and indeed in the same proportion as it produces goods.

This fact simply implies that the object produced by labour, its product, now stands opposed to it as an *alien being,* as a *power independent* of the producer. The product of labour is labour which has been embodied in an object and turned into a physical thing; this product is an *objectification* of labour. The performance of work is at the same time its objectification. The performance of work appears in the sphere of political economy as a *vitiation* of the worker, objectification as a *loss* and as *servitude to the object,* and appropriation as *alienation.*

So much does the performance of work appear as vitiation that the worker is vitiated to the point of starvation. So much does objectification appear as loss of the object that the worker is deprived of the most essential things not only of life but also of work. Labour itself becomes an object which he can acquire only by the greatest effort and with unpredictable interruptions. So much does the appropriation of the object appear as alienation that the more objects the worker produces the fewer he can possess and the more he falls under the domination of his product, of capital.

All these consequences follow from the fact that the worker is related to the *product of his labour* as to an *alien* object. For it is clear on this presupposition that the more the worker expends himself in work the more powerful becomes the world of objects which he creates in face of himself, the poorer he becomes in his inner life, and the less he belongs to himself. It is just the same as in religion. The more of himself man attributes to God the less he has left in himself. The worker puts his life into the object, and his life then belongs no longer to himself but to the object. The greater his activity, therefore, the less he possesses. What is embodied in the product of his labour is no longer his own. The greater this product is, therefore, the more he is diminished. The *alienation* of the worker in his product means not only that his labour becomes an object, assumes an *external* existence, but that it exists independently, *outside himself,* and alien to him, and that it stands opposed to him as an autonomous power. The life which he has given to the object sets itself against him as an alien and hostile force. Let us now examine more closely the phenomenon of *objectification;* the worker's production and the *alienation* and *loss* of the object it produces, which is involved in it. The worker can create nothing without *nature,* without the *sensuous external world.* The latter is the material in which his labour is realized, in which it is active, out of which and through which it produces things.

But just as nature affords the *means of existence* of labour, in the sense that labour cannot *live* without objects upon which it can be exercised, so also it provides the *means of existence* in a narrower sense; namely the means of physical existence for the *worker* himself. Thus, the more the worker *appropriates* the external world of sensuous nature by his labour the more he deprives himself of *means of existence,* in two respects: first, that the sensuous external world becomes progressively less an object belonging to his labour or a means of existence of his labour, and secondly, that it becomes progressively less a means of existence in the direct sense, a means for the physical subsistence of the worker.

In both respects, therefore, the worker becomes a slave of the object; first, in that he receives an *object of work,* i.e. receives *work,* and secondly, in that he receives *means of subsistence.* Thus the object enables him to exist, first as a *worker* and secondly, as a *physical subject.* The culmination of this enslavement is that he can only maintain himself as a *physical subject* so far as he is a *worker,* and that it is only as a *physical subject* that he is a worker.

(The alienation of the worker in his object is expressed as follows in the laws of political economy: the more the worker produces the less he has to consume; the more value he creates the more worthless he becomes; the more refined his product the more crude and misshapen the worker; the more civilized the product the more barbarous the worker; the more powerful the work the more feeble the worker; the more the work manifests intelligence the more the worker declines in intelligence and becomes a slave of nature.)

Political economy conceals the alienation in the nature of labour in so far as it does not examine the direct relationship between the worker (*work*) *and production.* Labour certainly produces marvels for the rich but it produces privation for the worker. It produces palaces, but hovels for the worker. It produces beauty, but deformity for the worker. It replaces labour by machinery, but it casts some of the workers back into a barbarous kind of work and turns the others into machines. It produces intelligence, but also stupidity and cretinism for the workers.

The direct relationship of labour to its products is the relationship of the worker to the objects of his production. The relationship of property owners to the objects of production and to production itself is merely a *consequence* of this first relationship and confirms it. We shall consider this second aspect later.

Thus, when we ask what is the important relationship of labour, we are concerned with the relationship of the *worker* to production.

So far we have considered the alienation of the worker only from one aspect; namely, *his relationship with the products of his labour.* However, alienation appears not merely in the result but also in the *process* of *production,* within *productive activity* itself. How could the worker stand in an alien relationship to the product of his activity if he did not alienate himself in the act of production itself? The product is indeed only the *résumé* of activity, of production. Consequently, if the product of labour is alienation, production itself must be active alienation—the alienation of activity and the activity of alienation. The alienation of the object of labour merely summarizes the alienation in the work activity itself.

What constitutes the alienation of labour? First, that the work is *external* to the worker, that it is not part of his nature; and that, consequently, he does not fulfil himself in his work but denies himself, has a feeling of misery rather than well-being, does not develop freely his mental and physical energies but is physically exhausted and mentally debased. The worker, therefore, feels himself at home only during his leisure time, whereas at work he feels homeless. His work is not voluntary but imposed, *forced labour.* It is not the satisfaction of a need, but only a *means* for satisfying other needs. Its alien character is clearly shown by the fact that as soon as there is no physical or other compulsion it is avoided like the plague. External labour, labour in which man alienates himself, is a labour of self-sacrifice, of mortification. Finally, the external character of work for the worker is shown by the fact that it is not his own work but work for someone else, that in work he does not belong to himself but to another person.

Just as in religion the spontaneous activity of human fantasy, of the human brain and heart, reacts independently as an alien activity of gods or devils upon the individual, so the activity of the worker is not his own spontaneous activity. It is another's activity and a loss of his own spontaneity.

We arrive at the result that man (the worker) feels himself to be freely active only in his animal functions—eating, drinking and procreating, or at most also in his dwelling and in personal adornment—while in his human functions he is reduced to an animal. The animal becomes human and the human becomes animal.

Eating, drinking and procreating are of course also genuine human functions. But abstractly considered, apart from the environment of human activities, and turned into final and sole ends, they are animal functions.

We have now considered the act of alienation of practical human activity, labour, from two aspects: (1) the relationship of the worker to the *product of labour* as an alien object which dominates him. This relationship is at the same time the relationship to the sensuous external world, to natural objects, as an alien and hostile world; (2) the relationship of labour to the *act of production* within *labour.* This is the relationship of the worker to his own activity as something alien and not belonging to him, activity as suffering (passivity), strength as powerlessness, creation as emasculation, the *personal* physical and mental energy of the worker, his personal life (for what is life but activity?), as an activity which is directed against himself, independent of him and not belonging to him. This is *self-alienation* as against the above-mentioned alienation of the *thing.*

We have now to infer a third characteristic of *alienated labour* from the two we have considered.

Man is a species-being not only in the sense that he makes the community (his own as well as those of other things) his object both practically and theoretically, but also (and this is simply another expression for the same thing) in the sense that he treats himself as the present, living species, as a *universal* and consequently free being.

Species-life, for man as for animals, has its physical basis in the fact that man (like animals) lives from inorganic nature, and since man is more universal than an animal so the range of inorganic nature from which he lives is more universal. Plants, animals, minerals, air, light, etc. constitute, from the theoretical aspect, a part of human consciousness as objects of natural science and art; they are man's spiritual inorganic nature, his intellectual means of life, which he must first prepare for enjoyment and perpetuation. So also, from the practical aspect, they form a part of human life and activity. In practice man lives only from these natural products, whether in the form of food, heating, clothing, housing, etc. The universality of man appears in practice in the universality which makes the whole of nature into his inorganic body: (1) as a direct means of life; and equally (2) as the material object and instrument of his life activity. Nature is the inorganic body of man; that is to say nature, excluding the human body itself. To say that man *lives* from nature means that nature is his *body* with which he must remain in a continuous interchange in order not to die. The statement that the physical and mental life of man, and nature, are interdependent means simply that nature is interdependent with itself, for man is a part of nature.

Since alienated labour: (1) alienates nature from man; and (2) alienates man from himself, from his own active function, his life activity; so it alienates him from the species. It makes *species-life* into a means of individual life. In the first place it alienates species-life and individual life, and secondly, it turns the latter, as an abstraction, into the purpose of the former, also in its abstract and alienated form.

For labour, *life activity, productive life,* now appear to man only as *means* for the satisfaction of a need, the need to maintain his physical existence. Productive life is, however, species-life. It is life creating life. In the type of life activity resides the whole character of a species, its species-character; and free, conscious activity is the species-character of human beings. Life itself appears only as a *means of life.*

The animal is one with its life activity. It does not distinguish the activity from itself. It is *its activity.* But man makes his life activity itself an object of his will and consciousness. He has a conscious life activity. It is not a determination with which he is completely identified. Conscious life activity distinguishes man from the life activity of animals. Only for this reason is he a species-being. Or rather, he is only a self-conscious being, i.e. his own life is an object for him, because he is a species-being. Only for this reason is his activity free activity. Alienated labour reverses the relationship, in that man because he is a self-conscious being makes his life activity, his *being,* only a means for his *existence.*

The practical construction of an *objective world,* the *manipulation* of inorganic nature, is the confirmation of man as a conscious species-being, i.e. a being who treats the species as his own being or himself as a species-being. Of course, animals also produce. They construct nests, dwellings, as in the case of bees, beavers, ants, etc. But they only produce what is strictly necessary for themselves or their young. They produce only in a single direction, while man produces universally. They produce only under the compulsion of direct physical needs, while man produces when he is free from physical need and only truly produces in freedom from such need. Animals produce only themselves, while man reproduces the whole of nature. The products of animal production belong directly to their physical bodies, while man is free in face of his product. Animals construct only in accordance with the standards and needs of the species to which they belong, while man knows how to produce in accordance with the standards of every species and knows how to apply the appropriate standard to the object. Thus man constructs also in accordance with the laws of beauty.

It is just in his work upon the objective world that man really proves himself as a *species-being.* This production is his active species-life. By means of it nature appears as *his* work and his reality. The object of labour is, therefore, the *objectification of man's species-life;* for he no longer reproduces himself merely intellectually, as in consciousness, but actively and in a real sense, and he sees his own reflection in a world which he has constructed. While, therefore, alienated labour takes away the object of production from man, it also takes away his *species-life,* his real objectivity as a species-being, and changes his advantage over animals into a disadvantage in so far as his inorganic body, nature, is taken from him.

Just as alienated labour transforms free and self-directed activity into a means, so it transforms the species-life of man into a means of physical existence.

Consciousness, which man has from his species, is transformed through alienation so that species-life becomes only a means for him. (3) Thus alienated labour turns the *species-life of man,* and also nature as his mental species-property, into an *alien* being and into a *means* for his *individual existence.* It alienates from man his own body, external nature, his mental life and his *human* life. (4) A direct consequence of the alienation of man from the product of his labour, from his life activity and from his species-life, is that *man* is *alienated* from other *men.* When man confronts himself he also confronts *other* men. What is true of man's relationship to his work, to the product of his work and to himself, is also true of his relationship to other men, to their labour and to the objects of their labour.

In general, the statement that man is alienated from his species-life means that each man is alienated from others, and that each of the others is likewise alienated from human life.

Human alienation, and above all the relation of man to himself, is first realized and expressed in the relationship between each man and other men. Thus in the relationship of alienated labour every man regards other men according to the standards and relationships in which he finds himself placed as a worker.

We began with an economic fact, the alienation of the worker and his production. We have expressed this fact in conceptual terms as *alienated labour,* and in analysing the concept we have merely analysed an economic fact.

Let us now examine further how this concept of alienated labour must express and reveal itself in reality. If the product of labour is alien to me and confronts me as an alien power, to whom does it belong? If my own activity does not belong to me but is an alien, forced activity, to whom does it belong? To a being *other* than myself. And who is this being? The *gods?* It is apparent in the earliest stages of advanced production, e.g. temple building, etc. in Egypt, India, Mexico, and in the service rendered to gods, that the product belonged to the gods. But the gods alone were never the lords of labour. And no more was *nature.* What a contradiction it would be if the more man subjugates nature by his labour, and the more the marvels of the gods are rendered superfluous by the marvels of industry, the more he should abstain from his joy in producing and his enjoyment of the product for love of these powers.

The *alien* being to whom labour and the product of labour belong, to whose service labour is devoted, and to whose enjoyment the product of labour goes, can only be *man* himself. If the product of labour does not belong to the worker, but confronts him as an alien power, this can only be because it belongs to *a man other than the worker.* If his activity is a torment to him it must be a source of *enjoyment* and pleasure to another. Not the gods, nor nature, but only man himself can be this alien power over men.

Consider the earlier statement that the relation of man to himself is first *realized, objectified,* through his relation to other men. If he is related to the product of his labour, his objectified labour, as to an *alien,* hostile, powerful and independent object, he is related in such a way that another alien, hostile, powerful and independent man is the lord of this object. If he is related to his own activity as to unfree activity, then he is related to it as activity in the service, and under the domination, coercion and yoke, of another man.

Every self-alienation of man, from himself and from nature, appears in the relation which he postulates between other men and himself and nature. Thus religious self-alienation is necessarily exemplified in the relation between laity and priest, or, since it is here a question of the spiritual world, between the laity and a mediator. In the real world of practice this self-alienation can only be expressed in the real, practical relation of man to his fellow men. The medium through which alienation occurs is itself a *practical* one. Through alienated labour, therefore, man not only produces his relation to the object and to the process of production as to alien and hostile men; he also produces the relation of other men to his production and his product, and the relation between himself and other men. Just as he creates his own production as a vitiation, a punishment, and his own product as a loss, as a product which does not belong to him, so he creates the domination of the non-producer over production and its product. As he alienates his own activity, so he bestows upon the stranger an activity which is not his own.

We have so far considered this relation only from the side of the worker, and later on we shall consider it also from the side of the non-worker.

Thus, through alienated labour the worker creates the relation of another man, who does not work and is outside the work process, to this labour. The relation of the worker to work also produces the relation of the capitalist (or whatever one likes to call the lord of labour) to work. *Private property* is, therefore, the product, the necessary result, of *alienated labour,* of the external relation of the worker to nature and to himself.

Private property is thus derived from the analysis of the concept of *alienated labour;* that is, alienated man, alienated labour, alienated life, and estranged man.

We have, of course, derived the concept of *alienated labour* (*alienated life*) from political economy, from an analysis of the *movement of private property.* But the analysis of this concept shows that although private property appears to be the basis and cause of alienated labour, it is rather a consequence of the latter, just as the gods are *fundamentally* not the cause but the product of confusions of human reason. At a later stage, however, there is a reciprocal influence.

Only in the final stage of the development of private property is its secret revealed, namely, that it is on one hand the *product* of alienated labour, and on the other hand the *means* by which labour is alienated, *the realization of this alienation.*

This elucidation throws light upon several unresolved controversies—

1. Political economy begins with labour as the real soul of production and then goes on to attribute nothing to labour and everything to private property. Proudhon, faced by this contradiction, has decided in favour of labour against private property. We perceive, however, that this apparent contradiction is the contradiction of *alienated labour* with itself and that political economy has merely formulated the laws of alienated labour.

We also observe, therefore, that *wages* and *private property* are identical, for wages, like the product or object of labour, labour itself remunerated, are only a necessary consequence of the alienation of labour. In the wage system labour appears not as an end in itself but as the servant of wages. We shall develop this point later on and here only bring out some of the consequences.

An enforced *increase in wages* (disregarding the other difficulties, and especially that such an anomaly could only be maintained by force) would be nothing more than a *better remuneration of slaves,* and would not restore, either to the worker or to the work, their human significance and worth.

Even the *equality of incomes* which Proudhon demands would only change the relation of the present-day worker to his work into a relation of all men to work. Society would then be conceived as an abstract capitalist.

2. From the relation of alienated labour to private property it also follows that the emancipation of society from private property, from servitude, takes the political form of the *emancipation of the workers;* not in the sense that only the latter's emancipation is involved, but because this emancipation includes the emancipation of humanity as a whole. For all human servitude is involved in the relation of the worker to production, and all the types of servitude are only modifications or consequences of this relation.

As we have discovered the concept of *private property* by an *analysis* of the concept of *alienated labour,* so with the aid of these two factors we can evolve all the *categories* of political economy, and in every category, e.g. trade, competition, capital, money, we shall discover only a particular and developed expression of these fundamental elements.

However, before considering this structure let us attempt to solve two problems.

1. To determine the general nature of *private property* as it has resulted from alienated labour, in its relation to *genuine human and social property.*

2. We have taken as a fact and analysed the *alienation of labour.* How does it happen, we may ask, that *man alienates his labour?* How is this alienation founded in the nature of human development? We have already done much to solve the problem in so far as we have *transformed* the question concerning the *origin of private property* into a question about the relation between *alienated labour* and the process of development of mankind. For in speaking of private property one believes oneself to be dealing with something external to mankind. But in speaking of labour one deals directly with mankind itself. This new formulation of the problem already contains its solution.

ad (1) *The general nature of private property and its relation to genuine human property.*

We have resolved alienated labour into two parts, which mutually determine each other, or rather, which constitute two different expressions of one and the same relation. *Appropriation* appears as *alienation* and *alienation* as *appropriation,* alienation as genuine acceptance in the community.

We have considered one aspect, *alienated* labour, in its bearing upon the *worker* himself, i.e. *the relation of alienated labour to itself.* And we have found as the necessary consequence of this relation the *property relation* of the *non-worker* to the *worker* and to labour. *Private property* as the material, summarized expression of alienated labour includes both relations; *the relation of the worker to labour, to the product of his labour and to the non-worker,* and the relation of the *non-worker to the worker and to the product of the latter's labour.*

We have already seen that in relation to the worker, who *appropriates* nature by his labour, appropriation appears as alienation, self-activity as activity for another and of another, living as the sacrifice of life, and production of the object as loss of the object to an alien power, an alien man. Let us now consider the relation to this *alien* man to the worker, to labour, and to the object of labour.

It should be noted first that everything which appears to the worker as an *activity of alienation,* appears to the non-worker as a *condition of alienation.* Secondly, the *real, practical* attitude (as a state of mind) of the worker in production and to the product appears to the non-worker who confronts him as a *theoretical* attitude.

Thirdly, the non-worker does everything against the worker which the latter does against himself, but he does not do against himself what he does against the worker.

Let us examine these three relationships more closely.[1]

[1] The manuscript was unfinished.

from

The Subjection of Women

John Stuart Mill

(1806-1873)

To Marx social conflict was entirely rational and dictated by class interest. Social institutions, such as religion or marriage, were in his view superstructures built on the basic economic relation between classes and generally served to reinforce existing economic conditions. Thus, established social institutions shared in the oppression of the worker and it behooved him to combat them if he was to regain what Marx would have called his full humanity. Marx, of course, was not the first to hold this view of social institutions, nor was he the last. Indeed, throughout the nineteenth century, the prevailing thought among liberal people was that social institutions were inherently oppressive and dehumanizing.

John Stuart Mill can easily be seen as the paradigm of nineteenth-century liberalism in England. Most of the major points in liberal thought were at one time or another touched on by him and were defended on the basis of their superior utility in gaining what Mill conceived to be the main goal of human endeavor, the good life, or as he would have put it, "human happiness." Unlike Marx, though, Mill believed that the conflict between classes or groups of people resulted from social relations that were originally imposed by force and subsequently fossilized by custom. To Mill there were no rational justifications for the continuance of these institutionalized relations. Also in contrast to Marx, Mill believed that social institutions had to be changed gradually, because of the irrational content underlying them, and through legislative processes rather than through revolutionary action. These differences have come down to the twentieth century and perhaps are the chief points of contention between contemporary radicals and liberals.

Mill's view of the origin and function of social institutions is rather fully stated in our selection from The Subjection of Women. *This work is generally considered the classic nineteenth-century exposition of feminism, much as his essay* On Liberty *is the classic argument for individual freedom and diversity of opinion. Some of Mill's other works are* Principles of Political Economy, Utilitarianism, *and* Systems of Logic.

THE object of this Essay is to explain, as clearly as I am able, the grounds of an opinion which I have held from the very earliest period when I had formed any opinions at all on social or political matters, and which, instead of being weakened or modified, has been constantly growing stronger by the progress of reflection and the experience of life: That the principle which regulates the existing social relations between the two sexes—the legal subordination of one sex to the other—is wrong in itself, and now one of the chief hindrances to human improvement; and that it ought to be replaced by a principle of perfect equality, admitting no power or privilege on the one side, nor disability on the other.

The very words necessary to express the task I have undertaken, show how arduous it is. But it would be a mistake to suppose that the difficulty of the case must lie in the insufficiency or obscurity of the grounds of reason on which my conviction rests. The difficulty is that which exists in all cases in which there is a mass of feeling to be contended against. So long as an opinion is strongly rooted in the feelings, it gains rather than loses in stability by having a preponderating weight of argument against it. For if it were accepted as a result of argument, the refutation of the argument might shake the solidity of the conviction; but when it rests solely on feeling, the worse it fares in argumentative contest, the more persuaded its adherents are that their feeling must have some deeper ground, which the arguments do not reach; and while the feeling remains, it is always throwing up fresh entrenchments of argument to repair any breach made in the old. And there are so many causes tending to make the feelings connected with this subject the most intense and most deeply-rooted of all those which gather round and protect old institutions and customs, that we need not wonder to find them as yet less undermined and loosened than any of the rest by the progress of the great modern spiritual and social transition; nor suppose that the barbarisms to which men cling longest must be less barbarisms than those which they earlier shake off.

In every respect the burthen is hard on those who attack an almost universal opinion. They must be very fortunate as well as unusually capable if they obtain a hearing at all. They have more difficulty in obtaining a trial, than any other litigants have in getting a verdict. If they do extort a hearing, they are subjected to a set of logical requirements totally different from those exacted from other people. In all other cases, the burthen of proof is supposed to lie with the affirmative. If a person is charged with a murder, it rests with those who accuse him to give proof of his guilt, not with himself to prove his innocence. If there is a difference of opinion about the reality of any alleged historical event, in which the feelings of men in general are not much interested, as the Siege of Troy for example, those who maintain that the event took place are expected to produce their proofs, before those who take the other side can be required to say anything; and at no time are these required to do more than show that the evidence produced by the others is of no value. Again, in practical matters, the burthen of proof is supposed to be with those who are against liberty; who contend for any restriction or prohibition; either any limitation of the general freedom of human action, or any disqualification or disparity of privilege affecting one person or kind of persons, as compared with others. The *a priori* presumption is in favour of freedom and impartiality. It is held that there should be no restraint not required by the general good, and that the law should be no respecter of persons, but should treat all alike, save where dissimilarity of treatment is required by positive reasons, either of justice or of policy. But of none of these rules of evidence will the benefit be allowed to those who maintain the opinion I profess. It is useless for me to say that those who maintain the doctrine that men have a right to command and women are under an obligation to obey, or that men are fit for government and women unfit, are on the affirmative side of the question, and that they are bound to show positive evidence for the assertions, or submit to their rejection. It is equally unavailing for me to say that those who deny to women any freedom or privilege rightly allowed to men, having the double presumption against them that they are opposing freedom and recommending partiality, must be held to the strictest proof of their case, and unless their success be such as to exclude all doubt, the judgement ought to go against them. These would be thought good pleas in any common case; but they will not be thought so in this instance. Before I could hope to make any impression, I should be expected not only to answer all that has ever been said by those who take the other side of the question, but to imagine all that could be said by them—to find them in reasons, as well as answer all I find: and besides refuting all arguments for the affirmative, I shall be called upon for invincible positive arguments to prove a negative. And even if I could do all this, and leave the opposite party with a host of unanswered arguments against them, and not a single unrefuted one on their side, I should be thought to have done little; for a cause supported on the one hand by universal usage, and on the other by so great a preponderance of popular sentiment, is supposed to have a presumption in its favour, superior to any conviction which an appeal to reason has power to produce in any intellects but those of a high class.

I do not mention these difficulties to complain of them; first, because it would be useless; they are inseparable from having to contend through people's understandings against the hostility of their feelings and practical tendencies: and truly the understandings of the majority of mankind would need to be much better cultivated than has ever yet been the case, before they can be asked to place such reliance in their own power of estimating arguments, as to give up practical principles in which they have been born and bred, and which are the basis of much of the existing order of the world, at the first argumentative attack which they are not capable of logically resisting. I do not therefore quarrel with them for having too little faith in argument, but for having too much faith in custom and the general feeling. It is one of the characteristic prejudices of the reaction of the nineteenth century against the eighteenth, to accord to the unreasoning elements in human nature the infallibility which the eighteenth century is supposed to have ascribed to the reasoning elements. For the apotheosis of Reason we have substituted that of Instinct; and we call everything instinct which we find in ourselves and for which we cannot trace any rational foundation. This idolatry, infinitely more degrading than the other, and the most pernicious of the false worships of the present day, of all of which it is now the main support, will probably hold its ground until it gives way before a sound psychology, laying bare the real root of much that is bowed down to as the intention of Nature and the ordinance of God. As regards the present question, I am willing to accept the unfavourable conditions which the prejudice assigns to me. I consent that established custom, and the general feeling, should be deemed conclusive against me, unless that custom and feeling from age to age can be shown to have owed their existence to other causes than their soundness, and to have derived their power from the worse rather than the better parts of human nature. I am willing that judgement should go against me, unless I can show that my judge has been tampered with. The concession is not so great as it might appear; for to prove this, is by far the easiest portion of my task.

The generality of a practice is in some cases a strong presumption that it is, or at all events once was, conducive to laudable ends. This is the case, when the practice was first adopted, or afterwards kept up, as a means to such ends, and was grounded on experience of the mode in which they could be most effectually attained. If the authority of men over women, when first established, had been the result of a conscientious comparison between different modes of constituting the government of society; if, after trying various other modes of social organization —the government of women over men, equality between the two, and such mixed and divided modes of government as might be invented—it had been decided, on the testimony of experience, that the mode in which women are wholly under the rule of men, having no share at all in public concerns, and each in private being under the legal obligation of obedience to the man with whom she has associated her destiny, was the arrangement most conducive to the happiness and well-being of both; its general adoption might then be fairly thought to be some evidence that, at the time when it was adopted, it was the best: though even then the considerations which recommended it may, like so many other primeval social facts of the greatest importance, have subsequently, in the course of ages, ceased to exist. But the state of the case is in every respect the reverse of this. In the first place, the opinion in favour of the present system, which entirely subordinates the weaker sex to the stronger, rests upon theory only; for their never has been trial made of any other: so that experience, in the sense in which it is vulgarly opposed to theory, cannot be pretended to have pronounced any verdict. And in the second place, the adoption of this system of inequality never was the result of deliberation, or forethought, or any social ideas, or any notion whatever of what conduced to the benefit of humanity or the good order of society. It arose simply from the fact that from the very earliest twilight of human society, every woman (owing to the value attached to her by men, combined with her inferiority in muscular strength) was found in a state of bondage to some man. Laws and systems of polity always begin by recognizing the relations they find already existing between individuals. They convert what was a mere physical fact into a legal right, give it the sanction of society, and principally aim at the substitution of public and organized means of asserting and protecting these rights, instead of the irregular and lawless conflict of physical strength. Those who had already been compelled to obedience became in this manner legally bound to it. Slavery, from being a mere affair of force between the master and the slave, became regularized and a matter of compact among the masters, who, binding themselves to one another for common protection, guaranteed by their collective strength the private possessions of each, including his slaves. In early times, the great majority of the male sex were slaves, as well as the whole of the female. And many ages elapsed, some of them ages of high cultivation, before any thinker was bold enough to question the rightfulness, and the absolute social necessity, either of the one slavery or of the other. By degrees such thinkers did arise: and (the general progress of society assisting) the slavery of the male sex has, in all the countries of Christian Europe at least (though, in one of them, only within the last few years) been at length abolished, and that of the female sex has been gradually changed into a milder form of dependence. But this dependence, as it exists at present, is not an original institution, taking a fresh start from considerations of justice and social expediency—it is the primitive state of slavery lasting on, through successive mitigations and modifications occasioned by the same causes which have softened the general manners, and brought all human relations more under the control of justice and the influence of humanity. It has not lost the taint of its brutal origin. No presumption in its favour, therefore, can be drawn from the fact of its existence. The only such presumption which it could be supposed to have, must be grounded on its having lasted till now, when so many other things which came down from the same odious source have been done away with. And this, indeed, is what makes it strange to ordinary ears, to hear it asserted that the inequality of rights between men and women has no other source than the law of the strongest.

That this statement should have the effect of a paradox, is in some respects creditable to the progress of civilization, and the improvement of the moral sentiments of mankind. We now live —that is to say, one or two of the most advanced nations of the world now live—in a state in which the law of the strongest seems to be entirely abandoned as the regulating principle of the world's affairs: nobody professes it, and, as regards most of the relations between human beings, nobody is permitted to practise it. When any one succeeds in doing so, it is under cover of some pretext which gives him the semblance of having some general social interest on his side. This being the ostensible state of things, people flatter themselves that the rule of mere force is ended; that the law of the strongest cannot be the reason of existence of anything which has remained in full operation down to the present time. However any of our present institutions may have begun, it can only, they think, have been preserved to this period of advanced civilization by a well-grounded feeling of its adaptation to human nature, and conduciveness to the general good. They do not understand the great vitality and durability of institutions which place right on the side of might; how intensely they are clung to; how the good as well as the bad propensities and sentiments of those who have power in their hands, become identified with retaining it; how slowly these bad institutions give way, one at a time, the weakest first, beginning with those which are least interwoven with the daily habits of life; and how very rarely those who have obtained legal power because they first had physical, have ever lost their hold of it until the physical power had passed over to the other side. Such shifting of the physical force not having taken place in the case of women; this fact, combined with all the peculiar and characteristic features of the particular case, made it certain from the first that this branch of the system of right founded on might, though softened in its most atrocious features at an earlier period than several of the others, would be the very last to disappear. It was inevitable that this one case of a social relation grounded on force would survive through generations of institutions grounded on equal justice, an almost solitary exception to the general character of their laws and customs; but which, so long as it does not proclaim its own origin, and as discussion has not brought out its true character, is not felt to jar with modern civilization, any more than domestic slavery among the Greeks jarred with their notion of themselves as a free people.

The truth is, that people of the present and the last two or three generations have lost all practical sense of the primitive condition of humanity; and only the few who have studied history accurately, or have much frequented the parts of the world occupied by the living representatives of ages long past, are able to form any mental picture of what society then was. People are not aware how entirely, in former ages, the law of superior strength was the rule of life; how publicly and openly it was avowed, I do not say cynically or shamelessly—for these words imply a feeling that there was something in it to be ashamed of, and no such notion could find a place in the faculties of any person in those ages, except a philosopher or a saint. History gives a cruel experience of human nature, in showing how exactly the regard due to the life, possessions, and entire earthly happiness of any class of persons, was measured by what they had the power of enforcing; how all who made any resistance to authorities that had arms in their hands, however dreadful might be the provocation, had not only the law of force but all other laws, and all the notions of social obligation against them; and, in the eyes of those whom they resisted, were not only guilty of crime, but of the worst of all crimes, deserving the most cruel chastisement which human beings could inflict. The first small vestige of a feeling of obligation in a superior to acknowledge any right in inferiors, began when he had been induced, for convenience, to make some promise to them. Though these promises, even when sanctioned by the most solemn oaths, were for many ages revoked or violated on the most trifling provocation or temptation, it is probable that this, except by persons of still worse than the average morality, was seldom done without some twinges of conscience. The ancient republics, being mostly grounded from the first upon some kind of mutual compact, or at any rate formed by an union of persons not very unequal in strength, afforded, in consequence, the first instance of a portion of human relations fenced round, and placed under the dominion of another law than that of force. And though the original law of force remained in full operation between them and their slaves, and also (except so far as limited by express compact) between a commonwealth and its subjects, or other independent commonwealths; the banishment of that primitive law, even from so narrow a field, commenced the regeneration of human nature, by giving birth to sentiments of which experience soon demonstrated the immense value even for material interests, and which thenceforward only required to be enlarged, not created. Though slaves were no part of the commonwealth, it was in the free states that slaves were first felt to have rights as human beings. The Stoics were, I believe, the first (except so far as the Jewish law constitutes an exception) who taught as a part of morality that men were bound by moral obligations to their slaves. No one, after Christianity became ascendant, could ever again have been a stranger to this belief, in theory; nor, after the rise of the Catholic Church, was it ever without persons to stand up for it. Yet to enforce it was the most arduous task which Christianity ever had to perform. For more than a thousand years the Church kept up the contest, with hardly any perceptible success. It was not for want of power over men's minds. Its power was prodigious. It could make kings and nobles resign their most valued possessions to enrich the Church. It could make thousands, in the prime of life and the height of worldly advantages, shut themselves up in convents to work out their salvation by poverty, fasting, and prayer. It could send hundreds of thousands across land and sea, Europe and Asia, to give their lives for the deliverance of the Holy Sepulchre. It could make kings relinquish wives who were the objects of their passionate attachment, because the Church declared that they were within the seventh (by our calculation the fourteenth) degree of relationship. All this it did; but it could not make men fight less with one another, nor tyrannize less cruelly over the serfs, and, when they were able, over burgesses. It could not make them renounce either of the applications of force; force militant, or force triumphant. This they could never be induced to do until they were themselves in their turn compelled by superior force. Only by the growing power of kings was an end put to fighting except between kings, or competitors for kingship; only by the growth of a wealthy and warlike bourgeoisie in the fortified towns, and of a plebeian infantry which proved more powerful in the field than the undisciplined chivalry, was the insolent tyranny of the nobles over the bourgeoisie and peasantry brought within some bounds. It was persisted in not only until, but long after, the oppressed had obtained a power enabling them often to take conspicuous vengeance; and on the Continent much of it continued to the time of the French Revolution, though in England the earlier and better organization of the democratic classes put an end to it sooner, by establishing equal laws and free national institutions.

If people are mostly so little aware how completely, during the greater part of the duration of our species, the law of force was the avowed rule of general conduct, any other being only a special and exceptional consequence of peculiar ties—and from how very recent a date it is that the affairs of society in general have been even pretended to be regulated according to any moral law; as little do people remember or consider, how institutions and customs which never had any ground but the law of force, last on into ages and states of general opinion which never would have permitted their first establishment. Less than forty years ago, Englishmen might still by law hold human beings in bondage as saleable property: within the present century they might kidnap them and carry them off, and work them literally to death. This absolutely extreme case of the law of force, condemned by those who can tolerate almost every other form of arbitrary power, and which, of all others, presents features the most revolting to the feelings of all who look at it from an impartial position, was the law of civilized and Christian England within the memory of persons now living: and in one half of Anglo-Saxon America three or four years ago, not only did slavery exist, but the slave trade, and the breeding of slaves expressly for it, was a general practice between slave states. Yet not only was there a greater strength of sentiment against it, but, in England at least, a less amount either of feeling or of interest in favour of it, than of any other of the customary abuses of force: for its motive was the love of gain, unmixed and undisguised; and those who profited by it were a very small numerical fraction of the country, while the natural feeling of all who were not personally interested in it, was unmitigated abhorrence. So extreme an instance makes it almost superfluous to refer to any other: but consider the long duration of absolute monarchy. In England at present it is the almost universal conviction that military despotism is a case of the law of force, having no other origin or justification. Yet in all the great nations of Europe except England it either still exists, or has only just ceased to exist, and has even now a strong party favourable to it in all ranks of the people, especially among persons of station and consequence. Such is the power of an established system, even when far from universal; when not only in almost every period of history there have been great and well-known examples of the contrary system, but these have almost invariably been afforded by the most illustrious and most prosperous communities. In this case, too, the possessor of the undue power, the person directly interested in it, is only one person, while those who are subject to it and suffer from it are literally all the rest. The yoke is naturally and necessarily humiliating to all persons, except the one who is on the throne, together with, at most, the one who expects to succeed to it. How different are these cases from that of the power of men over women! I am not now prejudging the question of its justifiableness. I am showing how vastly more permanent it could not but be, even if not justifiable, than these other dominations which have nevertheless lasted down to our own time. Whatever gratification of pride there is in the possession of power, and whatever personal interest in its exercise, is in this case not confined to a limited class, but common to the whole male sex. Instead of being, to most of its supporters, a thing desirable chiefly in the abstract, or, like the political ends usually contended for by factions, of little private importance to any but the leaders; it comes home to the person and hearth of every male head of a family, and of every one who looks forward to being so. The clodhopper exercises, or is to exercise, his share of the power equally with the highest nobleman. And the case is that in which the desire of power is the strongest: for every one who desires power, desires it most over those who are nearest to him, with whom his life is passed, with whom he has most concerns in common, and in whom any independence of his authority is oftenest likely to interfere with his individual preferences. If, in the other cases specified, powers manifestly grounded only on force, and having so much less to support them, are so slowly and with so much difficulty got rid of, much more must it be so with this, even if it rests on no better foundation than those. We must consider, too, that the possessors of the power have facilities in this case, greater than in any other, to prevent any uprising against it. Every one of the subjects lives under the very eye, and almost, it may be said, in the hands, of one of the masters—in closer intimacy with him than with any of her fellow subjects; with no means of combining against him, no power of even locally overmastering him, and, on the other hand, with the strongest motives for seeking his favour and avoiding to give him offence. In struggles for political emancipation, everybody knows how often its champions are bought off by bribes, or daunted by terrors. In the case of women, each individual of the subject-class is in a chronic state of bribery and intimidation combined. In setting up the standard of resistance, a large number of the leaders, and still more of the followers, must make an almost complete sacrifice of the pleasures or the alleviations of their own individual lot. If ever any system of privilege and enforced subjection had its yoke tightly riveted on the necks of those who are kept down by it, this has. I have not yet shown that it is a wrong system: but every one who is capable of thinking on the subject must see that even if it is, it was certain to outlast all other forms of unjust authority. And when some of the grossest of the other forms still exist in many civilized countries, and have only recently been got rid of in others, it would be strange if that which is so much the deepest-rooted had yet been perceptibly shaken anywhere. There is more reason to wonder that the protests and testimonies against it should have been so numerous and so weighty as they are.

Some will object, that a comparison cannot fairly be made between the government of the male sex and the forms of unjust power which I have adduced in illustration of it, since these are arbitrary, and the effect of mere usurpation, while it on the contrary is natural. But was there ever any domination which did not appear natural to those who possessed it? There was a time when the division of mankind into two classes, a small one of masters and a numerous one of slaves, appeared, even to the most cultivated minds, to be a natural, and the only natural, condition of the human race. No less an intellect, and one which contributed no less to the progress of human thought, than Aristotle, held this opinion without doubt or misgiving; and rested it on the same premisses on which the same assertion in regard to the dominion of men over women is usually based, namely that there are different natures among mankind, free natures, and slave natures; that the Greeks were of a free nature, the barbarian races of Thracians and Asiatics of a slave nature. But why need I go back to Aristotle? Did not the slave-owners of the Southern United States maintain the same doctrine, with all the fanaticism with which men cling to the theories that justify their passions and legitimate their personal interests? Did they not call heaven and earth to witness that the dominion of the white man over the black is natural, that the black race is by nature incapable of freedom, and marked out for slavery?—some even going so far as to say that the freedom of manual labourers is an unnatural order of things anywhere. Again, the theorists of absolute monarchy have always affirmed it to be the only natural form of government; issuing from the patriarchal, which was the primitive and spontaneous form of society, framed on the model of the paternal, which is anterior to society itself, and, as they contend, the most natural authority of all. Nay, for that matter, the law of force itself, to those who could not plead any other, has always seemed the most natural of all grounds for the exercise of authority. Conquering races hold it to be Nature's own dictate that the conquered should obey the conquerors, or, as they euphoniously paraphrase it, that the feebler and more unwarlike races should submit to the braver and manlier. The smallest acquaintance with human life in the Middle Ages shows how supremely natural the dominion of the feudal nobility over men of low condition appeared to the nobility themselves, and how unnatural the conception seemed, of a person of the inferior class claiming equality with them, or exercising authority over them. It hardly seemed less so to the class held in subjection. The emancipated serfs and burgesses, even in their most vigorous struggles, never made any pretension to a share of authority; they only demanded more or less of limitation to the power of tyrannizing over them. So true is it that unnatural generally means only uncustomary, and that everything which is usual appears natural. The subjection of women to men being a universal custom, any departure from it quite naturally appears unnatural. But how entirely, even in this case, the feeling is dependent on custom, appears by ample experience. Nothing so much astonishes the people of distant parts of the world, when they first learn anything about England, as to be told that it is under a queen: the thing seems to them so unnatural as to be almost incredible. To Englishmen this does not seem in the least degree unnatural, because they are used to it; but they do feel it unnatural that women should be soldiers or members of Parliament. In the feudal ages, on the contrary, war and politics were not thought unnatural to women, because not unusual; it seemed natural that women of the privileged classes should be of manly character, inferior in nothing but bodily strength to their husbands and fathers. The independence of women seemed rather less unnatural to the Greeks than to other ancients, on account of the fabulous Amazons (whom they believed to be historical), and the partial example afforded by the Spartan women; who, though no less subordinate by law than in other Greek states, were more free in fact, and being trained to bodily exercises in the same manner with men, gave ample proof that they were not naturally disqualified for them. There can be little doubt that Spartan experience suggested to Plato, among many other of his doctrines, that of the social and political equality of the two sexes.

But, it will be said, the rule of men over women differs from all these others in not being a rule of force: it is accepted voluntarily; women make no complaint, and are consenting parties to it. In the first place, a great number of women do not accept it. Ever since there have been women able to make their sentiments known by their writings (the only mode of publicity which society permits to them), an increasing number of them have recorded protests against their present social condition: and recently many thousands of them, headed by the most eminent women known to the public, have petitioned Parliament for their admission to the Parliamentary Suffrage. The claim of women to be educated as solidly, and in the same branches of knowledge, as men, is urged with growing intensity, and with a great prospect of success; while the demand for their admission into professions and occupations hitherto closed against them, becomes every year more urgent. Though there are not in this country, as there are in the United States, periodical Conventions and an organized party to agitate for the Rights of Women, there is a numerous and active Society organized and managed by women, for the more limited object of obtaining the political franchise. Nor is it only in our own country and in America that women are beginning to protest, more or less collectively, against the disabilities under which they labour. France, and Italy, and Switzerland, and Russia now afford examples of the same thing. How many more women there are who silently cherish similar aspirations, no one can possibly know; but there are abundant tokens how many *would* cherish them, were they not so strenuously taught to repress them as contrary to the proprieties of their sex. It must be remembered, also, that no enslaved class ever asked for complete liberty at once. When Simon de Montfort called the deputies of the commons to sit for the first time in Parliament, did any of them dream of demanding that an assembly, elected by their constituents, should make and destroy ministries, and dictate to the king in affairs of State? No such thought entered into the imagination of the most ambitious of them. The nobility had already these pretensions; the commons pretended to nothing but to be exempt from arbitrary taxation, and from the gross individual oppression of the king's officers. It is a political law of nature that those who are under any power of ancient origin never begin by complaining of the power itself, but only of its oppressive exercise. There is never any want of women who complain of ill usage by their husbands. There would be infinitely more, if complaint were not the greatest of all provocatives to a repetition and increase of the ill usage. It is this which frustrates all attempts to maintain the power but protect the woman against its abuses. In no other case (except that of a child) is the person who has been proved judicially to have suffered an injury, replaced under the physical power of the culprit who inflicted it. Accordingly wives, even in the most extreme and protracted cases of bodily ill usage, hardly ever dare avail themselves of the laws made for their protection: and if, in a moment of irrepressible indignation, or by the interference of neighbours, they are induced to do so, their whole effort afterwards is to disclose as little as they can, and to beg off their tyrant from his merited chastisement.

All causes, social and natural, combine to make it unlikely that women should be collectively rebellious to the power of men. They are so far in a position different from all other subject classes, that their masters require something more from them than actual service. Men do not want solely the obedience of women, they want their sentiments. All men, except the most brutish, desire to have, in the woman most nearly connected with them, not a forced slave but a willing one; not a slave merely, but a favourite. They have therefore put everything in practice to enslave their minds. The masters of all other slaves rely, for maintaining obedience, on fear; either fear of themselves, or religious fears. The masters of women wanted more than simple obedience, and they turned the whole force of education to effect their purpose. All women are brought up from the very earliest years in the belief that their ideal of character is the very opposite to that of men; not self-will, and government by self-control, but submission, and yielding to the control of others. All the moralities tell them that it is the duty of women, and all the current sentimentalities that it is their nature, to live for others; to make complete abnegation of themselves, and to have no life but in their affections. And by their affections are meant the only ones they are allowed to have—those to the men with whom they are connected, or to the children who constitute an additional and indefeasible tie between them and a man. When we put together three things—first, the natural attraction between opposite sexes; secondly, the wife's entire dependence on the husband, every privilege or pleasure she has being either his gift, or depending entirely on his will; and lastly, that the principal object of human pursuit, consideration, and all objects of social ambition, can in general be sought or obtained by her only through him—it would be a miracle if the object of being attractive to men had not become the polar star of feminine education and formation of character. And, this great means of influence over the minds of women having been acquired, an instinct of selfishness made men avail themselves of it to the utmost as a means of holding women in subjection, by representing to them meekness, submissiveness, and resignation of all individual will into the hands of a man, as an essential part of sexual attractiveness. Can it be doubted that any of the other yokes which mankind have succeeded in breaking, would have subsisted till now if the same means had existed, and had been as sedulously used, to bow down their minds to it? If it had been made the object of the life of every young plebeian to find personal favour in the eyes of some patrician, of every young serf with some seigneur; if domestication with him, and a share of his personal affections, had been held out as the prize which they all should look out for, the most gifted and aspiring being able to reckon on the most desirable prizes; and if, when this prize had been obtained, they had been shut out by a wall of brass from all interests not centring in him, all feelings and desires but those which he shared or inculcated; would not serfs and seigneurs, plebeians and patricians, have been as broadly distinguished at this day as men and women are? and would not all but a thinker here and there have believed the distinction to be a fundamental and unalterable fact in human nature?

The preceding considerations are amply sufficient to show that custom, however universal it may be, affords in this case no presumption, and ought not to create any prejudice, in favour of the arrangements which place women in social and political subjection to men. But I may go farther, and maintain that the course of history, and the tendencies of progressive human society, afford not only no presumption in favour of this system of inequality of rights, but a strong one against it; and that, so far as the whole course of human improvement up to this time, the whole stream of modern tendencies, warrants any inference on the subject, it is, that this relic of the past is discordant with the future, and must necessarily disappear.

For what is the peculiar character of the modern world—the difference which chiefly distinguishes modern institutions, modern social ideas, modern life itself, from those of times long past? It is, that human beings are no longer born to their place in life, and chained down by an inexorable bond to the place they are born to, but are free to employ their faculties, and such favourable chances as offer, to achieve the lot which may appear to them most desirable. Human society of old was constituted on a very different principle. All were born to a fixed social position, and were mostly kept in it by law, or interdicted from any means by which they could emerge from it. As some men are born white and others black, so some were born slaves and others freemen and citizens; some were born patricians, others plebeians; some were born feudal nobles, others commoners and *roturiers*. A slave or serf could never make himself free, nor, except by the will of his master, become so. In most European countries it was not till towards the close of the Middle Ages, and as a consequence of the growth of regal power, that commoners could be ennobled. Even among nobles, the eldest son was born the exclusive heir to the paternal possessions, and a long time elapsed before it was fully established that the father could disinherit him. Among the industrious classes, only those who were born members of a guild, or were admitted into it by its members, could lawfully practise their calling within its local limits; and nobody could practise any calling deemed important, in any but the legal manner—by processes authoritatively prescribed. Manufacturers have stood in the pillory for presuming to carry on their business by new and improved methods. In modern Europe, and most in those parts of it which have participated most largely in all other modern improvements, diametrically opposite doctrines now prevail. Law and government do not undertake to prescribe by whom any social or industrial operation shall or shall not be conducted, or what modes of conducting them shall be lawful. These things are left to the unfettered choice of individuals. Even the laws which required that workmen should serve an apprenticeship, have in this country been repealed: there being ample assurance that in all cases in which an apprenticeship is necessary, its necessity will suffice to enforce it. The old theory was, that the least possible should be left to the choice of the individual agent; that all he had to do should, as far as practicable, be laid down for him by superior wisdom. Left to himself he was sure to go wrong. The modern conviction, the fruit of a thousand years of experience, is, that things in which the individual is the person directly interested, never go right but as they are left to his own discretion; and that any regulation of them by authority, except to protect the rights of others, is sure to be mischievous. This conclusion, slowly arrived at, and not adopted until almost every possible application of the contrary theory had been made with disastrous result, now (in the industrial department) prevails universally in the most advanced countries, almost universally in all that have pretensions to any sort of advancement. It is not that all processes are supposed to be equally good, or all persons to be equally qualified for everything; but that freedom of individual choice is now known to be the only thing which procures the adoption of the best processes, and throws each operation into the hands of those who are best qualified for it. Nobody thinks it necessary to make a law that only a strong-armed man shall be a blacksmith. Freedom and competition suffice to make blacksmiths strong-armed men, because the weak-armed can earn more by engaging in occupations for which they are more fit. In consonance with this doctrine, it is felt to be an overstepping of the proper bounds of authority to fix beforehand, on some general presumption, that certain persons are not fit to do certain things. It is now thoroughly known and admitted that if some such presumptions exist, no such presumption is infallible. Even if it be well grounded in a majority of cases, which it is very likely not to be, there will be a minority of exceptional cases in which it does not hold: and in those it is both an injustice to the individuals, and a detriment to society, to place barriers in the way of their using their faculties for their own benefit and for that of others. In the cases, on the other hand, in which the unfitness is real, the ordinary motives of human conduct will on the whole suffice to prevent the incompetent person from making, or from persisting in, the attempt.

If this general principle of social and economical science is not true; if individuals, with such help as they can derive from the opinion of those who know them, are not better judges than the law and the government, of their own capacities and vocation; the world cannot too soon abandon this principle, and return to the old system of regulations and disabilities. But if the principle is true, we ought to act as if we believed it, and not to ordain that to be born a girl instead of a boy, any more than to be born black instead of white, or a commoner instead of a nobleman, shall decide the person's position through all life—shall interdict people from all the more elevated social positions, and from all, except a few, respectable occupations. Even were we to admit the utmost that is ever pretended as to the superior fitness of men for all the functions now reserved to them, the same argument applies which forbids a legal qualification for members of Parliament. If only once in a dozen years the conditions of eligibility exclude a fit person, there is a real loss, while the exclusion of thousands of unfit persons is no gain; for if the constitution of the electoral body disposes them to choose unfit persons, there are always plenty of such persons to choose from. In all things of any difficulty and importance, those who can do them well are fewer than the need, even with the most unrestricted latitude of choice: and any limitation of the field of selection deprives society of some chances of being served by the competent, without ever saving it from the incompetent.

At present, in the more improved countries, the disabilities of women are the only case, save one, in which laws and institutions take persons at their birth, and ordain that they shall never in all their lives be allowed to compete for certain things. The one exception is that of royalty. Persons still are born to the throne; no one, not of the reigning family, can ever occupy it, and no one even of that family can, by any means but the course of hereditary succession, attain it. All other dignities and social advantages are open to the whole male sex: many indeed are only attainable by wealth, but wealth may be striven for by any one, and is actually obtained by many men of the very humblest origin. The difficulties, to the majority, are indeed insuperable without the aid of fortunate accidents; but no male human being is under any legal ban: neither law nor opinion superadd artificial obstacles to the natural ones. Royalty, as I have said, is excepted: but in this case every one feels it to be an exception—an anomaly in the modern world, in marked opposition to its customs and principles, and to be justified only by extraordinary special expediencies, which, though individuals and nations differ in estimating their weight, unquestionably do in fact exist. But in this exceptional case, in which a high social function is, for important reasons, bestowed on birth instead of being put up to competition, all free nations contrive to adhere in substance to the principle from which they nominally derogate; for they circumscribe this high function by conditions avowedly intended to prevent the person to whom it ostensibly belongs from really performing it; while the person by whom it is performed, the responsible minister, does obtain the post by a competition from which no full-grown citizen of the male sex is legally excluded. The disabilities, therefore, to which women are subject from the mere fact of their birth, are the solitary examples of the kind in modern legislation. In no instance except this, which comprehends half the human race, are the higher social functions closed against any one by a fatality of birth which no exertions, and no change of circumstances, can overcome; for even religious disabilities (besides that in England and in Europe they have practically almost ceased to exist) do not close any career to the disqualified person in case of conversion.

The social subordination of women thus stands out an isolated fact in modern social institutions; a solitary breach of what has become their fundamental law; a single relic of an old world of thought and practice exploded in everything else, but retained in the one thing of most universal interest; as if a gigantic dolmen, or a vast temple of Jupiter Olympius, occupied the site of St.

Paul's and received daily worship, while the surrounding Christian churches were only resorted to on fasts and festivals. This entire discrepancy between one social fact and all those which accompany it, and the radical opposition between its nature and the progressive movement which is the boast of the modern world, and which has successively swept away everything else of an analogous character, surely affords, to a conscientious observer of human tendencies, serious matter for reflection. It raises a prima facie presumption on the unfavourable side, far outweighing any which custom and usage could in such circumstances create on the favourable; and should at least suffice to make this, like the choice between republicanism and royalty, a balanced question.

The least that can be demanded is, that the question should not be considered as prejudged by existing fact and existing opinion, but open to discussion on its merits, as a question of justice and expediency: the decision on this, as on any of the other social arrangements of mankind, depending on what an enlightened estimate of tendencies and consequences may show to be most advantageous to humanity in general, without distinction of sex. And the discussion must be a real discussion, descending to foundations, and not resting satisfied with vague and general assertions. It will not do, for instance, to assert in general terms, that the experience of mankind has pronounced in favour of the existing system. Experience cannot possibly have decided between two courses, so long as there has only been experience of one. If it be said that the doctrine of the equality of the sexes rests only on theory, it must be remembered that the contrary doctrine also has only theory to rest upon. All that is proved in its favour by direct experience, is that mankind have been able to exist under it, and to attain the degree of improvement and prosperity which we now see; but whether that prosperity has been attained sooner, or is now greater, than it would have been under the other system, experience does not say. On the other hand, experience does say, that every step in improvement has been so invariably accompanied by a step made in raising the social position of women, that historians and philosophers have been led to adopt their elevation or debasement as on the whole the surest test and most correct measure of the civilization of a people or an age. Through all the progressive period of human history, the condition of women has been approaching nearer to equality with men. This does not of itself prove that the assimilation must go on to complete equality; but it assuredly affords some presumption that such is the case.

Neither does it avail anything to say that the *nature* of the two sexes adapts them to their present functions and position, and renders these appropriate to them. Standing on the ground of common sense and the constitution of the human mind, I deny that any one knows, or can know, the nature of the two sexes, as long as they have only been seen in their persent relation to one another. If men had ever been found in society without women, or women without men, or if there had been a society of men and women in which the women were not under the control of the men, something might have been positively known about the mental and moral differences which may be inherent in the nature of each. What is now called the nature of women is an eminently artificial thing—the result of forced repression in some directions, unnatural stimulation in others. It may be asserted without scruple, that no other class of dependents have had their character so entirely distorted from its natural proportions by their relation with their masters; for, if conquered and slave races have been, in some respects, more forcibly repressed, whatever in them has not been crushed down by an iron heel has generally been let alone, and if left with any liberty of development, it has developed itself according to its own laws; but in the case of women, a hot-house and stove cultivation has always been carried on of some of the capabilities of their nature, for the benefit and pleasure of their masters. Then, because certain products of the general vital force sprout luxuriantly and reach a great development in this heated atmosphere and under this active nurture and watering, while other shoots from the same root, which are left outside in the wintry air, with ice purposely heaped all round them, have a stunted growth, and some are burnt off with fire and disappear; men, with that inability to recognize their own work which distinguishes the unanalytic mind, indolently believe that the tree grows of itself in the way they have made it grow, and that it would die if one half of it were not kept in a vapour bath and the other half in the snow.

Of all difficulties which impede the progress of thought, and the formation of well-grounded opinions on life and social arrangements, the greatest is now the unspeakable ignorance and inattention of mankind in respect to the influences which form human character. Whatever any portion of the human species now are, or seem to be, such, it is supposed, they have a natural tendency to be: even when the most elementary knowledge of the circumstances in which they have been placed, clearly points out the causes that made them what they are. Because a cottier deeply in arrears to his landlord is not industrious, there are people who think that the Irish are naturally idle. Because constitutions can be overthrown when the authorities appointed to execute them turn their arms against them, there are people who think the French incapable of free government. Because the Greeks cheated the Turks, and the Turks only plundered the Greeks, there are persons who think that the Turks are naturally more sincere: and because women, as is often said, care nothing about politics except their personalities, it is supposed that the general good is naturally less interesting to women than to men. History, which is now so much better understood than formerly, teaches another lesson: if only by showing the extraordinary susceptibility of human nature to external influences, and the extreme variableness of those of its manifestations which are supposed to be most universal and uniform. But in history, as in travelling, men usually see only what they already had in their own minds; and few learn much from history, who do not bring much with them to its study.

Hence, in regard to that most difficult question, what are the natural differences between the two sexes—a subject on which it is impossible in the present state of society to obtain complete and correct knowledge—while almost everybody dogmatizes upon it, almost all neglect and make light of the only means by which any partial insight can be obtained into it. This is, an analytic study of the most important department of psychology, the laws of the influence of circumstances on character. For, however great and apparently ineradicable the moral and intellectual differences between men and women might be, the evidence of their being natural differences could only be negative. Those only could be inferred to be natural which could not possibly be artificial—the residuum, after deducting every characteristic of either sex which can admit of being explained from education or external circumstances. The profoundest knowledge of the laws of the formation of character is indispensable to entitle any one to affirm even that there is any difference, much more what the difference is, between the two sexes considered as moral and rational beings; and since no one, as yet, has that knowledge (for there is hardly any subject which, in proportion to its importance, has been so little studied), no one is thus far entitled to any positive opinion on the subject. Conjectures are all that can at present be made; conjectures more or less probable, according as more or less authorized by such knowledge as we yet have of the laws of psychology, as applied to the formation of character.

Even the preliminary knowledge, what the differences between the sexes now are, apart from all question as to how they are made what they are, is still in the crudest and most incomplete state. Medical practitioners and physiologists have ascertained, to some extent, the differences in bodily constitution; and this is an important element to the psychologist: but hardly any medical practitioner is a psychologist. Respecting the mental characteristics of women; their observations are of no more worth than those of common men. It is a subject on which nothing final can be known, so long as those who alone can really know it, women themselves, have given but little testimony, and that little, mostly suborned. It is easy to know stupid women. Stupidity is much the same all the world over. A stupid person's notions and feelings may confidently be inferred from those which prevail in the circle by which the person is surrounded. Not so with those whose opinions and feelings are an emanation from their own nature and faculties. It is only a man here and there who has any tolerable knowledge of the character even of the women of his own family. I do not mean, of their capabilities; these nobody knows, not even themselves, because most of them have never been called out. I mean their actually existing thoughts and feelings. Many a man thinks he perfectly understands women, because he has had amatory relations with several, perhaps with many of them. If he is a good observer, and his experience extends to quality as well as quantity, he may have learnt something of one narrow department of their nature—an important department, no doubt. But of all the rest of it, few persons are generally more ignorant, because there are few from whom it is so carefully hidden. The most favourable case which a man can generally have for studying the character of a woman, is that of his own wife: for the opportunities are greater, and the cases of complete sympathy not so unspeakably rare. And in fact, this is the source from which any knowledge worth having on the subject has, I believe, generally come. But most men have not had the opportunity of studying in this way more than a single case: accordingly one can, to an almost laughable degree, infer what a man's wife is like, from his opinions about women in general. To make even this one case yield any result, the woman must be worth knowing, and the man not only a competent judge, but of a character so sympathetic in itself, and so well adapted to hers, that he can either read her mind by sympathetic intuition, or has nothing in himself which makes her shy of disclosing it. Hardly anything, I believe, can be more rare than this conjunction. It often happens that there is the most complete unity of feeling and community of interests as to all external things, yet the one has as little admission into the internal life of the other as if they were common acquaintance. Even with true affection, authority on the one side and subordination on the other prevent perfect confidence. Though nothing may be intentionally withheld, much is not shown. In the analogous relation of parent and child, the corresponding phenomenon must have been in the observation of every one. As between father and son, how many are the cases in which the father, in spite of real affection on both sides, obviously to all the world does not know, nor suspect, parts of the son's character familiar to his companions and equals. The truth is, that the position of looking up to another is extremely unpropitious to complete sincerity and openness with him. The fear of losing ground in his opinion or in his feelings is so strong, that even in an upright character, there is an unconscious tendency to show only the best side, or the side which, though not the best, is that which he most likes to see: and it may be confidently said that thorough knowledge of one another hardly ever exists, but between persons who, besides being intimates, are equals. How much more true, then, must all this be, when the one is not only under the authority of the other, but has it inculcated on her as a duty to reckon everything else subordinate to his comfort and pleasure, and to let him neither see nor feel anything coming from her, except what is agreeable to him. All these difficulties stand in the way of a man's obtaining any thorough knowledge even of the one woman whom alone, in general, he has sufficient opportunity of studying. When we further consider that to understand one woman is not necessarily to understand any other woman; that even if he could study many women of one rank, or of one country, he would not thereby understand women of other ranks or countries; and even if he did, they are still only the women of a single period of history; we may safely assert that the knowledge which men can acquire of women, even as they have been and are, without reference to what they might be, is wretchedly imperfect and superficial, and always will be so, until women themselves have told all that they have to tell.

And this time has not come; nor will it come otherwise than gradually. It is but of yesterday that women have either been qualified by literary accomplishments, or permitted by society, to tell anything to the general public. As yet very few of them dare tell anything, which men, on whom their literary success depends, are unwilling to hear. Let us remember in what manner, up to a very recent time, the expression, even by a male author, of uncustomary opinions, or what are deemed eccentric feelings, usually was, and in some degree still is, received; and we may form some faint conception under what impediments a woman, who is brought up to think custom and opinion her sovereign rule, attempts to express in books anything drawn from the depths of her own nature. The greatest woman who has left writings behind her sufficient to give her an eminent rank in the literature of her country, thought it necessary to prefix as a motto to her boldest work, 'Un homme peut braver l'opinion; une femme doit s'y soumettre.'[1] The greater part of what women write about women is mere sycophancy to men. In the case of unmarried women, much of it seems only intended to increase their chance of a husband. Many, both married and unmarried, overstep the mark, and inculcate a servility beyond what is desired or relished by any man, except the very vulgarest. But this is not so often the case as, even at a quite late period, it still was. Literary women are becoming more freespoken, and more willing to express their real sentiments. Unfortunately, in this country especially, they are themselves such artificial products, that their sentiments are compounded of a small element of individual observation and consciousness, and a very large one of acquired associations. This will be less and less the case, but it will remain true to a great extent, as long as social institutions do not admit the same free development of originality in women which is possible to men. When that time comes, and not before, we shall see, and not merely hear, as much as it is necessary to know of the nature of women, and the adaptation of other things to it.

[1] Title-page of Mme de Staël's *Delphine*.

I have dwelt so much on the difficulties which at present obstruct any real knowledge by men of the true nature of women, because in this as in so many other things 'opinio copiae inter maximas causas inopiae est'; and there is little chance of reasonable thinking on the matter, while people flatter themselves that they perfectly understand a subject of which most men know absolutely nothing, and of which it is at present impossible that any man, or all men taken together, should have knowledge which can qualify them to lay down the law to women as to what is, or is not, their vocation. Happily, no such knowledge is necessary for any practical purpose connected with the position of women in relation to society and life. For, according to all the principles involved in modern society, the question rests with women themselves—to be decided by their own experience, and by the use of their own faculties. There are no means of finding what either one person or many can do, but by trying—and no means by which any one else can discover for them what it is for their happiness to do or leave undone.

One thing we may be certain of—that what is contrary to women's nature to do, they never will be made to do by simply giving their nature free play. The anxiety of mankind to interfere in behalf of nature, for fear lest nature should not succeed in effecting its purpose, is an altogether unnecessary solicitude. What women by nature cannot do, it is quite superfluous to forbid them from doing. What they can do, but not so well as the men who are their competitors, competition suffices to exclude them from; since nobody asks for protective duties and bounties in favour of women; it is only asked that the present bounties and protective duties in favour of men should be recalled. If women have a greater natural inclination for some things than for others, there is no need of laws or social inculcation to make the majority of them do the former in preference to the latter. Whatever women's services are most wanted for, the free play of competition will hold out the strongest inducements to them to undertake. And, as the words imply, they are most wanted for the things for which they are most fit; by the apportionment of which to them, the collective faculties of the two sexes can be applied on the whole with the greatest sum of valuable result.

The general opinion of men is supposed to be, that the natural vocation of a woman is that of a wife and mother. I say, is supposed to be, because, judging from acts—from the whole of the present constitution of society—one might infer that their opinion was the direct contrary. They might be supposed to think that the alleged natural vocation of women was of all things the most repugnant to their nature; insomuch that if they are free to do anything else—if any other means of living, or occupation of their time and faculties, is open, which has any chance of appearing desirable to them—there will not be enough of them who will be willing to accept the condition said to be natural to them. If this is the real opinion of men in general, it would be well that it should be spoken out. I should like to hear somebody openly enunciating the doctrine (it is already implied in much that is written on the subject)—'It is necessary to society that women should marry and produce children. They will not do so unless they are compelled. Therefore it is necessary to compel them.' The merits of the case would then be clearly defined. It would be exactly that of the slaveholders of South Carolina and Louisiana. 'It is necessary that cotton and sugar should be grown. White men cannot produce them. Negroes will not, for any wages which we choose to give. *Ergo* they must be compelled.' An illustration still closer to the point is that of impressment. Sailors must absolutely be had to defend the country. It often happens that they will not voluntarily enlist. Therefore there must be the power of forcing them. How often has this logic been used! and, but for one flaw in it, without doubt it would have been successful up to this day. But it is open to the retort—First pay the sailors the honest value of their labour. When you have made it as well worth their while to serve you, as to work for other employers, you will have no more difficulty than others have in obtaining their services. To this there is no logical answer except 'I will not': and as people are now not only ashamed, but are not desirous, to rob the labourer of his hire, impressment is no longer advocated. Those who attempt to force women into marriage by closing all other doors against them, lay themselves open to a similar retort. If they mean what they say, their opinion must evidently be, that men do not render the married condition so desirable to women, as to induce them to accept it for its own recommendations. It is not a sign of one's thinking the boon one offers very attractive, when one allows only Hobson's choice, 'that or none.' And here, I believe, is the clue to the feelings of those men, who have a real antipathy to the equal freedom of women. I believe they are afraid, not lest women should be unwilling to marry, for I do not think that any one in reality has that apprehension; but lest they should insist that marriage should be on equal conditions; lest all women of spirit and capacity should prefer doing almost anything else, not in their own eyes degrading, rather than marry, when marrying is giving themselves a master, and a master too of all their earthly possessions. And truly, if this consequence were necessarily incident to marriage, I think that the apprehension would be very well founded. I agree in thinking it probable that few women, capable of anything else, would, unless under an irresistible *entrainement,* rendering them for the time insensible to anything but itself, choose such a lot, when any other means were open to them of filling a conventionally honourable place in life: and if men are determined that the law of marriage shall be a law of despotism, they are quite right, in point of mere policy, in leaving to women only Hobson's choice. But, in that case, all that has been done in the modern world to relax the chain on the minds of women, has been a mistake. They never should have been allowed to receive a literary education. Women who read, much more women who write, are, in the existing constitution of things, a contradiction and a disturbing element: and it was wrong to bring women up with any acquirements but those of an odalisque, or of a domestic servant.

The Grand Inquisitor

Fyodor Dostoevsky

(1821-1881)

In positing the irrational content underlying institutional beliefs, Mill worked from the assumption that these beliefs were nonetheless genuinely held. He was primarily concerned with the conventional sentiments shared by large masses of people and the problems these sentiments posed for the development of a more just and humane society. But what of the elites who lead these masses? Do they genuinely share the conventional notions of those they lead? Or do they simply manipulate these beliefs for their own ends? It is an age-old question that has taken many forms. We have previously seen it handled indirectly by Lucian with reference to philosophy (pages 19–34) and Rabelais with reference to religion (pages 163–79). In our excerpt from The Brothers Karamazov *Dostoevsky handles the question directly if rather ironically.*

The problem of belief, especially in relation to institutional-

ized religion, is central to Dostoevsky's novels. Throughout his works there is a persistent tension between the need for faith and the impossibility of finding it through orthodox channels. In The Brothers Karamazov *Dostoevsky has the purest of innocents, Alyosha, search for faith along the byways of institutionalized Christianity. In his search Alyosha periodically encounters the supreme skeptic, his brother Ivan, who at one point tells him the parable of "The Grand Inquisitor." It is interesting to note that although Ivan is a skeptic, Dostoevsky was not. Indeed, Dostoevsky advanced his religious beliefs in opposition to rationalism and socialism, which he frequently identified with atheism.*

In addition to The Brothers Karamazov, *Dostoevsky's other major novels are* Crime and Punishment, The Idiot, *and* The Possessed. *These works, together with* Notes from Underground, *deal essentially with a single theme which has been summed up in Renne Wellek's words as "a huge allegory of man's search for God and himself."*

"EVEN this must have a preface—that is, a literary preface," laughed Ivan, "and I am a poor hand at making one. You see, my action takes place in the sixteenth century, and at that time, as you probably learnt at school, it was customary in poetry to bring down heavenly powers on earth. Not to speak of Dante, in France, clerks, as well as the monks in the monasteries, used to give regular performances in which the Madonna, the saints, the angels, Christ, and God Himself were brought on the stage. In those days it was done in all simplicity. In Victor Hugo's *Notre Dame de Paris* an edifying and gratuitous spectacle was provided for the people in the Hôtel de Ville of Paris in the reign of Louis XI in honour of the birth of the dauphin. It was called *Le bon jugement de la très sainte et gracieuse Vierge Marie,* and she appears herself on the stage and pronounces her *bon jugement.* Similar plays, chiefly from the Old Testament, were occasionally performed in Moscow too, up to the times of Peter the

Great. But besides plays there were all sorts of legends and ballads scattered about the world, in which the saints and angels and all the powers of Heaven took part when required. In our monasteries the monks busied themselves in translating, copying, and even composing such poems—and even under the Tatars. There is, for instance, one such poem (of course, from the Greek), *The Wanderings of Our Lady through Hell,* with descriptions as bold as Dante's. Our Lady visits hell, and the Archangel Michael leads her through the torments. She sees the sinners and their punishment. There she sees among others one noteworthy set of sinners in a burning lake; some of them sink to the bottom of the lake so that they can't swim out, and 'these God forgets'—an expression of extraordinary depth and force. And so Our Lady, shocked and weeping, falls before the throne of God and begs for mercy for all in hell—for all she has seen there, indiscriminately. Her conversation with God is immensely interesting. She beseeches Him, she will not desist, and when God points to the hands and feet of her Son, nailed to the Cross, and asks, 'How can I forgive His tormentors?' she bids all the saints, all the martyrs, all the angels and archangels to fall down with her and pray for mercy on all without distinction. It ends by her winning from God a respite of suffering every year from Good Friday till Trinity Day, and the sinners at once raise a cry of thankfulness from hell, chanting, 'Thou art just, O Lord, in this judgment.' Well, my poem would have been of that kind if it had appeared at that time. He comes on the scene in my poem, but He says nothing, only appears and passes on. Fifteen centuries have passed since He promised to come in His glory, fifteen centuries since His prophet wrote, 'Behold, I come quickly'; 'Of that day and that hour knoweth no man, neither the Son, but the Father,' as He Himself predicted on earth. But humanity awaits him with the same faith and with the same love. Oh, with greater faith, for it is fifteen centuries since man has ceased to see signs from heaven.

No signs from heaven come to-day
To add to what the heart doth say.

There was nothing left but faith in what the heart doth say. It is true there were many miracles in those days. There were saints who performed miraculous cures; some holy people, according to their biographies, were visited by the Queen of Heaven herself. But the devil did not slumber, and doubts were already arising among men of the truth of these miracles. And just then there appeared in the north of Germany a terrible new heresy. 'A huge star like to a torch' (that is, to a church) 'fell on the sources of the waters and they became bitter.' These heretics began blasphemously denying miracles. But those who remained faithful were all the more ardent in their faith. The tears of humanity rose up to Him as before, awaited His coming, loved Him, hoped for Him, yearned to suffer and die for Him as before. And so many ages mankind had prayed with faith and fervour, 'O Lord our God, hasten Thy coming'; so many ages called upon Him, that in His infinite mercy He deigned to come down to His servants. Before that day He had come down, He had visited some holy men, martyrs, and hermits, as is written in their lives. Among us, Tyutchev, with absolute faith in the truth of his words, bore witness that

Bearing the Cross, in slavish dress,
Weary and worn, the Heavenly King
Our mother, Russia, came to bless,
And through our land went wandering.

And that certainly was so, I assure you.

"And behold, He deigned to appear for a moment to the people, to the tortured, suffering people, sunk in iniquity, but loving Him like children. My story is laid in Spain, in Seville, in the most terrible time of the Inquisition, when fires were lighted every day to the glory of God, and 'in the splendid *auto da fé* the wicked heretics were burnt.' Oh, of course, this was not the coming in which He will appear, according to His promise, at the end of time in all His heavenly glory, and which will be sudden 'as lightning flashing from east to west.' No, He visited His children only for a moment, and there where the flames were crackling round the heretics. In His infinite mercy He came once more among men in that human shape in which He walked among men for thirty-three years fifteen centuries ago. He came down to the 'hot pavements' of the southern town in which on the day before almost a hundred heretics had, *ad majorem gloriam Dei,* been burnt by the cardinal, the Grand Inquisitor, in a magnificent *auto da fé,* in the presence of the king, the court, the knights, the cardinals, the most charming ladies of the court, and the whole population of Seville.

"He came softly, unobserved, and yet, strange to say, everyone recognised Him. That might be one of the best passages in the poem. I mean, why they recognised Him. The people are irresistibly drawn to Him, they surround Him, they flock about Him, follow Him. He moves silently in their midst with a gentle smile of infinite compassion. The sun of love burns in His heart, light and power shine from His eyes, and their radiance, shed on the people, stirs their hearts with responsive love. He holds out His hands to them, blesses them, and a healing virtue comes from contact with Him, even with His garments. An old man in the crowd, blind from childhood, cries out, 'O Lord, heal me and I shall see Thee!' and, as it were, scales fall from his eyes and the blind man sees Him. The crowd weeps and kisses the earth under His feet. Children throw flowers before Him, sing, and cry hosannah. 'It is He—it is He!' all repeat. 'It must be He, it can be no one but Him!' He stops at the steps of the Seville cathedral at the moment when the weeping mourners are bringing in a little open white coffin. In it lies a child of seven, the only daughter of a prominent citizen. The dead child lies hidden in flowers. 'He will raise your child,' the crowd shouts to the weeping mother. The priest, coming to meet the coffin, looks perplexed, and frowns, but the mother of the dead child throws herself at His feet with a wail. 'If it is Thou, raise my child!' she cries, holding out her hands to Him. The procession halts, the coffin in laid on the steps at His feet. He looks with compassion, and His lips once more softly pronounce, 'Maiden, arise!' and the maiden arises. The little girl sits up in the coffin and looks round, smiling with wide-open wondering eyes, holding a bunch of white roses they had put in her hand.

"There are cries, sobs, confusion among the people, and at that moment the cardinal himself, the Grand Inquisitor, passes by the cathedral. He is an old man, almost ninety, tall and erect, with a withered face and sunken eyes, in which there is still a gleam of light. He is not dressed in his gorgeous cardinal's robes, as he was the day before, when he was burning the enemies of the Roman Church—at this moment he is wearing his coarse, old, monk's cassock. At a distance behind him come his gloomy assistants and slaves and the 'holy guard.' He stops at the sight of the crowd and watches it from a distance. He sees everything; he sees them set the coffin down at His feet, sees the child rise up, and his face darkens. He knits his thick grey brows and his eyes gleam with a sinister fire. He holds out his finger and bids the guards take Him. And such is his power, so completely are the people cowed into submission and trembling obedience to him, that the crowd immediately makes way for the guards, and in the midst of deathlike silence they lay hands on Him and lead Him away. The crowd instantly bows down to the earth, like one man, before the old Inquisitor. He blesses the people in silence and passes on. The guards lead their prisoner to the close, gloomy vaulted prison in the ancient palace of the Holy Inquisition and shut Him in it. The day passes and is followed by the dark, burning, 'breathless' night of Seville. The air is 'fragrant with laurel and lemon.' In the pitch darkness the iron door of the prison is suddenly opened and the Grand Inquisitor himself comes in with a light in his hand. He is alone; the door is closed at once behind him. He stands in the doorway and for a minute or two gazes into His face. At last he goes up slowly, sets the light on the table and speaks.

" 'Is it Thou? Thou?' but receiving no answer, he adds at once. 'Don't answer, be silent. What canst Thou say, indeed? I know too well what Thou wouldst say. And Thou has no right to add anything to what Thou hadst said of old. Why, then, art Thou come to hinder us? For Thou hast come to hinder us, and Thou knowest that. But dost Thou know what will be to-morrow? I know not who Thou art and care not to know whether it is Thou or only a semblance of Him, but to-morrow I shall condemn Thee and burn Thee at the stake as the worst of heretics. And the very people who have to-day kissed Thy feet, to-morrow at the faintest sign from me will rush to heap up the embers of Thy fire. Knowest Thou that? Yes, maybe Thou knowest it,' he added with thoughtful penetration, never for a moment taking his eyes off the Prisoner."

"I don't quite understand, Ivan. What does it mean?" Alyosha, who had been listening in silence, said with a smile. "Is it simply a wild fantasy, or a mistake on the part of the old man—some impossible *quid pro quo?*"

"Take it as the last," said Ivan, laughing, "if you are so corrupted by modern realism and can't stand anything fantastic. If you like it to be a case of mistaken identity, let it be so. It is true," he went on, laughing, "the old man was ninety, and he might well be crazy over his set idea. He might have been struck by the appearance of the Prisoner. It might, in fact, be simply his ravings, the delusion of an old man of ninety, over-excited by the *auto da fé* of a hundred heretics the day before. But does it matter to us after all whether it was a mistake of identity or a wild fantasy? All that matters is that the old man should speak out, that he should speak openly of what he has thought in silence for ninety years."

"And the Prisoner too is silent? Does He look at him and not say a word?"

"That's inevitable in any case," Ivan laughed again. "The old man has told Him He hasn't the right to add anything to what He has said of old. One may say it is the most fundamental feature of Roman Catholicism, in my opinion at least. 'All has been given by Thee to the Pope,' they say, 'and all, therefore, is still in the Pope's hands, and there is no need for Thee to come now at all. Thou must not meddle for the time, at least.' That's how they speak and write too—the Jesuits, at any rate. I have read it myself in the works of their theologians. 'Hast Thou the right to reveal to us one of the mysteries of that world from which Thou hast come?' my old man asks Him, and answers the question for Him. 'No, Thou hast not; that Thou mayest not add to what has been said of old, and mayest not take from men the freedom which Thou didst exalt when Thou wast on earth. Whatsoever Thou revealest anew will encroach on men's freedom of faith; for it will be manifest as a miracle, and the freedom of their faith was dearer to Thee than anything in those days fifteen hundred years ago. Didst Thou not often say then, "I will make you free"? But now Thou hast seen these "free" men,' the old man adds suddenly, with a pensive smile. 'Yes, we've paid dearly for it,' he goes on, looking sternly at Him, 'but at last we have completed that work in Thy name. For fifteen centuries we have been wrestling with Thy freedom, but now it is ended and over for good. Dost Thou not believe that it's over for good? Thou lookest meekly at me and deignest not even to be wroth with me. But let me tell Thee that now, to-day, people are more persuaded than ever that they have perfect freedom, yet they have brought their freedom to us and laid it humbly at our feet. But that has been our doing. Was this what Thou didst? Was this Thy freedom?' "

"I don't understand again." Alyosha broke in. "Is he ironical, is he jesting?"

"Not a bit of it! He claims it as a merit for himself and his Church that at last they have vanquished freedom and have done so to make men happy. 'For now' (he is speaking of the Inquisition, of course) 'for the first time it has become possible to think of the happiness of men. Man was created a rebel; and how can rebels be happy? Thou wast warned,' he says to Him. 'Thou hast had no lack of admonitions and warnings, but Thou didst not listen to those warnings; Thou didst reject the only way by which men might be made happy. But, fortunately, departing Thou didst hand on the work to us. Thou hast promised, Thou has established by Thy word, Thou hast given to us the right to bind and to unbind, and now, of course, Thou canst not think of taking it away. Why, then, hast Thou come to hinder us?' "

"And what's the meaning of 'no lack of admonitions and warnings'?" asked Alyosha.

"Why, that's the chief part of what the old man must say.

" 'The wise and dread spirit, the spirit of self-destruction and non-existence,' the old man goes on, 'the great spirit talked with Thee in the wilderness, and we are told in the books that he "tempted" Thee. Is that so? And could anything truer be said than what he revealed to Thee in three questions and what Thou didst reject, and what in the books is called "the temptation"? And yet if there has ever been on earth a real stupendous miracle, it took place on that day, on the day of the three temptations. The statement of those three questions was itself the miracle. If it were possible to imagine simply for the sake of argument that those three questions of the dread spirit had perished utterly from the books, and that we had to restore them and to invent them anew, and to do so had gathered together all the wise men of the earth—rulers, chief priests, learned men, philosophers, poets—and had set them the task to invent three questions, such as would not only fit the occasion, but express in three words, three human phrases, the whole future history of the world and of humanity—dost Thou believe that all the wisdom of the earth united could have invented anything in depth and force equal to the three questions which were actually put to Thee then by the wise and mighty spirit in the wilderness? From those questions alone, from the miracle of their statement, we can see that we have here to do not with the fleeting human intelligence, but with the absolute and eternal. For in those three questions the whole subsequent history of mankind is, as it were, brought together into one whole, and foretold, and in them are united all the unsolved historical contradictions of human nature. At the time it could not be so clear, since the future was unknown; but now that fifteen hundred years have passed, we see that everything in those three questions was so justly divined and foretold, and has been so truly fulfilled, that nothing can be added to them or taken from them.

" 'Judge Thyself who was right—Thou or he who questioned Thee then? Remember the first question; its meaning, in other words, was this: "Thou wouldst go into the world, and art going with empty hands, with some promise of freedom which men in their simplicity and their natural unruliness cannot even understand, which they fear and dread—for nothing has ever been more insupportable for a man and a human society than freedom. But seest Thou these stones in this parched and barren wilderness? Turn them into bread, and mankind will run after Thee like a flock of sheep, grateful and obedient, though for ever trembling, lest Thou withdraw Thy hand and deny them Thy bread." But Thou wouldst not deprive man of freedom and didst reject the offer, thinking, what is that freedom worth, if obedience is bought with bread? Thou didst reply that man lives not by bread alone. But dost Thou know that for the sake of that earthly bread the spirit of the earth will rise up against Thee and will strive with Thee and overcome Thee, and all will follow him, crying, "Who can compare with this beast? He has given us fire from heaven!" Dost Thou know that the ages will pass, and humanity will proclaim by the lips of their sages that there is no crime, and therefore no sin; there is only hunger? "Feed men, and then ask for them virtue!" that's what they'll write on the banner, which they will raise against Thee, and with which they will destroy Thy temple. Where Thy temple stood will rise a new building; the terrible tower of Babel will be built again, and though, like the one of old, it will not be finished, yet Thou mightest have prevented that new tower and have cut short the sufferings of men for a thousand years; for they will come back to us after a thousand years of agony with their tower. They will seek us again, hidden underground in the catacombs, for we shall be again persecuted and tortured. They will find us and cry to us, "Feed us, for those who have promised us fire from heaven haven't given it!" And then we shall finish building their tower, for he finishes the building who feeds them. And we alone shall feed them in Thy name, declaring falsely that it is in Thy name. Oh, never, never can they feed themselves without us! No science will give them bread so long as they remain free. In the end they will lay their freedom at our feet, and say to us, "Make us your slaves, but feed us." They will understand themselves, at last, that freedom and bread enough for all are inconceivable together, for never, never will they be able to share between them! They will be convinced, too, that they can never be free, for they are weak, vicious, worthless, and rebellious. Thou didst promise them the bread of Heaven, but, I repeat again, can it compare with earthly bread in the eyes of the weak, ever sinful and ignoble race of man? And if for the sake of the bread of Heaven thousands shall follow Thee, what is to become of the millions and tens of thousands of millions of creatures who will not have the strength to forego the earthly bread for the sake of the heavenly? Or dost Thou care only for the tens of thousands of the great and strong, while the millions, numerous as the sands of the sea, who are weak but love Thee, must exist only for the sake of the great and strong? No, we care for the weak too. They are sinful and rebellious, but in the end they too will become obedient. They will marvel at us and look on us as gods, because we are ready to endure the freedom which they have found so dreadful and to rule over them—so awful it will seem to them to be free. But we shall tell them that we are Thy servants and rule them in Thy name. We shall deceive them again, for we will not let Thee come to us again. That deception will be our suffering, for we shall be forced to lie.

" 'This is the significance of the first question in the wilderness, and this is what Thou hast rejected for the sake of that freedom which Thou hast exalted above everything. Yet in this question lies hid the great secret of this world. Choosing "bread," Thou wouldst have satisfied the universal and everlasting craving of humanity—to find someone to worship. So long as man remains free he strives for nothing so incessantly and so painfully as to find someone to worship. But man seeks to worship what is established beyond dispute, so that all men would agree at once to worship it. For these pitiful creatures are concerned not only to find what one or the other can worship, but to find something that all would believe in and worship; what is essential is that all may be *together* in it. This craving for *community* of worship is the chief misery of every man individually and of all humanity from the beginning of time. For the sake of common worship they've slain each other with the sword. They have set up gods and challenged one another, "Put away your gods and come and worship ours, or we will kill you and your gods!" And so it will be to the end of the world, even when gods disappear from the earth; they will fall down before idols just the same. Thou didst know, Thou couldst not but have known, this fundamental secret of human nature, but Thou didst reject the one infallible banner which was offered

Thee to make all men bow down to Thee alone—the banner of earthly bread; and Thou hast rejected it for the sake of freedom and the bread of Heaven. Behold what Thou didst further. And all again in the name of freedom! I tell Thee that man is tormented by no greater anxiety than to find someone quickly to whom he can hand over that gift of freedom with which the ill-fated creature is born. But only one who can appease their conscience can take over their freedom. In bread there was offered Thee an invincible banner; give bread, and man will worship thee, for nothing is more certain than bread. But if someone else gains possession of his conscience—oh! then he will cast away Thy bread and follow after him who has ensnared his conscience. In that Thou was right. For the secret of man's being is not only to live but to have something to live for. Without a stable conception of the object of life, man would not consent to go on living, and would rather destroy himself than remain on earth, though he had bread in abundance. That is true. But what happened? Instead of taking men's freedom from them, Thou didst make it greater than ever! Didst Thou forget that man prefers peace, and even death, to freedom of choice in the knowledge of good and evil? Nothing is more seductive for man than his freedom of conscience, but nothing is a greater cause of suffering. And behold, instead of giving a firm foundation for setting though Thou didst not love them at all—Thou didst choose all that is exceptional, vague and enigmatic; Thou didst choose what was utterly beyond the strength of men, acting as though Thou didst not love them at all—Thou who didst come to give Thy life for them! Instead of taking possession of men's freedom, Thou didst increase it, and burdened the spiritual kingdom of mankind with its sufferings for ever. Thou didst desire man's free love, that he should follow Thee freely, enticed and taken captive by Thee. In place of the rigid ancient law, man must hereafter with free heart decide for himself what is good and what is evil, having only Thy image before him as his guide. But didst Thou not know that he would at last reject even Thy image and Thy truth, if he is weighed down with the fearful burden of free choice? They will cry aloud at last that the truth is not in Thee, for they could not have been left in greater confusion and suffering than Thou hast caused, laying upon them so many cares and unanswerable problems.

" 'So that, in truth, Thou didst Thyself lay the foundation for the destruction of Thy kingdom, and no one is more to blame for it. Yet what was offered Thee? There are three powers, three powers alone, able to conquer and to hold captive for ever the conscience of these impotent rebels for their happiness—those forces are miracle, mystery and authority. Thou hast rejected all three and hast set the example for doing so. When the wise and dread spirit set Thee on the pinnacle of the temple and said to Thee, "If Thou wouldst know whether Thou art the Son of God then cast Thyself down, for it is written: the angels shall hold him up lest he fall and bruise himself, and Thou shalt know then whether Thou art the Son of God and shalt prove then how great is Thy faith in Thy Father." But Thou didst refuse and wouldst not cast Thyself down. Oh, of course. Thou didst proudly and well, like God; but the weak, unruly race of men, are they gods? Oh, Thou didst know then that in taking one step, in making one movement to cast Thyself down, Thou wouldst be tempting God and have lost all Thy faith in Him, and wouldst have been dashed to pieces against that earth which Thou didst come to save. And the wise spirit that tempted Thee would have rejoiced. But I ask again, are there many like Thee? And couldst Thou believe for one moment that men, too, could face such a temptation? Is the nature of men such, that they can reject miracle, and at the great moments of their life, the moments of their deepest, most agonising spiritual difficulties, cling only to the free verdict of the heart? Oh, Thou didst know that Thy deed would be recorded in books, would be handed down to remote times and the utmost ends of the earth, and Thou didst hope that man, following Thee, would cling to God and not ask for a miracle. But Thou didst not know that when man rejects miracle he rejects God too; for man seeks not so much God as the miraculous. And as man cannot bear to be without the miraculous, he will create new miracles of his own for himself, and will worship deeds of sorcery and witchcraft, though he might be a hundred times over a rebel, heretic and infidel. Thou didst not come down from the Cross when they shouted to Thee, mocking and reviling Thee, "Come down from the cross and we will believe that Thou art He." Thou didst not come down, for again Thou wouldst not enslave man by a miracle, and didst crave faith given freely, not based on miracle. Thou didst crave for free love and not the base raptures of the slave before the might that has overawed him for ever. But Thou didst think too highly of men therein, for they are slaves, of course, though rebellious by nature. Look round and judge;

fifteen centuries have passed, look upon them. Whom hast Thou raised up to Thyself? I swear, man is weaker and baser by nature than Thou hast believed him! Can he, can he do what Thou didst? By showing him so much respect, Thou didst, as it were, cease to feel for him, for Thou didst ask far too much from him—Thou who hast loved him more than Thyself! Respecting him less, Thou wouldst have asked less of him. That would have been more like love, for his burden would have been lighter. He is weak and vile. What though he is everywhere now rebelling against our power, and proud of his rebellion? It is the pride of a child and a schoolboy. They are little children rioting and barring out the teacher at school. But their childish delight will end; it will cost them dear. They will cast down temples and drench the earth with blood. But they will see at last, the foolish children, that, though they are rebels, they are impotent rebels, unable to keep up their own rebellion. Bathed in their foolish tears, they will recognise at last that He who created them rebels must have meant to mock at them. They will say this in despair, and their utterance will be a blasphemy which will make them more unhappy still, for man's nature cannot bear blasphemy, and in the end always avenges it on itself. And so unrest, confusion, and unhappiness—that is the present lot of man after Thou didst bear so much for their freedom! The great prophet tells in vision and in image, that he saw all those who took part in the first resurrection and that there were of each tribe twelve thousand. But if there were so many of them, they must have been not men but gods. They had borne Thy cross, they had endured scores of years in the barren, hungry wilderness, living upon locusts and roots—and Thou mayest indeed point with pride at those children of freedom, of free love, of free and splendid sacrifice for Thy name. But remember that they were only some thousands; and what of the rest? And how are the other weak ones to blame, because they could not endure what the strong have endured? How is the weak soul to blame that it is unable to receive such terrible gifts? Canst Thou have simply come to the elect and for the elect? But if so, it is a mystery and we cannot understand it. And if it is a mystery, we too have a right to preach a mystery, and to teach them that it's not the free judgment of their hearts, not love that matters, but a mystery which they must follow blindly, even against their conscience. So we have done. We have corrected Thy work and have founded it upon *miracle, mystery* and *authority*. And men rejoiced that they were again led like sheep, and that the terrible gift that had brought them such suffering was, at last, lifted from their hearts. Were we right teaching them this? Speak! Did we not love mankind, so meekly acknowledging their feebleness, lovingly lightening their burden, and permitting their weak nature even sin with our sanction? Why hast Thou come now to hinder us? And why dost Thou look silently and searchingly at me with Thy mild eyes? Be angry. I don't want Thy love, for I love Thee not. And what use is it for me to hide anything from Thee? Don't I know to Whom I am speaking? All that I can say is known to Thee already. And is it for me to conceal from Thee our mystery? Perhaps it is Thy will to hear it from my lips. Listen, then. We are not working with Thee, but with *him*—that is our mystery. It's long—eight centuries—since we have been on *his* side and not on Thine. Just eight centuries ago, we took from him what Thou didst reject with scorn, that last gift he offered Thee, showing Thee all the kingdoms of the earth. We took from him Rome and the sword of Caesar, and proclaimed ourselves sole rulers of the earth, though hitherto we have not been able to complete our work. But whose fault is that? Oh, the work is only beginning, but it has begun. It has long to await completion and the earth has yet much to suffer, but we shall triumph and shall be Caesars, and then we shall plan the universal happiness of man. But Thou mightest have taken even then the sword of Caesar. Why didst Thou reject that last gift? Hadst Thou accepted that last counsel of the mighty spirit, Thou wouldst have accomplished all that man seeks on earth—that is, someone to worship, someone to keep his conscience, and some means of uniting all in one unanimous and harmonious ant-heap, for the craving for universal unity is the third and last anguish of men. Mankind as a whole has always striven to organise a universal state. There have been many great nations with great histories, but the more highly they were developed the more unhappy they were, for they felt more acutely than other people the craving for world-wide union. The great conquerors, Timours and Ghenghis-Khans, whirled like hurricanes over the face of the earth striving to subdue its people, and they too were but the unconscious expression of the same craving for universal unity. Hadst Thou taken the world and Caesar's purple, Thou wouldst have founded the universal state and have given universal peace. For who can rule men if not he who holds their conscience and their bread in his hands? We have taken the sword of Caesar, and in taking it, of course, have rejected Thee and followed *him*. Oh, ages are yet to come of the confusion of free thought, of their science and cannibalism. For having begun to build their tower of Babel without us, they will end, of course, with cannibalism. But then the beast will crawl to us and lick our feet and spatter them with tears of blood. And we shall sit upon the beast and raise the cup, and on it will be written, "Mystery." But then, and only then, the reign of peace and happiness will come for men. Thou art proud of Thine elect, but Thou hast only the elect, while we give rest to all. And besides, how many of those elect, those mighty ones who could become elect, have grown weary waiting for Thee, and have transferred and will transfer the powers of their spirit and the warmth of their heart to the other camp, and end by raising their *free* banner against Thee. Thou didst Thyself lift up that banner. But with us all will be happy and will no more rebel nor destroy one another as under Thy freedom. Oh, we shall persuade them that they will only become free when they renounce their freedom to us and submit to us. And shall we be right or shall we be lying? They will be convinced that we are right, for they will remember the horrors of slavery and confusion to which Thy freedom brought them. Freedom, free thought, and science will lead them into such straits and will bring them face to face with such marvels and insoluble mysteries, that some of them, the fierce and rebellious, will destroy themselves, others, rebellious but weak, will destroy one another, while the rest, weak and unhappy, will crawl fawning to our feet and whine to us: "Yes, you were right, you alone possess His mystery, and we come back to you, save us from ourselves!"

" 'Receiving bread from us, they will see clearly that we take the bread made by their hands from them, to give it to them, without any miracle. They will see that we do not change the stones to bread, but in truth they will be more thankful for taking it from our hands than for the bread itself! For they will remember only too well that in old days, without our help, even the bread they made turned to stones in their hands, while since they have come back to us, the very stones have turned to bread in their hands. Too, too well will they know the value of complete submission! And until men know that, they will be unhappy. Who is most to blame for their not knowing it?—speak! Who scattered the flock and sent it astray on unknown paths? But the flock will come together again and will submit once more, and then it will be once for all. Then we shall give them the quiet humble happiness of weak creatures such as they are by nature. Oh, we shall persuade them at last not to be proud, for Thou didst lift them up and thereby taught them to be proud. We shall show them that they are weak, that they are only pitiful children, but that childlike happiness is the sweetest of all. They will become timid and will look to us and huddle close to us in fear, as chicks to the hen. They will marvel at us and will be awe stricken before us, and will be proud at our being so powerful and clever that we have been able to subdue such a turbulent flock of thousands of millions. They will tremble impotently before our wrath, their minds will grow fearful, they will be quick to shed tears like women and children, but they will be just as ready at a sign from us to pass to laughter and rejoicing, to happy mirth and childish song. Yes, we shall set them to work, but in their leisure hours we shall make their life like a child's game, with children's songs and innocent dance. Oh, we shall allow them even sin, they are weak and helpless, and they will love us like children because we allow them to sin. We shall tell them that every sin will be expiated, if it is done with our permission, that we allow them to sin because we love them, and the punishment for these sins we take upon ourselves. And we shall take it upon ourselves, and they will adore us as their saviours who have taken on themselves their sins before God. And they will have no secrets from us. We shall allow or forbid them to live with their wives and mistresses, to have or not to have children—according to whether they have been obedient or disobedient—and they will submit to us gladly and cheerfully. The most painful secrets of their conscience, all, all they will bring to us, and we shall have an answer for all. And they will be glad to believe our answer, for it will save them from the great anxiety and terrible agony they endure at present in making a free decision for themselves. And all will be happy, all the millions of creatures except the hundred thousand who rule over them. For only we, we who guard the mystery, shall be unhappy. There will be thousands of millions of happy babes, and a hundred thousand sufferers who have taken upon themselves the curse of the knowledge of good and evil. Peacefully they will die, peacefully they will expire in Thy name, and beyond the grave they will find nothing but death. But we shall keep the secret, and for their happiness we shall allure them with the reward of heaven and eternity. Though if there were anything in the other world, it certainly would not be for such as they. It is prophesied that Thou wilt come again in victory, Thou wilt come with Thy chosen, the proud and strong, but we will say that they have only saved themselves, but we have saved all. We are told that the harlot who sits upon the beast, and holds in her hands the *mystery,* shall be put to shame, that the weak will rise up again, and will rend her royal purple and will strip naked her loathsome body. But then I will stand up and point out to Thee the thousand millions of happy children who have known no sin. And we who have taken their sins upon us for their happiness will stand up before Thee and say: "Judge us if Thou canst and darest." Know that I fear Thee not. Know that I too have been in the wilderness, I too have lived on roots and locusts, I too prized the freedom with which Thou hast blessed men, and I too was striving to stand among Thy elect, among the strong and powerful, thirsting "to make up the number." But I awakened and would not serve madness. I turned back and joined the ranks of those *who have corrected Thy work.* I left the proud and went back to the humble, for the happiness of the humble. What I say to Thee will come to pass, and our dominion will be built up. I repeat, to-morrow Thou shalt see that obedient flock who at a sign from me will hasten to heap up the hot cinders about the pile on which I shall burn Thee for coming to hinder us. For if anyone has ever deserved our fires, it is Thou. To-morrow I shall burn Thee. *Dixi.*' "

Ivan stopped. He was carried away as he talked, and spoke with excitement; when he had finished, he suddenly smiled.

Alyosha had listened in silence; towards the end he was greatly moved and seemed several times on the point of interrupting, but restrained himself. Now his words came with a rush.

"But . . . that's absurd!" he cried, flushing. "Your poem is in praise of Jesus, not in blame of Him—as you meant it to be. And who will believe you about freedom? Is that the way to understand it? That's not the idea of it in the Orthodox Church. . . . That's Rome, and not even the whole of Rome, it's false—those are the worst of the Catholics, the Inquisitors, the Jesuits! . . . And there could not be such a fantastic creature as your Inquisitor. What are these sins of mankind they take on themselves? Who are these keepers of the mystery who have taken some curse upon themselves for the happiness of mankind? When have they been seen? We know the Jesuits, they are spoken ill of, but surely they are not what you describe? They are not that at all, not at all. . . . They are simply the Romish army for the earthly sovereignty of the world in the future, with the Pontiff of Rome for Emperor . . . that's their ideal, but there's no sort of mystery or lofty melancholy about it. . . . It's simple lust of power, of filthy earthly gain, of domination—something like a universal serfdom with them as masters—that's all they stand for. They don't even believe in God perhaps. Your suffering Inquisitor is a mere fantasy."

"Stay, stay," laughed Ivan, "how hot you are! A fantasy you say, let it be so! Of course it's a fantasy. But allow me to say: do you really think that the Roman Catholic movement of the last centuries is actually nothing but the lust of power, of filthy earthly gain? Is that Father Païssy's teaching?"

"No, no, on the contrary, Father Païssy did once say something rather the same as you . . . but of course it's not the same, not a bit the same," Alyosha hastily corrected himself.

"A precious admission, in spite of your 'not a bit the same.' I ask you why your Jesuits and Inquisitors have united simply for vile material gain? Why can there not be among them one martyr oppressed by great sorrow and loving humanity? You see, only suppose that there was one such man among all those who desire nothing but filthy material gain—if there's only one like my old Inquisitor, who had himself eaten roots in the desert and made frenzied efforts to subdue his flesh to make himself free and perfect. But yet all his life he loved humanity, and suddenly his eyes were opened, and he saw that it is no great moral blessedness to attain perfection and freedom, if at the same time one gains the conviction that millions of God's creatures have been created as a mockery, that they will never be capable of using their freedom, that these poor rebels can never turn into giants to complete the tower, that it was not for such geese that the great idealist dreamt his dream of harmony. Seeing all that he turned back and joined—the clever people. Surely that could have happened?"

"Joined whom, what clever people?" cried Alyosha, completely carried away. "They have no such great cleverness and no mysteries and secrets. . . . Perhaps nothing but Atheism, that's all their secret. Your Inquisitor does not believe in God, that's his secret!"

"What if it is so! At last you have guessed it. It's perfectly true, it's true that that's the whole secret, but isn't that suffering, at least for a man like that, who has wasted his whole life in the desert and yet could not shake off his incurable love of humanity? In his old age he reached the clear conviction that nothing but the advice of the great dread spirit could build up any tolerable sort of life for the feeble, unruly, 'incomplete, empirical creatures created in jest.' And so, convinced of this, he sees that he must follow the counsel of the wise spirit, the dread spirit of death and destruction, and therefore accept lying and deception, and lead men consciously to death and destruction, and yet deceive them all the way so that they may not notice where they are being led, that the poor blind creatures may at least on the way think themselves happy. And note, the deception is in the name of Him in Whose ideal the old man had so fervently believed all his life long. Is not that tragic? And if only one such stood at the head of the whole army 'filled with the lust of power only for the sake of filthy gain'—would not one such be enough to make a tragedy? More than that, one such standing at the head is enough to create the actual leading idea of the Roman Church with all its armies and Jesuits, its highest idea. I tell you frankly that I firmly believe that there has always been such a man among those who stood at the head of the movement. Who knows, there may have been some such even among the Roman Popes. Who knows, perhaps the spirit of that accursed old man who loves mankind so obstinately in his own way, is to be found even now in a whole multitude of such old men, existing not by chance but by agreement, as a secret league formed long ago for the guarding of the mystery, to guard it from the weak and the unhappy, so as to make them happy. No doubt it is so, and so it must be indeed. I fancy that even among the Masons there's something of the same mystery at the bottom, and that that's why the Catholics so detest the Masons as their rivals breaking up the unity of the idea, while it is so essential that there should be one flock and one shepherd. . . . But from the way I defend my idea I might be an author impatient of your criticism. Enough of it."

"You are perhaps a Mason yourself!" broke suddenly from Alyosha. "You don't believe in God," he added, speaking this time very sorrowfully. He fancied besides that his brother was looking at him ironically. "How does your poem end?" he asked, suddenly looking down. "Or was it the end?"

"I meant to end it like this. When the Inquisitor ceased speaking he waited some time for his Prisoner to answer him. His silence weighed down upon him. He saw that the Prisoner had listened intently all the time, looking gently in his face and evidently not wishing to reply. The old man longed for him to say something, however bitter and terrible. But He suddenly approached the old man in silence and softly kissed him on his bloodless aged lips. That was all his answer. The old man shuddered. His lips moved. He went to the door, opened it, and said to Him: 'Go, and come no more . . . come not at all, never, never!' And he let Him out into the dark alleys of the town. The Prisoner went away."

"And the old man?"

"The kiss glows in his heart, but the old man adheres to his idea."

"And you with him, you too?" cried Alyosha, mournfully.

Ivan laughed.

"Why, it's all nonsense, Alyosha. It's only a senseless poem of a senseless student, who could never write two lines of verse. Why do you take it so seriously? Surely you don't suppose I am going straight off to the Jesuits, to join the men who are correcting His work? Good Lord, it's no business of mine. I told you, all I want is to live on to thirty, and then . . . dash the cup to the ground!"

. . . . .

The Marriage of Heaven and Hell

William Blake

(1757-1827)

Ivan Karamazov's parable shows institutional religion, personified by the Grand Inquisitor, as a self-conscious falsification of truth. This falsification is carried out because of enormous "love for a humanity" that cannot bear the burden of a "true faith" that is in any case a falsehood for the mass of believers. Ivan's paradox haunts the modern view of institutionalized relations much as the Grand Inquisitor's reasoning echoes that of the contemporary public official who says, "We will bomb the people in order to preserve their freedom."

Through Ivan's parable Dostoevsky took orthodox Christian dogma and stood it on its head in order to comment on the relationship between institutional power and human need. Few writers, though, have inverted the conventional pieties of religion more consistently than William Blake in The Marriage of Heaven and Hell. *As with Dostoevsky, Blake's pur-*

pose extended beyond just simply an attack on conventional religion. For Blake, systematic thought, especially as it attempts to harmonize opposites and eliminate contradictions, distorts human capabilities and restricts the full development of human life. "Without Contraries is no progression. Attraction and Repulsion, Reason and Energy, Love and Hate, are necessary to Human existence."

Systematic thought, whether it is rationalism or empiricism, lies at the center of institutional behavior and Blake's attack on "Reason" represents a critique of institutions as such. At this juncture we have returned to the starting point of the unit: According to the liberal world view, "social institutions distort human character and are thus the source of much of society's ills." In doing so we have recovered a basic premise of John Locke, one of the founders of empirical philosophy, in the ideas of one of the most vehemently antirationalist mystics of English literature, William Blake. We can also hear in the Romantic poet, Blake, echoes of the anathema against institutional restraint pronounced by the Renaissance writer, Rabelais. But in their similarity there are differences, between Blake and Rabelais, Blake and Locke. What are these differences? What light do they throw on society and social aspirations?

THE ARGUMENT

RINTRAH roars, and shakes his fires in the burdened air;
Hungry clouds swag on the deep.
Once meek, and in a perilous path,
The just man kept his course along
The vale of death.
Roses are planted where thorns grow,
And on the barren heath
Sing the honey bees.

Then the perilous path was planted,
And a river and a spring
On every cliff and tomb,
And on the bleached bones
Red clay brought forth;
Till the villain left the paths of ease,
To walk in perilous paths, and drive
The just man into barren climes.
Now the sneaking serpent walks
In mild humility,
And the just man rages in the wilds
Where lions roam.

Rintrah roars, and shakes his fires in the burdened air;
Hungry clouds swag on the deep.

As a new heaven is begun, and it is now thirty-three years since its advent, the Eternal Hell revives. And lo! Swedenborg is the Angel sitting at the tomb: his writings are the linen clothes folded up. Now is the dominion of Edom, and the return of Adam into Paradise. See Isaiah xxxiv and xxxv chap.

Without Contraries is no progression. Attraction and Repulsion, Reason and Energy, Love and Hate, are necessary to Human existence.

From these contraries spring what the religious call Good and Evil. Good is the passive that obeys Reason. Evil is the active springing from Energy.

Good is Heaven. Evil is Hell.

THE VOICE OF THE DEVIL

All Bibles or sacred codes have been the causes of the following Errors:

1. That Man has two real existing principles: viz.: a Body and a Soul.

2. That Energy, called Evil, is alone from the Body; and that Reason, called Good, is alone from the Soul.

3. That God will torment Man in Eternity for following his Energies.

But the following Contraries to these are True:

1. Man has no Body distinct from his Soul; for that called

Body is a portion of Soul discerned by the five Senses, the chief inlets of Soul in this age.

2. Energy is the only life, and is from the Body; and Reason is the bound or outward circumference of Energy.

3. Energy is Eternal Delight.

Those who restrain Desire, do so because theirs is weak enough to be restrained; and the restrainer or Reason usurps its place and governs the unwilling.

And being restrained, it by degrees becomes passive, till it is only the shadow of Desire.

The history of this is written in *Paradise Lost,* and the Governor or Reason is called Messiah.

And the original Archangel, or possessor of the command of the Heavenly Host, is called the Devil or Satan, and his children are called Sin and Death.

But in the Book of Job, Milton's Messiah is called Satan.

For this history has been adopted by both parties.

It indeed appeared to Reason as if Desire was cast out; but the Devil's account is, that the Messiah fell, and formed a Heaven of what he stole from the Abyss.

This is shown in the Gospel, where he prays to the Father to send the Comforter, or Desire, that Reason may have Ideas to build on; the Jehovah of the Bible being no other than he who dwells in flaming fire.

Know that after Christ's death, he became Jehovah.

But in Milton, the Father is Destiny, the Son a Ratio of the five senses, and the Holy-ghost Vacuum!

Note: The reason Milton wrote in fetters when he wrote of Angels and God, and at liberty when of Devils and Hell, is because he was a true Poet and of the Devil's party without knowing it.

A MEMORABLE FANCY

As I was walking among the fires of Hell, delighted with the enjoyments of Genius, which to Angels look like torment and insanity, I collected some of their Proverbs, thinking that as the sayings used in a nation mark its character, so the Proverbs of Hell show the nature of Infernal wisdom better than any description of buildings or garments.

When I came home: on the abyss of the five senses, where a flat-sided steep frowns over the present world, I saw a mighty Devil folded in black clouds, hovering on the sides of the rock: with corroding fires he wrote the following sentence now perceived by the minds of men, and read by them on earth:

How do you know but every Bird that cuts the airy way,
Is an immense World of Delight, closed by your senses five?

PROVERBS OF HELL

In seed time learn, in harvest teach, in winter enjoy.

Drive your cart and your plough over the bones of the dead.

The road of excess leads to the palace of wisdom.

Prudence is a rich, ugly old maid courted by incapacity.

He who desires but acts not, breeds pestilence.

The cut worm forgives the plough.

Dip him in the river who loves water.

A fool sees not the same tree that a wise man sees.

He whose face gives no light, shall never become a star.

Eternity is in love with the productions of time.

The busy bee has no time for sorrow.

The hours of folly are measured by the clock; but of wisdom, no clock can measure.

All wholesome food is caught without a net or a trap.

Bring out number, weight and measure in a year of dearth.

No bird soars too high, if he soars with his own wings.

A dead body revenges not injuries.

The most sublime act is to set another before you.

If the fool would persist in his folly he would become wise.

Folly is the cloak of knavery.

Shame is Pride's cloak.

Prisons are built with stones of Law, brothels with bricks of Religion.

The pride of the peacock is the glory of God.

The lust of the goat is the bounty of God.

The wrath of the lion is the wisdom of God.

The nakedness of woman is the work of God.

Excess of sorrow laughs. Excess of joy weeps.

The roaring of lions, the howling of wolves, the raging of the stormy sea, and the destructive sword are portions of eternity, too great for the eye of man.

The fox condemns the trap, not himself.

Joys impregnate. Sorrows bring forth.

Let man wear the fell of the lion, woman the fleece of the sheep.

The bird a nest, the spider a web, man friendship.

The selfish, smiling fool, and the sullen, frowning fool shall be both thought wise, that they may be a rod.

What is now proved was once only imagined.

The rat, the mouse, the fox, the rabbit watch the roots; the lion, the tiger, the horse, the elephant watch the fruits.

The cistern contains: the fountain overflows.

One thought fills immensity.

Always be ready to speak your mind, and a base man will avoid you.

Everything possible to be believed is an image of truth.

The eagle never lost so much time as when he submitted to learn of the crow.

The fox provides for himself, but God provides for the lion.

Think in the morning. Act in the noon. Eat in the evening. Sleep in the night.

He who has suffered you to impose on him, knows you.

As the plough follows words, so God rewards prayers.

The tigers of wrath are wiser than the horses of instruction.

Expect poison from the standing water.

You never know what is enough unless you know what is more than enough.

Listen to the fool's reproach! it is a kingly title!

The eyes of fire, the nostrils of air, the mouth of water, the beard of earth.

The weak in courage is strong in cunning.

The apple tree never asks the beech how he shall grow, nor the lion, the horse, how he shall take his prey.

The thankful receiver bears a plentiful harvest.

If others had not been foolish, we should be so.

The soul of sweet delight can never be defiled.

When thou seest an eagle, thou seest a portion of Genius; lift up thy head!

As the caterpillar chooses the fairest leaves to lay her eggs on, so the priest lays his curse on the fairest joys.

To create a little flower is the labour of ages.

Damn braces. Bless relaxes.

The best wine is the oldest, the best water the newest.

Prayers plough not! Praises reap not!

Joys laugh not! Sorrows weep not!

The head Sublime, the heart Pathos, the genitals Beauty, the hands and feet Proportion.

As the air to a bird or the sea to a fish, so is contempt to the contemptible.

The crow wished everything was black, the owl that everything was white.

Exuberance is Beauty.

If the lion was advised by the fox, he would be cunning.

Improvement makes straight roads; but the crooked roads without improvement are roads of Genius.

Sooner murder an infant in its cradle than nurse unacted desires.

Where man is not, nature is barren.

Truth can never be told so as to be understood and not be believed.

Enough! or Too much.

The ancient Poets animated all sensible objects with Gods or Geniuses, calling them by the names and adorning them with the properties of woods, rivers, mountains, lakes, cities, nations, and whatever their enlarged and numerous senses could perceive.

And particularly they studied the Genius of each city and country, placing it under its Mental Deity;

Till a System was formed, which some took advantage of, and enslaved the vulgar by attempting to realize or abstract the Mental Deities from their objects: thus began Priesthood:

Choosing forms of worship from poetic tales.

And at length they pronounced that the Gods had ordered such things.

Thus men forgot that All Deities reside in the Human breast.

A MEMORABLE FANCY

The Prophets Isaiah and Ezekiel dined with me, and I asked them how they dared so roundly to assert that God spoke to them; and whether they did not think at the time that they would be misunderstood, and so be the cause of imposition.

Isaiah answered: "I saw no God, nor heard any, in a finite organical perception; but my senses discovered the infinite in everything, and as I was then persuaded, and remain confirmed, that the voice of honest indignation is the voice of God, I cared not for consequences, but wrote."

Then I asked: "Does a firm persuasion that a thing is so, make it so?"

He replied: "All Poets believe that it does, and in ages of imagination this firm persuasion removed mountains; but many are not capable of a firm persuasion of anything."

Then Ezekiel said: "The philosophy of the East taught the first principles of human perception. Some nations held one principle for the origin, and some another: we of Israel taught that the Poetic Genius (as you now call it) was the first principle and all the others merely derivative, which was the cause of our despising the Priests and Philosophers of other countries, and prophesying that all Gods would at last be proved to originate in ours and to be the tributaries of the Poetic Genius; it was this that our great poet, King David, desired so fervently and invokes so pathetically, saying by this he conquers enemies and governs kingdoms; and we so loved our God; that we cursed in his name all the Deities of surrounding nations, and asserted that they had rebelled: from these opinions the vulgar came to think that all nations would at last be subject to the Jews."

"This," said he, "like all firm persuasions, is come to pass; for all nations believe the Jews' code and worship the Jews' god, and what greater subjection can be?"

I heard this with some wonder, and must confess my own conviction. After dinner I asked Isaiah to favour the world with his lost works; he said none of equal value was lost. Ezekiel said the same of his.

I also asked Isaiah what made him go naked and barefoot three years? He answered: "The same that made our friend Diogenes, the Grecian."

I then asked Ezekiel why he ate dung, and lay so long on his right and left side. He answered, "The desire of raising other men into a perception of the infinite: this the North American tribes practise, and is he honest who resists his genius or conscience only for the sake of present ease or gratification?"

The ancient tradition that the world will be consumed in fire at the end of six thousand years is true, as I have heard from Hell.

For the cherub with his flaming sword is hereby commanded

to leave his guard at tree of life; and when he does, the whole creation will be consumed and appear infinite and holy, whereas it now appears finite and corrupt.

This will come to pass by an improvement of sensual enjoyment.

But first the notion that man has a body distinct from his soul is to be expunged; this I shall do by printing in the infernal method, by corrosives, which in Hell are salutary and medicinal, melting apparent surfaces away, and displaying the infinite which was hid.

If the doors of perception were cleansed everything would appear to man as it is, infinite.

For man has closed himself up till he sees all things through narrow chinks of his cavern.

A MEMORABLE FANCY

I was in a Printing-house in Hell, and saw the method in which knowledge is transmitted from generation to generation.

In the first chamber was a Dragon-Man, clearing away the rubbish from a cave's mouth; within, a number of Dragons were hollowing the cave.

In the second chamber was a Viper folding round the rock and the cave, and others adorning it with gold, silver, and precious stones.

In the third chamber was an Eagle with wings and feathers of air: he caused the inside of the cave to be infinite; around were numbers of Eagle-like men who built palaces in the immense cliffs.

In the fourth chamber were Lions of flaming fire, raging around and melting the metals into living fluids.

In the fifth chamber were Unnamed forms, which cast the metals into the expanse.

There they were received by Men who occupied the sixth chamber, and took the forms of books and were arranged in libraries.

The Giants who formed this world into its sensual existence, and now seem to live in it in chains, are in truth the causes of its life and the sources of all activity; but the chains are the cunning of weak and tame minds which have power to resist energy. According to the proverb, the weak in courage is strong in cunning.

Thus one portion of being is the Prolific, the other the Devouring: to the Devourer it seems as if the producer was in his chains; but it is not so, he only takes portions of existence and fancies that the whole.

But the Prolific would cease to be Prolific unless the Devourer, as a sea, received the excess of his delights.

Some will say: "Is not God alone the Prolific?" I answer: "God only Acts and Is, in existing beings or Men."

These two classes of men are always upon earth, and they should be enemies: whoever tries to reconcile them seeks to destroy existence.

Religion is an endeavour to reconcile the two.

Note: Jesus Christ did not wish to unite, but to separate them, as in the Parable of sheep and goats! And he says: "I came not to send Peace, but a Sword."

Messiah or Satan or Tempter was formerly thought to be one of the Antediluvians who are our Energies.

A MEMORABLE FANCY

An Angel came to me and said: "O pitiable foolish young man! O horrible! O dreadful state! Consider the hot burning dungeon thou art preparing for thyself to all Eternity, to which thou art going in such career."

I said: "Perhaps you will be willing to show me my eternal lot, and we will contemplate together upon it, and see whether your lot or mine is most desirable."

So he took me through a stable and through a church and down into the church vault, at the end of which was a mill: through the mill we went, and came to a cave: down the winding cavern we groped our tedious way, till a void boundless as a nether sky appeared beneath us, and we held by the roots of trees and hung over this immensity; but I said: "If you please, we will commit ourselves to this void, and see whether Providence is here also: if you will not, I will." But he answered: "Do not presume, O young man, but as we here remain, behold thy lot which will soon appear when the darkness passes away."

So I remained with him, sitting in the twisted root of an oak;

he was suspended in a fungus, which hung with the head downward into the deep.

By degrees we beheld the infinite Abyss, fiery as the smoke of a burning city; beneath us, at an immense distance, was the sun, black but shining; round it were fiery tracks on which revolved vast spiders, crawling after their prey, which flew, or rather swam, in the infinite deep, in the most terrific shapes of animals sprung from corruption; and the air was full of them, and seemed composed of them: these are Devils, and are called Powers of the Air. I now asked my companion which was my eternal lot? He said: "Between the black and white spiders."

But now, from between the black and white spiders, a cloud and fire burst and rolled through the deep, blackening all beneath, so that the nether deep grew black as a sea, and rolled with a terrible noise; beneath us was nothing now to be seen but a black tempest, till looking East between the clouds and the waves, we saw a cataract of blood mixed with fire, and not many stones' throw from us appeared and sunk again the scaly fold of a monstrous serpent. At last, to the East, distant about three degrees, appeared a fiery crest above the waves. Slowly it reared like a ridge of golden rocks, till we discovered two globes of crimson fire, from which the sea fled away in clouds of smoke; and now we saw it was the head of Leviathan. His forehead was divided into streaks of green and purple like those on a tiger's forehead. Soon we saw his mouth and red gills hang just above the raging foam, tinging the black deep with beams of blood, advancing toward us with all the fury of a Spiritual Existence.

My friend the Angel climbed up from his station into the mill: I remained alone; and then this appearance was no more, but I found myself sitting on a pleasant bank beside a river by moonlight, hearing a harper, who sung to the harp; and his theme was: "The man who never alters his opinion is like standing water, and breeds reptiles of the mind."

But I arose and sought for the mill, and there I found my Angel, who, surprised, asked me how I escaped.

I answered: "All that we saw was owing to your metaphysics; for when you ran away, I found myself on a bank by moonlight hearing a harper. But now we have seen my eternal lot, shall I show you yours?" He laughed at my proposal; but I by force suddenly caught him in my arms, and flew westerly through the night, till we were elevated above the earth's shadow; then I flung myself with him directly into the body of the sun; here I clothed myself in white, and taking in my hand Swedenborg's volumes, sunk from the glorious clime, and passed all the planets till we came to Saturn: here I stayed to rest, and then leaped into the void between Saturn and the fixed stars.

"Here," said I, "is your lot, in this space—if space it may be called." Soon we saw the stable and the church, and I took him to the altar and opened the Bible, and lo! it was a deep pit, into which I descended, driving the Angel before me. Soon we saw seven houses of brick. One we entered; in it were a number of monkeys, baboons, and all of that species, chained by the middle, grinning and snatching at one another, but withheld by the shortness of their chains. However, I saw that they sometimes grew numerous, and then the weak were caught by the strong, and with a grinning aspect, first coupled with, and then devoured, by plucking off first one limb and then another, till the body was left a helpless trunk. This, after grinning and kissing it with seeming fondness, they devoured too; and here and there I saw one savourily picking the flesh off of his own tail. As the stench terribly annoyed us both, we went into the mill, and I in my hand brought the skeleton of a body, which in the mill was Aristotle's Analytics.

So the Angel said: "Thy phantasy has imposed upon me, and thou oughtest to be ashamed."

I answered: "We impose on one another, and it is but lost time to converse with you whose works are only Analytics."

I have always found that Angels have the vanity to speak of themselves as the Only Wise; this they do with a confident insolence sprouting from systematic reasoning.

Thus Swedenborg boasts that what he writes is new: though it is only the Contents or Index of already published books.

A man carried a monkey about for a show, and because he was a little wiser than the monkey, grew vain, and conceived himself as much wiser than seven men. It is so with Swedenborg: he shows the folly of churches, and exposes hypocrites, till he imagines that all are religious, and himself the single one on earth that ever broke a net.

Now hear a plain fact: Swedenborg has not written one new truth. Now hear another: he has written all the old falsehoods.

And now hear the reason. He conversed with Angels who are all religious, and conversed not with Devils who all hate religion, for he was incapable through his conceited notions.

Thus Swedenborg's writings are a recapitulation of all superficial opinions, and an analysis of the more sublime—but no further.

Have now another plain fact. Any man of mechanical talents may, from the writings of Paracelsus or Jacob Behmen, produce ten thousand volumes of equal value with Swedenborg's, and from those of Dante or Shakespeare an infinite number.

But when he has done this, let him not say that he knows better than his master, for he only holds a candle in sunshine.

A MEMORABLE FANCY

Once I saw a Devil in a flame of fire, who arose before an Angel that sat on a cloud, and the Devil uttered these words:

"The worship of God is: Honouring his gifts in other men, each according to his genius, and loving the greatest men best: those who envy or calumniate great men hate God; for there is no other God."

The Angel hearing this became almost blue; but mastering himself he grew yellow, and at last white, pink, and smiling, and then replied:

"Thou Idolater! is not God One? and is not he visible in Jesus Christ? and has not Jesus Christ given his sanction to the law of ten commandments? and are not all other men fools, sinners, and nothings?"

The Devil answered: "Bray a fool in a mortar with wheat, yet shall not his folly be beaten out of him; if Jesus Christ is the greatest man, you ought to love him in the greatest degree; now hear how he has given his sanction to the law of ten commandments: did he not mock at the sabbath, and so mock the sabbath's God? murder those who were murdered because of him? turn away the law from the woman taken in adultery? steal the labour of others to support him? bear false witness when he omitted making a defence before Pilate? covet when he prayed for his disciples, and when he bid them shake off the dust of their feet against such as refused to lodge them? I tell you, no virtue can exist without breaking these ten commandments. Jesus was all virtue, and acted from impulse, not from rules."

When he had so spoken, I beheld the Angel, who stretched out his arms, embracing the flame of fire, and he was consumed and arose as Elijah.

Note: This Angel, who is now become a Devil, is my particular friend; we often read the Bible together in its infernal or diabolical sense, which the world shall have if they behave well.

I have also The Bible of Hell, which the world shall have whether they will or no.

One Law for the Lion and Ox is Oppression.

A SONG OF LIBERTY

1. The Eternal Female groan'd! it was heard over all the Earth.

2. Albion's coast is sick, silent; the American meadows faint!

3. Shadows of Prophecy shiver along by the lakes and the rivers, and mutter across the ocean: France, rend down by dungeon!

4. Golden Spain, burst the barriers of old Rome!

5. Cast thy keys, O Rome, into the deep, down falling, even to eternity down falling,

6. And weep.

7. In her trembling hand she took the new born terror, howling.

8. On those infinite mountains of light, now barr'd out by the atlantic sea, the new born fire stood before the starry king!

9. Flag'd with grey brow'd snows and thunderous visages, the jealous wings wav'd over the deep.

10. The speary hand burned aloft, unbuckled was the shield; forth went the hand of jealousy among the flaming hair, and hurl'd the new born wonder thro' the starry night.

11. The fire, the fire is falling!

12. Look up! look up! O citizen of London, enlarge thy countenance! O Jew, leave counting gold! return to thy oil and wine. O African! black African! (go, winged thought, widen his forehead.)

13. The fiery limbs, the flaming hair, shot like the sinking sun into the western sea.

14. Wak'd from his eternal sleep, the hoary element roaring fled away.

15. Down rush'd, beating his wings in vain, the jealous king; his grey brow'd councellors, thunderous warriors, curl'd veterans, among helms, and shields, and chariots, horses, elephants, banners, castles, slings, and rocks.

16. Falling, rushing, ruining! buried in the ruins, on Urthona's dens;

17. All night beneath the ruins; then, their sullen flames faded, emerge round the gloomy King.

18. With thunder and fire, leading his starry hosts thro' the waste wilderness, he promulgates his ten commands, glancing his beamy eyelids over the deep in dark dismay.

19. Where the son of fire in his eastern cloud, while the morning plumes her golden breast,

20. Spurning the clouds written with curses, stamps the stony law to dust, loosing the eternal horses from the dens of night, crying:

Empire is no More! and Now the Lion & Wolf Shall Cease.

CHORUS

Let the Priests of the Raven of dawn no longer, in deadly black, with hoarse note curse the sons of joy. Nor his accepted brethren—whom, tyrant, he calls free—lay the bound or build the roof. Nor pale religious letchery call that virginity that wishes but acts not!

For every thing that lives is Holy.

Literature and Art

On the Feeling of Immortality in Youth

William Hazlitt

(1778-1830)

If we had to characterize all the preceding selections in one phrase we might say they were "dissenting voices from the past." But it is also important to recognize that not one of our authors remained on a purely negative level of dissent. In each instance they offered, either explicitly or implicitly, an alternative that was seen as superior. All, in one way or another, pointed toward an ideal of excellence, in education, political relations, or social organization.

Perhaps the one human activity that seems to embody most completely the highest ideals of excellence in Western civilization is art, whether we call it literature, painting, dance, or music. The problem, of course, is to define our various excellences. Romantic esthetics defined excellence as the intensity of feeling communicated in art and experienced in life. William Hazlitt, one of the most brilliant of Romantic essayists, asserted that strong emotion is "proof against the canker of time." He further stated, "We take out a new lease of existence from the objects on which we set our affections, and become abstracted, impassive, immortal in them." The arts served Hazlitt as the prime examples of human aspiration as he cried "perfection is slow of attainment, and . . . no limit should be put to our endeavours."

Hazlitt's essay not only provides us with a definition of excellence but is itself an example of excellence in a particular form. "On the Feeling of Immortality in Youth" is a superb instance of the familiar essay, and we can see in our selection the strong personal tone so characteristic of this form. Hazlitt's long footnote on Lady Mary Wortley Montague, a leading snob of the Augustan Age, recalls to mind some of Jefferson's comments on what he called "natural aristocracy" and clearly indicates the quality of Hazlitt's own "unrepentant radicalism."

Some of Hazlitt's other writings that do some of the same things as in our selection can be found in his collections of essays titled, Table Talk, The Spirit of the Age, *and* The Plain Speaker. *Hazlitt was and still is considered one of the most perceptive literary critics in the English language. His critical writings can be found in* Characters of Shakespeare's Plays *and the three collections of lectures on the dramatic literature of the Elizabethan age, on English poets, and on comic writers.*

Life is a pure flame, and we live by an invisible sun within us.

—SIR THOMAS BROWN

No young man believes he shall ever die. It was a saying of my brother's, and a fine one. There is a feeling of Eternity in youth, which makes us amends for every thing. To be young is to be as one of the Immortal Gods. One half of time indeed is flown—the other half remains in store for us with all its countless treasures; for there is no line drawn, and we see no limit to our hopes and wishes. We make the coming age our own.—

The vast, the unbounded prospect lies before us.

Death, old age, are words without a meaning, that pass by us like the idle air which we regard not. Others may have undergone, or may still be liable to them—we 'bear a charmed life,' which laughs to scorn all such sickly fancies. As in setting out on a delightful journey, we strain our eager gaze forward—

Bidding the lovely scenes at distance hail,—

and see no end to the landscape, new objects presenting themselves as we advance; so, in the commencement of life, we set no bounds to our inclinations, nor to the unrestricted opportunities of gratifying them. We have as yet found no obstacle, no disposition to flag; and it seems that we can go on so for ever. We look round in a new world, full of life, and motion, and ceaseless progress; and feel in ourselves all the vigour and spirit to keep pace with it, and do not foresee from any present symptoms how we shall be left behind in the natural course of things, decline into old age, and drop into the grave. It is the simplicity, and as it were *abstractedness* of our feelings in youth, that (so to speak) identifies us with nature, and (our experience being slight and our passions strong) deludes us into a belief of being immortal like it. Our short-lived connection with existence, we fondly flatter ourselves, is an indissoluble and lasting union—a honey-moon that knows neither coldness, jar, nor separation. As infants smile and sleep, we are rocked in the cradle of our wayward fancies, and lulled into security by the roar of the universe around us—we quaff the cup of life with eager haste without draining it, instead of which it only overflows the more—objects press around us, filling the mind with their magnitude and with the throng of desires that wait upon them, so that we have no room for the thoughts of death. From that plenitude of our being, we cannot change all at once to dust and ashes, we cannot imagine 'this sensible, warm motion, to become a kneaded clod'—we are too much dazzled by the brightness of the waking dream around us to look into the darkness of the tomb. We no more see our end than our beginning: the one is lost in oblivion and vacancy, as the other is hid from us by the crowd and hurry of approaching events. Or the grim shadow is seen lingering in the horizon, which we are doomed never to overtake, or whose last, faint, glimmering outline touches upon Heaven and translates us to the skies! Nor would the hold that life has taken of us permit us to detach our thoughts from present objects and pursuits, even if we would. What is there more opposed to health, than sickness; to strength and beauty, than decay and dissolution; to the active search of knowledge than mere oblivion? Or is there none of the usual advantage to bar the approach of Death, and mock his idle threats; Hope supplies their place, and draws a veil over the abrupt termination of all our cherished schemes. While the spirit of youth remains unimpaired, ere the 'wine of life is drank up,' we are like people intoxicated or in a fever, who are hurried away by the violence of their own sensations: it is only as present objects begin to pall upon the sense, as we have been disappointed in our favourite pursuits, cut off from our closest ties, that passion loosens its hold upon the breast, that we by degrees become weaned from the world, and allow ourselves to contemplate, 'as in a glass, darkly,' the possibility of parting with it for good. The example of others, the voice of experience, has no effect upon us whatever. Casualties we must avoid: the slow and deliberate advances of age we can play at *hide-and-seek* with. We think ourselves too lusty and too nimble for that blear-eyed decrepit old gentleman to catch us. Like the foolish fat scullion, in Sterne, when she hears that Master Bobby is dead, our only reflection is—'So am not I!' The idea of death, instead of staggering our confidence, rather seems to strengthen and enhance our possession and our enjoyment of life. Others may fall around us like leaves, or be mowed down like flowers by the scythe of Time: these are but tropes and figures to the unreflecting ears and overweening presumption of youth. It is not till we see the flowers of Love, Hope, and Joy, withering around us, and our own pleasures cut up by the roots, that we bring the moral home to ourselves, that we abate something of the wanton extravagance of our pretensions, or that the emptiness and dreariness of the prospect before us reconciles us to the stillness of the grave!

Life! thou strange thing, that hast a power to feel
Thou art, and to perceive that others are.

Well might the poet begin his indignant invective against an art, whose professed object is its destruction, with this animated apostrophe to life. Life is indeed a strange gift, and its privileges are most miraculous. Nor is it singular that when the splendid boon is first granted us, our gratitude, our admiration, and our delight should prevent us from reflecting on our own nothingness, or from thinking it will ever be recalled. Our first and strongest impressions are taken from the mighty scene that is opened to us, and we very innocently transfer its durability as well as magnificence to ourselves. So newly found, we cannot make up our minds to parting with it yet and at least put off that consideration to an indefinite term. Like a clown at a fair, we are full of amazement and rapture, and have no thoughts of going home, or that it will soon be night. We know our existence only from external objects, and we measure it by them. We can never be satisfied with gazing; and nature will still want us to look on and applaud. Otherwise, the sumptuous entertainment, 'the feast of reason and the flow of soul,' to which we were invited, seems little better than a mockery and a cruel insult. We do not go from a play till the scene is ended, and the lights are ready to be extinguished. But the fair face of things still shines on; shall we be called away, before the curtain falls, or ere we have scarce had a glimpse of what is going on? Like children, our step-mother Nature holds us up to see the raree-show of the universe; and then, as if life were a burthen to support, lets us instantly down again. Yet in that short interval, what 'brave sublunary things' does not the spectacle unfold; like a bubble, at one minute reflecting the universe, and the next, shook to air!—To see the golden sun and the azure sky, the outstretched ocean, to walk upon the green earth, and to be lord of a thousand creatures, to look down giddy precipices or over distant flowery vales, to see the world spread out under one's finger in a map, to bring the stars near, to view the smallest insects in a microscope, to read history, and witness the revolutions of empires and the succession of generations, to hear of the glory of Sidon and Tyre, of Babylon and Susa, as of a faded pageant, and to say all these were, and are now nothing, to think that we exist in such a point of time, and in such a corner of space, to be at once spectators and a part of the moving scene, to watch the return of the seasons, of spring and autumn, to hear

—The stockdove plain amid the forest deep,
That drowsy rustles to the sighing gale—

to traverse desert wilderness, to listen to the midnight choir, to visit lighted halls, or plunge into the dungeon's gloom, or sit in crowded theatres and see life itself mocked, to feel heat and cold, pleasure and pain, right and wrong, truth and falsehood, to study the works of art and refine the sense of beauty to agony, to worship fame and to dream of immortality, to have read Shakespear and belong to the same species as Sir Isaac Newton;[1]

[1] Lady Wortley Montague says, in one of her letters, that 'she would much rather be a rich *effendi,* with all his ignorance, than Sir Isaac Newton, with all his knowledge.' This was not perhaps an impolitic choice, as she had a better chance of becoming one than the other, there being many rich effendis to one Sir Isaac Newton. The wish was not a very intellectual one. The same petulance of rank and sex breaks out every where in these *Letters.* She is constantly reducing the poets or philosophers who have the misfortune of her acquaintance, to the figure they might make at her Ladyship's levee or toilette, not considering that the public mind does not sympathise with this process of a fastidious imagination. In the same spirit, she declares of Pope and Swift, that 'had it not been for the *good-nature* of mankind, these two superior beings were entitled, by their birth and hereditary fortune, to be only a couple of link-boys.' Gulliver's Travels, and the Rape of the Lock, go for nothing in this critical estimate, and the world raised the authors to the rank of superior beings, in spite of their disadvantages of birth and fortune, *out of pure good-nature!* So, again, she says of Richardson, that he had never got beyond the servants' hall, and was utterly unfit to describe the manners of people of quality; till in the capricious workings of her vanity, she persuades herself that Clarissa is very like what she was at her age, and that Sir Thomas and Lady Grandison strongly resembled what she had heard of her mother and remembered of her father. It is one of the beauties and advantages of literature, that it is the means of abstracting the mind from the narrowness of local and personal prejudices, and of enabling us to judge of truth and excellence by their inherent merits alone. Woe be to the pen that would undo this fine illusion (the only reality), and teach us to regulate our notions of genius and virtue by the circumstances in which they happen to be placed! You would not expect a person whom you saw in a servants' hall, or behind a counter, to write Clarissa; but after he had written the work, to *pre-judge* it from the situation of the writer, is an unpardonable piece of injustice and folly. His merit could only be the greater from the contrast. If literature is an elegant accomplishment, which none but persons of birth and fashion should be allowed to excel in, or to exercise with advantage to the public, let them by all means take upon them the task of enlightening and refining mankind: if they decline this responsibility as too heavy for their shoulders, let those who do the drudgery in their stead, however inadequately, for want of their polite example, receive the meed that is their due, and not be treated as low pretenders who have encroached on the province of their betters. Suppose Richardson to have been acquainted with the great man's steward, or valet, instead of the great man himself, I will venture to say that there was more difference between him who lived in an *ideal world,* and had the genius and felicity to open that world to others, and his friend the steward, than between the lacquey and the mere lord, or between those who lived in different rooms of the same house, who dined on the same luxuries at different tables, who rode outside or inside of the same coach, and were proud of wearing or of be-

to be and to do all this, and then in a moment to be nothing, to have it all snatched from one like a juggler's ball or a phantasmagoria; there is something revolting and incredible to sense in the transition, and no wonder that, aided by youth and warm blood, and the flush of enthusiasm, the mind contrives for a long time to reject it with disdain and loathing as a monstrous and improbable fiction, like a monkey on a house-top, that is loath, amidst its fine discoveries and specious antics, to be tumbled head-long into the street, and crushed to atoms, the sport and laughter of the multitude!

The change, from the commencement to the close of life, ap-

---

stowing the same tawdry livery. If the lord is distinguished from his valet by any thing else, it is by education and talent, which he has in common with our author. But if the latter shews these in the highest degree, it is asked what are his pretensions? Not birth or fortune, for neither of these would enable him to write a Clarissa. One man is born with a title and estate, another with genius. That is sufficient; and we have no right to question the genius for want of the *gentility,* unless the former ran in families, or could be bequeathed with a fortune, which is not the case. Were it so, the flowers of literature, like jewels and embroidery, would be confined to the fashionable circles; and there would be no pretenders to taste or elegance but those whose names were found in the court list. No one objects to Claude's Landscapes as the work of a pastrycook, or withholds from Raphael the epithet of *divine,* because his parents were not rich. This impertinence is confined to men of letters; the evidence of the senses baffles the envy and foppery of mankind. No quarter ought to be given to this *aristocratic* tone of criticism whenever it appears. People of quality are not contented with carrying all the external advantages for their own share, but would persuade you that all the intellectual ones are packed up in the same bundle. Lord Byron was a later instance of this double and unwarrantable style of pretension—*monstrum ingens, biforme.* He could not endure a lord who was not a wit, nor a poet who was not a lord. Nobody but himself answered to his own standard of perfection. Mr. Moore carries a proxy in his pocket from some noble persons to estimate literary merit by the same rule. Lady Mary calls Fielding names, but she afterwards makes atonement by doing justice to his frank, free, hearty nature, where she says 'his spirits gave him raptures with his cook-maid, and cheerfulness when he was starving in a garret, and his happy constitution made him forget every thing when he was placed before a venison-pasty or over a flask of champagne.' She does not want shrewdness and spirit when her petulance and conceit do not get the better of her, and she has done ample and merited execution on Lord Bolingbroke. She is, however, very angry at the freedoms taken with the Great; *smells a rat* in this indiscriminate scribbling, and the familiarity of writers with the reading public; and inspired by her Turkish costume, foretells a French or English revolution as the consequence of transferring the patronage of letters from the *quality* to the mob, and of supposing that ordinary writers or readers can have any notions in common with their superiors.

pears like a fable, after it has taken place; how should we treat it otherwise than as a chimera before it has come to pass? There are some things that happened so long ago, places or persons we have formerly seen, of which such dim traces remain, we hardly know whether it was sleeping or waking they occurred; they are like dreams within the dream of life, a mist, a film before the eye of memory, which, as we try to recall them more distinctly, elude our notice altogether. It is but natural that the lone interval that we thus look back upon, should have appeared long and endless in prospect. There are others so distinct and fresh, they seem but of yesterday—their very vividness might be deemed a pledge of their permanence. Then, however far back our impressions may go, we find others still older (for our years are multiplied in youth); descriptions of scenes that we had read, and people before our time, Priam and the Trojan war; and even then, Nestor was old and dwelt delighted on his youth, and spoke of the race of heroes that were no more;—what wonder that, seeing this long line of being pictured in our minds, and reviving as it were in us, we should give ourselves involuntary credit for an indeterminate period of existence? In the Cathedral at Peterborough there is a monument to Mary, Queen of Scots, at which I used to gaze when a boy, while the events of the period, all that had happened since, passed in review before me. If all this mass of feeling and imagination could be crowded into a moment's compass, what might not the whole of life be supposed to contain? We are heirs of the past; we count upon the future as our natural reversion. Besides, there are some of our early impressions so exquisitely tempered, it appears that they must always last—nothing can add to or take away from their sweetness and purity—the first breath of spring, the hyacinth dipped in the dew, the mild lustre of the evening-star, the rainbow after a storm—while we have the full enjoyment of these, we must be young; and what can ever alter us in this respect? Truth, friendship, love, books, are also proof against the canker of time; and while we live, but for them, we can never grow old. We take out a new lease of existence from the objects on which we set our affections, and become abstracted, impassive, immortal in them. We cannot conceive how certain sentiments should ever decay or grow cold in our breasts; and, consequently, to maintain them in their first youthful glow and vigour, the flame of life must continue to burn as bright as ever, or rather, they are the fuel that feed the sacred lamp, that kindle 'the purple light of love,' and spread a golden cloud around our heads! Again, we not only flourish and survive in our affections (in which we will not listen to the possibility of a change, any more than we foresee the wrinkles on the brow of a mistress), but we have a farther guarantee against the thoughts of death in our favourite studies and pursuits, and in their continual advance. Art we know is long; life, we feel, should be so too. We see no end of the difficulties we have to encounter: perfection is slow of attainment, and we must have time to accomplish it in. Rubens complained that when he had just learnt his art, he was snatched away from it: we trust we shall be more fortunate! A wrinkle in an old head takes whole days to finish it properly: but to catch 'the Raphael grace, the Guido air,' no limit should be put to our endeavours. What a prospect for the future! What a task we have entered upon! and shall we be arrested in the middle of it? We do not reckon our time thus employed lost, or our pains thrown away, or our progress slow—we do not droop or grow tired, but 'gain new vigour at our endless task';—and shall Time grudge us the opportunity to finish what we have auspiciously begun, and have formed a sort of compact with nature to achieve? The fame of the great names we look up to is also imperishable; and shall not we, who contemplate it with such intense yearnings, imbibe a portion of ethereal fire, the *divinae particula aurae,* which nothing can extinguish? I remember to have looked at a print of Rembrandt for hours together, without being conscious of the flight of time, trying to resolve it into its component parts, to connect its strong and sharp gradations, to learn the secret of its reflected lights, and found neither satiety nor pause in the prosecution of my studies. The print over which I was pouring would last long enough; why should the idea in my mind, which was finer, more impalpable, perish before it? At this, I redoubled the ardour of my pursuit, and by the very subtlety and refinement of my inquiries, seemed to bespeak for them an exemption from corruption and the rude grasp of Death.[2]

Objects, on our first acquaintance with them, have that singleness and integrity of impression that it seems as if nothing could

[2] Is it not this that frequently keeps artists alive so long, *viz,* the constant occupation of their minds with vivid images, with little of the *wear-and-tear* of the body?

destroy or obliterate them, so firmly are they stamped and rivetted on the brain. We repose on them with a sort of voluptuous indolence, in full faith and boundless confidence. We are absorbed in the present moment, or return to the same point—idling away a great deal of time in youth, thinking we have enough and to spare. There is often a local feeling in the air, which is as fixed as if it were of marble; we loiter in dim cloisters, losing ourselves in thought and in their glimmering arches; a winding road before us seems as long as the journey of life, and as full of events. Time and experience dissipate this illusion; and by reducing them to detail, circumscribe the limits of our expectations. It is only as the pageant of life passes by, and the masques turn their backs upon us, that we see through the deception, or believe that the train will have an end. In many cases, the slow progress and monotonous texture of our lives, before we mingle with the world and are embroiled in its affairs, has a tendency to aid the same feeling. We have a difficulty, when left to ourselves, and without the resource of books or some more lively pursuit, to 'beguile the slow and creeping hours of time,' and argue that if it moves on always at this tedious snail's-pace, it can never come to an end. We are willing to skip over certain portions of it that separate us from favourite objects, that irritate ourselves at the unnecessary delay. The young are prodigal of life from a superabundance of it; the old are tenacious on the same score, because they have little left, and cannot enjoy even what remains of it.

For my part, I set out in life with the French Revolution, and that event had considerable influence on my early feelings, as on those of others. Youth was then doubly such. It was the dawn of a new era, a new impulse had been given to men's minds, and the sun of Liberty rose upon the sun of Life in the same day, and both were proud to run their race together. Little did I dream, while my first hopes and wishes went hand in hand with those of the human race, that long before my eyes should close, that dawn would be overcast, and set once more in the night of despotism—'total eclipse!' Happy that I did not. I felt for years, and during the best part of my existence, *heart-whole* in that cause, and triumphed in the triumphs over the enemies of man! At that time, while the fairest aspirations of the human mind seemed about to be realised, ere the image of man was defaced and his breast mangled in scorn, philosophy took a higher, poetry could afford a deeper range. At that time, to read the 'ROBBERS' was indeed delicious, and to hear

> *From the dungeon of the tower time-rent,*
> *That fearful voice, a famish'd father's cry,*

could be borne only amidst the fulness of hope, the crash of the fall of the strong holds of power, and the exulting sounds of the march of human freedom. What feelings the death-scene in Don Carlos sent into the soul! In that headlong career of lofty enthusiasm, and the joyous opening of the prospects of the world and our own, the thought of death crossing it, smote doubly cold upon the mind; there was a stifling sense of oppression and confinement, an impatience of our present knowledge, a desire to grasp the whole of our existence in one strong embrace, to sound the mystery of life and death, and in order to put an end to the agony of doubt and dread, to burst through our prison-house, and confront the King of Terrors in his grisly palace! . . . As I was writing out this passage, my miniature-picture when a child lay on the mantle-piece, and I took it out of the case to look at it. I could perceive few traces of myself in it; but there was the same placid brow, the dimpled mouth, the same timid, inquisitive glance as ever. But its careless smile did not seem to reproach me with having become a recreant to the sentiments that were then sown in my mind, or with having written a sentence that could call up a blush in this image of ingenuous youth!

'That time is past with all its giddy raptures.' Since the future was barred to my progress, I have turned for consolation to the past, gathering up the fragments of my early recollections, and putting them into a form that might live. It is thus, that when we find our personal and substantial identity vanishing from us, we strive to gain a reflected and substituted one in our thoughts: we do not like to perish wholly, and wish to bequeath our names at least to posterity. As long as we can keep alive our cherished thoughts and nearest interests in the minds of others, we do not appear to have retired altogether from the stage, we still occupy a place in the estimation of mankind, [and] exercise a powerful influence over them, and it is only our bodies that are trampled into dust or dispersed to air. Our darling speculations still find favour and encouragement, and we make as good a figure in the eyes of our descendants, nay, perhaps, a better than we did in our life-time. This is one point gained; the demands of our self-love are so far satisfied. Besides, if by the proofs of intellectual superiority we survive ourselves in this world, by exemplary virtue or unblemished faith, we are taught to ensure an interest in another and a higher state of being, and to anticipate at the same time the applauses of men and angels.

Even from the tomb the voice of nature cries;
Even in our ashes live their wonted fires.

As we advance in life, we acquire a keener sense of the value of time. Nothing else, indeed, seems of any consequence; and we become misers in this respect. We try to arrest its few last tottering steps, and to make it linger on the brink of the grave. We can never leave off wondering how that which has ever been should cease to be, and would still live on, that we may wonder at our own shadow, and when 'all the life of life is flown,' dwell on the retrospect of the past. This accompanied by a mechanical tenaciousness of whatever we possess, by a distrust and a sense of fallacious hollowness in all we see. Instead of the full, pulpy feeling of youth, every thing is flat and insipid. The world is a painted witch, that puts us off with false shews and tempting appearances. The ease, the jocund gaiety, the unsuspecting security of youth are fled: nor can we, without flying in the face of common sense,

From the last dregs of life, hope to receive
What its first sprightly runnings could not give.

If we can slip out of the world without notice or mischance, can tamper with bodily infirmity, and frame our minds to the becoming composure of *still-life,* before we sink into total insensibility, it is as much as we ought to expect. We do not in the regular course of nature die all at once: we have mouldered away gradually long before; faculty after faculty, attachment after attachment, we are torn from ourselves piece-meal while living; year after year takes something from us; and death only consigns the last remnant of what we were to the grave. The revulsion is not so great, and a quiet *euthanasia* is a winding-up of the plot, that is not out of reason or nature.

That we should thus in a manner outlive ourselves, and dwindle imperceptibly into nothing, is not surprising, when even in our prime the strongest impressions leave so little traces of themselves behind, and the last object is driven out by the succeeding one. How little effect is produced on us at any time by the books we have read, the scenes we have witnessed, the sufferings we have gone through! Think only of the variety of feelings we experience in reading an interesting romance, or being present at a fine play—what beauty, what sublimity, what soothing, what heart-rending emotions! You would suppose these would last for ever, or at least subdue the mind to a correspondent tone and harmony—while we turn over the page, while the scene is passing before us, it seems as if nothing could ever after shake our resolution, that 'treason domestic, foreign levy, nothing could touch us farther!' The first splash of mud we get, on entering the street, the first pettifogging shop-keeper that cheats us out of twopence, and the whole vanishes clean out of our remembrance, and we become the idle prey of the most petty and annoying circumstances. The mind soars by an effort to the grand and lofty: it is at home in the grovelling, the disagreeable, and the little. This happens in the height and hey-day of our existence, when novelty gives a stronger impulse to the blood and takes a faster hold of the brain, (I have known the impression on coming out of a gallery of pictures then last half a day)—as we grow old, we become more feeble and querulous, every object 'reverbs its own hollowness,' and both worlds are not enough to satisfy the peevish importunity and extravagant presumption of our desires! There are a few superior, happy beings, who are born with a temper exempt from every trifling annoyance. This spirit sits serene and smiling as in its native skies, and a divine harmony (whether heard or not) plays around them. This is to be at peace. Without this, it is in vain to fly into deserts, or to build a hermitage on the top of rocks, if regret and ill-humour follow us there: and with this, it is needless to make the experiment. The only true retirement is that of the heart; the only true leisure is the repose of the passions. To such persons it makes little difference whether they are young or old; and they die as they have lived, with graceful resignation.

Traffic

John Ruskin

(1819-1900)

In Hazlitt the excellence of art is ultimately due to the psychological effect it can produce—how deeply it can move or absorb us. According to this notion, the quality of art did not necessarily possess any moral virtue, other than that it enhanced life or at least induced a temporary state of "immortality." Hazlitt arrived at his esthetic values from a moral view of life, true enough, but he did not in turn propound a moral view of art. John Ruskin, however, did propound a stringent morality of art that in large measure reflected his moral views on life. His central thesis, in our selection as well as in his other writings, is "that good architecture [and art generally] is essentially . . . the production of a faithful and virtuous, not of an infidel and corrupted people." To Ruskin the genre picture of the Flemish painter David Teniers is "evil" because it depicts a "vile thing" and reflects "the taste of the devils."

One had best be careful about the art one liked around Ruskin. No wonder he lost his court case against the American painter J. A. M. Whistler. Few people could bear so heavy a burden as Ruskin imposed on esthetic judgment.

Ruskin did not only attack art and artists. He began his five volume Modern Painters *in order to advocate the superiority of the landscapes of his friend the English painter J. M. W. Turner and later defended the works of the struggling young artists of the Pre-Raphaelite school. In addition to* Modern Painters, *Ruskin's* Stones of Venice *and* The Seven Lamps of Architecture *are his major works in art criticism.*

Delivered in the Town Hall, Bradford
April 21, 1864

My good Yorkshire friends, you asked me down here among your hills that I might talk to you about this Exchange you are going to build: but, earnestly and seriously asking you to pardon me, I am going to do nothing of the kind. I cannot talk, or at least can say very little, about this same Exchange. I must talk of quite other things, though not willingly;—I could not deserve your pardon, if, when you invited me to speak on one subject, I *willfully* spoke on another. But I cannot speak, to purpose, of anything about which I do not care; and most simply and sorrowfully I have to tell you, in the outset, that I do *not* care about this Exchange of yours.

If, however, when you sent me your invitation, I had answered, "I won't come, I don't care about the Exchange of Bradford," you would have been justly offended with me, not knowing the reasons of so blunt a carelessness. So I have come down, hoping that you will patiently let me tell you why, on this, and many other such occasions, I now remain silent, when formerly I should have caught at the opportunity of speaking to a gracious audience.

In a word, then, I do not care about this Exchange—because *you* don't; and because you know perfectly well I cannot make you. Look at the essential conditions of the case, which you, as business men, know perfectly well, though perhaps you think I forget them. You are going to spend £30,000, which to you, collectively, is nothing; the buying a new coat is, as to the cost of it, a much more important matter of consideration to me, than building a new Exchange is to you. But you think you may as well have the right thing for your money. You know there are a great many odd styles of architecture about; you don't want to do anything ridiculous; you hear of me, among others, as a respectable architectural man-milliner; and you send for me, that I may tell you the leading fashion; and what is, in our shops, for the moment, the newest and sweetest thing in pinnacles.

Now, pardon me for telling you frankly, you cannot have good architecture merely by asking people's advice on occasion. All good architecture is the expression of national life and character; and it is produced by a prevalent and eager national taste, or desire for beauty. And I want you to think a little of the deep significance of this word "taste"; for no statement of mine has been more earnestly or oftener controverted than that good taste is essentially a moral quality. "No," say many of my antagonists, "taste is one thing, morality is another. Tell us what is pretty: we shall be glad to know that; but we need no sermons—even were you able to preach them, which may be doubted."

Permit me, therefore, to fortify this old dogma of mine somewhat. Taste is not only a part and an index of morality;—it is the ONLY morality. The first, and last, and closest trial question to any living creature is, "What do you like?" Tell me what you like, and I'll tell you what you are. Go out into the street, and ask the first man or woman you meet, what their "taste" is; and if they answer candidly, you know them, body and soul. "You, my friend in the rags, with the unsteady gait, what do *you* like?" "A pipe, and a quartern of gin." I know you. "You, good woman, with the quick step and tidy bonnet, what do you like?" "A swept hearth, and a clean tea-table; and my husband opposite me, and a baby at my breast." Good, I know you also. "You, little girl with the golden hair and the soft eyes, what do you like?" "My canary, and a run among the wood hyacinths." "You, little boy with the dirty hands, and the low forehead, what do you like?" "A shy at the sparrows, and a game at pitch farthing." Good; we know them all now. What more need we ask?

"Nay," perhaps you answer; "we need rather to ask what these people and children do, than what they like. If they *do* right, it is no matter that they like what is wrong; and if they *do* wrong, it is no matter that they like what is right. Doing is the great thing; and it does not matter that the man likes drinking, so that he does not drink; nor that the little girl likes to be kind to her canary, if she will not learn her lessons; nor that the little boy likes throwing stones at the sparrows, if he goes to the Sunday school." Indeed, for a short time, and in a provisional sense, this is true. For if, resolutely, people do what is right, in time to come they like doing it. But they only are in a right moral state when they *have* come to like doing it; and as long as they don't like it, they are still in a vicious state. The man is not in health of body who is always thinking of the bottle in the cupboard, though he bravely bears his thirst; but the man who heartily enjoys water in the morning, and wine in the evening, each in its proper quantity and time. And the entire object of true education is to make people not merely *do* the right things, but *enjoy* the right things:—not merely industrious, but to love industry—not merely learned, but to love knowledge—not merely pure, but to love purity—not merely just, but to hunger and thirst after justice.

But you may answer or think, "Is the liking for outside ornaments,—for pictures, or statues, or furniture, or architecture, a moral quality?" Yes, most surely, if a rightly set liking. Taste for *any* pictures or statues is not a moral quality, but taste for good ones is. Only here again we have to define the word "good." I don't mean by "good," clever—or learned—or difficult in the doing. Take a picture by Teniers, of sots quarrelling over their dice; it is an entirely clever picture; so clever that nothing in its kind has ever been done equal to it; but it is also an entirely base and evil picture. It is an expression of delight in the prolonged contemplation of a vile thing, and delight in that is an "unmannered," or "immoral" quality. It is "bad taste" in the profoundest sense—it is the taste of the devils. On the other hand, a picture of Titian's, or a Greek statue, or a Greek coin, or a Turner landscape, expresses delight in the perpetual contemplation of a good and perfect thing. That is an entirely moral quality—it is the taste of the angels. And all delight in fine art, and all love of it, resolve themselves into simple love of that which deserves love. That deserving is the quality which we call "loveliness"—(we ought to have an opposite word, hateliness, to be said of the things which deserve to be hated); and it is not an indifferent nor optional thing whether we love this or that;

but it is just the vital function of all our being. What we *like* determines what we *are,* and is the sign of what we are; and to teach taste is inevitably to form character.

As I was thinking over this, in walking up Fleet Street the other day, my eye caught the title of a book standing open in a bookseller's window. It was—"On the necessity of the diffusion of taste among all classes." "Ah," I thought to myself, "my classifying friend, when you have diffused your taste, where will your classes be? The man who likes what you like, belongs to the same class with you, I think. Inevitably so. You may put him to other work if you choose; but, by the condition you have brought him into, he will dislike the work as much as you would yourself. You get hold of a scavenger or a costermonger, who enjoyed the Newgate Calendar for literature, and 'Pop goes the Weasel' for music. You think you can make him like Dante and Beethoven? I wish you joy of your lessons; but if you do, you have made a gentleman of him:—he won't like to go back to his costermongering."

And so completely and unexceptionally is this so, that, if I had time to-night, I could show you that a nation cannot be affected by any vice, or weakness, without expressing it, legibly, and for ever, either in bad art, or by want of art; and that there is no national virtue, small or great, which is not manifestly expressed in all the art which circumstances enable the people possessing that virtue to produce. Take, for instance, your great English virtue of enduring and patient courage. You have at present in England only one art of any consequence—that is, ironworking. You know thoroughly well how to cast and hammer iron. Now, do you think, in those masses of lava which you build volcanic cones to melt, and which you forge at the mouths of the Infernos you have created; do you think, on those iron plates, your courage and endurance are not written for ever,—not merely with an iron pen, but on iron parchment? And take also your great English vice—European vice—vice of all the world—vice of all other worlds that roll or shine in heaven, bearing with them yet the atmosphere of hell—the vice of jealousy, which brings competition into your commerce, teachery into your councils, and dishonour into your wars—that vice which has rendered for you, and for your next neighbouring nation, the daily occupations of existence no longer possible, but with the mail upon your breasts and the sword loose in its sheath; so that at last, you have realised for all the multitudes of the two great peoples who lead the so-called civilization of the earth,—you have realised for them all, I say, in person and in policy, what was once true only of the rough Border riders of your Cheviot hills—

They carved at the meal
With gloves of steel,
And they drank the red wine through the helmet barr'd;—

do you think that this national shame and dastardliness of heart are not written as legibly on every rivet of your iron armour as the strength of the right hands that forged it?

Friends, I know not whether this thing be the more ludicrous or the more melancholy. It is quite unspeakably both. Suppose, instead of being now sent for by you, I had been sent for by some private gentleman, living in a suburban house, with his garden separated only by a fruit wall from his next door neighbour's; and he had called me to consult with him on the furnishing of his drawing-room. I begin looking about me, and find the walls rather bare; I think such and such a paper might be desirable—perhaps a little fresco here and there on the ceiling—a damask curtain or so at the windows. "Ah," says my employer, "damask curtains, indeed! That's all very fine, but you know I can't afford that kind of thing just now!" "Yet the world credits you with a splendid income!" "Ah, yes," says my friend, "but do you know, at present I am obliged to spend it nearly all in steel-traps?" "Steel-traps! for whom?" "Why, for that fellow on the other side the wall, you know: we're very good friends, capital friends; but we are obliged to keep our traps set on both sides of the wall; we could not possibly keep on friendly terms without them, and our spring guns. The worst of it is, we are both clever fellows enough; and there's never a day passes that we won't find out a new trap, or a new gun-barrel, or something; we spend about fifteen millions a year each in our traps, take it altogether; and I don't see how we're to do with less." A highly comic state of life for two private gentlemen! but for two nations, it seems to me, not wholly comic. Bedlam would be comic, perhaps, if there were only one madman in it; and your Christmas pantomime is comic, when there is only one clown in it; but when the whole world turns clown, and paints itself red with its own heart's blood instead of vermilion, it is something else than comic, I think.

Mind, I know a great deal of this is play, and willingly allow for that. You don't know what to do with yourselves for a sensation: fox-hunting and cricketing will not carry you through the whole of this unendurably long mortal life: you liked pop-guns when you were schoolboys, and rifles and Armstrongs are only the same things better made: but then the worst of it is, that what was play to you when boys, was not play to the sparrows; and what is play to you now, is not play to the small birds of State neither; and for the black eagles, you are somewhat shy of taking shots at them, if I mistake not.

I must get back to the matter in hand, however. Believe me, without farther instance, I could show you, in all time, that every nation's vice, or virtue, was written in its art: the soldiership of early Greece; the sensuality of late Italy; the visionary religion of Tuscany; the splendid human energy of Venice. I have no time to do this to-night (I have done it elsewhere before now); but I proceed to apply the principle to ourselves in a more searching manner.

I notice that among all the new buildings which cover your once wild hills, churches and schools are mixed in due, that is to say, in large proportion, with your mills and mansions; and I notice also that the churches and schools are almost always Gothic, and the mansions and mills are never Gothic. May I ask the meaning of this? for, remember, it is peculiarly a modern phenomenon. When Gothic was invented, houses were Gothic as well as churches; and when the Italian style superseded the Gothic, churches were Italian as well as houses. If there is a Gothic spire to the cathedral of Antwerp, there is a Gothic belfry to the Hôtel de Ville at Brussels; if Indigo Jones builds an Italian Whitehall, Sir Christopher Wren builds an Italian St. Paul's. But now you live under one school of architecture, and worship under another. What do you mean by doing this? Am I to understand that you are thinking of changing your architecture back to Gothic; and that you treat your churches experimentally, because it does not matter what mistakes you make in a church? Or am I to understand that you consider Gothic a pre-eminently sacred and beautiful mode of building, which you think, like the fine frankincense, should be mixed for the tabernacle only, and reserved for your religious services? For if this be the feeling, though it may seem at first as if it were graceful and reverent, at the root of the matter, it signifies neither more nor less than that you have separated your religion from your life.

For consider what a wide significance this fact has; and remember that it is not you only, but all the people of England, who are behaving thus, just now.

You have all got into the habit of calling the church "the house of God." I have seen, over the doors of many churches, the legend actually carved, "*This* is the house of God and this is the gate of heaven." Now, note where the legend comes from, and of what place it was first spoken. A boy leaves his father's house to go on a long journey on foot, to visit his uncle: he has to cross a wild hill-desert; just as if one of your own boys had to cross the wolds to visit an uncle at Carlisle. The second or third day your boy finds himself between Hawes and Brough, in the midst of the moors, at sunset. It is stony ground, and boggy; he cannot go one foot farther that night. Down he lies, to sleep, on Wharnside, where best he may, gathering a few of the stones together to put under his head;—so wild the place is, he cannot get anything but stones. And there, lying under the broad night, he has a dream; and he sees a ladder set up on the earth, and the top of it reaches to heaven, and the angels of God are seen ascending and descending upon it. And when he wakes out of his sleep, he says, "How dreadful is this place; surely this is none other than the house of God, and this is the gate of heaven." This PLACE, observe; not this church; not this city; not this stone, even, which he puts up for a memorial—the piece of flint on which his head was lain. But this *place;* this windy slope of Wharnside; this moorland hollow, torrent-bitten, snow-blighted! this *any* place where God lets down the ladder. And how are you to know where that will be? or how are you to determine where it may be, but by being ready for it always? Do you know where the lightning is to fall next? You *do* know that, partly; you can guide the lightning; but you cannot guide the going forth of the Spirit, which is as that lightning when it shines from the east to the west.

But the perpetual and insolent warping of that strong verse to serve a merely ecclesiastical purpose, is only one of the thousand instances in which we sink back into gross Judaism. We call our churches "temples." Now, you know perfectly well they are *not* temples. They have never had, never can have, anything whatever to do with temples. They are "synagogues"—"gathering places"—where you gather yourselves together as an assembly; and by not calling them so, you again miss the force of another mighty text—"Thou, when thou prayest, shalt not be as the hypocrites are; for they love to pray standing in the *churches* [we should translate it],[1] that they may be seen of men. But thou, when thou prayest, enter into thy closet, and when thou hast shut thy door, pray to thy Father,"—which is, not in chancel nor in aisle, but "in secret."

Now, you feel, as I say this to you—I know you feel—as if I were trying to take away the honor of your churches. Not so; I am trying to prove to you the honour of your houses and your hills; not that the Church is not sacred—but that the whole Earth is. I would have you feel what careless, what constant, what infectious sin there is in all modes of thought, whereby, in calling your churches only "holy," you call your hearths and homes "profane"; and have separated yourselves from the heathen by casting all your household gods to the ground, instead of recognizing, in the places of their many and feeble Lares, the presence of your One and Mighty Lord and Lar.

"But what has all this to do with our Exchange?" you ask me, impatiently. My dear friends, it has just everything to do with it; on these inner and great questions depend all the outer and little ones; and if you have asked me down here to speak to you, because you had before been interested in anything I have written, you must know that all I have yet said about architecture was to show this. The book I called *The Seven Lamps* was to show that certain right states of temper and moral feeling were the magic powers by which all good architecture, without exception, had been produced. *The Stones of Venice* had, from beginning to end, no other aim than to show that the Gothic architecture of Venice had arisen out of, and indicated in all its features, a state of pure national faith, and of domestic virtue; and that its Renaissance architecture had arisen out of, and in all its features indicated, a state of concealed national infidelity, and of domestic corruption. And now, you ask me what style is best to build in, and how can I answer, knowing the meaning of the two styles but by another question—do you mean to build as Christians or as infidels? And still more—do you mean to build as honest Christians or as honest infidels? as thoroughly and confessedly either one or the other? You don't like to be asked such rude questions. I cannot help it; they are of much more

1 Text inserted by Ruskin in 1873.

importance than this Exchange business; and if they can be at once answered, the Exchange business settles itself in a moment. But before I press them farther, I must ask leave to explain one point clearly.

In all my past work, my endeavour has been to show that good architecture is essentially religious—the production of a faithful and virtuous, not of an infidel and corrupted people. But in the course of doing this, I have had also to show that good architecture is not *ecclesiastical.* People are so apt to look upon religion as the business of the clergy, not their own, that the moment they hear of anything depending on "religion," they think it must also have depended on the priesthood; and I have had to take what place was to be occupied between these two errors, and fight both, often with seeming contradiction. Good architecture is the work of good and believing men; therefore, you say, at least some people say, "Good architecture must essentially have been the work of the clergy, not of the laity." No—a thousand times no; good architecture has always been the work of the commonalty, *not* of the clergy. "What," you say, "those glorious cathedrals—the pride of Europe—did their builders not form Gothic architecture?" No; they corrupted Gothic architecture. Gothic was formed in the baron's castle, and the burgher's street. It was formed by the thoughts, and hands, and powers of labouring citizens and warrior kings. By the monk it was used as an instrument for the aid of his superstition: when that superstition became a beautiful madness, and the best hearts of Europe vainly dreamed and pined in the cloister, and vainly raged and perished in the crusade,—through that fury of perverted faith and wasted war, the Gothic rose also to its loveliest, most fantastic, and, finally, most foolish dreams; and in those dreams was lost.

I hope, now, that there is no risk of your misunderstanding me when I come to the gist of what I want to say to-night;—when I repeat, that every great national architecture has been the result and exponent of a great national religion. You can't have bits of it here, bits there—you must have it everywhere or nowhere. It is not the monopoly of a clerical company—it is not the exponent of a theological dogma—it is not the hieroglyphic writing of an initiated priesthood; it is the manly language of a people inspired by resolute and common purpose, and rendering resolute and common fidelity to the legible laws of an undoubted God.

Now there have as yet been three distinct schools of European architecture. I say, European, because Asiatic and African architectures belong so entirely to other races and climates, that there is no question of them here; only, in passing, I will simply assure you that whatever is good or great in Egypt, and Syria, and India, is just good or great for the same reasons as the buildings on our side of the Bosphorus. We Europeans, then, have had three great religions: the Greek, which was the worship of the God of Wisdom and Power; the Mediaeval, which was the worship of the God of Judgment and Consolation; the Renaissance, which was the worship of the God of Pride and Beauty: these three we have had—they are past,—and now, at last, we English have got a fourth religion, and a God of our own, about which I want to ask you. But I must explain these three old ones first.

I repeat, first, the Greeks essentially worshipped the God of Wisdom; so that whatever contended against their religion,—to the Jews a stumbling-block,—was, to the Greeks—*Foolishness.*

The first Greek idea of deity was that expressed in the word, of which we keep the remnant in our words "*Di*-urnal" and "*Di*-vine"—the god of *Day,* Jupiter the revealer. Athena is his daughter, but especially daughter of the Intellect, springing armed from the head. We are only with the help of recent investigation beginning to penetrate the depth of meaning couched under the Athenaic symbols: but I may note rapidly, that her aegis, the mantle with the serpent fringes, in which she often, in the best statues, is represented as folding up her left hand, for better guard; and the Gorgon, on her shield, are both representative mainly of the chilling horror and sadness (turning men to stone, as it were), of the outmost and superficial spheres of knowledge—that knowledge which separates, in bitterness, hardness, and sorrow, the heart of the full-grown man from the heart of the child. For out of imperfect knowledge spring terror, dissension, danger, and disdain; but from perfect knowledge, given by the full-revealed Athena, strength and peace, in sign of which she is crowned with the olive spray, and bears the resistless spear.

This, then, was the Greek conception of purest Deity; and every habit of life, and every form of his art developed themselves from the seeking this bright, serene, resistless wisdom; and setting himself, as a man, to do things evermore rightly and strongly; not with any ardent affection or ultimate hope; but with a resolute and continent energy of will, as knowing that for failure there was no consolation, and for sin there was no remission. And the Greek architecture rose unerring, bright, clearly defined, and self-contained.

Next followed in Europe the great Christian faith, which was essentially the religion of Comfort. Its great doctrine is the remission of sins; for which cause, it happens, too often, in certain phases of Christianity, that sin and sickness themselves are partly glorified, as if, the more you had to be healed of, the more divine was the healing. The practical result of this doctrine, in art, is a continual contemplation of sin and disease, and of imaginary states of purification from them; thus we have an architecture conceived in a mingled sentiment of melancholy and aspiration, partly severe, partly luxuriant, which will bend itself to every one of our needs, and every one of our fancies, and be strong or weak with us, as we are strong or weak ourselves. It is, of all architecture, the basest, when base people build it—of all, the noblest, when built by the noble.

And now note that both these religions—Greek and Mediaeval—perished by falsehood in their own main purpose. The Greek religion of Wisdom perished in a false philosophy—"Oppositions of science, falsely so called." The Mediaeval religion of Consolation perished in false comfort; in remission of sins given lyingly. It was the selling of absolution that ended the Mediaeval faith; and I can tell you more, it is the selling of absolution which, to the end of time, will mark false Christianity. Pure Christianity gives her remission of sins only by *ending* them; but false Christianity gets her remission of sins by *compounding for* them. And there are many ways of compounding for them. We English have beautiful little quiet ways of buying absolution, whether in low Church or high, far more cunning than any of Tetzel's trading.

Then, thirdly, there followed the religion of Pleasure, in which all Europe gave itself to luxury, ending in death. First, *bals masqués* in every saloon, and then guillotines in every square. And all these three worships issue in vast temple building. Your Greek worshipped Wisdom, and built you the Parthenon—the Virgin's temple. The Mediaeval worshipped Consolation, and built you Virgin temples also—but to our Lady of Salvation. Then the Revivalist worshipped beauty, of a sort, and built you Versailles and the Vatican. Now, lastly, will you tell me what *we* worship, and what *we* build?

You know we are speaking always of the real, active, continual, national worship; that by which men act, while they live; not that which they talk of, when they die. Now, we have, indeed, a nominal religion, to which we pay tithes of property and sevenths of time; but we have also a practical and earnest religion, to which we devote nine-tenths of our property, and six-sevenths of our time. And we dispute a great deal about the nominal religion: but we are all unanimous about this practical one; of which I think you will admit that the ruling goddess may be best described as the "Goddess of Getting-on," or "Britannia of the Market." The Athenians had an "Athena Agoraia," or Athena of the Market; but she was a subordinate type of their goddess, while our Britannia Agoraia is the principal type of ours. And all your great architectural works are, of course, built to her. It is long since you built a great cathedral; and how you would laugh at me if I proposed building a cathedral on the top of one of these hills of yours, to make it an Acropolis! But your railroad mounds, vaster than the walls of Babylon; your railroad stations, vaster than the temple of Ephesus, and innumerable; your chimneys, how much more mighty and costly than cathedral spires! your harbour-piers; your warehouses; your exchanges!—all these are built to your great Goddess of "Getting-on"; and she has formed, and will continue to form, your architecture, as long as you worship her; and it is quite vain to ask me to tell you how to build to *her;* you know far better than I.

There might, indeed, on some theories, be a conceivably good architecture for Exchanges—that is to say, if there were any heroism in the fact or deed of exchange, which might be typically carved on the outside of your building. For, you know, all beautiful architecture must be adorned with sculpture or painting; and for sculpture or painting, you must have a subject. And hitherto it has been a received opinion among the nations of the world that the only right subjects for either, were *heroisms* of some sort. Even on his pots and his flagons, the Greek put a Hercules slaying lions, or an Apollo slaying serpents, or Bacchus slaying melancholy giants, and earthborn despondencies. On his temples, the Greek put contests of great warriors in founding states, or of gods with evil spirits. On his houses and temples alike, the Christian put carvings of angels conquering devils; or of hero-martyrs exchanging this world for another: subject inappropriate, I think, to our direction of exchange here. And the Master of Christians not only left His followers without any orders as to the sculpture of affairs of exchange on the outside of buildings, but gave some strong evidence of His dislike of affairs of exchange within them. And yet there might surely be a heroism in such affairs; and all commerce become a kind of selling of doves, not impious. The wonder has always been great to me, that heroism has never been supposed to be in anywise consistent with the practice of supplying people with food, or clothes; but rather with that of quartering one's self upon them for food, and stripping them of their clothes. Spoiling of armour is an heroic deed in all ages; but the selling of clothes, old, or new, has never taken any colour of magnanimity. Yet one does not see why feeding the hungry and clothing the naked should ever become base businesses, even, when engaged in on a large scale. If one could contrive to attach the notion of conquest to them anyhow! so that, supposing there were anywhere an obstinate race, who refused to be comforted, one might take some pride in giving them compulsory comfort! and, as it were, "*occupying* a country" with one's gifts, instead of one's armies? If one could only consider it as much a victory to get a barren field sown, as to get an eared field stripped; and contend who should build villages, instead of who should "carry" them! Are not all forms of heroism conceivable in doing these serviceable deeds? You doubt who is strongest? It might be ascertained by push of spade, as well as push of sword. Who is wisest? There are witty things to be thought of in planning other business than campaigns. Who is bravest? There are always the elements to fight with, stronger than men; and nearly as merciless.

The only absolutely and unapproachably heroic element in the soldier's work seems to be—that he is paid little for it—and regularly: while you traffickers, and exchangers, and others occupied in presumably benevolent business, like to be paid much for it—and by chance. I never can make out how it is that a *knight*-errant does not expect to be paid for his trouble, but a *pedlar*-errant always does;—that people are willing to take hard knocks for nothing, but never to sell ribands cheap; that they are ready to go on fervent crusades, to recover the tomb of a buried God, but never on any travels to fulfil the orders of a living one;—that they will go anywhere barefoot to preach their faith, but must be well bribed to practise it, and are perfectly ready to give the Gospel gratis, but never the loaves and fishes.

If you chose to take the matter up on any such soldierly principle; to do your commerce, and your feeding of nations, for fixed salaries; and to be as particular about giving people the best food, and the best cloth, as soldiers are about giving them the best gunpowder, I could carve something for you on your exchange worth looking at. But I can only at present suggest decorating its frieze with pendant purses; and making its pillars broad at the base, for the sticking of bills. And in the innermost chambers of it there might be a statue of Britannia of the Market, who may have, perhaps advisably, a partridge for her crest, typical at once of her courage in fighting for noble ideas, and of her interest in game; and round its neck, the inscription in golden letters, "Perdix fovit quae non peperit." Then, for her spear, she might have a weaver's beam; and on her shield, instead of St. George's Cross, the Milanese boar, semi-fleeced, with the town of Gennesaret proper, in the field; and the legend, "In the best market," and her corslet, of leather, folded over her heart in the shape of a purse, with thirty slits in it, for a piece of money to go in at, on each day of the month. And I doubt not but that people would come to see your exchange, and its goddess, with applause.

Nevertheless, I want to point out to you certain strange characters in this goddess of yours. She differs from the great Greek and Mediaeval deities essentially in two things—first, as to the continuance of her presumed power; secondly, as to the extent of it.

1st, as to the Continuance.

The Greek Goddess of Wisdom gave continual increase of wisdom, as the Christian Spirit of Comfort (or Comforter) continual increase of comfort. There was no question, with these, of any limit or cessation of function. But with your Agora Goddess, that is just the most important question. Getting on—but where to? Gathering together—but how much? Do you mean to gather always—never to spend? If so, I wish you joy of your goddess, for I am just as well off as you, without the trouble of worshipping her at all. But if you do not spend, somebody else will—somebody else must. And it is because of this (among many other such errors) that I have fearlessly declared your so-called science of Political Economy to be no science; because, namely, it has omitted the study of exactly the most important branch of the business—the study of *spending.* For spend you must, and as much as you make, ultimately. You gather corn:—will you bury England under a heap of grain; or will you, when you have gathered, finally eat? You gather gold:—will you make your house-roofs of it, or pave your streets with it? That is still one way of spending it. But if you keep it, that you may get more, I'll give you more; I'll give you all the gold you want—all you can imagine—if you can tell me what you'll do with it. You shall have thousands of gold pieces;—thousand of thousands—millions—mountains, of gold: where will you keep them? Will you put an Olympus of silver upon a golden Pelion—make Ossa like a wart? Do you think the rain and dew would then come down to you, in the streams from such mountains, more blessedly than they will down the mountains which God has made for you, of moss and whinstone? But it is not gold that you want to gather! What is it? greenbacks? No; not those neither. What is it then—is it ciphers after a capital I? Cannot you practise writing ciphers, and write as many as you want! Write ciphers for an hour every morning, in a big book, and say every evening, I am worth all those noughts more than I was yesterday. Won't that do? Well, what in the name of Plutus is it you want? Not gold, not greenbacks, not ciphers after a capital I? You will have to answer, after all, "No; we want, somehow or other, money's *worth*." Well, what is that? Let your Goddess of Getting-on discover it, and let her learn to stay therein.

II. But there is yet another question to be asked respecting this Goddess of Getting-on. The first was of the continuance of her power; the second is of its extent.

Pallas and the Madonna were supposed to be all the world's Pallas, and all the world's Madonna. They could teach all men, and they could comfort all men. But, look strictly into the nature of the power of your Goddess of Getting-on; and you will find she is the Goddess—not of everybody's getting on—but only of somebody's getting on. This is a vital, or rather deathful, distinction. Examine it in your own ideal of the state of national life which this Goddess is to evoke and maintain. I asked you what it was, when I was last here;—you have never told me. Now, shall I try to tell you?

Your ideal of human life then is, I think, that it should be passed in a pleasant undulating world, with iron and coal everywhere underneath it. On each pleasant bank of this world is to be a beautiful mansion, with two wings; and stables, and coach-houses; a moderately-sized park; a large garden and hot-houses; and pleasant carriage drives through the shrubberies. In this mansion are to live the favoured votaries of the Goddess; the English gentleman, with his gracious wife, and his beautiful family; he always able to have the boudoir and the jewels for the wife, and the beautiful ball dresses for the daughters, and hunters for the sons, and a shooting in the Highlands for himself. At the bottom of the bank, is to be the mill; not less than a quarter of a mile long, with one steam engine at each end, and two in the middle, and a chimney three hundred feet high. In this mill are to be in constant employment from eight hundred to a thousand workers, who never drink, never strike, always go to church on Sunday, and always express themselves in respectful language.

Is not that, broadly, and in the main features, the kind of thing you propose to yourselves? It is very pretty indeed, seen from above; not at all so pretty, seen from below. For, observe, while to one family this deity is indeed the Goddess of Getting-on, to a thousand families she is the Goddess of *not* Getting-on. "Nay," you say, "they have all their chance." Yes, so has every one in a lottery, but there must always be the same number of blanks. "Ah! but in a lottery it is not skill and intelligence which take the lead, but blind chance." What then! do you think the old practice, that "they should take who have the power, and they should keep who can," is less iniquitous, when the power has become power of brains instead of fist? and that, though we may not take advantage of a child's or a woman's weakness, we may of a man's foolishness? "Nay, but finally, work must be done, and some one must be at the top, some one at the bottom." Granted, my friends. Work must always be, and captains of work must always be; and if you in the least remember the tone of any of my writings, you must know that they are thought unfit for this age, because they are always insisting on need of government, and speaking with scorn of liberty. But I beg you to observe that there is a wide difference between being captains or governors of work, and taking the profits of it. It does not follow, because you are general of an army, that you are to take all the treasure, or land, it wins; (if it fight for treasure or land;) neither, because you are king of a nation, that you are to consume all the profits of the nation's work. Real kings on the contrary, are known invariably by their doing quite the reverse of this,—by their taking the least possible quantity of the nation's work for themselves. There is no test of real kinghood so infallible as that. Does the crowned creature live simply, bravely, unostentatiously? probably he *is* a King. Does he cover his body with jewels, and his table with delicates?

in all probability he is *not* a King. It is possible he may be, as Solomon was; but that is when the nation shares his splendour with him. Solomon made gold, not only to be in his own palace as stones, but to be in Jerusalem as stones. But, even so, for the most part, these splendid kinghoods expire in ruin, and only the true kinghoods live, which are of royal labourers governing loyal labourers; who, both leading rough lives, establish the true dynasties. Conclusively you will find that because you are king of a nation, it does not follow that you are to gather for yourself all the wealth of that nation; neither, because you are king of a small part of the nation, and lord over the means of its maintenance—over field, or mill, or mine,—are you to take all the produce of that piece of the foundation of national existence for yourself.

You will tell me I need not preach against these things, for I cannot mend them. No, good friends, I cannot; but you can, and you will; or something else can and will. Even good things have no abiding power—and shall these evil things persist in victorious evil? All history shows, on the contrary, that to be the exact thing they never can do. Change *must* come; but it is ours to determine whether change of growth, or change of death. Shall the Parthenon be in ruins on its rock, and Bolton priory in its meadow, but these mills of yours be the consummation of the buildings of the earth, and their wheels be as the wheels of eternity? Think you that "men may come, and men may go," but —mills—go on for ever? Not so; out of these, better or worse shall come; and it is for you to choose which.

I know that none of this wrong is done with deliberate purpose. I know, on the contrary, that you wish your workmen well; that you do much for them, and that you desire to do more for them, if you saw your way to such benevolence safely. I know that even all this wrong and misery are brought about by a warped sense of duty, each of you striving to do his best; but, unhappily, not knowing for whom this best should be done. And all our hearts have been betrayed by the plausible impiety of the modern economist, telling us that, "To do the best for ourselves, is finally to do the best for others." Friends, our great Master said not so; and most absolutely we shall find this world is not made so. Indeed, to do the best for others, is finally to do the best for ourselves; but it will not do to have our eyes fixed on that issue. The Pagans had got beyond that. Hear what a Pagan says of this matter; hear what were, perhaps, the last written words of Plato,—if not the last actually written (for this we cannot know), yet assuredly in fact and power his parting words—in which, endeavouring to give full crowning and harmonious close to all his thoughts, and to speak the sum of them by the imagined sentence of the Great Spirit, his strength and his heart fail him, and the words cease, broken off for ever.

They are at the close of the dialogue called *Critias,* in which he describes, partly from real tradition, partly in ideal dream, the early state of Athens; and the genesis, and order, and religion, of the fabled isle of Atlantis; in which genesis he conceives the same first perfection and final degeneracy of man, which in our own Scriptural tradition is expressed by saying that the Sons of God inter-married with the daughters of men, for he supposes the earliest race to have been indeed the children of God; and to have corrupted themselves, until "their spot was not the spot of his children." And this, he says, was the end; that indeed "through many generations, so long as the God's nature in them yet was full, they were submissive to the sacred laws, and carried themselves lovingly to all that had kindred with them in divineness; for their uttermost spirit was faithful and true, and in every wise great; so that, in *all meekness of wisdom, they dealt with each other,* and took all the chances of life; and despising all things except virtue, they cared little what happened day by day, and *bore lightly the burden* of gold and of possessions; for they saw that, if *only their common love and virtue increased, all these things would be increased together with them;* but to set their esteem and ardent pursuit upon material possession would be to lose that first, and their virtue and effection together with it. And by such reasoning, and what of the divine nature remained in them, they gained all this greatness of which we have already told; but when the God's part of them faded and became extinct, being mixed again and again, and effaced by the prevalent mortality; and the human nature at last exceeded, they then became unable to endure the courses of fortune; and fell into shapelessness of life, and baseness in the sight of him who could see, having lost everything that was fairest of their honour; while to the blind hearts which could not discern the true life, tending to happiness, it seemed that they were then chiefly noble and happy, being filled with all iniquity of inordinate possession and power. Whereupon, the God of Gods, whose Kinghood is in laws, beholding a once just nation thus cast into misery, and desiring to lay such punishment upon them as might make them repent into restraining, gathered together all the gods into his dwelling place, which from heaven's centre overlooks whatever has part in creation; and having assembled them, he said"—

The rest is silence. Last words of the chief wisdom of the heathen, spoken of this idol of riches; this idol of yours; this golden image, high by measureless cubits, set up where your green fields of England are furnace-burnt into the likeness of the plain of Dura: this idol, forbidden to us, first of all idols, by our own Master and faith; forbidden to us also by every human lip that has ever, in any age or people, been accounted of as able to speak according to the purposes of God. Continue to make that forbidden deity your principal one, and soon no more art, no more science, no more pleasure will be possible. Catastrophe will come; or, worse than catastrophe, slow mouldering and withering into Hades. But if you can fix some conception of a true human state of life to be striven for—life, good for all men, as for yourselves; if you can determine some honest and simple order of existence; following those trodden ways of wisdom, which are pleasantness, and seeking her quiet and withdrawn paths, which are peace;—then, and so sanctifying wealth into "commonwealth," all your art, your literature, your daily labours, your domestic affection, and citizen's duty, will join and increase into one magnificent harmony. You will know then how to build, well enough; you will build with stone well, but with flesh better; temples not made with hands, but riveted of hearts; and that kind of marble, crimson-veined, is indeed eternal.

from

The Birth of Tragedy

Friedrich Nietzsche

(1844-1900)

We can no longer accept Ruskin's notion that "good" art is angelic, mainly because it is too simple-minded a view of art and life as well as much too syrupy a conception for modern tastes. We prefer today that our art have more pungency and reflect a more complex vision than was allowed for by Ruskin. In large measure our current preference for a complex, astringent vision stems from the writings of Friedrich Nietzsche.

To Nietzsche art was a mixture of good and evil, of joy and terror, of total individuation and complete self-abnegation, of dream and reality, and of restraint and licentiousness. In other words, Nietzsche saw art as the marriage of heaven and hell, albeit these qualities are in conflict. Nietzsche held that in classical art, the "Apollonian consciousness"—representing the first term in each of the above pairs—"like a veil, hid this Dionysian world"—representing the second term in each of the above pairs. Although the Dionysian vision underlay Apollonian form, these two necessary "impulses" were in competition for artistic dominance. If one successfully dominates the other we have either lifelessness or formlessness in art. Both must be present and Nietzsche would say that the highest art is that which holds the Apollonian and Dionysian impulses in appropriate tension (he would never have used the word "balance").

The Birth of Tragedy, *Nietzsche's first book, was written when he was about twenty-six and grew out of his studies in classical philology. The book was roundly condemned by the academics of his day, but has had a profound influence on subsequent studies of the ancients, as well as an enormous impact on contemporary esthetics. Moreover, Nietzsche's notion of the Dionysian substratum in all art presages Freud's later psychoanalytic theories and can be seen as a pioneering work in modern psychology.*

Unlike Blake, whom he much resembles in his dualism, and unlike most of the other authors in this anthology, Nietzsche's radicalism came from the right rather than the left of the political spectrum. Scion of a long line of Lutheran ministers who held strong royalist views, Nietzsche propounded an elitist doctrine in opposition to the "slave mentality" produced by what he must have seen as "creeping democracy." His political and social theories can be found in his major works, Thus Spake Zarathustra, Beyond Good and Evil, Ecce Homo, *and* The Will to Power.

I

WE shall do a great deal for the science of esthetics, once we perceive not merely by logical inference, but with the immediate certainty of intuition, that the continuous development of art is bound up with the *Apollonian* and *Dionysian* duality: just as procreation depends on the duality of the sexes, involving perpetual strife with only periodically intervening reconciliations. The terms Dionysian and Apollonian we borrow from the Greeks, who disclose to the discerning mind the profound mysteries of their view of art, not, to be sure, in concepts, but in the impressively clear figures of their gods. Through Apollo and Dionysus, the two art-deities of the Greeks, we come to recognize that in the Greek world there existed a sharp opposition, in origin and aims, between the Apollonian art of sculpture, and the non-plastic, Dionysian, art of music. These two distinct tendencies run parallel to each other, for the most part openly at variance; and they continually incite each other to new and more powerful births, which perpetuate an antagonism, only superficially reconciled by the common term "Art"; till at last, by a metaphysical miracle of the Hellenic will, they appear coupled with each other, and through this coupling eventually generate the art-product, equally Dionysian and Apollonian, of Attic tragedy.

In order to grasp these two tendencies, let us first conceive of them as the separate art-worlds of *dreams* and *drunkenness.* These physiological phenomena present a contrast analogous to that existing between the Apollonian and the Dionysian. It was in dreams, says Lucretius, that the glorious divine figures first appeared to the souls of men; in dreams the great shaper beheld the splendid corporeal structure of superhuman beings; and the Hellenic poet, if questioned about the mysteries of poetic inspiration, would likewise have suggested dreams and he might have given an explanation like that of Hans Sachs in the *Mastersingers:*

> *Mein Freund, das grad' ist Dichters Werk,*
> *dess er sein Träumen deut' and merk'.*
> *Glaubt mir, des Menschen wahrster Wahn*
> *wird ihm im Traume aufgethan:*
> *all' Dichtkunst und Poëterei*
> *ist nichts als Wahrtraum-Deuterei.*[1]

The beautiful appearance of the dream-worlds, in creating which every man is a perfect artist, is the prerequisite of all plastic art, and in fact, as we shall see, of an important part of poetry also. In our dreams we delight in the immediate apprehension of form; all forms speak to us; none are unimportant, none are superfluous. But, when this dream-reality is most in-

[1] "My friend, that is exactly the poet's task, to mark his dreams and to attach meanings to them. Believe me, man's most profound illusions are revealed to him in dreams; and all versifying and poetizing is nothing but an interpretation of them."

tense, we also have, glimmering through it, the sensation of its appearance: at least this is my experience, as to whose frequency, aye, normality, I could adduce many proofs, in addition to the sayings of the poets. Indeed, the man of philosophic mind has a presentiment that underneath this reality in which we live and have our being, is concealed another and quite different reality, which, like the first, is an appearance; and Schopenhauer actually indicates as the criterion of philosophical ability the occasional ability to view men and things as mere phantoms or dream-pictures. Thus the esthetically sensitive man stands in the same relation to the reality of dreams as the philosopher does to the reality of existence; he is a close and willing observer, for these pictures afford him an interpretation of life, and it is by these processes that he trains himself for life. And it is not only the agreeable and friendly pictures that he experiences in himself with such perfect understanding: but the serious, the troubled, the sad, the gloomy, the sudden restraints, the tricks of fate, the uneasy presentiments, in short, the whole Divine Comedy of life, and the Inferno, also pass before him, not like mere shadows on the wall—for in these scenes he lives and suffers—and yet not without that fleeting sensation of appearance. And perhaps many will, like myself, recall that amid the dangers and terrors of dream-life they would at times, cry out in self-encouragement, and not without success. "It is only a dream! I will dream on!" I have likewise heard of persons capable of continuing one and the same dream for three and even more successive nights: facts which indicate clearly that our innermost beings, our common subconscious experiences, express themselves in dreams because they must do so and because they take profound delight in so doing.

This joyful necessity of the dream-experience has been embodied by the Greeks in their Apollo: for Apollo, the god of all plastic energies, is at the same time the soothsaying god. He, who (as the etymology of the name indicates) is the "shining one," the deity of light, is also ruler over the fair appearance of the inner world of fantasy. The higher truth, the perfection of these states in contrast to the incompletely intelligible everyday world, this deep consciousness of nature, healing and helping in sleep and dreams, is at the same time the symbolical analogue of the soothsaying faculty and of the arts generally, which make life possible and worth living. But we must also include in our picture of Apollo that delicate boundary, which the dream-picture must not overstep—lest it act pathologically (in which case appearance would impose upon us as pure reality). We must keep in mind that measured restraint, that freedom from the wilder emotions, that philosophical calm of the sculptor-god. His eye must be "sunlike," as befits his origin; even when his glance is angry and distempered, the sacredness of his beautiful appearance must still be there. And so, in one sense, we might apply to Apollo the words of Schopenhauer when he speaks of the man wrapped in the veil of Mâyâ: *Welt als Wille und Vorstellung,* I. p. 416: "Just as in a stormy sea, unbounded in every direction, rising and falling with howling mountainous waves, a sailor sits in a boat and trusts in his frail barque: so in the midst of a world of sorrows the individual sits quietly, supported by and trusting in his *principium individuationis.*" In fact, we might say of Apollo, that in him the unshaken faith in this *principium* and the calm repose of the man wrapped therein receive their sublimest expression; and we might consider Apollo himself as the glorious divine image of the *principium individuationis,* whose gestures and expression tell us of all the joy and wisdom of "appearance," together with its beauty.

In the same work Schopenhauer has depicted for us the terrible *awe* which seizes upon man, when he is suddenly unable to account for the cognitive forms of a phenomenon, when the principle of reason, in some one of its manifestations, seems to admit of an exception. If we add to this awe the blissful ecstasy which rises from the innermost depths of man, aye, of nature, at this very collapse of the *principium individuationis,* we shall gain an insight into the nature of the *Dionysian,* which is brought home to us most intimately perhaps by the analogy of *drunkenness.* It is either under the influence of the narcotic draught, which we hear of in the songs of all primitive men and peoples, or with the potent coming of spring penetrating all nature with joy, that these Dionysian emotions awake, which, as they intensify, cause the subjective to vanish into complete self-forgetfulness. So also in the German Middle Ages singing and dancing crowds, ever increasing in number, were whirled from place to place under this same Dionysian impulse. In these dancers of St. John and St. Vitus, we rediscover the Bacchic choruses of the Greeks, with their early history in Asia Minor, as far back as Babylon and the orgiastic Sacaea. There are some, who, from obtuseness, or lack of experience, will deprecate such phenomena as "folk-diseases," with contempt or pity born of the consciousness of their own "healthy-mindedness." But, of course, such poor wretches can not imagine how anemic and ghastly their so-called "healthy-mindedness" seems in contrast to the glowing life of the Dionysian revellers rushing past them.

Under the charm of the Dionysian not only is the union between man and man reaffirmed, but Nature which has become estranged, hostile, or subjugated, celebrates once more her reconciliation with her prodigal son, man. Freely earth proffers her gifts, and peacefully the beasts of prey approach from desert and mountain. The chariot of Dionysus is bedecked with flowers and garlands; panthers and tigers pass beneath his yoke. Transform Beethoven's "Hymn to Joy" into a painting; let your imagination conceive the multitudes bowing to the dust, awestruck—then you will be able to appreciate the Dionysian. Now the slave is free; now all the stubborn, hostile barriers, which necessity, caprice or "shameless fashion" have erected between man and man, are broken down. Now, with the gospel of universal harmony, each one feels himself not only united, reconciled, blended with his neighbor, but as one with him; he feels as if the veil of Mâyâ had been torn aside and were now merely fluttering in tatters before the mysterious Primordial Unity. In song and in dance man expresses himself as a member of a higher community; he has forgotten how to walk and speak; he is about to take a dancing flight into the air. His very gestures bespeak enchantment. Just as the animals now talk, just as the earth yields milk and honey, so from him emanate supernatural sounds. He feels himself a god, he himself now walks about enchanted, in ecstasy, like to the gods whom he saw walking about in his dreams. He is no longer an artist, he has become a work of art: in these paroxysms of intoxication the artistic power of all nature reveals itself to the highest gratification of the Primordial Unity. The noblest clay, the most costly marble, man, is here kneaded and cut, and to the sound of the chisel strokes of the Dionysian world-artist rings out the cry of the Eleusinian mysteries: "Do ye bow in the dust, O millions? Do you divine your creator, O world?"

II

Thus far we have considered the Apollonian and its antithesis, the Dionysian, as artistic energies which burst forth from nature herself, *without the mediation of the human artist;* energies in which nature's art-impulses are satisfied in the most immediate and direct way: first, on the one hand, in the pictorial world of dreams, whose completeness is not dependent upon the intellectual attitude or the artistic culture of any single being; and, on the other hand, as drunken reality, which likewise does not heed the single unit, but even seeks to destroy the individual and redeem him by a mystic feeling of Oneness. With reference to these immediate art-states of nature, every artist is an "imitator," that is to say, either an Apollonian artist in dreams, or a Dionysian artist in ecstasies, or finally—as for example in Greek tragedy—at once artist in both dreams and ecstasies: so we may perhaps picture him sinking down in his Dionysian drunkenness and mystical self-abnegation, alone, and apart from the singing revelers, and we may imagine how now, through Apollonian dream-inspiration, his own state, *i.e.,* his oneness with the primal nature of the universe, is revealed to him in a *symbolical dream-picture.*

So much for these general premises and contrasts. Let us now approach the *Greeks* in order to learn how highly these *art-impulses of nature* were developed in them. Thus we shall be in a position to understand and appreciate more deeply that relation of the Greek artist to his archetypes, which, according to the Aristotelian expression, is "the imitation of nature." In spite of all the dream-literature and the numerous dream-anecdotes of the Greeks, we can speak only conjecturally, though with reasonable assurance, of their *dreams.* If we consider the incredibly precise and unerring plastic power of their eyes, together with their vivid, frank delight in colors, we can hardly refrain (to the shame of all those born later) from assuming even for their dreams a certain logic of line and contour, colors and groups, a certain pictorial sequence reminding us of their finest bas-reliefs, whose perfection would certainly justify us, if a comparison were possible, in designating the dreaming Greeks as Homers and Homer as a dreaming Greek: in a deeper sense than that in which modern man, speaking of his dreams, ventures to compare himself with Shakespeare.

On the other hand, there is no conjecture as to the immense gap which separates the *Dionysian Greek* from the Dionysian barbarian. From all quarters of the Ancient World,—to say nothing here of the modern,—from Rome to Babylon, we can point to the existence of Dionysian festivals, types which bear, at best, the same relation to the Greek festivals as the bearded satyr, who borrowed his name and attributes from the goat, does to Dionysus himself. In nearly every case these festivals centered in extravagant sexual licentiousness, whose waves overwhelmed all family life and its venerable traditions; the most savage natural instincts were unleashed, including even that horrible mixture of sensuality and cruelty which has always seemed to me to be the genuine "witches' brew." For some time, however, it would appear that the Greeks were perfectly insulated and guarded against the feverish excitements of these festivals by the figure of Apollo himself rising here in full pride, who could not have held out the Gorgon's head to any power more dangerous than this grotesquely uncouth Dionysian. It is in Doric art that this majestically-rejecting attitude of Apollo is eternized. The opposition between Apollo and Dionysus became more hazardous and even impossible, when, from the deepest roots of the Hellenic nature, similar impulses finally burst forth and made a path for themselves: the Delphic god, by a seasonably effected reconciliation, now contented himself with taking the destructive weapons from the hands of his powerful antagonist. This reconciliation is the most important moment in the history of the Greek cult: wherever we turn we note the revolutions resulting from this event. The two antagonists were reconciled; the boundary lines thenceforth to be observed by each were sharply defined, and there was to be a periodical exchange of gifts of esteem. At bottom, however, the chasm was not bridged over. But if we observe how, under the pressure of this treaty of peace, the Dionysian power revealed itself, we shall now recognize in the Dionysian orgies of the Greeks, as compared with the Babylonian Sacaea with their reversion of man to the tiger and the ape, the significance of festivals of world-redemption and days of transfiguration. It is with them that nature for the first time attains her artistic jubilee; it is with them that the destruction of the *principium individuationis* for the first time becomes an artistic phenomenon. The horrible "witches' brew" of sensuality and cruelty becomes ineffective: only the curious blending and duality in the emotions of the Dionysian revelers remind us—as medicines remind us of deadly poisons—of the phenomenon that pain begets joy, that ecstasy may wring sounds of agony from us. At the very climax of joy there sounds a cry of horror or a yearning lamentation for an irretrievable loss. In these Greek festivals, nature seems to reveal a sentimental trait; it is as if she were heaving a sigh at her dismemberment into individuals. The song and pantomime of such dually-minded revelers was something new and unheard-of for the Homeric-Grecian world: and the Dionysian *music* in particular excited awe and terror. If music, as it would seem, had been known previously as an Apollonian art, it was so, strictly speaking, only as the wave-beat of rhythm, whose formative power was developed for the representation of Apollonian states. The music of Apollo was Doric architectonics in tones, but in tones that were merely suggestive, such as those of the cithara. The very element which forms the essence of Dionysian music (and hence of music in general) is carefully excluded as un-Apollonian; namely, the emotional power of the tone, the uniform flow of the melos, and the utterly incomparable world of harmony. In the Dionysian dithyramb man is incited to the greatest exaltation of all his symbolic faculties; something never before experienced struggles for utterance—the annihilation of the veil of Mâyâ, Oneness as the soul of the race, and of nature itself. The essence of nature is now to be expressed symbolically; we need a new world of symbols; for once the entire symbolism of the body is called into play, not the mere symbolism of the lips, face, and speech, but the whole pantomime of dancing, forcing every member into rhythmic movement. Thereupon the other symbolic powers suddenly press forward, particularly those of music, in rhythmics, dynamics, and harmony. To grasp this collective release of all the symbolic powers, man must have already attained that height of self-abnegation which wills to express itself symbolically through all these powers: and so the dithyrambic votary of Dionysus is understood only by his peers! With what astonishment must the Apollonian Greek have beheld him! With an astonishment that was all the greater the more it was mingled with the shuddering suspicion that all this was actually not so very alien to him after all, in fact, that it was only his Apollonian consciousness which, like a veil, hid this Dionysian world from his vision.

III

To understand this, it becomes necessary to level the artistic structure of the *Apollonian culture,* as it were, stone by stone, till the foundations on which it rests become visible. First of all we see the glorious *Olympian* figures of the gods, standing on the gables of this structure. Their deeds, pictured in brilliant reliefs, adorn its friezes. We must not be misled by the fact that

Apollo stands side by side with the others as an individual deity, without any claim to priority of rank. For the same impulse which embodied itself in Apollo gave birth in general to this entire Olympian world, and so in this sense Apollo is its father. What terrific need was it that could produce such an illustrious company of Olympian beings?

He who approaches these Olympians with another religion in his heart, seeking among them for moral elevation, even for sanctity, for disincarnate spirituality, for charity and benevolence, will soon be forced to turn his back on them, discouraged and disappointed. For there is nothing here that suggests asceticism, spirituality, or duty. We hear nothing but the accents of an exuberant, triumphant life, in which all things, whether good or bad, are deified. And so the spectator may stand quite bewildered before this fantastic superfluity of life, asking himself what magic potion these mad glad men could have imbibed to make life so enjoyable that, wherever they turned, their eyes beheld the smile of Helen, the ideal picture of their own existence, "floating in sweet sensuality." But to this spectator, who has his back already turned, we must perforce cry: "Go not away, but stay and hear what Greek folk-wisdom has to say of this very life, which with such inexplicable gayety unfolds itself before your eyes. There is an ancient story that King Midas hunted in the forest a long time for the wise *Silenus,* the companion of Dionysus, without capturing him. When Silenus at last fell into his hands, the king asked what was the best and most desirable of all things for man. Fixed and immovable, the demigod said not a word; till at last, urged by the king, he gave a shrill laugh and broke out into these words: 'Oh, wretched ephemeral race, children of chance and misery, why do ye compel me to tell you what it were most expedient for you not to hear? What is best of all is beyond your reach forever: not to be born, not to *be,* to be *nothing*. But the second best for you—is quickly to die.' "

How is the Olympian world of deities related to this folk-wisdom? Even as the rapturous vision of the tortured martyr to his suffering.

Now it is as if the Olympian magic mountain had opened before us and revealed its roots to us. The Greek knew and felt the terror and horror of existence. That he might endure this terror at all, he had to interpose between himself and life the radiant dream-birth of the Olympians. That overwhelming dismay in the face of the titanic powers of nature, the Moira enthroned inexorably over all knowledge, the vulture of the great lover of mankind, Prometheus, the terrible fate of the wise Oedipus, the family curse of the Atridae which drove Orestes to matricide: in short, that entire philosophy of the sylvan god, with its mythical exemplars, which caused the downfall of the melancholy Etruscans—all this was again and again overcome by the Greeks with the aid of the Olympian *middle world* of art; or at any rate it was veiled and withdrawn from sight. It was out of the direst necessity to live that the Greeks created these gods. Perhaps we may picture the process to ourselves somewhat as follows: out of the original Titan thearchy of terror the Olympian thearchy of joy gradually evolved through the Apollonian impulse towards beauty, just as roses bud from thorny bushes. How else could this people, so sensitive, so vehement in its desires, so singularly constituted for *suffering,* how could they have endured existence, if it had not been revealed to them in their gods, surrounded with a higher glory? The same impulse which calls art into being, as the complement and consummation of existence, seducing one to a continuation of life, was also the cause of the Olympian world which the Hellenic "will" made use of as a transfiguring mirror. Thus do the gods justify the life of man, in that they themselves live it—the only satisfactory Theodicy! Existence under the bright sunshine of such gods is regarded as desirable in itself, and the real *grief* of the Homeric men is caused by parting from it, especially by early parting: so that now, reversing the wisdom of Silenus, we might say of the Greeks that "to die early is worst of all for them, the next worst —some day to die at all." Once heard, it will ring out again; forget not the lament of the short-lived Achilles, mourning the leaflike change and vicissitude of the race of men and the decline of the heroic age. It is not unworthy of the greatest hero to long for a continuation of life, aye, even though he live as a slave. At the Apollonian stage of development, the "will" longs so vehemently for this existence, the Homeric man feels himself so completely at one with it, that lamentation itself becomes a song of praise.

Here we should note that this harmony which is contemplated with such longing by modern man, in fact, this oneness of man with nature (to express which Schiller introduced the technical term "naïve"), is by no means a simple condition, resulting naturally, and as if inevitably. It is not a condition which, like a terrestrial paradise, *must* necessarily be found at the gate of every culture. Only a romantic age could believe this, an age which conceived of the artist in terms of Rousseau's *Emile* and imagined that in Homer it had found such an artist Emile, reared in Nature's bosom. Wherever we meet with the "naïve" in art, we recognize the highest effect of the Apollonian culture, which in the first place has always to overthrow some Titanic empire and slay monsters, and which, through its potent dazzling representations and its pleasurable illusions, must have triumphed over a terrible depth of world-contemplation and a most keen sensitivity to suffering. But how seldom do we attain to the naïve—that complete absorption in the beauty of appearance! And hence how inexpressibly sublime is *Homer,* who, as individual being, bears the same relation to this Apollonian folk-culture as the individual dream-artist does to the dream-faculty of the people and of Nature in general. The Homeric "naïveté" can be understood only as the complete victory of the Apollonian illusion: an illusion similar to those which Nature so frequently employs to achieve her own ends. The true goal is veiled by a phantasm: and while we stretch out our hands for the latter, Nature attains the former by means of your illusion. In the Greeks the "will" wished to contemplate itself in the transfiguration of genius and the world of art; in order to glorify themselves, its creatures had to feel themselves worthy of glory; they had to behold themselves again in a higher sphere, without this perfect world of contemplation acting as a command or a reproach. Such is the sphere of beauty, in which they saw their mirrored images, the Olympians. With this mirroring of beauty the Hellenic will combated its artistically correlative talent for suffering and for the wisdom of suffering: and, as a monument of its victory, we have Homer, the naïve artist.

IV

Now the dream-analogy may throw some light on the problem of the naïve artist. Let us imagine the dreamer: in the midst of the illusion of the dream-world and without disturbing it, he calls out to himself: "It is a dream, I will dream on." What must we infer? That he experiences a deep inner joy in dream-contemplation; on the other hand, to be at all able to dream with this inner joy in contemplation he must have completely lost sight of the waking reality and its ominous obtrusiveness. Guided by the dream-reading Apollo, we may interpret all these phenomena to ourselves somewhat in this way. Though it is certain that of the two halves of our existence, the waking and the dreaming states, the former appeals to us as infinitely preferable, important, excellent and worthy of being lived, indeed, as that which alone is lived: yet, in relation to that mysterious substratum of our nature of which we are the phenomena, I should, paradoxical as it may seem, maintain the very opposite estimate of the value of dream life. For the more clearly I perceive in Nature those omnipotent art impulses, and in them an ardent longing for release, for redemption through release, the more I feel myself impelled to the metaphysical assumption that the Truly-Existent and Primal Unity, eternally suffering and divided against itself, has need of the rapturous vision, the joyful appearance, for its continuous salvation: which appearance we, completely wrapped up in it and composed of it, are compelled to apprehend as the True Non-Being,—*i.e.,* as a perpetual becoming in time, space and causality,—in other words, as empiric reality. If, for the moment, we do not consider the question of our own "reality," if we conceive of our empirical existence, and that of the world in general, as a continuously manifested representation of the Primal Unity, we shall then have to look upon the dream as an *appearance of appearance,* hence as a still higher appeasement of the primordial desire for appearance. And that is why the innermost heart of Nature feels that ineffable joy in the naïve artist and the naïve work of art, which is likewise only "an appearance of appearance." In a symbolic painting, *Raphael,* himself one of these immortal "naïve" ones, has represented for us this devolution of appearance to appearance, the primitive process of the naïve artist and of Apollonian culture. In his "Transfiguration," the lower half of the picture, with the possessed boy, the despairing bearers, the bewildered, terrified disciples, shows us the reflection of suffering, primal and eternal, the sole basis of the world: the "appearance" here is the counter-appearance of eternal contradiction, the father of things. From this appearance now arises, like ambrosial vapor, a new visionary world of appearances, invisible to those wrapped in the first appearance—a radiant floating in purest bliss, a serene contemplation beaming from wide-open eyes. Here we have presented, in the most sublime artistic symbolism, that Apollonian world of beauty and its substratum, the terrible wisdom of Silenus; and intuitively we comprehend their necessary interdependence. Apollo, however, again appears to us as the apotheosis of the *principium individuationis,* in which alone is consummated the perpetually attained goal of the Primal Unity, its redemption through appearance. With his sublime gestures, he shows us how necessary is the entire world of suffering, that by means of it the individual may be impelled to realize the redeeming vision, and then, sunk in contemplation of it, sit quietly in his tossing barque, amid the waves.

If we at all conceive of it as imperative and mandatory, this apotheosis of individuation knows but one law—the individual, *i.e.,* the delimiting of the boundaries of the individual, *measure* in the Hellenic sense. Apollo, as ethical deity, exacts measure of his disciples, and, that to this end, he requires self-knowledge. And so, side by side with the esthetic necessity for beauty, there occur the demands "know thyself" and "nothing overmuch"; consequently pride and excess are regarded as the truly inimical demons of the non-Apollonian sphere, hence as characteristics of the pre-Apollonian age—that of the Titans; and of the extra-Apollonian world—that of the barbarians. Because of his Titan-like love for man, Prometheus must be torn to pieces by vultures; because of his excessive wisdom, which could solve the riddle of the Sphinx, Oedipus must be plunged into a bewildering vortex of crime. Thus did the Delphic god interpret the Greek past.

Similarly the effects wrought by the *Dionysian* seemed "titan-like" and "barbaric" to the Apollonian Greek: while at the same time he could not conceal from himself that he too was inwardly related to these overthrown Titans and heroes. Indeed, he had to recognize even more than this: despite all its beauty and moderation, his entire existence rested on a hidden substratum of suffering and of knowledge, which was again revealed to him by the Dionysian. And lo! Apollo could not live without Dionysus! The "titanic" and the "barbaric" were in the last analysis as necessary as the Apollonian.

And now let us take this artistically limited world, based on appearance and moderation; let us imagine how into it there penetrated, in tones ever more bewitching and alluring, the ecstatic sound of the Dionysian festival; let us remember that in these strains all of Nature's excess in joy, sorrow, and knowledge become audible, even in piercing shrieks; and finally, let us ask ourselves what significance remains to the psalmodizing artist of Apollo, with his phantom harp-sound, once it is compared with this demonic folk-song! The muses of the arts of "appearance" paled before an art which, in its intoxication, spoke the truth. The wisdom of Silenus cried "Woe! woe!" to the serene Olympians. The individual, with all his restraint and proportion, succumbed to the self-oblivion of the Dionysian state, forgetting the precepts of Apollo. Excess revealed itself as truth. Contradiction, the bliss born of pain, spoke out from the very heart of Nature. And so, wherever the Dionysian prevailed, the Apollonian was checked and destroyed. But, on the other hand, it is equally certain that, wherever the first Dionysian onslaught was successfully withstood, the authority and majesty of the Delphic god exhibited itself as more rigid and menacing than ever. For to me the *Doric* state and Doric art are explicable only as a permanent citadel of the Apollonian. For an art so defiantly prim, and so encompassed with bulwarks, a training so warlike and rigorous, a political structure so cruel and relentless, could endure for any length of time only by incessant opposition to the titanic-barbaric nature of the Dionysian.

Up to this point we have simply enlarged upon the observation made at the beginning of this essay: that the Dionysian and the Apollonian, in new births ever following and mutually augmenting one another, controlled the Hellenic genius; that from out the age of "bronze," with its wars of the Titans and its rigorous folk-philosophy, the Homeric world developed under the sway of the Apollonian impulse to beauty; that this "naïve" splendor was again overwhelmed by the influx of the Dionysian; and that against this new power the Apollonian rose to the austere majesty of Doric art and the Doric view of the world. If, then, amid the strife of these two hostile principles, the older Hellenic history thus falls into four great periods of art, we are now impelled to inquire after the *final goal* of these developments and processes, lest perchance we should regard the last-attained period, the period of Doric art, as the climax and aim of these artistic impulses. And here the sublime and celebrated art of *Attic tragedy* and the dramatic dithyramb presents itself as the common goal of both these tendencies, whose mysterious union, after many and long precursory struggles, found glorious consummation in this child,—at once Antigone and Cassandra.

V

We now approach the real goal of our investigation, which is directed towards acquiring a knowledge of the Dionysian-Apollonian genius and its art-product, or at least an anticipatory understanding of its mysterious union. Here we shall first of all inquire after the first evidence in Greece of that new germ which subsequently developed into tragedy and the dramatic dithyramb. The ancients themselves give us a symbolic answer, when they place the faces of *Homer* and *Archilochus* as the forefathers and torchbearers of Greek poetry side by side on gems, sculptures, etc., with a sure feeling that consideration should be given only to these two thoroughly original compeers, from whom a stream of fire flows over the whole of later Greek history. Homer, the aged self-absorbed dreamer, the type of the Apollonian naïve artist, now beholds with astonishment the passionate genius of the war-like votary of the muses, Archilochus, passing through life with fury and violence; and modern esthetics, by way of interpretation, can only add that here the first "objective" artist confronts the first "subjective" artist. But this interpretation helps us but little, because we know the subjective artist only as the poor artist, and throughout the entire range of art we demand specially and first of all the conquest of the Subjective, the release from the ego and the silencing of the individual will and desire; indeed, we find it impossible to believe in any truly artistic production, however insignificant, if it is without objectivity, without pure, detached contemplation. Hence our esthetic must first solve the problem of how the "lyrist" is possible as an artist—he who, according to the experience of all ages, is continually saying "I" and running through the entire chromatic scale of his passions and desires. Compared with Homer, this very Archilochus appalls us by his cries of hatred and scorn, by his drunken outbursts of desire. Therefore is not he, who has been called the first subjective artist, essentially the non-artist? But in this case, how explain the reverence which was shown to him—the poet—in very remarkable utterances by the Delphic oracle itself, the center of "objective" art?

Schiller has thrown some light on the poetic process by a psychological observation, inexplicable to himself, yet apparently valid. He admits that before the act of creation he did not perhaps have before him or within him any series of images accompanied by an ordered thought-relationship; but his condition was rather that of a *musical mood.* ("With me the perception has at first no clear and definite object; this is formed later. A certain musical mood of mind precedes, and only after this ensues the poetical idea.") Let us add to this the natural and most important phenomenon of all ancient lyric poetry, *the union,* indeed, the *identity,* of the *lyrist with the musician,*—compared with which our modern lyric poetry appears like the statue of a god without a head,—with this in mind we may now, on the basis of our metaphysics of esthetics set forth above, explain the lyrist to ourselves in this manner: In the first place, as Dionysian artist he has identified himself with the Primal Unity, its pain and contradiction. Assuming that music has been correctly termed a repetition and a recast of the world, we may say that he produces the copy of this Primal Unity as music. Now, however, under the Apollonian dream-inspiration, this music reveals itself to him again as a *symbolic dream-picture.* The inchoate, intangible reflection of the primordial pain in music, with its redemption in appearance, now produces a second mirroring as a specific symbol or example. The artist has already surrendered his subjectivity in the Dionysian process. The picture which now shows him his identity with the heart of the world, is a dream-scene, which embodies the primordial contradiction and primordial pain, together with the primordial joy, of appearance. The "I" of the lyrist therefore sounds from the depth of his being: its "subjectivity," in the sense of the modern esthetes, is pure imagination. When Archilochus, the first Greek lyrist, proclaims to the daughters of Lycambes both his mad love and his contempt, it is not his passion alone which dances before us in orgiastic frenzy; but we see Dionysus and the Maenads, we see the drunken reveler Archilochus sunk down in slumber —as Euripides depicts it in the *Bacchae,* the sleep on the high mountain pasture, in the noonday sun. And now Apollo approaches and touches him with the laurel. Then the Dionyso-musical enchantment of the sleeper seems to emit picture sparks, lyrical poems, which in their highest form are called tragedies and dramatic dithyrambs.

The plastic artist, as also the epic poet, who is related to him, is sunk in the pure contemplation of images. The Dionysian musician is, without any images, himself pure primordial pain and its primordial reëchoing. The lyric genius is conscious of a world of pictures and symbols—growing out of his state of mystical self-abnegation and oneness. This state has a coloring, a causality and a velocity quite different from that of the world of the plastic artist and the epic poet. For the latter lives in these pictures, and only in them, with joyful satisfaction. He never grows tired of contemplating lovingly even their minutest traits. Even the picture of the angry Achilles is only a picture to him, whose angry expression he enjoys with the dream-joy in appearance. Thus, by this mirror of appearance, he is protected against being united and blended with his figures. In direct contrast to this, the pictures of the *lyrist* are nothing but *his very* self and, as it were, only different projections of himself, by force of which he, as the moving center of this world, may say "I": only of course this self is not the same as that of the waking, empirically real man, but the only truly existent and eternal self resting at the basis of things, and with the help of whose images, the lyric genius can penetrate to this very basis.

Now let us suppose that among these images he also beholds *himself* as non-genius, *i.e.,* his subject, the whole throng of subjective passions and agitations directed to a definite object which appears real to him. It may now seem as if the lyric genius and the allied non-genius were one, as if the former had of its own accord spoken that little word "I." But this identity is but superficial and it will no longer be able to lead us astray, as it certainly led astray those who designated the lyrist as the subjective poet. For, as a matter of fact, Archilochus, the passionately inflamed, loving and hating man, is but a vision of the genius, who by this time is no longer merely Archilochus, but a world-genius expressing his primordial pain symbolically in the likeness of the man Archilochus: while the subjectively willing and desiring man, Archilochus, can never at any time be a poet. It is by no means necessary, however, that the lyrist should see nothing but the phenomenon of the man Archilochus before him as a reflection of eternal being; and tragedy shows how far the visionary world of the lyrist may be removed from this phenomenon, which, of course, is intimately related to it.

Schopenhauer, who did not conceal from himself the difficulty the lyrist presents in the philosophical contemplation of art, thought he had found a solution, with which, however, I am not in entire accord. (Actually, it was in his profound metaphysics of music that he alone held in his hands the means whereby this difficulty might be definitely removed: as I believe I have removed it here in his spirit and to his honor.) In contrast to our view, he describes the peculiar nature of song as follows (*Welt als Wille und Vorstellung,* I. 295):

"It is the subject of will, *i.e.,* his own volition, which the consciousness of the singer feels; often as a released and satisfied desire (joy), but still oftener as a restricted desire (grief), always as an emotion, a passion, a moved frame of mind. Besides this, however, and along with it, by the sight of surrounding nature, the singer becomes conscious of himself as the subject of pure will-less knowing, whose unbroken, blissful peace now appears, in contrast to the stress of desire, which is always restricted and always needy. The feeling of this contrast, this alternation, is really what the lyric as a whole expresses and what principally constitutes the lyrical state of mind. In it pure knowing comes to us as it were to deliver us from desire and its strain; we follow, but only for an instant; desire, the remembrance of our own personal ends, tears us anew from peaceful contemplation; yet ever again the next beautiful surrounding in which the pure will-less knowledge presents itself to us, allures us away from desire. Therefore, in the lyric and the lyrical mood, desire (the personal interest of the ends) and pure perception of the surrounding presented are wonderfully mingled with each other; connections between them are sought for and imagined; the subjective disposition, the affection of the will, imparts its own hue to the perceived surrounding, and conversely, the surroundings communicate the reflex of their color to the will. The true lyric is the expression of the whole of this mingled and divided state of mind."

Who could fail to recognize in this description that lyric poetry is here characterized as an incompletely attained art, which arrives at its goal infrequently and only as it were by leaps? Indeed, it is described as a semi-art, whose essence is said to consist in this, that desire and pure contemplation, *i.e.,* the unesthetic and the esthetic condition, are wonderfully mingled with each other. It follows that Schopenhauer still classifies the arts as subjective or objective, using the antithesis as if it were a criterion of value. But it is our contention, on the contrary, that this antithesis between the subjective and the objective is especially irrelevant in esthetics, since the subject, the desiring individual furthering his own egoistic ends, can be conceived of only as the antagonist, not as the origin of art. In so far as the subject is the artist, however, he has already been released from his individual will, and has become as it were the medium through which the one truly existent Subject celebrates his release in appearance. For, above all, to our humiliation *and* exaltation, one thing must be clear to us. The entire comedy of art is neither performed for our betterment or education nor are we the true authors of this art-world. On the contrary, we may assume that we are merely pictures and artistic projections for the true author, and that we have our highest dignity in our significance as works of art—for it is only as an *esthetic phenomenon* that existence and the world are eternally *justified*—while of course our consciousness of our own significance hardly differs from that which the soldiers painted on canvas have of the battle represented on it. Thus all our knowledge of art is basically quite illusory, because as knowing beings we are not one and identical with that Being who, as the sole author and spectator of this comedy of art, prepares a perpetual entertainment for himself. Only in so far as the genius in the act of artistic creation coalesces with this primordial artist of the world, does he catch sight of the eternal essence of art; for in this state he is, in a marvelous manner, like the weird picture of the fairy-tale which can turn its eyes at will and behold itself; he is now at once subject and object, at once poet, actor, and spectator.

Literature and Science

Matthew Arnold

(1822-1888)

But why art? Yes, certainly we agree that art is the highest expression of human capabilities. We can agree with Hazlitt that art makes some few of us immortal, at least for a little while, we can even agree with Ruskin that art is our only morality, and perhaps also agree with Nietzsche that art is our ultimate reality. Indeed, we are by now accustomed to thinking of art as the very pinnacle of human endeavor. But unfortunately, most of us poor souls do not live on mountain tops, like Empedocles; we spend most of our time in the valleys of this world preoccupied with the humdrum tasks of everyday life. What practical value can art have for us?

Although this question has been present throughout the history of art, it came to special prominence during the nineteenth century. In large measure the question of the social value of art underlay Ruskin's polemic in "Traffic." *Essenti-*

ally, he argued that art provides us with clues to our major social values, and for the most part we would still agree with his damnation of the vulgar eclecticism and self-righteous mercantilism that pervaded Victorian society. The writer who confronted the social problem of art most directly, however, was not Ruskin but his more conservative contemporary, Matthew Arnold.

The classic instance of this confrontation is Arnold's "Literature and Science," originally delivered as a lecture while he was on a speaking tour in the United States. In this talk Arnold addressed himself chiefly to the attack on the preeminence of literature and humanistic studies in education by the brilliant popularizer of Darwin's theories, Thomas Huxley. Huxley contended that science, not literature or the humanities, supplied the kind of knowledge needed by a "practical age." Wrong, said Arnold, in somewhat gentler accents. In every age, "practical" or otherwise, people need to know how to conduct their affairs and to derive satisfaction from life. Only literature and the humanities can satisfy this need, says Arnold. He was not alone in this feeling, and much of the Arnold-Huxley controversy has come down to our own day via the "two cultures" concept of C. P. Snow. We can also hear echoes of Arnold's argument in Alfred North Whitehead's "Aims of Education."

Arnold, son of an eminent Victorian, was an inspector of schools as well as a poet of considerable stature. He was thus professionally interested in the educational program of his day and wrote a number of influential reports on the problems involved in education. His views on education are also present in his major critique of Victorian society, Culture and Anarchy. Essays in Criticism *is Arnold's major work on literature.*

PRACTICAL people talk with a smile of Plato and of his absolute ideas; and it is impossible to deny that Plato's ideas do often seem unpractical and unpracticable, and especially when one views them in connexion with the life of a great work-a-day world like the United States. The necessary staple of the life of such a world Plato regards with disdain; handicraft and trade and the working professions he regards with disdain; but what becomes of the life of an industrial modern community if you take handicraft and trade and the working professions out of it? The base mechanic arts and handicrafts, says Plato, bring about a natural weakness in the principle of excellence in a man, so that he cannot govern the ignoble growths in him, but nurses them, and cannot understand fostering any other. Those who exercise such arts and trades, as they have their bodies, he says, marred by their vulgar businesses, so they have their souls, too, bowed and broken by them. And if one of these uncomely people has a mind to seek self-culture and philosophy, Plato compares him to a bald little tinker, who has scraped together money, and has got his release from service, and has had a bath, and bought a new coat, and is rigged out like a bridegroom about to marry the daughter of his master who has fallen into poor and helpless estate.

Nor do the working professions fare any better than trade at the hands of Plato. He draws for us an inimitable picture of the working lawyer, and of his life of bondage; he shows how this bondage from his youth up has stunted and warped him, and made him small and crooked of soul, encompassing him with difficulties which he is not man enough to rely on justice and truth as means to encounter, but has recourse, for help out of them, to falsehood and wrong. And so, says Plato, this poor creature is bent and broken, and grows up from boy to man without a particle of soundness in him, although exceedingly smart and clever in his own esteem.

One cannot refuse to admire the artist who draws these pictures. But we say to ourselves that his ideas show the influence of a primitive and obsolete order of things, when the warrior caste and the priestly caste were alone in honour, and the humble work of the world was done by slaves. We have now changed all that; the modern majesty consists in work, as Emerson declares; and in work, we may add, principally of such plain and dusty kind as the work of cultivators of the ground, handicraftsmen, men of trade and business, men of the working professions. Above all is this true in a great industrious community such as that of the United States.

Now education, many people go on to say, is still mainly governed by the ideas of men like Plato, who lived when the warrior caste and the priestly or philosophical class were alone in honour, and the really useful part of the community were slaves. It is an education fitted for persons of leisure in such a community. This education passed from Greece and Rome to the feudal communities of Europe, where also the warrior caste and the priestly caste were alone held in honour, and where the really useful and working part of the community, though not nominally slaves as in the pagan world, were practically not much better off than slaves, and not more seriously regarded. And how absurd it is, people end by saying, to inflict this education upon an industrious modern community, where very few indeed are persons of leisure, and the mass to be considered has not leisure, but is bound, for its own great good, and for the great good of the world at large, to plain labour and to industrial pursuits, and the education in question tends necessarily to make men dissatisfied with these pursuits and unfitted for them!

That is what is said. So far I must defend Plato, as to plead that his view of education and studies is in the general, as it seems to me, sound enough, and fitted for all sorts and conditions of men, whatever their pursuits may be. "An intelligent man," says Plato, "will prize those studies which result in his soul getting soberness, righteousness, and wisdom, and will less value the others." I cannot consider *that* a bad description of the aim of education, and of the motives which should govern us in the choice of studies, whether we are preparing ourselves for a hereditary seat in the English House of Lords or for the pork trade in Chicago.

Still I admit that Plato's world was not ours, that his scorn of trade and handicraft is fantastic, that he had no conception of a great industrial community such as that of the United States, and that such a community must and will shape its education to suit its own needs. If the usual education handed down to it from the past does not suit it, it will certainly before long drop this and try another. The usual education in the past has been mainly literary. The question is whether the studies which were long supposed to be the best for all of us are practically the best now; whether others are not better. The tyranny of the past, many think, weighs on us injuriously in the predominance given to letters in education. The question is raised whether, to meet the needs of our modern life, the predominance ought not now to pass from letters to science; and naturally the question is nowhere raised with more energy than here in the United States. The design of abasing what is called "mere literary instruction and education," and of exalting what is called "sound, extensive, and practical scientific knowledge," is, in this intensely modern world of the United States, even more perhaps than in Europe, a very popular design, and makes great and rapid progress.

I am going to ask whether the present movement for ousting letters from their old predominance in education, and for transferring the predominance in education to the natural sciences, whether this brisk and flourishing movement ought to prevail, and whether it is likely that in the end it really will prevail. An objection may be raised which I will anticipate. My own studies have been almost wholly in letters, and my visits to the field of the natural sciences have been very slight and inadequate, although those sciences have always strongly moved my curiosity. A man of letters, it will perhaps be said, is not competent to discuss the comparative merits of letters and natural science as means of education. To this objection I reply, first of all, that his incompetence, if he attempts the discussion but is really incompetent for it, will be abundantly visible; nobody will be taken in; he will have plenty of sharp observers and critics to save mankind from that danger. But the line I am going to follow is, as you will soon discover, so extremely simple, that perhaps it may be followed without failure even by one who for a more ambitious line of discussion would be quite incompetent.

Some of you may possibly remember a phrase of mine which has been the object of a good deal of comment; an observation to the effect that in our culture, the aim being *to know ourselves and the world,* we have, as the means to this end, *to know the best which has been thought and said in the world.* A man of science, who is also an excellent writer and the very prince of debaters, Professor Huxley, in a discourse at the opening of Sir Josiah Mason's college at Birmingham, laying hold of this phrase, expanded it by quoting some more words of mine, which are these: "The civilised world is to be regarded as now being, for intellectual and spiritual purposes, one great confederation, bound to a joint action and working to a common result; and whose members have for their proper outfit a knowledge of Greek, Roman, and Eastern antiquity, and of one another. Special local and temporary advantages being put out of account, that modern nation will in the intellectual and spiritual sphere make most progress, which most thoroughly carries out this programme."

Now on my phrase, thus enlarged, Professor Huxley remarks that when I speak of the above-mentioned knowledge as enabling us to know ourselves and the world, I assert *literature* to contain the materials which suffice for thus making us know ourselves and the world. But it is not by any means clear, says he, that after having learnt all which ancient and modern literatures have to tell us, we have laid a sufficiently broad and deep foundation for that criticism of life, that knowledge of ourselves and the world, which constitutes culture. On the contrary, Professor Huxley declares that he finds himself "wholly unable to admit that either nations or individuals will really advance, if their outfit draws nothing from the stories of physical science. An army without weapons of precision, and with no particular base of operations, might more hopefully enter upon a campaign on the Rhine, than a man, devoid of a knowledge of what physical science has done in the last century, upon a criticism of life."

This shows how needful it is for those who are to discuss any matter togther, to have a common understanding as to the sense of the terms they employ,—how needful, and how difficult. What Professor Huxley says, implies just the reproach which is so often brought against the study of *belles lettres,* as they are called: that the study is an elegant one, but slight and ineffectual; a smattering of Greek and Latin and other ornamental things, of little use for any one whose object is to get at truth, and to be a practical man. So, too, M. Renan talks of the "superficial humanism" of a school-course which treats us as if we were all going to be poets, writers, preachers, orators, and he opposes this humanism to positive science, or the critical search after truth. And there is always a tendency in those who are remonstrating against the predominance of letters in education, to understand by letters *belles lettres,* and by *belles lettres* a superficial humanism, the opposite of science or true knowledge.

But when we talk of knowing Greek and Roman antiquity, for instance, which is the knowledge people have called the humanities, I for my part mean a knowledge which is something more than a superficial humanism, mainly decorative. "I call all teaching *scientific,*" says Wolf, the critic of Homer, "which is systematically laid out and followed up to its original sources. For example: a knowledge of classical antiquity is scientific when the remains of classical antiquity are correctly studied in the original languages." There can be no doubt that Wolf is perfectly right; that all learning is scientific which is systematically laid out and followed up to its original sources, and that a genuine humanism is scientific.

When I speak of knowing Greek and Roman antiquity, therefore, as a help to knowing ourselves and the world, I mean more than a knowledge of so much vocabulary, so much grammar, so many portions of authors in the Greek and Latin languages. I mean knowing the Greeks and Romans, and their life and genius, and what they were and did in the world; what we get from them, and what is its value. That, at least, is the ideal; and when we talk of endeavouring to know Greek and Roman antiquity, as a help to knowing ourselves and the world, we mean endeavouring so to know them as to satisfy this ideal, however much we may still fall short of it.

The same also as to knowing our own and other modern nations, with the like aim of getting to understand ourselves and the world. To know the best that has been thought and said by the modern nations, is to know, says Professor Huxley, "only what modern *literatures* have to tell us; it is the criticism of life contained in modern literature." And yet "the distinctive character of our times," he urges, "lies in the vast and constantly increasing part which is played by natural knowledge." And how, therefore, can a man, devoid of knowledge of what physical science has done in the last century, enter hopefully upon a criticism of modern life?

Let us, I say, be agreed about the meaning of the terms we are using. I talk of knowing the best which has been thought and uttered in the world; Professor Huxley says this means knowing *literature.* Literature is a large word; it may mean everything written with letters or printed in a book. Euclid's *Elements* and Newton's *Principia* are thus literature. All knowledge that reaches us through books is literature. But by literature Professor Huxley means *belles lettres*. He means to make me say, that knowing the best which has been thought and said by the modern nations is knowing their *belles lettres* and no more. And this is no sufficient equipment, he argues, for a criticism of modern life. But as I do not mean, by knowing ancient Rome, knowing merely more or less of Latin *belles lettres,* and taking no account of Rome's military, and political, and legal, and administrative work in the world; and as, by knowing ancient Greece, I understand knowing her as the giver of Greek art, and the guide to a free and right use of reason and to scientific method, and the founder of our mathematics and physics and astronomy and biology,—I understand knowing her as all this, and not merely knowing certain Greek poems, and histories, and treatises, and speeches,—so as to the knowledge of modern nations also. By knowing modern nations, I mean not merely knowing their *belles lettres,* but knowing also what has been done by such men as Copernicus, Galileo, Newton, Darwin. "Our ancestors learned," says Professor Huxley, "that the earth is the centre of the visible universe, and that man is the cynosure of things terrestrial; and more especially was it inculcated that the course of nature had no fixed order, but that it could be, and constantly was, altered." "But for us now," continues Professor Huxley, "the notions of the beginning and the end of the world entertained by our forefathers are no longer credible. It is very certain that the earth is not the chief body in the material universe, and that the world is not subordinated to man's use. It is even more certain that nature is the expression of a definite order, with which nothing interferes." "And yet," he cries, "the purely classical education advocated by the representatives of the humanists in our day gives no inkling of all this."

In due place and time I will just touch upon that vexed question of classical education; but at present the question is as to what is meant by knowing the best which modern nations have thought and said. It is not knowing their *belles lettres* merely which is meant. To know Italian *belles lettres* is not to know Italy, and to know English *belles lettres* is not to know England. Into knowing Italy and England there comes a great deal more, Galileo and Newton amongst it. The reproach of being a superficial humanism, a tincture of *belles lettres,* may attach rightly enough to some other disciplines; but to the particular discipline recommended when I proposed knowing the best that has been thought and said in the world, it does not apply. In that best I certainly include what in modern times has been thought and said by the great observers and knowers of nature.

There is, therefore, really no question between Professor Huxley and me as to whether knowing the great results of the modern scientific study of nature is not required as a part of our culture, as well as knowing the products of literature and art. But to follow the processes by which those results are reached, ought, say the friends of physical science, to be made the staple of education for the bulk of mankind. And here there does arise a question between those whom Professor Huxley calls with playful sarcasm "the Levites of culture," and those whom the poor humanist is sometimes apt to regard as its Nebuchadnezzars.

The great results of the scientific investigation of nature we are agreed upon knowing, but how much of our study are we bound to give to the processes by which those results are reached? The results have their visible bearing on human life. But all the processes, too, all the items of fact, by which those results are reached and established, are interesting. All knowledge is interesting to a wise man, and the knowledge of nature is interesting to all men. It is very interesting to know, that, from the albuminous white of the egg, the chick in the egg gets the materials for its flesh, bones, blood, and feathers; while, from the fatty yolk of the egg, it gets the heat and energy which enable it at length to break its shell and begin the world. It is less interesting, perhaps, but still it is interesting, to know that when a taper burns, the wax is converted into carbonic acid and water. Moreover, it is quite true that the habit of dealing with facts, which is given by the study of nature, is, as the friends of physical science praise it for being, an excellent discipline. The appeal, in the study of nature, is constantly to observation and experiment; not only is it said that the thing is so, but we can be made to see that it is so. Not only does a man tell us that when a taper burns the wax is converted into carbonic acid and water, as a man may tell us, if he likes, that Charon is punting his ferry-boat on the river Styx, or that Victor Hugo is a sublime poet, or Mr. Gladstone the most admirable of statesmen; but we are made to see that the conversion into carbonic acid and water does actually happen. This reality of natural knowledge it is, which makes the friends of physical science contrast it, as a knowledge of things, with the humanist's knowledge, which is, say they, a knowledge of words. And hence Professor Huxley is moved to lay it down that, "for the purpose of attaining real culture, an exclusively scientific education is at least as effectual as an exclusively literary education." And a certain President of the Section for Mechanical Science in the British Association is, in Scripture phrase, "very bold," and declares that if a man, in his mental training, "has substituted literature and history for natural science, he has chosen the less useful alternative." But whether we go these lengths or not, we must all admit that in natural science the habit gained of dealing with facts is a most valuable discipline, and that every one should have some experience of it.

More than this, however, is demanded by the reformers. It is proposed to make the training in natural science the main part of education, for the great majority of mankind at any rate. And here, I confess, I part company with the friends of physical science, with whom up to this point I have been agreeing. In differing from them, however, I wish to proceed with the utmost caution and diffidence. The smallness of my own acquaintance with the disciplines of natural science is ever before my mind, and I am fearful of doing these disciplines an injustice. The ability and pugnacity of the partisans of natural science make them formidable persons to contradict. The tone of tentative inquiry, which befits a being of dim faculties and bounded knowledge, is the tone I would wish to take and not to depart from. At present it seems to me, that those who are for giving to natural knowledge, as they call it, the chief place in the education of the majority of mankind, leave one important thing out of their account: the constitution of human nature. But I put this forward on the strength of some facts not at all recondite, very far from it; facts capable of being stated in the simplest possible fashion, and to which, if I so state them, the man of science will, I am sure, be willing to allow their due weight.

Deny the facts altogether, I think, he hardly can. He can hardly deny, that when we set ourselves to enumerate the powers which go to the building up of human life, and say that they are the power of conduct, the power of intellect and knowledge, the power of beauty, and the power of social life and manners,—he can hardly deny that this scheme, though drawn in rough and plain lines enough, and not pretending to scientific exactness, does yet give a fairly true representation of the matter. Human nature is built up by these powers; we have the need for them all. When we have rightly met and adjusted the claims of them all, we shall then be in a fair way for getting soberness and righteousness, with wisdom. This is evident enough, and the friends of physical science would admit it.

But perhaps they may not have sufficiently observed another thing: namely, that the several powers just mentioned are not isolated, but there is, in the generality of mankind, a perpetual tendency to relate them one to another in divers ways. With one such way of relating them I am particularly concerned now. Following our instinct for intellect and knowledge, we acquire pieces of knowledge; and presently, in the generality of men, there arises the desire to relate these pieces of knowledge to our sense of conduct, to our sense for beauty,—and there is weariness and dissatisfaction if the desire is baulked. Now in this desire lies, I think, the strength of that hold which letters have upon us.

All knowledge is, as I said just now, interesting; and even items of knowledge which from the nature of the case cannot well be related, but must stand isolated in our thoughts, have their interest. Even lists of exceptions have their interest. If we are studying Greek accents, it is interesting to know that *pais* and *pas,* and some other monosyllables of the same form of declension, do not take the circumflex upon the last syllable of the genitive plural, but vary, in this respect, from the common rule. If we are studying physiology, it is interesting to know that the pulmonary artery carries dark blood and the pulmonary vein carries bright blood, departing in this respect from the common rule for the division of labour between the veins and the arteries. But every one knows how we seek naturally to combine the pieces of our knowledge together, to bring them under general rules, to relate them to principles; and how unsatisfactory and tiresome it would be to go on for ever learning lists of exceptions, or accumulating items of fact which must stand isolated.

Well, that same need of relating our knowledge, which operates here within the sphere of our knowledge itself, we shall find operating, also, outside that sphere. We experience, as we go on learning and knowing,—the vast majority of us experience, —the need of relating what we have learnt and known to the sense which we have in us for conduct, to the sense which we have in us for beauty.

A certain Greek prophetess of Mantineia in Arcadia, Diotima by name, once explained to the philosopher Socrates that love, and impulse, and bent of all kinds, is, in fact, nothing else but the desire in men that good should for ever be present to them. This desire for good, Diotima assured Socrates, is our fundamental desire, of which fundamental desire every impulse in us is only some one particular form. And therefore this fundamental desire it is, I suppose,—this desire in men that good should be for ever present to them,—which acts in us when we feel the impulse for relating our knowledge to our sense for conduct and to our sense for beauty. At any rate, with men in general the instinct exists. Such is human nature. And the instinct, it will be admitted, is innocent, and human nature is preserved by our following the lead of its innocent instincts. Therefore, in seeking to gratify this instinct in question, we are following the instinct of self-preservation in humanity.

But, no doubt, some kinds of knowledge cannot be made to directly serve the instinct in question, cannot be directly related to the sense for beauty, to the sense for conduct. These are instrument-knowledges; they lead on to other knowledges, which can. A man who passes his life in instrument knowledges is a specialist. They may be invaluable as instruments to something beyond, for those who have the gift thus to employ them; and they may be disciplines in themselves wherein it is useful for every one to have some schooling. But it is inconceivable that the generality of men should pass all their mental life with Greek accents or with formal logic. My friend Professor Sylvester, who is one of the first mathematicians in the world, holds transcendental doctrines as to the virtue of mathematics, but those doctrines are not for common men. In the very Senate House and heart of our English Cambridge I once ventured, though not without an apology for my profaneness, to hazard the opinion that for the majority of mankind a little of mathematics, even, goes a long way. Of course this is quite consistent with their being of immense importance as an instrument to something else; but it is the few who have the aptitude for thus using them, not the bulk of mankind.

The natural sciences do not, however, stand on the same footing with these instrument-knowledges. Experience shows us that the generality of men will find more interest in learning that, when a taper burns, the wax is converted into carbonic acid and water, or in learning the explanation of the phenomenon of dew, or in learning how the circulation of the blood is carried on, than they find in learning that the genitive plural of *pais* and *pas* does not take the circumflex on the termination. And one piece of natural knowledge is added to another, and others are added to that, and at last we come to propositions so interesting as Mr. Darwin's famous proposition that "our ancestor was a hairy quadruped furnished with a tail and pointed ears, probably arboreal in his habits." Or we come to propositions of such reach and magnitude as those which Professor Huxley delivers, when he says that the notions of our forefathers about the beginning and the end of the world were all wrong, and that nature is the expression of a definite order with which nothing interferes.

Interesting, indeed, these results of science are, important they are, and we should all of us be acquainted with them. But what I now wish you to mark is, that we are still, when they are propounded to us and we receive them, we are still in the sphere of intellect and knowledge. And for the generality of men there will be found, I say, to arise, when they have duly taken in the proposition that their ancestor was "a hairy quadruped furnished with a tail and pointed ears, probably arboreal in his habits," there will be found to arise an invincible desire to relate this proposition to the sense in us for conduct, and to the sense in us for beauty. But this the men of science will not do for us, and will hardly even profess to do. They will give us other pieces of knowledge, other facts, about other animals and their ancestors, or about plants, or about stones, or about stars; and they may finally bring us to those great "general conceptions of the universe, which are forced upon us all," says Professor Huxley, "by the progress of physical science." But still it will be *knowledge* only which they give us; knowledge not put for us into relation with our sense for conduct, our sense for beauty, and touched with emotion by being so put; not thus put for us, and therefore, to the majority of mankind, after a certain while, unsatisfying, wearying.

Not to the born naturalist, I admit. But what do we mean by a born naturalist? We mean a man in whom the zeal for observing nature is so uncommonly strong and eminent, that it marks him off from the bulk of mankind. Such a man will pass his life happily in collecting natural knowledge and reasoning upon it, and will ask for nothing, or hardly anything, more. I have heard it said that the sagacious and admirable naturalist whom we lost not very long ago, Mr. Darwin, once owned to a friend that for his part he did not experience the necessity for two things which most men find so necessary to them,—religion and poetry; science and the domestic affections, he thought, were enough. To a born naturalist, I can well understand that this should seem so. So absorbing is his occupation with nature, so strong his love for his occupation, that he goes on acquiring natural knowledge and reasoning upon it, and has little time or inclination for thinking about getting it related to the desire in man for conduct, the desire in man for beauty. He relates it to them for himself as he goes along, so far as he feels the need; and he draws from the domestic affections all the additional solace necessary. But then Darwins are extremely rare. Another great and admirable master of natural knowledge, Faraday, was a Sandemanian. That is to say, he related his knowledge to his instinct for conduct and to his instinct for beauty, by the aid of that respectable Scottish sectary, Robert Sandeman. And so strong, in general, is the demand of religion and poetry to have their share in a man, to associate themselves with his knowing, and to relieve and rejoice it, that, probably, for one man amongst us with the disposition to do as Darwin did in this respect, there are at least fifty with the disposition to do as Faraday.

Education lays hold upon us, in fact, by satisfying this demand. Professor Huxley holds up to scorn mediaeval education, with its neglect of the knowledge of nature, its poverty even of literary studies, its formal logic devoted to "showing how and why that which the Church said was true and must be true." But the great mediaeval Universities were not brought into being, we may be sure, by the zeal for giving a jejune and contemptible education. Kings have been their nursing fathers, and queens have been their nursing mothers, but not for this. The mediaeval Universities came into being, because the supposed knowledge, delivered by Scripture and the Church, so deeply engaged men's hearts, by so simply, easily, and powerfully relating itself to their desire for conduct, their desire for beauty. All other knowledge was dominated by this supposed knowledge and was subordinated to it, because of the surpassing strength of the hold which it gained upon the affections of men, by allying itself profoundly with their sense for conduct, their sense for beauty.

But now, says Professor Huxley, conceptions of the universe fatal to the notions held by our forefathers have been forced upon us by physical science. Grant to him that they are thus fatal, that the new conceptions must and will soon become current everywhere, and that every one will finally perceive them to be fatal to the beliefs of our forefathers. The need of humane letters, as they are truly called, because they serve the paramount desire in men that good should be for ever present to them,—the need of humane letters, to establish a relation between the new conceptions, and our instinct for beauty, our instinct for conduct, is only the more visible. The Middle Age could do without humane letters, as it could do without the study of nature, because its supposed knowledge was made to engage its emotions so powerfully. Grant that the supposed knowledge disappears, its power of being made to engage the emotions will of course disappear along with it,—but the emotions themselves, and their claim to be engaged and satisfied, will remain. Now if we find by experience that humane letters have an undeniable power of engaging the emotions, the importance of humane letters in a man's training becomes not less, but greater, in proportion to the success of modern science in extirpating what it calls "mediaeval thinking."

Have humane letters, then, have poetry and eloquence, the power here attributed to them of engaging the emotions, and do they exercise it? And if they have it and exercise it, *how* do they exercise it, so as to exert an influence upon man's sense for conduct, his sense for beauty? Finally, even if they both can and do exert an influence upon the senses in question, how are they to relate to them the results,—the modern results,—of natural science? All these questions may be asked. First, have poetry and eloquence the power of calling out the emotions? The appeal is to experience. Experience shows that for the vast majority of men, for mankind in general, they have the power. Next, do they exercise it? They do. But then, *how* do they exercise it so as to affect man's sense for conduct, his sense for beauty? And this is perhaps a case for applying the Preacher's words: "Though a man labour to seek it out, yet he shall not find it; yea, farther, though a wise man think to know it, yet shall he not be able to find it." Why should it be one thing, in its effect upon the emotions, to say, "Patience is a virtue," and quite another thing, in its effect upon the emotions, to say with Homer,

τλητὸν γὰρ Μοῖραι θυμὸν θέσαν ἀνθρώποισιν.—

"for an enduring heart have the destinies appointed to the children of men"? Why should it be one thing, in its effect upon the emotions, to say with the philosopher Spinoza, *Felicitas in eo consistit quod homo suum esse conservare potest*—"Man's happiness consists in his being able to preserve his own essence," and quite another thing, in its effect upon the emotions, to say with the Gospel, "What is a man advantaged, if he gain the whole world, and lose himself, forfeit himself?" How does this difference of effect arise? I cannot tell, and I am not much concerned to know; the important thing is that it does arise, and that we can profit by it. But how, finally, are poetry and eloquence to exercise the power of relating the modern results of natural science to man's instinct for conduct, his instinct for beauty? And here again I answer that I do not know *how* they will exercise it, but that they can and will exercise it I am sure. I do not mean that modern philosophical poets and modern philosophical moralists are to come and relate for us, in express terms, the results of modern scientific research to our instinct for conduct, our instinct for beauty. But I mean that we shall find, as a matter of experience, if we know the best that has been thought and uttered in the world, we shall find that the art and poetry and eloquence of men who lived, perhaps, long ago, who had the most limited natural knowledge, who had the most erroneous conceptions about many important matters, we shall find that this art, and poetry, and eloquence, have in fact not only the power of refreshing and delighting us, they have also the power, —such is the strength and worth, in essentials, of their authors' criticism of life,—they have a fortifying, and elevating, and quickening, and suggestive power, capable of wonderfully helping us to relate the results of modern science to our need for conduct, our need for beauty. Homer's conceptions of the physical universe were, I imagine, grotesque; but really, under the shock of hearing from modern science that "the world is not subordinated to man's use, and that man is not the cynosure of things terrestrial," I could, for my own part, desire no better comfort than Homer's line which I quoted just now,

τλητὸν γὰρ Μοῖραι θυμὸν θέσαν ἀνθρώποισιν·—

"for an enduring heart have the destinies appointed to the children of men"!

And the more that men's minds are cleared, the more that the results of science are frankly accepted, the more that poetry and eloquence come to be received and studied as what in truth they really are,—the criticism of life by gifted men, alive and active with extraordinary power at an unusual number of points;—so much the more will the value of humane letters, and of art also, which is an utterance having a like kind of power with theirs, be felt and acknowledged, and their place in education be secured.

Let us therefore, all of us, avoid indeed as much as possible any invidious comparison between the merits of humane letters, as means of education, and the merits of the natural sciences. But when some President of a Section for Mechanical Science insists on making the comparison, and tells us that "he who in his training has substituted literature and history for natural science has chosen the less useful alternative," let us make answer to him that the student of humane letters only, will, at least, know also the great conceptions brought in by modern physical science; for science, as Professor Huxley says, forces them upon us all. But the student of the natural sciences only, will, by our very hypothesis, know nothing of humane letters; not to mention that in setting himself to be perpetually accumulating natural knowledge, he sets himself to do what only specialists have in general the gift for doing genially. And so he will probably be unsatisfied, or at any rate incomplete, and even more incomplete than the student of humane letters only.

I once mentioned in a school-report, how a young man in one of our English training colleges having to paraphrase the passage in *Macbeth* beginning,

Can'st thou not minister to a mind diseased?

turned this line into, "Can you not wait upon the lunatic?" And I remarked what a curious state of things it would be, if every pupil of our national schools knew, let us say, that the moon is two thousand one hundred and sixty miles in diameter, and thought at the same time that a good paraphrase for

Can'st thou not minister to a mind diseased?

was, "Can you not wait upon the lunatic?" If one is driven to choose, I think I would rather have a young person ignorant about the moon's diameter, but aware that "Can you not wait upon the lunatic?" is bad, than a young person whose education had been such as to manage things the other way.

Or to go higher than the pupils of our national schools. I have in my mind's eye a member of our British Parliament who comes to travel here in America, who afterwards relates his travels, and who shows a really masterly knowledge of the geology of this great country and of its mining capabilities, but who ends by gravely suggesting that the United States should borrow a prince from our Royal Family, and should make him their king, and should create a House of Lords of great landed proprietors after the pattern of ours; and then America, he thinks, would have her future happily and perfectly secured. Surely, in this case, the President of the Section for Mechanical Science would himself hardly say that our member of Parliament, by concentrating himself upon geology and mineralogy, and so on, and not attending to literature and history, had "chosen the more useful alternative."

If then there is to be separation and option between humane letters on the one hand, and the natural sciences on the other, the great majority of mankind, all who have not exceptional and overpowering aptitudes for the study of nature, would do well, I cannot but think, to choose to be educated in humane letters rather than in the natural sciences. Letters will call out their being at more points, will make them live more.

I said that before I ended I would just touch on the question of classical education, and I will keep my word. Even if literature is to retain a large place in our education, yet Latin and Greek, say the friends of progress, will certainly have to go. Greek is the grand offender in the eyes of these gentlemen. The attackers of the established course of study think that against Greek, at any rate, they have irresistible arguments. Literature may perhaps be needed in education, they say; but why on earth should it be Greek literature? Why not French or German? Nay, "has not an Englishman models in his own literature of every kind of excellence?" As before, it is not on any weak pleadings of my own that I rely for convincing the gainsayers; it is on the constitution of human nature itself, and on the instinct of self-preservation in humanity. The instinct for beauty is set in human nature, as surely as the instinct for knowledge is set there, or the instinct for conduct. If the instinct for beauty is served by Greek literature and art as it is served by no other literature and art, we may trust to the instinct of self-preservation in humanity for keeping Greek as part of our culture. We may trust to it for even making the study of Greek more prevalent than it is now. Greek will come, I hope, some day to be studied more rationally than at present; but it will be increasingly studied as men increasingly feel the need in them for beauty, and how powerfully Greek art and Greek literature can serve this need. Women will again study Greek, as Lady Jane Grey did; I believe that in that chain of forts, with which the fair host of the Amazons are now engirdling our English universities, I find that here in America, in colleges like Smith College in Massachusetts, and Vassar College in the

State of New York, and in the happy families of the mixed universities out West, they are studying it already.

Defuit una mihi symmetria prisca,—"The antique symmetry was the one thing wanting to me," said Leonardo da Vinci; and he was an Italian. I will not presume to speak for the Americans, but I am sure that, in the Englishman, the want of this admirable symmetry of the Greeks is a thousand times more great and crying than in any Italian. The results of the want show themselves most glaringly, perhaps, in our architecture, but they show themselves, also, in all our art. *Fit details strictly combined, in view of a large general result nobly conceived;* that is just the beautiful *symmetria prisca* of the Greeks, and it is just where we English fail, where all our art fails. Striking ideas we have, and well-executed details we have; but that high symmetry which, with satisfying and delightful effect, combines them, we seldom or never have. The glorious beauty of the Acropolis at Athens did not come from single fine things stuck about on that hill, a statue here, a gateway there;—no, it arose from all things being perfectly combined for a supreme total effect. What must not an Englishman feel about our deficiencies in this respect, as the sense for beauty, whereof this symmetry is an essential element, awakens and strengthens within him! what will not one day be his respect and desire for Greece and its *symmetria prisca,* when the scales drop from his eyes as he walks the London streets, and he sees such a lesson in meanness as the Strand, for instance, in its true deformity! But here we are coming to our friend Mr. Ruskin's province, and I will not intrude upon it, for he is its very sufficient guardian.

And so we at last find, it seems, we find flowing in favour of the humanities the natural and necessary stream of things, which seemed against them when we started. The "hairy quadruped furnished with a tail and pointed ears, probably arboreal in his habits," this good fellow carried hidden in his nature, apparently, something destined to develop into a necessity for humane letters. Nay, more; we seem finally to be even led to the further conclusion that our hairy ancestor carried in his nature, also, a necessity for Greek.

And therefore, to say the truth, I cannot really think that humane letters are in much actual danger of being thrust out from their leading place in education, in spite of the array of authorities against them at this moment. So long as human nature is what it is, their attractions will remain irresistible. As with Greek, so with letters generally: they will some day come, we may hope, to be studied more rationally, but they will not lose their place. What will happen will rather be that there will be crowded into education other matters besides, far too many; there will be, perhaps, a period of unsettlement and confusion and false tendency; but letters will not in the end lose their leading place. If they lose it for a time, they will get it back again. We shall be brought back to them by our wants and aspirations. And a poor humanist may possess his soul in patience, neither strive nor cry, admit the energy and brilliancy of the partisans of physical science, and their present favour with the public, to be far greater than his own, and still have a happy faith that the nature of things works silently on behalf of the studies which he loves, and that, while we shall all have to acquaint ourselves with the great results reached by modern science, and to give ourselves as much training in its disciplines as we can conveniently carry, yet the majority of men will always require humane letters; and so much the more, as they have the more and the greater results of science to relate to the need in man for conduct, and to the need in him for beauty.

Tonio Kröger

Thomas Mann

(1875-1955)

So far we have considered art primarily in terms of its social value and concentrated on its function and character. But what of the artist? What is his relationship to art and society? What does he think art is and how does he see its function? Does he see himself writing a guide to the socially perplexed, as suggested by Matthew Arnold? These questions have moved to the center of the literary stage in the twentieth century.

One of the major writers of the modern period who addressed himself most consistently to the problem of artistic identity and function was Thomas Mann. In his youth, Mann, as most German writers of the time, was deeply influenced by the thought of Nietzsche. The metaphysical and psychological ambivalences in the Nietzschean esthetic were concretized and particularized by these writers and can be seen at work in Mann's "Tonio Kröger." For Mann the central problem was the conflicting demands made upon the artist by life and art. In his view the artist is simultaneously attracted and repelled by both.

"Tonio Kröger" can be thought of as a miniature Bildungsroman, *a type of novel dealing with the psychological development of a young hero and much favored by contemporary writers dealing with the search for identity theme. Two well-known works that fall into this class are James Joyce's* Portrait of the Artist as a Young Man *and Marcel Proust's* Remembrance of Things Past. *Mann's own* Buddenbrooks *is a classic of the kind. Each of these works depicts the growing estrangement of a perceptive young man from the society around him. Mann was fascinated with the problem of the sensitive person in a gross and vigorous society and dealt with it in several major works beside* Buddenbrooks. *Chief among these are* The Magic Mountain, *the tetralogy* Joseph and His Brothers, *and* Dr. Faustus.

THE winter sun, poor ghost of itself, hung milky and wan behind layers of cloud above the huddled roofs of the town. In the gabled streets it was wet and windy and there came in gusts a sort of soft hail, not ice, not snow.

School was out. The hosts of the released streamed over the paved court and out at the wrought-iron gate, where they broke up and hastened off right and left. Elder pupils held their books in a strap high on the left shoulder and rowed, right arm against the wind, towards dinner. Small people trotted gaily off, splashing the slush with their feet, the tools of learning rattling amain in their walrus-skin satchels. But one and all pulled off their caps and cast down their eyes in awe before the Olympian hat and ambrosial beard of a master moving homewards with measured stride . . .

"Ah, there you are at last, Hans," said Tonio Kröger. He had been waiting a long time in the street and went up with a smile to the friend he saw coming out of the gate in talk with other boys and about to go off with them . . . "What?" said Hans, and looked at Tonio. "Right-oh! We'll take a little walk, then."

Tonio said nothing and his eyes were clouded. Did Hans forget, had he only just remembered that they were to take a walk together today? And he himself had looked forward to it with almost incessant joy.

"Well, good-bye, fellows," said Hans Hansen to his comrades. "I'm taking a walk with Kröger." And the two turned to their left, while the others sauntered off in the opposite direction.

Hans and Tonio had time to walk after school because in neither of their families was dinner served before four o'clock. Their fathers were prominent business men, who held public office and were of consequence in the town. Hans's people had owned for some generations the big wood-yards down by the river, where powerful machine-saws hissed and spat and cut up timber; while Tonio was the son of Consul Kröger, whose grain-sacks with the firm name in great black letters you might see any day driven through the streets; his large, old ancestral home was the finest house in all the town. The two friends had to keep taking off their hats to their many acquaintances; some folk did not even wait for the fourteen-year-old lads to speak first, as by rights they should.

Both of them carried their satchels across their shoulders and both were well and warmly dressed: Hans in a short sailor jacket, with the wide blue collar of his sailor suit turned out over shoulders and back, and Tonio in a belted gray overcoat. Hans wore a Danish sailor cap with black ribbons, beneath which streamed a shock of straw-colored hair. He was uncommonly handsome and well built, broad in the shoulders and narrow in the hips, with keen, far-apart, steel-blue eyes; while beneath Tonio's round fur cap was a brunette face with the finely chiselled features of the south; the dark eyes, with delicate shadows and too heavy lids, looked dreamily and a little timorously on the world. Tonio's walk was idle and uneven, whereas the other's slim legs in their black stockings moved with an elastic, rhythmic tread.

Tonio did not speak. He suffered. His rather oblique brows were drawn together in a frown, his lips were rounded to whistle, he gazed into space with his head on one side. Posture and manner were habitual.

Suddenly Hans shoved his arm into Tonio's, with a sideways look—he knew very well what the trouble was. And Tonio, though he was silent for the next few steps, felt his heart soften.

"I hadn't forgotten, you see, Tonio," Hans said, gazing at the pavement, "I only thought it wouldn't come off today because it was so wet and windy. But I don't mind that at all, and it's jolly of you to have waited. I thought you had gone home, and I was cross. . . ."

Everything in Tonio leaped and jumped for joy at the words.

"All right; let's go over the wall," he said with a quaver in his voice. "Over the Millwall and the Holstenwall, and I'll go as far as your house with you, Hans. Then I'll have to walk back alone, but that doesn't matter; next time you can go round my way."

At bottom he was not really convinced by what Hans said; he quite knew the other attached less importance to this walk than he did himself. Yet he saw Hans was sorry for his remissness and willing to be put in a position to ask pardon, a pardon that Tonio was far indeed from withholding.

The truth was, Tonio loved Hans Hansen, and had already suffered much on his account. He who loves the more is the inferior and must suffer; in this hard and simple fact his fourteen-year-old soul had already been instructed by life; and he was so organized that he received such experiences consciously, wrote them down as it were inwardly, and even, in a certain way, took pleasure in them, though without ever letting them mould his conduct, indeed, or drawing any practical advantage from them. Being what he was, he found this knowledge far more important and far more interesting than the sort they made him learn in school; yes, during his lesson hours in the vaulted Gothic classrooms he was mainly occupied in feeling his way about among these intuitions of his and penetrating them. The process gave him the same kind of satisfaction as that he felt when he moved about in his room with his violin—for he played the violin—and made the tones, brought out as softly as ever he knew how, mingle with the plashing of the fountain that leaped and danced down there in the garden beneath the branches of the old walnut tree.

The fountain, the old walnut tree, his fiddle, and away in the distance the North Sea, within sound of whose summer murmurings he spent his holidays—these were the things he loved, within these he enfolded his spirit, among these things his inner life took its course. And they were all things whose names were effective in verse and occurred pretty frequently in the lines Tonio Kröger sometimes wrote.

The fact that he had a note-book full of such things, written by himself, leaked out through his own carelessness and injured him no little with the masters as well as among his fellows. On the one hand, Consul Kröger's son found their attitude both cheap and silly, and despised his schoolmates and his masters as well, and in his turn (with extraordinary penetration) saw through and disliked their personal weaknesses and bad breeding. But then, on the other hand, he himself felt his verse-making extravagant and out of place and to a certain extent agreed with those who considered it an unpleasing occupation. But that did not enable him to leave off.

As he wasted his time at home, was slow and absent-minded at school, and always had bad marks from the masters, he was in the habit of bringing home pitifully poor reports, which troubled and angered his father, a tall, fastidiously dressed man, with thoughtful blue eyes, and always a wild flower in his buttonhole. But for his mother, she cared nothing about the reports—Tonio's beautiful black-haired mother, whose name was Consuelo, and who was so absolutely different from the other ladies in the town, because father had brought her long ago from some place far down on the map.

Tonio loved his dark, fiery mother, who played the piano and mandolin so wonderfully, and he was glad his doubtful standing among men did not distress her. Though at the same time he found his father's annoyance a more dignified and respectable attitude, and despite his scolding understood him very well, whereas his mother's blithe indifference always seemed just a little wanton. His thoughts at times would run something like this: "It is true enough that I am what I am and will not and cannot alter: heedless, self-willed, with my mind on things nobody else thinks of. And so it is right they should scold and punish me and not smother things all up with kisses and music. After all, we are not gypsies living in a green wagon; we're respectable people, the family Consul Kröger." And not seldom he would think: "Why is it I am different, why do I fight everything, why am I at odds with my masters and like a stranger among the other boys? The good scholars, and the solid majority—they don't find the masters funny, they don't write verses, their thoughts are all about things that people do think about and can talk about out loud. How regular and comfortable they must feel, knowing that everybody knows just where they stand! It must be nice! But what is the matter with me, and what will be the end of it all?"

These thoughts about himself and his relation to life played an important part in Tonio's love for Hans Hansen. He loved him, in the first place, because he was so handsome; but in the next, because he was in every respect his own opposite and foil. Hans Hansen was a capital scholar, and a jolly chap to boot, who was head at drill, rode and swam to perfection, and lived in the sunshine of popularity. The masters were almost tender with him, they called him Hans and were partial to him in every way; the other pupils curried favor with him; even grown people stopped him on the street, twitched the shock of hair beneath his Danish sailor cap, and said: "Ah, here you are, Hans Hansen, with your pretty blond hair! Still head of the school? Remember me to your father and mother, that's a fine lad!"

Such was Hans Hansen and ever since Tonio Kröger had known him, from the very minute he set eyes on him, he had burned inwardly with a heavy, envious longing. "Who else has blue eyes like yours, or lives in such friendliness and harmony with all the world? You are always spending your time with some right and proper occupation. When you have done your prep you take your riding-lesson, or make things with a fret-saw, even in the holidays, at the seashore, you row and sail and swim all the time, while I wander off somewhere and lie down in the sand and stare at the strange and mysterious changes that whisk over the face of the sea. And all that is why your eyes are so clear. To be like you. . . ."

He made no attempt to be like Hans Hansen, and perhaps hardly even seriously wanted to. What he did ardently, painfully want, was that just as he was, Hans Hansen should love him; and he wooed Hans Hansen in his own way, deeply, lingeringly, devotedly, with a melancholy that gnawed and burned more terribly than all the sudden passion one might have expected from his exotic looks.

And he wooed not in vain. Hans respected Tonio's superior power of putting certain difficult matters into words; moreover, he felt the lively presence of an uncommonly strong and tender feeling for himself; he was grateful for it, and his response gave Tonio much happiness—though also many pangs of jealousy and disillusion over his futile efforts to establish a communion of spirit between them. For the queer thing was that Tonio, who after all envied Hans Hansen for being what he was, still kept on trying to draw him over to his own side; though of course he could succeed in this at most only at moments and superficially. . . .

"I have just been reading something so wonderful and splendid . . ." he said. They were walking and eating together out of a bag of fruit toffees that they had bought at Iverson's sweetshop in Mill Street for ten pfennigs. "You must read it, Hans, it is Schiller's *Don Carlos* . . . I'll lend it you if you like. . . ."

"Oh, no," said Hans Hansen, "you needn't, that's not anything for me. I'll stick to my horse books. There are wonderful cuts in them, let me tell you. I'll show them to you when you come to see me. They are instantaneous photography—the horse in motion; you can see him trot and canter and jump, in all positions, that you never can get to see in life, because they happen so fast. . . ."

"In all positions?" asked Tonio politely. "Yes, that must be great. But about *Don Carlos*—it is beyond anything you could possibly dream of. There are places in it that are so lovely they make you jump . . . as though it were an explosion—"

"An explosion?" asked Hans Hansen. "What sort of an explosion?"

"For instance, the place where the king has been crying because the marquis betrayed him . . . but the marquis did it only out of love for the prince, you see, he sacrifices himself for his sake. And the word comes out of the cabinet into the antechamber that the king has been weeping. 'Weeping? The king been weeping?' All the courtiers are fearfully upset, it goes through and through you, for the king has been so frightfully stiff and stern. But it is so easy to understand why he cried, and I feel sorrier for him than for the prince and the marquis put together. He is always so alone, nobody loves him, and then he thinks he has found one man, and then *he* betrays him. . . ."

Hans Hansen looked sideways into Tonio's face, and something in it must have won him to the subject, for suddenly he shoved his arm once more into Tonio's and said:

"How had he betrayed him, Tonio?"

Tonio went on.

"Well," he said, "you see all the letters for Brabant and Flanders—"

"There comes Irwin Immerthal," said Hans.

Tonio stopped talking. If only the earth would open and swallow Immerthal up! "Why does he have to come disturbing us?

If he only doesn't go with us all the way and talk about the riding-lessons!" For Irwin Immerthal had riding-lessons too. He was the son of the bank president and lived close by, outside the city wall. He had already been home and left his bag, and now he walked towards them through the avenue. His legs were crooked and his eyes like slits,

" 'lo, Immerthal," said Hans. "I'm taking a little walk with Kröger. . . ."

"I have to go into town on an errand," said Immerthal. "But I'll walk a little way with you. Are those fruit toffees you've got? Thanks. I'll have a couple. Tomorrow we have our next lesson, Hans." He meant the riding-lesson.

"What larks!" said Hans. "I'm going to get the leather gaiters for a present, because I was top lately in our papers."

"You don't take riding-lessons, I suppose, Kröger?" asked Immerthal, and his eyes were only two gleaming cracks.

"No . . ." answered Tonio, uncertainly.

"You ought to ask your father," Hans Hansen remarked, "so you could have lessons, too, Kröger."

"Yes . . ." said Tonio. He spoke hastily and without interest; his throat had suddenly contracted, because Hans had called him by his last name. Hans seemed conscious of it, too, for he first said by way of explanation: "I call you Kröger because your first name is so crazy. Don't mind my saying so, I can't do with it at all. Tonio—why, what sort of name is that? Though of course I know it's not your fault in the least."

"No, they probably called you that because it sounds so foreign and sort of something special," and Immerthal, obviously with intent to say just the right thing.

Tonio's mouth twitched. He pulled himself together and said:

"Yes, it's a silly name—Lord knows I'd rather be called Heinrich or Wilhelm. It's all because I'm named after my mother's brother Antonio. She comes from down there, you know. . . ."

There he stopped and let the others have their say about horses and saddles. Hans had taken Immerthal's arm; he talked with a fluency that *Don Carlos* could never have roused in him . . . Tonio felt a mounting desire to weep, pricking his nose from time to time; he had hard work to control the trembling of his lips.

Hans could not stand his name—what was to be done? He himself was called Hans, and Immerthal was called Irwin; two good, sound familiar names, offensive to nobody. And Tonio was foreign and queer. Yes, there was always something queer about him, whether he would or no, and he was alone, the regular and usual would none of him; although after all he was no gypsy in a green wagon, but the son of Consul Kröger, a member of the Kröger family. But why did Hans call him Tonio as long as they were alone and then feel ashamed as soon as anybody else was by? Just now he had won him over, they had been close together, he was sure. "How had he betrayed him, Tonio?" Hans asked, and took his arm. But he had breathed easier directly Immerthal came up, he had dropped him like a shot, even gratuitously taunted him with his outlandish name. How it hurt to have to see through all this! . . . Hans Hansen did like him a little, when they were alone, that he knew. But he let a third person come, he was ashamed, and offered up his friend. And again he was alone. He thought of King Philip. The king had wept. . . .

"Goodness, I have to go," said Irwin Immerthal. "Good-bye, and thanks for the toffee." He jumped upon a bench that stood by the way, ran along it with his crooked legs, jumped down, and trotted off.

"I like Immerthal," said Hans, with emphasis. He had a spoilt and arbitrary way of announcing his likes and dislikes, as though graciously pleased to confer them like an order on this person and that. . . . He went on talking about the riding-lessons where he had left off. Anyhow, it was not very much farther to his house; the walk over the walls was not a long one. They held their caps and bent their heads before the strong, damp wind that rattled and groaned in the leafless trees. And Hans Hansen went on talking, Tonio throwing in a forced yes or no from time to time. Hans talked eagerly, had taken his arm again; but the contact gave Tonio no pleasure. The nearness was only apparent, not real; it meant nothing. . . .

They struck away from the walls close to the station, where they saw a train puff busily past, idly counted the coaches, and waved to the man who was perched on top of the last one, bundled in a leather coat. They stopped in front of the Hansen villa on the Lindenplatz, and Hans went into detail about what fun it was to stand on the bottom rail of the garden gate and let it swing on its creaking hinges. After that they said good-bye.

"I must go in now," said Hans. "Good-bye, Tonio. Next time I'll take you home, see if I don't."

"Good-bye, Hans," said Tonio. "It was a nice walk."

They put out their hands, all wet and rusty from the garden gate. But as Hans looked up into Tonio's eyes, he bethought himself, a look of remorse came over his charming face.

"And I'll read *Don Carlos* pretty soon, too," he said quickly. "That bit about the king in his cabinet must be nuts." Then he took his bag under his arm and ran off through the front garden. Before he disappeared he turned and nodded once more.

And Tonio went off as though on wings. The wind was at his back; but it was not the wind alone that bore him along so lightly.

Hans would read *Don Carlos,* and then they would have something to talk about, and neither Irwin Immerthal nor another could join in. How well they understood each other! Perhaps—who knew?—some day he might even get Hans to write poetry! . . . No, no, that he did not ask. Hans must not become like Tonio, he must stop just as he was, so strong and bright, everybody loved him as he was, and Tonio most of all. But it would do him no harm to read *Don Carlos* . . . Tonio passed under the squat old city gate, along by the harbor, and up the steep, wet, windy, gabled street to his parents' house. His heart beat richly: longing was awake in it, and a gentle envy; a faint contempt, and no little innocent bliss.

Ingeborg Holm, blonde little Inge, the daughter of Dr. Holm, who lived on Market Square opposite the tall old Gothic fountain with its manifold spires—she it was Tonio Kröger loved when he was sixteen years old.

Strange how things come about! He had seen her a thousand times; then one evening he saw her again; saw her in a certain light, talking with a friend in a certain saucy way, laughing and tossing her head; saw her lift her arm and smooth her back hair with her schoolgirl hand, that was by no means particularly fine or slender, in such a way that the thin white sleeve slipped down from her elbow; heard her speak a word or two, a quite indifferent phrase, but with a certain intonation, with a warm ring in her voice; and his heart throbbed with ecstasy, far stronger than that he had once felt, when he looked at Hans Hansen long ago, when he was still a little, stupid boy.

That evening he carried away her picture in his eye: the thick blond plait, the longish, laughing blue eyes, the saddle of pale freckles across the nose. He could not go to sleep for hearing that ring in her voice; he tried in a whisper to imitate the tone in which she had uttered the commonplace phrase, and felt a shiver run through and through him. He knew by experience that this was love. And he was accurately aware that love would surely bring him much pain, affliction, and sadness, that it would certainly destroy his peace, filling his heart to overflowing with melodies which would be no good to him because he would never have the time or tranquility to give them permanent form. Yet he received this love with joy, surrendered himself to it, and cherished it with all the strength of his being; for he knew that love made one vital and rich, and he longed to be vital and rich, far more than he did to work tranquilly on anything to give it permanent form.

Tonio Kröger fell in love with merry Ingeborg Holm in Frau Consul Hustede's drawing-room on the evening when it was emptied of furniture for the weekly dancing-class. It was a private class, attended only by members of the first families; it met by turns in the various parental houses to receive instruction from Knaak, the dancing-master, who came from Hamburg expressly for the purpose.

François Knaak was his name, and what a man he was! *"J'ai l'honneur de me vous representer,"* he would say, *"mon nom est Knaak. . . .* This is not said during the bowing, but after you have finished and are standing up straight again. In a low voice, but distinctly. Of course one does not need to introduce oneself in French every day in the week, but if you can do it correctly and faultlessly in French you are not likely to make a mistake when you do it in German." How marvelously the silky black frock-coat fitted his chubby hips! His trouser-legs fell down in soft folds upon his patent-leather pumps with their wide satin bows, and his brown eyes glanced about him with languid pleasure in their own beauty.

All this excess of self-confidence and good form was positively overpowering. He went trippingly—and nobody tripped like him, so elastically, so weavingly, rockingly, royally—up to the mistress of the house, made a bow, waited for a hand to be put forth. This vouchsafed, he gave murmurous voice to his gratitude, stepped buoyantly back, turned on his left foot, swiftly drawing the right one backwards on its toe-tip, and moved away, with his hips shaking.

When you took leave of a company you must go backwards out at the door; when you fetched a chair, you were not to shove it along the floor or clutch it by one leg; but gently, by the back, and set it down without a sound. When you stood, you were not to fold your hands on your tummy, or seek with your tongue the corners of your mouth. If you did, Herr Knaak had a way of showing you how it looked that filled you with disgust for that particular gesture all the rest of your life.

This was deportment. As for dancing, Herr Knaak was, if possible, even more of a master at that. The salon was emptied of furniture and lighted by a gas-chandelier in the middle of the ceiling and candles on the mantel-shelf. The floor was strewn with talc, and the pupils stood about in a dumb semicircle. But in the next room, behind the portières, mothers and aunts sat on plush-upholstered chairs and watched Herr Knaak through their lorgnettes, as in little springs and hops, curtsying slightly, the hem of his frock-coat held up on each side by two fingers, he demonstrated the single steps of the mazurka. When he wanted to dazzle his audience completely, he would suddenly and unexpectedly spring from the ground, whirling his two legs about each other with bewildering swiftness in the air, as it were, trilling with them, and then, with a subdued bump, which nevertheless shook everything within him to its depths, returned to earth.

"What an unmentionable monkey!" thought Tonio Kröger to himself. But he saw the absorbed smile on jolly little Inge's face as she followed Herr Knaak's movements; and that, though not that alone, roused in him something like admiration of all this wonderfully controlled corporeality. How tranquil, how imperturbable was Herr Knaak's gaze! His eyes did not plumb the depths of things to the place where life becomes complex and melancholy; they knew nothing save that they were beautiful brown eyes. But that was just why his bearing was so proud. To be able to walk like that, one must be stupid; then one was loved, then one was lovable. He should so well understand how it was that Inge, blonde, sweet little Inge, looked at Herr Knaak as she did. But would never a girl look at him like that?

Oh, yes, there would, and did. For instance, Magdalena Vermehren, Attorney Vermehren's daughter, with the gentle mouth and the great, dark, brilliant eyes, so serious and adoring. She often fell down in the dance; but when it was "ladies' choice" she came up to him; she knew he wrote verses and twice she had asked him to show them to her. She often sat at a distance, with drooping head, and gazed at him. He did not care. It was Inge he loved, blonde, jolly Inge, who most assuredy despised him for his poetic effusions . . . he looked at her, looked at her narrow blue eyes full of fun and mockery, and felt an envious longing; to be shut away from her like this, to be forever strange—he felt it in his breast, like a heavy, burning weight.

"First couple *en avant,*" said Herr Knaak; and no words can tell how marvelously he pronounced the nasal. They were to practise the quadrille, and to Tonio Kröger's profound alarm he found himself in the same set with Inge Holm. He avoided her where he could, yet somehow was forever near her; kept his eyes away from her person and yet found his gaze ever on her. There she came, tripping up hand-in-hand with red-headed Ferdinand Matthiessen; she flung back her braid, drew a deep breath, and took her place opposite Tonio. Herr Heinzelmann, at the piano, laid bony hands upon the keys, Herr Knaak waved his arm, the quadrille began.

She moved to and fro before his eyes, forwards and back, pacing and swinging; he seemed to catch a fragrance from her hair or the folds of her thin white frock, and his eyes grew sadder and sadder. "I love you, dear, sweet Inge," he said to himself, and put into his words all the pain he felt to see her so intent upon the dance with not a thought of him. Some lines of an exquisite poem by Storm came into his mind: "I would sleep, but thou must dance." It seemed against all sense, and most depressing, that he must be dancing when he was in love. . . .

"First couple *en avant,*" said Herr Knaak; it was the next figure. *"Compliment! Moulinet des dames! Tour de main!"* and he swallowed the silent *e* in the *de,* with quite indescribable ease and grace.

"Second couple *en avant!*" This was Tonio Kröger and his partner. *"Compliment!"* And Tonio Kröger bowed. *"Moulinet des dames!"* And Tonio Kröger, with bent head and gloomy brows, laid his hand on those of the four ladies, on Ingeborg Holm's hand, and danced the *moulinet.*

Roundabout rose a tittering and laughing. Herr Knaak took a ballet pose conventionally expressive of horror. "Oh, dear! Oh, dear!" he cried. "Stop! Stop! Kröger among the ladies! *En arrière,* Fräulein Kröger, step back, *fi donc!* Everybody else understood it but you. Shoo! Get out! Get away!" He drew out his yellow silk handkerchief and flapped Tonio Kröger back to his place.

Everyone laughed, the girls and the boys and the ladies beyond the portières: Herr Knaak had made something too utterly funny out of the little episode, it was as amusing as a play. But Herr Heinzelmann at the piano sat and waited, with a dry, business-like air, for a sign to go on; he was hardened against Herr Knaak's effects.

Then the quadrille went on. And the intermission followed. The parlor-maid came clinking in with a tray of wine-jelly glasses, the cook followed in her wake with a load of plum-cake. But Tonio Kröger stole away. He stole out into the corridor and stood there, his hands behind his back, in front of a window with the blind down. He never thought that one could not see through the blind and that it was absurd to stand there as though one were looking out.

For he was looking within, into himself, the theater of so much pain and longing. Why, why was he here? Why was he not sitting by the window in his own room, reading Storm's *Immensee* and lifting his eyes to the twilight garden outside, where the old walnut-tree moaned? That was the place for him! Others might dance, others bend their fresh and lively minds upon the pleasure in hand! . . . But, no, no, after all, his place was here, where he could feel near Inge, even although he stood lonely and aloof, seeking to distinguish the warm notes of her voice amid the buzzing, clattering, and laughter within. Oh, lovely Inge, blonde Inge of the narrow, laughing blue eyes! So lovely and laughing as you are one can only be if one does not read *Immensee* and never tries to write things like it. And that was just the tragedy!

Ah, she *must* come! She *must* notice where he had gone, must feel how he suffered! She must slip out to him, even pity must bring her, to lay her hand on his shoulder and say: "Do come back to us, ah, don't be sad—I love you, Tonio." He listened behind him and waited in frantic suspense. But not in the least. Such things did not happen on this earth.

Had she laughed at him too like all the others? Yes, she had, however gladly he would have denied it for both their sakes. And yet it was only because he had been so taken up with her that he had danced the *moulinet des dames*. Suppose he had—what did that matter? Had not a magazine accepted a poem of his a little while ago—even though the magazine had failed before his poem could be printed? The day was coming when he would be famous, when they would print everything he wrote; and *then* he would see if that made any impression on Inge Holm! No, it would make no impression at all; that was just it. Magdalena Vermehren, who was always falling down in the dances, yes, she would be impressed. But never Ingeborg Holm, never blue-eyed, laughing Inge. So what was the good of it?

Tonio Kröger's heart contracted painfully at the thought. To feel stirring within you the wonderful and melancholy play of strange forces and to be aware that those others you yearn for are blithely inaccessible to all that moves you—what a pain is this! And yet! He stood there aloof and alone, staring hopelessly at a drawn blind and making, in his distraction, as though he could look out. But yet he was happy. For he lived. His heart was full; hotly and sadly it beat for thee, Ingeborg Holm, and his soul embraced thy blonde, simple, pert, commonplace little personality in blissful self-abnegation.

Often after that he stood thus, with burning cheeks, in lonely corners, whither the sound of the music, the tinkling of glasses and fragrance of flowers came but faintly, and tried to distinguish the ringing tones of thy voice amid the distant happy din; stood suffering for thee—and still was happy! Often it angered him to think that he might talk with Magdalena Vermehren, who always fell down in the dance. She understood him, she laughed or was serious in the right places; while Inge the fair, let him sit never so near her, seemed remote and estranged, his speech not being her speech. And still—he was happy. For happiness, he told himself, is not in being loved—which is a satisfaction of the vanity and mingled with disgust. Happiness is in loving, and perhaps in snatching fugitive little approaches to the beloved object. And he took inward note of this thought, wrote it down in his mind; followed out all its implications and felt it to the depths of his soul.

"Faithfulness," thought Tonio Kröger. "Yes, I will be faithful, I will love thee, Ingeborg, as long as I live!" He said this in the honesty of his intentions. And yet a still small voice whispered misgivings in his ear: after all, he had forgotten Hans Hansen utterly, even though he saw him every day! And the hateful, the pitiable fact was that this still, small, rather spiteful voice was right: time passed and the day came when Tonio Kröger was no longer so unconditionally ready as once he had been to die for the lively Inge, because he felt in himself desires and powers to accomplish in his own way a host of wonderful things in this world.

And he circled with watchful eye the sacrificial altar, where flickered the pure, chaste flame of his love; knelt before it and tended and cherished it in every way, because he so wanted to be faithful. And in a little while, unobservably, without sensation or stir, it went out after all.

But Tonio Kröger still stood before the cold altar, full of regret and dismay at the fact that faithfulness was impossible upon this earth. Then he shrugged his shoulders and went his way.

He went the way that go he must, a little idly, a little irregularly, whistling to himself, gazing into space with his head on one side; and if he went wrong it was because for some people there is no such thing as a right way. Asked what in the world he meant to become, he gave various answers, for he was used to say (and had even already written it) that he bore within himself the possibility of a thousand ways of life, together with the private conviction that they were all sheer impossibilities.

Even before he left the narrow streets of his native city, the threads that bound him to it had gently loosened. The old Kröger family gradually declined, and some people quite rightly considered Tonio Kröger's own existence and way of life as one of the signs of decay. His father's mother, the head of the family, had died, and not long after his own father followed, the tall, thoughtful, carefully dressed gentleman with the field-flower in his buttonhole. The great Kröger house, with all its stately tradition, came up for sale, and the firm was dissolved. Tonio's mother, his beautiful, fiery mother, who played the piano and mandolin so wonderfully and to whom nothing mattered at all, she married again after a year's time, married a musician, moreover, a virtuoso with an Italian name, and went away with him into remote blue distances. Tonio Kröger found this a little irregular, but who was he to call her to order, who wrote poetry himself and could not even give an answer when asked what he meant to do in life?

And so he left his native town and its tortuous, gabled streets with the damp wind whistling through them; left the fountain in the garden and the ancient walnut-tree, familiar friends of his youth; left the sea too, that he loved so much, and felt no pain to go. For he was grown up and sensible and had come to realize how things stood with him; he looked down on the lowly and vulgar life he had led so long in these surroundings.

He surrendered utterly to the power that to him seemed the highest on earth, to whose service he felt called, which promised him elevation and honors; the power of intellect, the power of the Word, that lord it with a smile over the unconscious and inarticulate. To this power he surrendered with all the passion of youth, and it rewarded him with all it had to give, taking from him inexorably, in return, all that it is wont to take.

It sharpened his eyes and made him see through the large words which puff out the bosoms of mankind; it opened for him men's souls and his own, made him clairvoyant, showed him the inwardness of the word and the ultimate behind men's words and deeds. And all that he saw could be put in two words: the comedy and the tragedy of life.

And then, with knowledge, its torment and its arrogance, came solitude; because he could not endure the blithe and innocent with their darkened understanding, while they in turn were troubled by the sign on his brow. But his love of the word kept growing sweeter and sweeter, and his love of form; for he used to say (and had already said it in writing) that knowledge of the soul would unfailingly make use melancholy if the pleasures of expression did not keep us alert and of good cheer.

He lived in large cities and in the south, promising himself a luxuriant ripening of his art by southern suns; perhaps it was the blood of his mother's race that drew him thither. But his heart being dead and loveless, he fell into adventures of the flesh, descended into the depths of lust and searing sin, and suffered unspeakably thereby. It might have been his father in him, that tall, thoughtful, fastidiously dressed man with the wild flower in his buttonhole, that made him suffer so down there in the south; now and again he would feel a faint, yearning memory of a certain joy that was of the soul; once it had been his own, but now, in all his joys, he could not find it again.

Then he would be seized with disgust and hatred of the senses; pant after purity and seemly peace, while still he breathed the air of art, the tepid, sweet air of permanent spring, heavy with fragrance where it breeds and brews and burgeons in the mysterious bliss of creation. So for all result he was flung to and fro forever between two crass extremes: between icy intellect and scorching sense, and what with his pangs of conscience led an exhausting life, rare, extraordinary, excessive, which at bottom he, Tonio Kröger, despised. "What a labyrinth!" he sometimes thought. "How could I possibly have got into all these fantastic adventures? As though I had a wagonful of traveling gypsies for my ancestors!"

But as his health suffered from these excesses, so his artistry was sharpened; it grew fastidious, precious, refined, morbidly sensitive in questions of tact and taste, rasped by the banal. His first appearance in print elicited much applause; there was joy among the elect, for it was a good and workmanlike performance, full of humor and acquaintance with pain. In no long time his name—the same by which his masters had reproached him, the same he had signed to his earliest verses on the walnut tree and the fountain and the sea, those syllables compact of the north and the south, that good middle-class name with the exotic twist to it—became a synonym for excellence; for the painful thoroughness of the experiences he had gone through, combined with a tenacious ambition and a persistent industry, joined battle with the irritable fastidiousness of his taste and under grinding torments issued in work of a quality quite uncommon.

He worked, not like a man who works that he may live; but as one who is bent on doing nothing but work; having no regard for himself as a human being but only as a creator; moving about gray and unobtrusive among his fellows like an actor without his make-up, who counts for nothing as soon as he stops representing someone else. He worked withdrawn out of sight and sound of the small fry, for whom he felt nothing but contempt, because to them a talent was a social asset like another; who, whether they were poor or not, went about ostentatiously shabby or else flaunted startling cravats, all the time taking good care to amuse themselves, to be artistic and charming without the smallest notion of the fact that good work only comes out under pressure of a bad life; that he who lives does not work; that one must die to live in order to be utterly a creator.

"Shall I disturb you?" asked Tonio Kröger on the threshold of the atelier. He held his hat in his hand and bowed with some ceremony, although Lisabeta Ivanovna was a good friend of his, to whom he told all his troubles.

"Mercy on you, Tonio Kröger! Don't be so formal," answered she, with her lilting intonation. "Everybody knows you were taught good manners in your nursery." She transferred her brush to her left hand, that held the palette, reached him her right, and looked him in the face, smiling and shaking her head.

"Yes, but you are working," he said. "Let's see. Oh, you've

been getting on," and he looked at the color-sketches leaning against chairs at both sides of the easel and from them to the large canvas covered with a square linen mesh, where the first patches of color were beginning to appear among the confused and schematic lines of the charcoal sketch.

This was in Munich, in a back building in Schellingstrasse, several stories up. Beyond the wide window facing the north were blue sky, sunshine, birds twittering; the young sweet breath of spring streaming through an open pane mingled with the smells of paint and fixative. The afternoon light, bright golden, flooded the spacious emptiness of the atelier; it made no secret of the bad flooring or the rough table under the window, covered with little bottles, tubes, and brushes; it illumined the unframed studies on the unpapered walls, the torn silk screen that shut off a charmingly furnished little living-corner near the door; it shone upon the inchoate work on the easel, upon the artist and the poet there before it.

She was about the same age as himself—slightly past thirty. She sat there on a low stool, in her dark-blue apron, and leant her chin in her hand. Her brown hair, compactly dressed, already a little gray at the sides, was parted in the middle and waved over the temples, framing a sensitive, sympathetic, dark-skinned face, which was Slavic in its facial structure, with flat nose, strongly accentuated cheekbones, and little bright black eyes. She sat there measuring her work with her head on one side and her eyes screwed up; her features were drawn with a look of misgiving, almost of vexation.

He stood beside her, his right hand on his hip, with the other furiously twirling his brown moustache. His dress, reserved in cut and a soothing shade of gray, was punctilious and dignified to the last degree. He was whistling softly to himself, in the way he had, and his slanting brows were gathered in a frown. The dark-brown hair was parted with severe correctness, but the labored forehead beneath showed a nervous twitching, and the chiselled southern features were sharpened as though they had been gone over again with a graver's tool. And yet the mouth—how gently curved it was, the chin how softly formed! . . . After a little he drew his hand across his brow and eyes and turned away.

"I ought not to have come," he said.

"And why not, Tonio Kröger?"

"I've just got up from my desk, Lisabeta, and inside my head it looks just the way it does on this canvas. A scaffolding, a faint first draft smeared with corrections and a few splotches of color; yes, and I come up here and see the same thing. And the same conflict and contradiction in the air," he went on, sniffing, "that has been torturing me at home. It's extraordinary. If you are possessed by an idea, you find it expressed everywhere, you even *smell* it. Fixative and the breath of spring; art and—what? Don't say nature, Lisabeta, 'nature' isn't exhausting. Ah, no, I ought to have gone for a walk, though it's doubtful if it would have made me feel better. Five minutes ago, not far from here, I met a man I know, Adalbert, the novelist. 'God damn the spring!' says he in the aggressive way he has. 'It is and always has been the most ghastly time of the year. Can you get hold of a single sensible idea, Kröger? Can you sit still and work out even the smallest effect, when your blood tickles till it's positively indecent and you are teased by a whole host of irrelevant sensations that when you look at them turn out to be unworkable trash? For my part, I am going to a café. A café is neutral territory, the change of the seasons doesn't affect it; it represents, so to speak, the detached and elevated sphere of the literary man, in which one is only capable of refined ideas.' And he went into the café . . . and perhaps I ought to have gone with him."

Lisabeta was highly entertained.

"I like that, Tonio Kröger. That part about the indecent tickling is good. And he is right, too, in a way, for spring is really not very conducive to work. But now listen. Spring or no spring, I will just finish this little place—work out this little effect, as your friend Adalbert would say. Then we'll go into the 'salon' and have tea, and you can talk yourself out, for I can perfectly well see you are too full for utterance. Will you just compose yourself somewhere—on that chest, for instance, if you are not afraid for your aristocratic garments—"

"Oh, leave my clothes alone, Lisabeta Ivanovna! Do you want me to go about in a ragged velveteen jacket or a red waistcoat? Every artist is as bohemian as the deuce, inside! Let him at least wear proper clothes and behave outwardly like a respectable being. No, I am not too full for utterance," he said as he watched her mixing her paints, "I've told you, it is only that I have a problem and a conflict, that sticks in my mind and disturbs me at my work. . . . Yes, what was it we were just saying? We were talking about Adalbert, the novelist, that stout and forthright man. 'Spring is the most ghastly time of the year,' says he, and goes into a café. A man has to know what he needs, eh? Well, you see he's not the only one; the spring makes me nervous, too; I get dazed with the triflingness and sacredness of the memories and feelings it evokes; only that I don't succeed in looking down on it, for the truth is it makes me ashamed; I quail before its sheer naturalness and triumphant youth. And I don't know whether I should envy Adalbert or despise him for his ignorance. . . .

"Yes, it is true; spring is a bad time for work; and why? Because we are feeling too much. Nobody but a beginner imagines that he who creates must feel. Every real and genuine artist smiles at such naive blunders as that. A melancholy enough smile, perhaps, but still a smile. For what an artist talks about is never the main point; it is the raw material, in and for itself indifferent, out of which, with bland and serene mastery, he creates the work of art. If you care too much about what you have to say, if your heart is too much in it, you can be pretty sure of making a mess. You get pathetic, you wax sentimental; something dull and doddering, without roots or outlines, with no sense of humor—something tiresome and banal grows under your hand, and you get nothing out of it but apathy in your audience and disappointment and misery in yourself. For so it is, Lisabeta; feeling, warm, heartfelt feeling, is always banal and futile; only the irritations and icy ecstasies of the artist's corrupted nervous system are artistic. The artist must be unhuman, extra-human; he must stand in a queer aloof relationship to our humanity; only so is he in a position, I ought to say only so would he be tempted, to represent it, to present it, to portray it to good effect. The very gift of style, of form and expression, is nothing else than this cool and fastidious attitude towards humanity; you might say there has to be this impoverishment and devastation as a preliminary condition. For sound natural feeling, say what you like, has no taste. It is all up with the artist as soon as he becomes a man and begins to feel. Adalbert knows that; that's why he betook himself to the café, the neutral territory—God help him!"

"Yes, God help him, Batuschka," said Lisabeta, as she washed her hands in a tin basin. "You don't need to follow his example."

"No, Lisabeta, I am not going to; and the only reason is that I am now and again in a position to feel a little ashamed of the springtime of my art. You see sometimes I get letters from strangers, full of praise and thanks and admiration from people whose feelings I have touched. I read them and feel touched myself at these warm if ungainly emotions I have called up; a sort of pity steals over me at this naive enthusiasm; and I positively blush at the thought of how these good people would freeze up if they were to look behind the scenes. What they, in their innocence, cannot comprehend is that a properly constituted, healthy, decent man never writes, acts, or composes—all of which does not hinder me from using his admiration for my genius to goad myself on; nor from taking it in deadly earnest and aping the airs of a great man. Oh, don't talk to me, Lisabeta. I tell you I am sick to death of depicting humanity without having any part or lot in it. . . . Is an artist a male, anyhow? Ask the females! It seems to me we artists are all of us something like those unsexed papal singers . . . we sing like angels, but—"

"Shame on you, Tonio Kröger. But come to tea. The water is just on the boil, and here are some *papyros*. You were talking about singing soprano, do go on. But really you ought to be ashamed of yourself. If I did not know your passionate devotion to your calling and how proud you are of it—"

"Don't talk about 'calling,' Lisabeta Ivanovna. Literature is not a calling, it is a curse, believe me! When does one begin to feel the curse? Early, horribly early. At a time when one ought by rights still to be living in peace and harmony with God and the world. It begins by your feeling yourself set apart, in a curious sort of opposition to the nice, regular people; there is a gulf of ironic sensibility, of knowledge, skepticism, disagreement, between you and the others; it grows deeper and deeper, you realize that you are alone; and from then on any *rapprochement* is simply hopeless! What a fate! That is, if you still have enough heart, enough warmth of affections, to feel how frightful it is! . . . Your self-consciousness is kindled, because you among thousands feel the sign on your brow and know that everyone else sees it. I once knew an actor, a man of genius, who had to struggle with a morbid self-consciousness and instability. When he had no rôle to play, nothing to represent, this man, consummate artist but impoverished human being, was overcome by an exaggerated consciousness of his ego. A genuine artist—not one who has taken up art as a profession like another, but artist foreordained and damned—you can pick out, without boasting very sharp perceptions, out of a group of men. The sense of being set apart and not belonging, of being known and observed, something both regal and incongruous shows in his face. You might see something of the same sort on the features of a prince walking through a crowd in ordinary clothes. But no civilian clothes are any good here, Lisabeta. You can disguise yourself, you can dress up like an attaché or a lieutenant of the guard on leave; you hardly need to give a glance or speak a word before everyone knows you are not a human being, but something else: something queer, different, inimical.

"But what is it, to be an artist? Nothing shows up the general dislike of thinking, and man's innate craving to be comfortable, better than his attitude to this question. When these worthy people are affected by a work of art; they say humbly that that sort of thing is a 'gift.' And because in their innocence they assume that beautiful and uplifting results must have beautiful and uplifting causes, they never dream that the 'gift' in question is a very dubious affair and rests upon extremely sinister foundations. Everybody knows that artists are 'sensitive' and easily wounded; just as everybody knows that ordinary people, with a normal bump of self-confidence, are not. Now you see, Lisabeta, I cherish at the bottom of my soul all the scorn and suspicion of the artist-gentry—translated into terms of the intellectual—that my upright old forebears there on the Baltic would have felt for any juggler or mountebank that entered their houses. Listen to this. I know a banker, gray-haired business man, who has a gift for writing stories. He employs this gift in his idle hours, and some of his stories are of the first rank. But despite—I say despite—this excellent gift his withers are by no means unwrung: on the contrary, he has had to serve a prison sentence, on anything but trifling grounds. Yes, it was actually first *in prison* that he became conscious of his gift, and his experience as a convict is the main theme in all his works. One might be rash enough to conclude that a man has to be at home in some kind of jail in order to become a poet. But can you escape the suspicion that the source and essence of his being an artist had less to do with his life in prison than they had with the reasons that *brought him there?* A banker who writes—that is a rarity, isn't it? But a banker who isn't a criminal, who is irreproachably respectable, and yet writes—he doesn't exist. Yes, you are laughing, and yet I am more than half serious. No problem, none in the world, is more tormenting than this of the artist and his human aspect. Take the most miraculous case of all, take the most typical and therefore the most powerful of artists, take such a morbid and profoundly equivocal work as *Tristan and Isolde,* and look at the effect it has on a healthy young man of thoroughly normal feelings. Exaltation, encouragement, warm, downright enthusiasm, perhaps incitement to 'artistic' creation of his own. Poor young dilettante! In us artists it looks fundamentally different from what he wots of, with his 'warm heart' and 'honest enthusiasm.' I've seen women and youth go mad over artists . . . and I *knew* about them. . . ! The origin, the accompanying phenomena, and the conditions of the artist life—good Lord, what I haven't observed about them, over and over!"

"Observed, Tonio Kröger? If I may ask, only 'observed'?"

He was silent, knitting his oblique brown brows and whistling softly to himself.

"Let me have your cup, Tonio. The tea is weak. And take another cigarette. Now you perfectly know that you are looking at things as they do not necessarily have to be looked at. . . ."

"That is Horatio's answer, dear Lisabeta. ' 'Twere to consider too curiously, to consider so.' "

"I mean, Tonio Kröger, that one can consider them just exactly as well from another side. I am only a silly painting female, and if I can contradict you at all, if I can defend your own profession a little against you, it is not by saying anything new, but simply by reminding you of some things you very well know yourself: of the purifying and healing influence of letters, the subduing of the passions by knowledge and eloquence; literature as the guide to understanding, forgiveness, and love, the redeeming power of the word, literary art as the noblest manifestation of the human mind, the poet as the most highly developed of human beings, the poet as saint. Is it to consider things not curiously enough, to consider them so?"

"You may talk like that, Lisabeta Ivanovna, you have a perfect right. And with reference to Russian literature, and the works of your poets, one can really worship them; they really come close to being that elevated literature you are talking about. But I am not ignoring your objections, they are part of the things I have in my mind today. . . . Look at me, Lisabeta. I don't look any too cheerful, do I? A little old and tired and pinched, eh? Well, now to come back to the 'knowledge.' Can't you imagine a man, born orthodox, mild-mannered, well-meaning, a bit sentimental, just simply over-stimulated by his psychological clairvoyance, and going to the dogs? Not to let the sadness of the world unman you; to read, mark, learn, and put to account even the most torturing things and to be of perpetual good cheer, in the sublime consciousness of moral superiority over the horrible invention of existence—yea, thank you! But despite all the joys of expression once in a while the thing gets on your nerves, *'Tout comprendre, c'est tout pardonner.'* I don't know about that. There is something I call being sick of knowledge, Lisabeta: when it is enough for you to see through a thing in order to be sick to death of it, and not in the least in a forgiving mood. Such was the case of Hamlet the Dane, that typical literary man. He knew what it meant to be called to knowledge without being born to it. To see things clear, if even through your tears, to recognize, notice, observe—and have to put it all down with a smile, at the very moment when hands are clinging, and lips meeting, and the human gaze is blinded with feeling—it is infamous, Lisabeta, it is indecent, outrageous—but what good does it do to be outraged?

"Then another and no less charming side of the thing, of course, is your ennui, your indifferent and ironic attitude towards truth. It is a fact that there is no society in the world so dumb and hopeless as a circle of literary people who are hounded to death as it is. All knowledge is old and tedious to them. Utter some truth that it gave you considerable youthful joy to conquer and possess—and they will all chortle at you for your naiveté. Oh, yes, Lisabeta, literature is a wearing job. In human society, I do assure you, a reserved and skeptical man can be taken for stupid, whereas he is really only arrogant and perhaps lacks courage. So much for 'knowledge.' Now for the 'Word.' It isn't so much a matter of the 'redeeming power' as it is of putting your emotions on ice and serving them up chilled! Honestly, don't you think there's a good deal of cool cheek in the prompt and superficial way a writer can get rid of his feelings by turning them into literature? If your heart is too full, if you are overpowered with the emotions of some sweet or exalted moment—nothing simpler! Go to the literary man, he will put it straight for you instanter. He will analyze and formulate your affair, label it and express it and discuss it and polish it off and make you indifferent to it for time and eternity—and not charge you a farthing. You will go home quite relieved, cooled off, enlightened; and wonder what it was all about and why you were so mightily moved. And will you seriously enter the lists in behalf of this vain and frigid charlatan? What is uttered, so runs this *credo,* is finished and done with. If the whole world could be expressed, it would be saved, finished and done . . . Well and good. But I am not a nihilist—"

"You are not a—" said Lisabeta. . . . She was lifting a teaspoonful of tea to her mouth and paused in the act to stare at him.

"Come, come, Lisabeta, what's the matter? I say I am not a nihilist, with respect, that is, to lively feeling. You see, the literary man does not understand that life may go on living, unashamed, even after it has been expressed and therewith finished. No matter how much it has been redeemed by becoming literature, it keeps right on sinning—for all action is sin in the mind's eye—

"I'm nearly done, Lisabeta. Please listen. I love life—this is an admission. I present it to you, you may have it. I have never made it to anyone else. People say—people have even written and printed—that I hate life, or fear or despise or abominate it. I liked to hear this, it has always flattered me; but that does not make it true. I love life. You smile; and I know why, Lisabeta. But I implore you not to take what I am saying for literature. Don't think of Caesar Borgia or any drunken philosophy that has him for a standard-bearer. He is nothing to me, your Caesar Borgia. I have no opinion of him, and I shall never comprehend how one can honor the extraordinary and daemonic as an ideal. No, life as the eternal antinomy of mind and art does not represent itself to us as a vision of savage greatness and ruthless beauty; we who are set apart and different do not conceive it as, like us, unusual; it is the normal, respectable, and admirable that is the kingdom of our longing: life, in all its seductive banality! That man is very far from being an artist, my dear, whose last and deepest enthusiasm is the refined, the eccentric and satanic; who does not know a longing for the innocent, the simple, and the living, for a little friendship, devotion, familiar human happiness—the gnawing, surreptitious hankering, Lisabeta, for the bliss of the commonplace. . . .

"A genuine human friend. Believe me, I should be proud and happy to possess a friend among men. But up to now all the friends I have had have been demons, kobolds, impious monsters, and specters dumb with excess of knowledge—that is to say, literary men.

"I may be standing upon some platform, in some hall in front of people who have come to listen to me. And I find myself looking round among my hearers, I catch myself secretly peering about the auditorium, and all the while I am thinking who it is that has come here to listen to me, whose grateful applause is in my ears, with whom my art is making me one. . . . I do not find what I seek, Lisabeta. I find the herd. The same old community, the same old gathering of early Christians, so to speak: people with fine souls in uncouth bodies, people who are always falling down in the dance, if you know what I mean; the kind to whom poetry serves as a sort of mild revenge on life. Always and only the poor and suffering, never any of the others, the blue-eyed ones, Lisabeta—they do not need mind. . . .

"And, after all, would it not be a lamentable lack of logic to want it otherwise? It is against all sense to love life and yet bend all the powers you have to draw it over to your own side, to the side of finesse and melancholy and the whole sickly aristocracy of letters. The kingdom of art increases and that of health and innocence declines on this earth. What there is left of it ought to be carefully preserved; one ought not to tempt people to read poetry who would much rather read books about the instantaneous photography of horses.

"For, after all, what more pitiable sight is there than life led astray by art? We artists have a consummate contempt for the dilettante, the man who is leading a living life and yet thinks he can be an artist too if he gets the chance. I am speaking from personal experience, I do assure you. Suppose I am in a company in a good house, with eating and drinking going on, and plenty of conversation and good feeling; I am glad and grateful to be able to lose myself among good regular people for a while. Then all of a sudden—I am thinking of something that actually happened—an officer gets up, a lieutenant, a stout, good-looking chap, whom I could never have believed guilty of any conduct unbecoming his uniform, and actually in good set terms asks the company's permission to read some verses of his own composition. Everybody looks disconcerted, they laugh and tell him to go on, and he takes them at their word and reads from a sheet of paper he has up to now been hiding in his coat-tail pocket—something about love and music, as deeply felt as it is inept. But I ask you: a lieutenant! A man of the world! He surely did not need to. . . . Well, the inevitable result is long faces, silence, a little artificial applause, everybody thoroughly uncomfortable. The first sensation I am conscious of is guilt—I feel partly responsible for the disturbance this rash youth has brought upon the company; and no wonder, for I, as a member of the same guild, am a target for some of the unfriendly glances. But next minute I realize something else: this man for whom just now I felt the greatest respect has suddenly sunk in my eyes. I feel a benevolent pity. Along with some other brave and good-natured gentlemen I go up and speak to him. 'Congratulations, Herr Lieutenant,' I say, 'that is a very pretty talent you have. It was charming.' And I am within an ace of clapping him on the shoulder. But is that the way one is supposed to feel towards a lieutenant—benevolent? . . . It was his own fault. There he stood, suffering embarrassment for the mistake of thinking that one may pluck a single leaf from the laurel tree of art without paying for it with his life. No, there I go with my colleague, the convict banker—but don't you find, Lisabeta, that I have quite a Hamlet-like flow of oratory today?"

"Are you done, Tonio Kröger?"

"No. But there won't be any more."

"And quite enough too. Are you expecting a reply?"

"Have you one ready?"

"I should say. I have listened to you faithfully, Tonio, from beginning to end, and I will give you the answer to everything you have said this afternoon and the solution of the problem that has been upsetting you. Now: the solution is that you, as you sit there, are, quite simply, a bourgeois."

"Am I?" he asked, a little crestfallen.

"Yes; that hits you hard, it must. So I will soften the judgment just a little. You are a bourgeois on the wrong path, a bourgeois *manqué*."

Silence. Then he got up resolutely and took his hat and stick.

"Thank you, Lisabeta Ivanovna; now I can go home in peace. I am expressed."

Towards autumn Tonio Kröger said to Lisabeta Ivanovna:

"Well, Lisabeta, I think I'll be off. I need a change of air. I must get away, out into the open."

"Well, well, well, little Father! Does it please your Highness to go down to Italy again?"

"Oh, get along with your Italy, Lisabeta. I'm fed up with Italy, I spew it out of my mouth. It's a long time since I imagined I could belong down there. Art, eh? Blue-velvet sky, ardent wine, the sweets of sensuality. In short, I don't want it—I decline with thanks. The whole *bellezza* business makes me nervous. All those frightfully animated people down there with the black animal-like eyes. No, I'm going to take a trip to Denmark."

"To Denmark?"

"Yes. I'm quite sanguine of the results. I happen never to have been there, though I lived all my youth so close to it. Still I have always known and loved the country. I suppose I must have this northern tendency from my father, for my mother was really more for the *bellezza,* in so far, that is, as she cared very much one way or the other. But just take the books that are written up there, that clean, meaty, whimsical Scandinavian literature, Lisabeta, there's nothing like it. I love it. Or take the Scandinavian meals, those incomparable meals, which can only be digested in strong sea air (I don't know whether I can digest them in any sort of air); I know them from my home, too, because we ate that way up there. Take even the names, the given names that people rejoice in up north; we have a good many of them in my part of the country too: Ingeborg, for instance, isn't it the purest poetry—like a harp-tone? And then the sea—up there it's the Baltic! . . . In a word, I am going, Lisabeta. I want to see the Baltic again and read the books and hear the names on their native heath; I want to stand on the terrace at Kronberg, where the ghost appeared to Hamlet, bringing despair and death to that poor, noble-souled youth. . . ."

"How are you going, Tonio, if I may ask? What route are you taking?"

"The usual one," he said, shrugging his shoulders, and blushed perceptibly. "Yes, I shall touch my—my point of departure, Lisabeta, after thirteen years, and that may turn out rather funny."

She smiled.

"That is what I wanted to hear, Tonio Kröger. Well, be off, then, in God's name. Be sure to write to me, do you hear? I shall expect a letter full of your experiences in—Denmark."

And Tonio Kröger traveled north. He traveled in comfort (for he was wont to say that anyone who suffered inwardly more than other people had a right to a little outward ease); and he did not stay until the towers of the little town he had left rose up in the gray air. Among them he made a short and singular stay.

The dreary afternoon was merging into evening when the train pulled into the narrow, reeking shed, so marvelously familiar. The volumes of thick smoke rolled up to the dirty glass roof and wreathed to and fro there in long tatters, just as they had, long ago, on the day when Tonio Kröger, with nothing but derision in his heart, had left his native town.—He arranged to have his baggage sent to his hotel and walked out of the station.

There were the cabs, those enormously high, enormously wide black cabs drawn by two horses, standing in a rank. He did not take one, he only looked at them, as he looked at everything: the narrow gables, and the pointed towers peering above the roofs close at hand; the plump, fair, easy-going populace, with their broad yet rapid speech. And a nervous laugh mounted in him, mysteriously akin to a sob.—He walked on, slowly, with the damp wind constantly in his face, across the bridge, with the mythological statues on the railings, and some distance along the harbor.

Good Lord, how tiny and close it all seemed! The comical little gabled streets were climbing up just as of yore from the port to the town! And on the ruffled waters the smoke-stacks and masts of the ships dipped gently in the wind and twilight. Should he go up that next street, leading, he knew, to a certain house? No, tomorrow. He was too sleepy. His head was heavy from the journey, and slow, vague trains of thought passed though his mind.

Sometimes in the past thirteen years, when he was suffering from indigestion, he had dreamed of being back home in the echoing old house in the steep, narrow street. His father had been there too, and reproached him bitterly for his dissolute manner of life, and this, each time, he had found quite as it should be. And now the present refused to distinguish itself in any way from one of those tantalizing dream-fabrications in which the dreamer asks himself if this be delusion or reality and is driven to decide for the latter, only to wake up after all in the end. . . . He paced through the half-empty streets with his head inclined against the wind, moving as though in his sleep in the direction of the hotel, the first hotel in the town, where he meant to sleep. A bow-legged man, with a pole at the end of which burned a tiny fire, walked before him with a rolling, seafaring gait and lighted the gas-lamps.

What was at the bottom of this? What was it burning darkly beneath the ashes of his fatigue, refusing to burst out into a clear blaze? Hush, hush, only no talk. Only don't make words!

He would have liked to go on so, for a long time, in the wind, through the dusky, dreamily familiar streets—but everything was so little and close together here. You reached your goal at once.

In the upper town there were arc-lamps, just lighted. There was the hotel with the two black lions in front of it; he had been afraid of them as a child. And there they were, still looking at each other as though they were about to sneeze; only they seemed to have grown much smaller. Tonio Kröger passed between them into the hotel.

As he came on foot, he was received with no great ceremony. There was a porter, and a lordly gentleman dressed in black, to do the honors; the latter, shoving back his cuffs with his little fingers, measured him from the crown of his head to the soles of his boots, obviously with intent to place him, to assign him to his proper category socially and hierarchically speaking and then mete out the suitable degree of courtesy. He seemed not to come to any clear decision and compromised on a moderate display of politeness. A mild-mannered waiter with yellow-white side-whiskers, in a dress suit shiny with age, and rosettes on his soundless shoes, led him up two flights into a clean old room furnished in patriarchal style. Its windows gave on a twilt view of courts and gables, very medieval and picturesque, with the fantastic bulk of the old church close by. Tonio Kröger stood awhile before this window; then he sat down on the wide sofa, crossed his arms, drew down his brows, and whistled to himself.

Lights were brought, and his baggage came up. The mild-mannered waiter laid the hotel register on the table, and Tonio Kröger, his head on one side, scrawled something on it that might be taken for a name, a station, and a place of origin. Then he ordered supper and went on gazing into space from his sofa-corner. When it stood before him he let it wait long untouched, then took a few bites and walked up and down an hour in his room, stopping from time to time and closing his eyes. Then he very slowly undressed and went to bed. He slept long and had curiously confused and ardent dreams.

It was broad day when he woke. Hastily he recalled where he was and got up to draw the curtains; the pale-blue sky, already with a hint of autumn, was streaked with frayed and tattered cloud; still, above his native city the sun was shining.

He spent more care than usual upon his toilette, washed and shaved and made himself fresh and immaculate as though about to call upon some smart family where a well-dressed and flawless appearance was *de rigueur;* and while occupied in this wise he listened to the anxious beating of his heart.

How bright it was outside! He would have liked better a twilight air like yesterday's, instead of passing through the streets in the broad sunlight, under everybody's eye. Would he meet people he knew, be stopped and questioned and have to submit to be asked how he had spent the last thirteen years? No, thank goodness, he was known to nobody here; even if anybody remembered him, it was unlikely he would be recognized—for certainly he had changed in the meantime! He surveyed himself in the glass and felt a sudden sense of security behind his mask, behind his work-worn face, that was older than his years. . . . He sent for breakfast, and after that he went out; he passed under the disdainful eye of the porter and the gentleman in black, through the vestibule and between the two lions, and so into the street.

Where was he going? He scarcely knew. It was the same yesterday. Hardly was he in the midst of this long-familiar scene, this stately conglomeration of gables, turrets, arcades, and fountains, hardly did he feel once more the wind in his face, that strong current wafting a faint and pungent aroma from far-off dreams, than the same mistiness laid itself like a veil about his senses. . . . The muscles of his face relaxed, and he looked at men and things with a look grown suddenly calm. Perhaps right there, on that street corner, he might wake up after all. . . .

Where was he going? It seemed to him the direction he took had a connection with his sad and strangely rueful dreams of the night. . . . He went to Market Square, under the vaulted arches of the Rathaus, where the butchers were weighing out their wares red-handed, where the tall old Gothic fountain stood with its manifold spires. He pushed in front of a house, a plain narrow building, like many another, with a fretted baroque gable; stood there lost in contemplation. He read the plate on the door, his eyes rested a little while on each of the windows. Then he slowly turned away.

Where did he go? Towards home. But he took a roundabout way outside the walls—for he had plenty of time. He went over the Millwall and over the Holstenwall, clutching his hat, for the wind was rushing and moaning through the trees. He left the wall near the station, where he saw a train puffing busily past, idly counted the coaches, and looked after the man who sat perched upon the last. In the Lindenplatz he stopped at one of the pretty villas, peered long into the garden and up at the windows, lastly conceived the idea of swinging the gate to and fro upon its hinges till it creaked. Then he looked awhile at his moist, rust-stained hand and went on, went through the squat old gate, along the harbor, and up the steep, windy street to his parents' house.

It stood aloof from its neighbors, its gable towering above them: gray and somber, as it had stood these three hundred years; and Tonio Kröger read the pious, half-illegible motto above the entrance. Then he drew a long breath and went in.

His heart gave a throb of fear, lest his father might come out of one of the doors on the ground floor, in his office coat, with the pen behind his ear, and take him to task for his excesses. He would have found the reproach quite in order; but he got past unchidden. The inner door was ajar, which appeared to him reprehensible, though at the same time he felt as one does in certain broken dreams, where obstacles melt away of themselves, and one presses onward in marvelous favor with fortune. The wide entry, paved with great square flags, echoed to his tread. Opposite the silent kitchen was the curious projecting structure, of rough boards, but cleanly varnished, that had been the servants' quarters. It was quite high up and could only be reached by a sort of ladder from the entry. But the great cupboards and carven presses were gone. The son of the house climbed the majestic staircase, with his hand on the white-enamelled, fretwork balustrade. At each step he lifted his hand, and put it down again with the next as though testing whether he could call back his ancient familiarity with the stout old railing. . . . But at the landing of the entresol he stopped. For on the entrance door was a white plate; and on it in black letters he read: "Public Library."

"Public Library?" thought Tonio Kröger. What were either literature or the public doing here? He knocked . . . heard a "Come in," and obeying it with gloomy suspense gazed upon a scene of most unhappy alteration.

The story was three rooms deep, and all the doors stood open. The walls were covered nearly all the way up with long rows of books in uniform bindings, standing in dark-colored bookcases. In each room a poor creature of a man sat writing behind a sort of counter. The farthest two just turned their heads, but the nearest got up in haste and, leaning with both hands on the table, stuck out his head, pursed his lips, lifted his brows, and looked at the visitor with eagerly blinking eyes.

"I beg pardon," said Tonio Kröger without turning his eyes from the book-shelves. "I am a stranger here, seeing the sights. So this is your Public Library? May I examine your collection a little?"

"Certainly, with pleasure," said the official, blinking still more violently. "It is open to everybody. . . . Pray look about you. Should you care for a catalogue?"

"No, thanks," answered Tonio Kröger. "I shall soon find my way about." And he began to move slowly along the walls, with the appearance of studying the rows of books. After a while he took down a volume, opened it, and posted himself at the window.

This was the breakfast-room. They had eaten here in the morning instead of in the big dining room upstairs, with its white statues of gods and goddesses standing out against the blue walls. . . . Beyond there had been a bedroom, where his father's mother had died—only after a long struggle, old as she was, for she had been of a pleasure-loving nature and clung to life. And his father too had drawn his last breath in the same room: that tall, correct, slightly melancholy and pensive gentleman with the wild flower in his buttonhole. . . . Tonio had sat at the foot of his death-bed, quite given over to unutterable feelings of love and grief. His mother had knelt at the bedside, his lovely, fiery mother, dissolved in hot tears; and after that she had withdrawn with her artist into the far blue south. . . . And beyond still, the small third room, likewise full of books and presided over by a shabby man—that had been for years on end his own. Thither he had come after school and a walk—like today's; against that wall his table had stood with the drawer where he had kept his clumsy, heartfelt attempts at verse. . . . The walnut tree . . . a pang went through him. He gave a sidewise glance out at the window. The garden lay desolate, but there stood the old walnut tree where it used to stand, groaning and creaking heavily in the wind. And Tonio Kröger let his gaze fall upon the book he had in his hands, an excellent piece of work, and very familiar. He followed the black lines of print, the paragraphs, the flow of words that flowed with so much art, mounting in the ardor of creation to a certain climax and effect and then as artfully breaking off. . . .

"Yes, that was well done," he said; put back the book and

turned away. Then he saw that the functionary still stood bold upright, blinking with a mingled expression of zeal and misgiving.

"A capital collection, I see," said Tonio Kröger. "I have already quite a good idea of it. Much obliged to you. Good-bye." He went out; but it was a poor exit, and he felt sure the official would stand there perturbed and blinking for several minutes.

He felt no desire for further researches. He had been home. Strangers were living upstairs in the large rooms behind the pillared hall; the top of the stairs was shut off by a glass door which used not to be there, and on the door was a plate. He went away, down the steps, across the echoing corridor, and left his parental home. He sought a restaurant, sat down in a corner, and brooded over a heavy, greasy meal. Then he returned to his hotel.

"I am leaving," he said to the fine gentleman in black. "This afternoon." And he asked for his bill, and for a carriage to take him down to the harbor where he should take the boat for Copenhagen. Then he went up to his room and sat there stiff and still, with his cheek on his hand, looking down on the table before him with absent eyes. Later he paid his bill and packed his things. At the appointed hour the carriage was announced and Tonio Kröger went down in travel array.

At the foot of the stairs the gentleman in black was waiting.

"Beg pardon," he said, shoving back his cuffs with his little fingers . . . "Beg pardon, but we must detain you just a moment. Herr Seehaase, the proprietor, would like to exchange two words with you. A matter of form . . . He is back there . . . If you will have the goodness to step this way . . . It is *only* Herr Seehaase, the proprietor."

And he ushered Tonio Kröger into the background of the vestibule . . . There, in fact, stood Herr Seehaase. Tonio Kröger recognized him from old time. He was small, fat, and bowlegged. His shaven side-whisker was white, but he wore the same old low-cut dress coat and little velvet cap embroidered in green. He was not alone. Beside him, at a little high desk fastened into the wall, stood a policeman in a helmet, his gloved right hand resting on a document in colored inks; he turned towards Tonio Kröger with his honest, soldierly face as though he expected Tonio to sink into the earth at his glance.

Tonio Kröger looked at the two and confined himself to waiting.

"You came from Munich?" the policeman asked at length in a heavy, good-natured voice.

Tonio Kröger said he had.

"You are going to Copenhagen?"

"Yes, I am on the way to a Danish seashore resort."

"Seashore resort? Well, you must produce your papers," said the policeman. He uttered the last word with great satisfaction.

"Papers . . . ?" He had no papers. He drew out his pocket-book and looked into it; but aside from notes there was nothing there but some proof-sheets of a story which he had taken along to finish reading. He hated relations with officials and had never got himself a passport.

"I am sorry," he said, "but I don't travel with papers."

"Ah!" said the policeman. "And what might be your name?"

Tonio answered.

"Is that a fact?" asked the policeman, suddenly erect, and expanding his nostrils as wide as he could . . .

"Yes, that is a fact," answered Tonio Kröger.

"And what are you, anyhow?"

Tonio Kröger gulped and gave the name of his profession in a firm voice. Herr Seehaase lifted his head and looked him curiously in the face.

"H'm," said the policeman. "And you give out that you are not identical with an individdle named"—he said "individdle" and then, referring to his document in colored inks, spelled out an involved, fantastic name which mingled all the sounds of all races—Tonio Kröger forgot it the next minute—"of unknown parentage and unspecified means," he went on, "wanted by the Munich police for various shady transactions, and probably in flight towards Denmark?"

"Yes, I give out all that and more," said Tonio Kröger, wriggling his shoulders. The gesture made a certain impression.

"What? Oh, yes, of course," said the policeman. "You say you can't show any papers—"

Herr Seehaase threw himself into the breach.

"It is only a formality," he said pacifically, "nothing else. You must bear in mind the official is only doing his duty. If you could only identify yourself somehow—some document . . ."

They were all silent. Should he make an end of the business, by revealing to Herr Seehaase that he was no swindler without specified means, no gypsy in a green wagon, but the son of the late Consul Kröger, a member of the Kröger family? No, he felt no desire to do that. After all, were not these guardians of civic order within their right? He even agreed with them—up to a point. He shrugged his shoulders and kept quiet.

"What have you got, then?" asked the policeman. "In your portfoly, I mean?"

"Here? Nothing. Just a proof-sheet," answered Tonio Kröger.

"Proof-sheet? What's that? Let's see it."

And Tonio Kröger handed over his work. The policeman spread it out on the shelf and began reading. Herr Seehaase drew up and shared it with him. Tonio Kröger looked over their shoulders to see what they read. It was a good moment, a little effect he had worked out to a perfection. He had a sense of self-satisfaction.

"You see," he said, "there is my name. I wrote it, and it is going to be published, you understand."

"All right, that will answer," said Herr Seehaase with decision, gathered up the sheets and gave them back. "That will have to answer, Peterson," he repeated crisply, shutting his eyes and shaking his head as though to see and hear no more. "We must not keep the gentleman any longer. The carriage is waiting. I implore you to pardon this little inconvenience, sir. The officer has only done his duty, but I told him at once he was on the wrong track . . ."

"Indeed!" thought Tonio Kröger.

The officer seemed still to have his doubts; he muttered something else about individdle and document. But Herr Seehaase, overflowing with regrets, led his guest through the vestibule, accompanied him past the two lions to the carriage, and himself, with many respectful bows, closed the door upon him. And then the funny, high, wide old cab rolled and rattled and bumped down the steep, narrow street to the quay.

And such was the manner of Tonio Kröger's visit to his ancestral home.

Night fell and the moon swam up with silver gleam as Tonio Kröger's boat reached the open sea. He stood at the prow wrapped in his cloak against a mounting wind, and looked beneath into the dark going and coming of the waves as they hovered and swayed and came on, to meet with a clap and shoot erratically away in a bright gush of foam.

He was lulled in a mood of still enchantment. The episode at the hotel, their wanting to arrest him for a swindler in his own home, had cast him down a little, even although he found it quite in order—in a certain way. But after he came on board he had watched, as he used to do as a boy with his father, the lading of goods into the deep bowels of the boat, amid shouts of mingled Danish and Plattdeutsch; not only boxes and bales, but also a Bengal tiger and a polar bear were lowered in cages with stout iron bars. They had probably come from Hamburg and were destined for a Danish menagerie. He had enjoyed these distractions. And as the boat glided along between flat river-banks he quite forgot Officer Peterson's inquisition; while all the rest—his sweet, sad, rueful dreams of the night before, the walk he had taken, the walnut tree—had welled up again in his soul. The sea opened out and he saw in the distance the beach where he as a lad had been let to listen to the ocean's summer dreams; saw the flashing of the lighthouse tower and the lights of the Kurhaus where he and his parents had lived . . . The Baltic! He bent his head to the strong salt wind; it came sweeping on, it enfolded him, made him faintly giddy and a little deaf; and in that mild confusion of the senses all memory of evil, of anguish and error, effort and exertion of the will, sank away into joyous oblivion and were gone. The roaring, foaming, flapping, and slapping all about him came to his ears like the groan and rustle of an old walnut tree, the creaking of a garden gate . . . More and more the darkness came on.

"The stars! Oh, my Lord, look at the stars!" a voice suddenly said, with a heavy singsong accent that seemed to come out of the inside of a tun. He recognized it. It belonged to a young man with red-blond hair who had been Tonio Kröger's neighbor at dinner in the salon. His dress was very simple, his eyes were red, and he had the moist and chilly look of a person who has just bathed. With nervous and self-conscious movements he had taken unto himself an astonishing quantity of lobster omelet. Now he leaned on the rail beside Tonio Kröger and looked up at the skies, holding his chin between thumb and forefinger. Beyond a doubt he was in one of those rare and festal and edifying moods that cause the barriers between man and man to fall; when the heart opens even to the stranger, and the mouth utters that which otherwise it would blush to speak . . .

"Look, by dear sir, just look at the stars. There they stand and glitter, by goodness, the whole sky is full of theb! And I ask you, when you stand and look up at theb, and realize that bany of theb are a huddred tibes larger thad the earth, how does it bake you feel? Yes, we had idvehted the telegraph and the telephode and all the triuphs of our bodern tibes. But whed we look up there, after all we have to recogdize and uhderstad that we are worbs, biserable worbs, and dothing else. Ab I right, sir, or ab I wrog? Yes, we are worbs," he answered himself, and nodded meekly and abjectly in the direction of the firmament.

"Ah, no, he has no literature in his belly," thought Tonio Kröger. And he recalled something he had lately read, an essay by a famous French writer on cosmological and psychological philosophies, a very delightful *causerie.*

He made some sort of reply to the young man's feeling remarks, and they went on talking, leaning over the rail, and looking into the night with its movement and fitful lights. The young man, it seemed, was a Hamburg merchant on his holiday.

"Y'ought to travel to Copedhagen on the boat, thigks I, and so here I ab, and so far it's been fide. But they shouldn't have given us the lobster obelet, sir, for it's going to be storby—the captain said so hibself—and that's do joke with indigestible food like that in your stobach . . ."

Tonio Kröger listened to all this engaging artlessness and was privately drawn to it.

"Yes," he said, "all the food up here is too heavy. It makes one lazy and melancholy."

"Belancholy?" repeated the young man, and looked at him, taken aback. Then he asked, suddenly: "You are a stradger up here, sir?"

"Yes, I come from a long way off," answered Tonio Kröger vaguely, waving his arm.

"But you're right," said the youth; "Lord kdows you are right about the belancholy. I am dearly always belancholy, but specially on evedings like this when there are stars in the sky." And he supported his chin again with thumb and forefinger.

"Surely this man writes verses," thought Tonio Kröger; "business man's verses, full of deep feeling and single-mindedness."

Evening drew on. The wind had grown so violent as to prevent them from talking. So they thought they would sleep a bit, and wished each other good night.

Tonio Kröger stretched himself out on the narrow cabin bed, but he found no repose. The strong wind with its sharp tang had power to rouse him; he was strangely restless with sweet anticipations. Also he was violently sick with the motion of the ship as she glided down a steep mountain of wave and her screw vibrated as in agony, free of the water. He put on all his clothes again and went up to the deck.

Clouds raced across the moon. The sea danced. It did not come on in full-bodied, regular waves; but far out in the pale and flickering light the water was lashed, torn, and tumbled; leaped upward with great licking flames; hung in jagged and fantastic shapes above dizzy abysses, where the foam seemed to be tossed by the playful strength of colossal arms and flung upward in all directions. The ship had a heavy passage; she lurched and stamped and groaned through the welter; and far down in her bowels the tiger and the polar bear voiced their acute discomfort. A man in an oilskin, with the hood drawn over his head and a lantern strapped to his chest, went straddling painfully up and down the deck. And at the stern, leaning far out, stood the young man from Hamburg suffering the worst. "Lord!" he said in a hollow, quavering voice, when he saw Tonio Kröger. "Look at the uproar of the elebents, sir!" But he could say no more—he was obliged to turn hastily away.

Tonio Kröger clutched at a taut rope and looked abroad into the arrogance of the elements. His exultation outvied storm and wave; within himself he chanted a song to the sea, instinct with love of her: "O thou wild friend of my youth, Once more I behold thee—" But it got no further; he did not finish it. It was not fated to receive a final form nor in tranquility to be welded to a perfect whole. For his heart was too full . . .

Long he stood; then stretched himself out on a bench by the pilot-house and looked up at the sky, where stars were flickering. He even slept a little. And when the cold foam splashed his face, it seemed in his half-dreams like a caress.

Perpendicular chalk-cliffs, ghostly in the moonlight came in sight. They were nearing the island of Möen. Then sleep came again, broken by salty showers of spray that bit into his face and made it stiff . . . When he really roused, it was broad day, fresh and palest gray, and the sea had gone down. At breakfast he saw the young man from Hamburg again, who blushed rosy-red for shame of the poetic indiscretions he had been betrayed into by the dark, ruffled up his little red-blond moustache with all five fingers, and called out a brisk and soldierly good-morning—after that he studiously avoided him.

And Tonio Kröger landed in Denmark. He arrived in Copenhagen, gave tips to everybody who laid claim to them, took a room at a hotel, and roamed the city for three days with an open guide-book and the air of an intelligent foreigner bent on improving his mind. He looked at the king's New Market and the "Horse" in the middle of it, gazed respectfully up the columns of the Frauenkirch, stood long before Thorwaldsen's noble and beautiful statuary, climbed the round tower, visited castles, and spent two lively evenings in the Tivoli. But all this was not exactly what he saw.

The doors of the houses—so like those in his native town, with open-work gables of baroque shape—bore names known to him of old; names that had a tender and precious quality, and withal in their syllables an accent of plaintive reproach, of repining after the lost and gone. He walked, he gazed, drawing deep, lingering draughts of moist sea air; and everywhere he saw eyes as blue, hair as blond, faces as familiar, as those that had visited his rueful dreams the night he had spent in his native town. There in the open street it befell him that a glance, a ringing word, a sudden laugh would pierce him to his marrow.

He could not stand the bustling city for long. A restlessness, half memory and half hope, half foolish and half sweet, possessed him; he was moved to drop the rôle of ardently inquiring tourist and lie somewhere, quite quietly, on a beach. So he took ship once more and traveled under a cloudy sky, over a black water, northwards along the coast of Seeland towards Helsingör. Thence he drove, at once, by carriage, for three-quarters of an hour, along and above the sea, reaching at length his ultimate goal, the little white "bath-hotel!" with green blinds. It stood surrounded by a settlement of cottages, and its shingled turret tower looked out on the beach and the Swedish coast. Here he left the carriage, took possession of the light room they had ready for him, filled shelves and presses with his kit, and prepared to stop awhile.

It was well on in September; not many guests were left in Aalsgard. Meals were served on the ground-floor, in the great beamed dining-room, whose lofty windows led out upon the veranda and the sea. The landlady presided, an elderly spinster with white hair and faded eyes, a faint color in her cheek and a feeble twittering voice. She was forever arranging her red hands to look well upon the tablecloth. There was a short-necked old gentleman, quite blue in the face, with a gray sailor beard; a fish-dealer he was, from the capital, and strong at the German. He seemed entirely congested and inclined to apoplexy; breathed in short gasps, kept putting his beringed first finger to one nostril, and snorting violently to get a passage of air through the other. Notwithstanding, he addressed himself constantly to the whisky-bottle, which stood at his place at luncheon and dinner, and breakfast as well. Besides him the company consisted only of three tall American youths with their governor or tutor, who kept adjusting his glasses in unbroken silence. All day long he played football with his charges, who had narrow, taciturn faces and reddish-yellow hair parted in the middle. "Please pass the *wurst,"* said one. "That's not *wurst,* it's *schinken,"* said the other, and this was the extent of their conversation, as the rest of the time they sat there dumb, drinking hot water.

Tonio Kröger could have wished himself no better table-companions. He revelled in the peace and quiet, listened to the Danish palatals, the clear and the clouded vowels in which the fish-dealer and the landlady desultorily conversed; modestly exchanged views with the fish-dealer on the state of the barometer, and then left the table to go through the veranda and onto the beach once more, where he had already spent long, long morning hours.

Sometimes it was still and summery there. The sea lay idle and smooth, in stripes of blue and russet and bottle-green, played all across with glittering silvery lights. The seaweed shrivelled in the sun, and the jelly-fish lay steaming. There was a faintly stagnant smell and a whiff of tar from the fishing-boat against which Tonio Kröger leaned, so standing that he had before his eyes not the Swedish coast but the open horizon, and in his face the pure, fresh breath of the softly breathing sea.

Then gray, stormy days would come. The waves lowered their heads like bulls and charged against the beach; they ran and ramped high up the sands and left them strewn with shining wet sea-grass, driftwood, and mussels. All abroad beneath an overcast sky extended ranges of billows, and between them foaming valleys palely green; but above the spot where the sun hung behind the cloud, a patch like white velvet lay on the sea.

Tonio Kröger stood wrapped in wind and tumult, sunk in the continual dull, drowsy uproar that he loved. When he turned away it seemed suddenly warm and silent all about him. But he was never unconscious of the sea at his back; it called, it lured, it beckoned him. And he smiled.

He went landward, by lonely meadow-paths, and was swallowed up in the beech-groves that clothed the rolling landscape near and far. Here he sat down on the moss, against a tree, and gazed at the strip of water he could see between the trunks. Sometimes the sound of surf came on the wind—a noise like boards collapsing at a distance. And from the treetops over his head a cawing—hoarse, desolate, forlorn. He held a book on his knee, but did not read a line. He enjoyed profound forgetfulness, hovered disembodied above space and time; only now and again his heart would contract with a fugitive pain, a stab of longing and regret, into whose origin he was too lazy to inquire.

Thus passed some days. He could not have said how many and had no desire to know. But then came one on which something happened; happened while the sun stood in the sky and people were about; and Tonio Kröger, even, felt no vast surprise.

The very opening of the day had been rare and festal. Tonio Kröger woke early and suddenly from his sleep, with a vague and exquisite alarm; he seemed to be looking at a miracle, a magic illumination. His room had a glass door and balcony facing the sound: a thin white gauze curtain divided it into living- and sleeping-quarters, both hung with delicately tinted paper and furnished with an airy good taste that gave them a sunny and friendly look. But now to his sleep-drunken eyes it lay bathed in a serene and roseate light, an unearthly brightness that gilded walls and furniture and turned the gauze curtain to radiant pink cloud. Tonio Kröger did not at once understand. Not until he stood at the glass door and looked out did he realize that this was the sunrise.

For several days there had been clouds and rain; but now the sky was like a piece of pale-blue silk, spanned shimmering above sea and land, and shot with light from red and golden clouds. The sun's disk rose in splendor from a crisply glittering sea that seemed to quiver and burn beneath it. So began the day. In a joyous daze Tonio Kröger flung on his clothes, and breakfasting in the veranda before everybody else, swam from the little wooden bath-house some distance out into the sound, then walked for an hour along the beach. When he came back, several omnibuses were before the door, and from the dining room he could see people in the parlor next door where the piano was, in the veranda, and on the terrace in front; quantities of people sitting at little tables enjoying beer and sandwiches amid lively discourse. There were whole families, there were old and young, there were even a few children.

At second breakfast—the table was heavily laden with cold viands, roast, pickled, and smoked—Tonio Kröger inquired what was going on.

"Guests," said the fish-dealer. "Tourists and ball-guests from Helsingör. Lord help us, we shall get no sleep this night! There will be dancing and music, and I fear me it will keep up till late. It is a family reunion, a sort of celebration and excursion combined; they all subscribe to it and take advantage of the good weather. They came by boat and bus and they are having breakfast. After that they go on with their drive, but at night they will all come back for a dance here in the hall. Yes, damn it, you'll see we shan't get a wink of sleep."

"Oh, it will be a pleasant change," said Tonio Kröger.

After that there was nothing more said for some time. The landlady arranged her red fingers on the cloth, the fish-dealer blew through his nostril, the Americans drank hot water and made long faces.

Then all at once a thing came to pass: *Hans Hansen and Ingeborg Holm walked through the room.*

Tonio Kröger, pleasantly fatigued after his swim and rapid walk, was leaning back in his chair and eating smoked salmon on toast; he sat facing the veranda and the ocean. All at once the door opened, and the two entered hand-in-hand—calm and unhurried. Ingeborg, blonde Inge, was dressed just as she used to be at Herr Knaak's dancing-class. The light flowered frock reached down to her ankles, and it had a tulle fichu draped with a pointed opening that left her soft throat free. Her hat hung by its ribbons over her arm. She, perhaps, was a little more grown up than she used to be, and her wonderful plait of hair was wound round her head; but Hans Hansen was the same as ever. He wore his sailor overcoat with gilt buttons, and his wide blue sailor collar lay across his shoulders and back; the sailor cap with its short ribbons he was dangling carelessly in his hand. Ingeborg's narrow eyes were turned away; perhaps she felt shy before the company at table. But Hans Hansen turned his head straight towards them, and measured one after another defiantly with his steel-blue eyes; challengingly, with a sort of contempt. He even dropped Ingeborg's hand and swung his cap harder than ever, to show what manner of man he was. Thus the two, against the silent, blue-dyed sea, measured the length of the room and passed through the opposite door into the parlor.

This was at half past eleven in the morning. While the guests of the house were still at table the company in the veranda broke up and went away by the side-door. No one else came into the dining-room. The guests could hear them laughing and joking as they got into the omnibuses, which rumbled away one by one . . . "So they are coming back?" asked Tonio Kröger.

"That they are," said the fish-dealer. "More's the pity. They have ordered music, let me tell you—and my room is right above the dining-room."

"Oh well, it's a pleasant change," repeated Tonio Kröger. Then he got up and went away.

That day he spent as he had the others, on the beach and in the wood, holding a book on his knee and blinking into the sun. He had but one thought; they were coming back to have a dance in the hall, the fish-dealer had promised they would; and he did nothing but be glad of this, with a sweet and timorous gladness such as he had not felt through all these long dead years. Once he happened, by some chance association, to think of his friend Adalbert, the novelist, the man who had known what he wanted and betaken himself to the café to get away from the spring. Tonio Kröger shrugged his shoulders at the thought of him.

Luncheon was served earlier than usual, also supper, which they ate in the parlor because the dinning-room was being got ready for the ball, and the whole house flung in disorder for the occasion. It grew dark; Tonio Kröger, sitting in his room, heard on the road and in the house the sounds of approaching festivity. The picnickers were coming back; from Helsingör, by bicycle and carriage, new guests were arriving; a fiddle and a nasal clarinet might be heard practising down in the dining-room. Everything promised a brilliant ball . . .

Now the little orchestra struck up a march; he could hear the notes, faint but lively. The dancing opened with a polonaise. Tonio Kröger sat for a while and listened. But when he heard the march-tune go over into a waltz, he got up and slipped noiselessly out of his room.

From his corridor it was possible to go by the side stairs to the side entrance of the hotel, and thence to the veranda without passing through a room. He took this route, softly and stealthily as though on forbidden paths, feeling along through the dark, relentlessly drawn by this stupid jigging music, that now came up to him loud and clear.

The veranda was empty and dim, but the glass door stood open into the hall, where shone two large oil lamps, furnished with bright reflectors. Thither he stole on soft feet; and his skin prickled with the thievish pleasure of standing unseen in the dark and spying on the dancers there in the brightly lighted room. Quickly and eagerly he glanced about for the two whom he sought . . .

Even though the ball was only half an hour old, the merriment seemed in full swing; however, the guests had come hither already warm and merry, after a whole day of carefree, happy companionship. By bending forward a little, Tonio Kröger could see into the parlor from where he was. Several old gentlemen sat there smoking, drinking, and playing cards; others were with their wives on the plush-upholstered chairs in the foreground watching the dance. They sat with their knees apart and their hands resting on them, puffing out their cheeks with a prosperous air; the mothers, with bonnets perched on their parted hair, with their hands folded over their stomachs and their heads on one side, gazed into the whirl of dancers. A platform had been erected on the long side of the hall, and on it the musicians were doing their utmost. There was even a trumpet, that blew with a certain caution, as though afraid of its own voice, and yet after all kept breaking and cracking. Couples were dipping and circling about, others walked arm-in-arm up and down the room. No one wore ballroom clothes; they were dressed as for an outing in the summertime; the men in countrified suits which were obviously their Sunday wear; the girls in light-colored frocks with bunches of wild-flowers in their bodices. Even a few children were there, dancing with each other in their own way, even after the music stopped. There was a long-legged man in a coat with a little swallow-tail, a provincial lion with an eye-glass and frizzed hair, a post-office clerk or some such thing; he was like a comic figure stepped bodily out of a Danish novel; and he seemed to be the leader and manager of the ball. He was everywhere at once, bustling, perspiring, officious, utterly absorbed; setting down his feet, in shiny, pointed, military half-boots, in a very artificial and involved manner, toes first; waving his arms to issue an order, clapping his hands for the music to begin; here, there, and everywhere, and glancing over his shoulder in pride at his great bow of office, the streamers of which fluttered grandly in his rear.

Yes, there they were, those two, who had gone by Tonio Kröger in the broad light of day; he saw them again—with a joyful start he recognized them almost at the same moment. Here was Hans Hansen by the door; his legs apart, a little bent over, he was eating with circumspection a large piece of sponge-cake, holding his hand cupwise under his chin to catch the crumbs. And there by the wall sat Ingeborg Holm, Inge the fair, the post-office clerk was just mincing up to her with an exaggerated bow and asking her to dance. He laid one hand on his back and gracefully shoved the other into his bosom. But she was shaking her head in token that she was a little out of breath and must rest awhile, whereat the post-office clerk sat down by her side.

Tonio Kröger looked at them both, these two for whom he had in time past suffered love—at Hans and Ingeborg. They were Hans and Ingeborg not so much by virtue of individual traits and similarity of costume as by similarity of race and type. This was the blond, fair-haired breed of the steel-blue eyes, which stood to him for the pure, the blithe, the untroubled in life; for a virginal aloofness that was at once both simple and full of pride . . . He looked at them. Hans Hansen was standing there in his sailor suit, lively and well built as ever, broad in the shoulders and narrow in the hips; Ingeborg was laughing and tossing her head in a certain high-spirited way she had; she carried her hand, a schoolgirl hand, not at all slender, not at all particularly aristocratic, to the back of her head in a certain manner so that the thin sleeve fell away from her elbow—and suddenly such a pang of homesickness shook his breast that involuntarily he drew farther back into the darkness, lest someone might see his features twitch.

"Had I forgotten you?" he asked. "No, never. Not thee, Hans, not thee, Inge the fair! It was always you I worked for; when I heard applause I always stole a look to see if you were there . . . Did you read *Don Carlos,* Hans Hansen, as you promised me at the garden gate? No, don't read it! I do not ask it any more. What have you to do with a king who weeps for loneliness? You must not cloud your clear eyes or make them dreamy and dim by peering into melancholy poetry . . . To be like you! To begin again, to grow up like you, regular like you, simple and normal and cheerful, in conformity and understanding with God and man, beloved of the innocent and happy. To take you, Ingeborg Holm, to wife, and have a son like you, Hans Hansen—to live free from the curse of knowledge and the torment of creation, live and praise God in blessed mediocrity! Begin again? But it would do no good. It would turn out the same—everything would turn out the same as it did before. For some go of necessity astray, because for them there is no such thing as a right path."

The music ceased; there was a pause in which refreshments were handed round. The post-office assistant tripped about in person with a trayful of herring salad and served the ladies; but before Ingeborg Holm he even went down on one knee as he passed her the dish, and she blushed for pleasure.

But now those within began to be aware of a spectator behind the glass door; some of the flushed and pretty faces turned to measure him with hostile glances; but he stood his ground. Ingeborg and Hans looked at him too, at almost the same time, both with that utter indifference in their eyes that looks so like contempt. And he was conscious too of a gaze resting on him from a different quarter; turned his head and met with his own the eyes that had sought him out. A girl stood not far off, with a fine, pale little face—he had already noticed her. She had not danced much, she had few partners, and he had seen her sitting there against the wall, her lips closed in a bitter line. She was standing alone now too; her dress was a thin light stuff, like the others, but beneath the transparent frock her shouders showed angular and poor, and the thin neck was thrust down so deep between those meager shoulders that as she stood there motionless she might almost be thought a little deformed. She was holding her hands in their thin mitts across her flat breast, with the finger-tips touching; her head was drooped, yet she was looking up at Tonio Kröger with black, swimming eyes. He turned away . . .

Here, quite close to him, were Ingeborg and Hans. He had sat down beside her—she was perhaps his sister—and they ate and drank together, surrounded by other rosy-cheeked folk; they chattered and made merry, called to each other in ringing voices, and laughed aloud. Why could he not go up and speak to them? Make some trivial remark to him or her, to which they might at least answer with a smile? It would make him happy—he longed to do it; he would go back more satisfied to his room if he might feel he had established a little contact with them. He thought out what he might say; but he had not the courage to say it. Yes, this too was just as it had been: they would not understand him, they would listen like strangers to anything he was able to say. For their speech was not his speech.

It seemed the dance was about to begin again. The leader developed a comprehensive activity. He dashed hither and thither, adjuring everybody to get partners; helped the waiters to push chairs and glasses out of the way, gave orders to the musicians, even took some awkward people by the shoulders and shoved them aside . . . What was coming? They formed squares of four couples each . . . A frightful memory brought the color to Tonio Kröger's cheeks. They were forming for a quadrille.

The music struck up, the couples bowed and crossed over. The leader called off; he called off—Heaven save us—in French! And pronounced the nasals with great distinction. Ingeborg Holm danced close by, in the set nearest the glass door. She moved to and fro before him, forwards and back, pacing and turning; he caught a waft from her hair or the thin stuff of her frock, and it made him close his eyes with the old, familiar feeling, the fragrance and bitter-sweet enchantment he had faintly felt in all these days, that now filled him utterly with irresistible sweetness. And what was the feeling? Longing, tenderness? Envy? Self-contempt? . . . *Moulinet des dames!* "Did you laugh, Ingeborg the blonde, did you laugh at me when I disgraced myself by dancing the *moulinet?* And would you still laugh today even after I have become something like a famous man? Yes, that you would, and you would be right to laugh. Even if I in my own person had written the nine symphonies and *The World as Will and Idea* and painted the Last Judgment, you would still be eternally right to laugh . . ." As he looked at her he thought of a line of verse once so familiar to him, now long forgotten: "I would sleep, but thou must dance." How well he knew it, that melancholy northern mood it evoked—its heavy inarticulateness. To sleep . . . To long to be allowed to live the life of simple feeling, to rest sweetly and passively in feeling alone, without compulsion to act and achieve—and yet to be forced to dance, dance the cruel and perilous sword-dance of art; without even being allowed to forget the melancholy conflict within oneself; to be forced to dance, the while one loved . . .

A sudden wild extravagance had come over the scene. The sets had broken up, the quadrille was being succeeded by a galop, and all the couples were leaping and gliding about. They flew past Tonio Kröger to a maddeningly quick tempo, crossing, advancing, retreating, with quick, breathless laughter. A couple came rushing and circling towards Tonio Kröger; the girl had a pale, refined face and lean, high shoulders. Suddenly, directly in front of him, they tripped and slipped and stumbled . . . The pale girl fell, so hard and violently it almost looked dangerous;

and her partner with her. He must have hurt himself badly, for he quite forgot her, and, half rising, began to rub his knee and grimace; while she, quite dazed, it seemed, lay still on the floor. Then Tonio Kröger came forward, took her gently by the arms, and lifted her up. She looked dazed, bewildered, wretched; then suddenly her delicate face flushed pink.

"Tak, O, mange tak!" she said, and gazed up at him with dark, swimming eyes.

"You should not dance any more, Fräulein," he said gently. Once more he looked round at *them,* at Ingeborg and Hans, and then he went out, left the ball and the veranda and returned to his own room.

He was exhausted with jealousy, worn out with the gaiety in which he had had no part. Just the same, just the same as it had always been. Always with burning cheeks he had stood in his dark corner and suffered for you, you blond, you living, you happy ones! And then quite simply gone away. Somebody *must* come now! Ingeborg *must* notice he had gone, must slip after him, lay a hand on his shoulder and say: "Come back and be happy. I love you!" But she came not at all. No, such things did not happen. Yes, all was as it had been, and he too was happy, just as he had been. For his heart was alive. But between the past and this present what had happened to make him become that which he now was? Icy desolation, solitude: mind, and art, forsooth!

He undressed, lay down, put out the light. Two names he whispered into his pillow, the few chaste northern syllables that meant for him his true and native way of love, of longing and happiness; that meant to him life and home, meant simple and heartfelt feeling. He looked back on the years that had passed. He thought of the dreamy adventures of the senses, nerves, and mind in which he had been involved; saw himself eaten up with intellect and introspection, ravaged and paralyzed by insight, half worn out by the fevers and frosts of creation, helpless and in anguish of conscience between two extremes, flung to and fro between austerity and lust; refined, impoverished, exhausted by frigid and artificially heightened ecstasies; erring, forsaken, martyred, and ill—and sobbed with nostalgia and remorse.

Here in his room it was still and dark. But from below life's lulling, trivial waltz-rhythm came faintly to his ears.

Tonio Kröger sat up in the north, composing his promised letter to his friend Lisabeta Ivanovna.

"Dear Lisabeta down there in Arcady, whither I shall shortly return," he wrote: "Here is something like a letter, but it will probably disappoint you, for I mean to keep it rather general. Not that I have nothing to tell; for indeed, in my way, I have had experiences; for instance, in my native town they were even going to arrest me . . . but of that by word of mouth. Sometimes now I have days when I would rather state things in general terms than go on telling stories.

"You probably still remember, Lisabeta, that you called me a *bourgeois,* a *bourgeois manqué*? You called me that in an hour when, led on by other confessions I had previously let slip, I confessed to you my love of life, or what I call life. I ask myself if you were aware how very close you came to the truth, how much my love of 'life' is one and the same thing as my being a *bourgeois.* This journey of mine has given me much occasion to ponder the subject.

"My father, you know, had the temperament of the north: solid, reflective, puritanically correct, with a tendency to melancholia. My mother, of indeterminate foreign blood, was beautiful, sensuous, naive, passionate, and careless at once, and, I think, irregular by instinct. The mixture was no doubt extraordinary and bore with it extraordinary dangers. The issue of it, a *bourgeois* who strayed off into art, a bohemian who feels nostalgic yearnings for respectability, an artist with a bad conscience. For surely it is my *bourgeois* conscience that makes me see in the artist life, in all irregularity and all genius, something profoundly suspect, profoundly disreputable; that fills me with this lovelorn weakness for the simple and good, the comfortably normal, the average unendowed respectable human being.

"I stand between two worlds. I am at home in neither, and I suffer in consequence. You artists call me a *bourgeois,* and the *bourgeois* try to arrest me . . . I don't know which makes me feel worse. The *bourgeois* are stupid; but you adorers of the beautiful, who call me phlegmatic and without aspirations, you ought to realize that there is a way of being an artist that goes so deep and is so much a matter of origins and destinies that no longing seems to it sweeter and more worth knowing than longing after the bliss of the commonplace.

"I admire those proud, cold beings who adventure upon the paths of great and daemonic beauty and despite 'mankind'; but I do not envy them. For if anything is capable of making a poet of a literary man, it is my *bourgeois* love of the human, the living and usual. It is the source of all warmth, goodness, and humor; I even almost think it is itself the love of which it stands written that one may speak with the tongues of men and of angels and yet having it not is as sounding brass and tinkling cymbals.

"The work I have so far done is nothing or not much—as good as nothing. I will do better, Lisabeta—this is a promise. As I write, the sea whispers to me and I close my eyes. I am looking into a world unborn and formless, that needs to be ordered and shaped; I see into a whirl of shadows of human figures who beckon to me to weave spells to redeem them: tragic and laughable figures and some that are both together—and to these I am drawn. But my deepest and secretest love belongs to the blond and blue-eyed, the fair and living, the happy, lovely, and commonplace.

"Do not chide this love, Lisabeta; it is good and fruitful. There is longing in it, and a gentle envy; a touch of contempt and no little innocent bliss."

A 2
B 3
C 4
D 5
E 6
F 7
G 8
H 9
I 0
J 1